D1264484

THE PRISON

STUDIES IN

INSTITUTIONAL

ORGANIZATION

AND CHANGE

With Contributions by

JOHAN GALTUNG, Ph.D.
COLUMBIA UNIVERSITY AND THE
UNIVERSITY OF OSLO

DONALD L. GARRITY, Ph.D.
SAN FRANCISCO STATE COLLEGE

DANIEL GLASER, Ph.D., and JOHN R. STRATTON
UNIVERSITY OF ILLINOIS

ERVING GOFFMAN, Ph.D.
UNIVERSITY OF CALIFORNIA, BERKELEY

RICHARD H. McCLEERY, Ph.D.
ANTIOCH COLLEGE

CLARENCE SCHRAG, Ph.D.
UNIVERSITY OF WASHINGTON

GEORGE H. WEBER, Ph.D.
UNITED STATES CHILDREN'S BUREAU

STANTON WHEELER, Ph.D.
HARVARD UNIVERSITY

THE PRISON

STUDIES IN
INSTITUTIONAL
ORGANIZATION
AND CHANGE

DONALD R. CRESSEY, Ph.D., EDITOR
UNIVERSITY OF CALIFORNIA, LOS ANGELES

HOLT, RINEHART AND WINSTON, INC.
NEW YORK

3   4   5   6   7   8   9

PREFACE

In one sense, this book represents a continuation of the type of research conducted in the 1930's by Donald Clemmer, whose book *The Prison Community* was published in 1940. Clemmer viewed the prison as a laboratory in which some of the conditions and processes in the broader society are observable. His study focused on the inmate community, and was one of the first attempts to examine the idea that the events occurring in social organizations take place because there is an organizational "place" for them to occur. It showed in some detail that the behavior of neither inmates nor staff members in an institution can be efficiently observed if the researcher confines his attention to organizational charts and official lines of command.

In about 1950, other large-scale studies of institutions and institutional life, some of which are reported in this book, began to supplement Clemmer's work and the work of a few scholars who had studied smaller aspects of the prison world. By 1955, at least a dozen American social scientists were engaged in studies of organization and change in correctional institutions and agencies. Clemmer's volume was out of print by that time, and, since heavy reliance was being placed on it, Rinehart was persuaded to reissue *The Prison Community* in 1958. Because I wrote the Foreword for this reissued edition, a number of social scientists communicated to me the need for a companion volume which would show the approach and results of more recent research. Others—Professor John I. Kitsuse of Northwestern University was prominent among them—communicated with Rinehart, and I was persuaded to ask a number of my friends for chapters. The present volume is the result.

v

In another sense, however, the chapters in this book represent an enterprise quite different from the one in which Clemmer was engaged. *The Prison Community* could not make certain kinds of observations, for the simple reason that making them was not part of the social science culture of the 1930's. Since World War II, social scientists and business administrators have shown tremendous concern for the effectiveness and efficiency of various kinds of organization, and they have made numerous studies of the conditions under which various types of organization arise, persist, and change. Moreover, they have shown increasing concern for the effects of organization on the behavior of individual participants. Because of these concerns, the authors of the present volume have at hand a vast storehouse of knowledge and theory which was not available to Clemmer. Accordingly, in examining organizations and organizational problems they use frames of reference which enable them to contribute as much to general organizational theory as to an elaboration of any study of a prison or, for that matter, to an elaboration of prison studies generally.

From the standpoint of organizational theory, then, these are studies of organizational stability and change which just "happen" to use prison data as subject matter, just as similar studies have just "happened" to use data on factories, military establishments, governmental bureaus, hospitals, and similar systems. Nevertheless, anyone using prison data in an organizational study must possess some degree of special concern for prisons. Entering prison is a trying process, even for research workers. Men who study prisons must, at a minimum, be so interested in them that they are willing to try to secure data under difficult circumstances. The authors join me in extending thanks to the officials and inmates who, sometimes at considerable risk, gave us permission to use their prisons for research purposes.

DONALD R. CRESSEY

Los Angeles
January, 1961

ABOUT THE AUTHORS

DONALD R. CRESSEY is Professor of Sociology and Chairman of the Department of Anthropology and Sociology at the University of California, Los Angeles. He is the author of one book, *Other People's Money* (1953), and co-author of two others, *Principles of Criminology* (Fifth Edition, 1955; Sixth Edition, 1960), and *Theoretical Studies in Social Organization of the Prison* (1960). He also has published extensively in sociological, psychological, legal, and correctional journals. His "Introduction" to this volume is based in part upon research he conducted during 1955 and 1956, when he was on sabbatical leave from his university and attached to the Center for Education and Research in Corrections, University of Chicago. During the academic year 1961–1962 he will continue his research on the social organization of correctional agencies while in the position of Visiting Fellow at the University of Cambridge, England.

ERVING GOFFMAN is Associate Professor of Sociology at the University of California, Berkeley. He is author of numerous sociological and social psychological articles. His book, *The Presentation of Self in Everyday Life,* won a wide reputation as a "classic" within a few years after publication, and it was recently reissued as a paperback (Anchor Books, 1959). Goffman's two chapters on total institutions serve as a general introduction to the subsequent chapters, which are more specifically oriented to prisons. His chapters grew out of his experiences as a researcher in mental hospitals, where he was struck with the unique character of institutions where men live together twenty-four hours a day, and where the organization directly meets all of the personal needs that are

vii

going to be met at all. Social relations in such organizations take on a peculiar form, and the relationships in one type of total institution resemble the relationships in other total institutions.

JOHAN GALTUNG has in recent years been alternating between his position as Assistant Professor of Sociology at Columbia University and a similar position at the University of Oslo. His chapter grew out of his experiences as an inmate in a Norwegian prison, which led him to make a sociological analysis of the structure and functioning of prisons generally. This analysis, which was based both on his observations as a prisoner and on subsequent interviews with prison staff members and inmates, was published as a book in 1959, *Fengselssamfunnet* (*The Prison Community*), by the Oslo University Press. In his chapter, he shows that society has assigned purposes and conditions to prisons which are of such a nature that prisons provide a fruitful setting for study of what might be called "the sociology of dilemma." Basic to the many dilemmas confronting persons concerned with prisons is that which holds that the public should understand prisons and help them rehabilitate criminals, but also holds that the prison must be rejected by the public because it is a place where "bad" men are confined.

RICHARD H. MC CLEERY gives our volume an interdisciplinary flavor, for he is the only contributor who is not a sociologist. He is Assistant Professor of Government at Antioch College; earlier, he was in the departments of Political Science at Michigan State University and the University of North Carolina. Despite the fact that he has written a number of papers and three books based on observations of prisons (*The Strange Journey,* 1953; *Policy Change in Prison Management,* 1957; and *Theoretical Studies in Social Organization of the Prison* [co-author], 1960), McCleery is not interested in prisons. Instead, he is interested in governmental processes, and he has shown special concern for the relationships between communication and power. Governmental processes are studied in prisons because studying them there is more efficient than studying them in a larger social system.

Perhaps McCleery's orientation can be most accurately indicated by a quotation from a letter he wrote in connection with his Chapter 4: "The first significance of the chapter for me is the way it revitalizes the political theory of Hobbes that has been obscured by a concentration on his discussion of force in government. Hobbes' theory also contains several explicit passages to the effect that all government rests on the opinions of mankind and an assertion that the critical role of government is that of providing definitions. The function of force—and this is what is normally missed in Hobbes —is in the enforcement of those definitions. For Hobbes, government was necessarily arbitrary because definitions are necessarily arbitrary."

GEORGE H. WEBER is the only contributor who is not now attached to a university. His graduate training in sociology at the University of Kansas and his extensive experience as a clinical psychologist in a boys' school are utilized in his position as chief of the Technical Aid Branch, Delinquency Services, in the United States Children's Bureau. He has published numerous papers on institutions for children. His chapter may be considered an extension of an earlier paper, published in the *Journal of Criminal Law and Criminology* in 1957, "Conflict between Professional and Non-Professional Personnel in Institutional Delinquency Treatment." In that paper, he established the fact of conflict; in Chapter 5 he shows that both conflict and various reactions to conflict occur because there is an organizational place for them to occur.

STANTON WHEELER is Assistant Professor of Social Relations at Harvard University. He received his Ph.D. at the University of Washington, and his chapter is based on his Ph.D. dissertation. His research has concentrated on the processes by which persons take on the values, attitudes, norms, and other behaviors of the groups in which they have membership, and he has studied these processes by focusing on the "prisonization" of new inmates and on the role conflicts occurring in institutions. Currently, Dr. Wheeler is serving on a Fulbright grant in Norway, where he is attached to the Institutes of Sociology and Criminology at the University of Oslo. His chapter examines the degree of conflict between inmates and staff members in their privately expressed conceptions of appropriate conduct in the institution. It then goes on to examine the differences in perceptions, by inmates and staff members, of the attitudes that personnel and inmates are believed to have in reference to appropriate conduct. The results suggest that there is less conflict between inmates and staff on a private attitudinal level than is usually reported on the basis of observations of conduct. Yet the social organization of the prison operates to create a *perception* of severe conflict in role expectations.

CLARENCE SCHRAG is Professor of Sociology at the University of Washington, where he recently returned after a lengthy tour of duty as Director of Institutions and Agencies for the state of Washington. Like Dr. Weber, he has had extensive "practical" experience in correctional institutions, as well as academic training and experience in sociology. He is co-author of *Sociology* (New York: Harper, 1954) and co-editor of *Readings in General Sociology* (Boston: Houghton Mifflin, 1957). He has written numerous papers on criminology and correction. Currently, he is President of the Pacific Sociological Association. His chapter summarizes some of the work in criminological theory, outlines a conceptual framework for analysis of prisons, and then goes on to explore the implications of that theory and framework for rehabilitation of prisoners. Among other things, he shows that the organization of close-custody prisons places severe limitations on treatment potential and may be a greater barrier to resocialization of offenders than are the bars and walls that attract so much adverse comment from prison reformers.

DONALD L. GARRITY is Chairman of the Sociology Department at San Francisco State College, where he is engaged in research on delinquency, crime, and correction. His chapter, which is an extension of his Ph.D. dissertation, shows the extraordinary impact of prison experiences on some types of inmates. He shows that among prison inmates there is a broadly defined social structure that includes a normative system stemming from the common problems of adjustment; it tends to be dominated by antisocial convicts. He goes on to show that the impact of imprisonment on inmates varies with the kind and extent of participation in this structure. Most significant, perhaps, is his finding that exposing inmates to the experience of associating with other criminals in prison does not necessarily increase the probability that they will engage in subsequent criminal behavior, as has quite commonly been assumed.

DANIEL GLASER and JOHN R. STRATTON are both at the University of Illinois, where the former is Professor of Sociology and Director of a four-year study, financed by the Ford Foundation, of the Federal correctional system. Mr. Stratton is Research Assistant for the study. Dr. Glaser has had extensive experience as both a researcher and an employee in prisons, and he has done pioneering and highly significant work in developing parole prediction instruments. He also has published numerous articles on criminological theory. In their chapter, Glaser and Stratton summarize some of the ways in which sociological theory and research may be utilized in developing measures of inmate change in institutions, and then report some of the preliminary findings of their own research. These findings are consistent with those of Garrity.

CONTENTS

PART THREE

Rehabilitation in the Prison Community

THE PRISON

STUDIES IN

INSTITUTIONAL

ORGANIZATION

AND CHANGE

DONALD R. CRESSEY

| | | | | | | | | | |

Introduction

In the ten-year period, 1950–1959, over three-quarters of a million men and women entered the state and federal prisons and reformatories of the United States. They did not "end up" in prison. The vast majority have been discharged from the institution to which they were committed, so that only 207,500 inmates were confined in American prisons and reformatories at the end of 1959. Within the next ten years, almost all the remainder will return to the free community.

These prisoners, and thousands who preceded them to prison, were forcibly removed from the social relations in which they were participating and were locked in institutions where, we are prone to say, they "served their time," "paid their debt to society," and, perhaps, "learned their lesson." But they did more than pay, and serve, and learn in the institutions. They *lived* in them. For varying periods of time, each prisoner participated in an extraordinarily complex set of social relations, including a wide variety of social contacts, associations, bonds, alliances, compromises, and conflicts between hundreds of prisoners, guards, administrators, teachers, tradesmen, and professional personnel like social workers, psychologists, and physicians.

During the period of participation in this set of social relations, some prisoners were apparently "reformed" or "rehabilitated," while others became "confirmed" or "hardened" criminals. For still others, prison life had no discernible effect on subsequent criminality or noncriminality. No one knows how or why a particular prisoner happens to remain neutral, to become "hardened," or to become "reformed" during his prison experience. Social scientists are beginning to suspect, however, that the answer lies in the specific nature of the particular prisoner's participation in the social organization which is his prison. In the chapters to follow—especially in the three by Garrity, Glaser and Stratton, and Wheeler—this suspicion will be confirmed.

However, "nature of participation" and "social organization" are rather meaningless as explanatory concepts when they stand alone. They serve only to indicate in a general way, to oversimplify, and to dramatize social interactions which are so confused, entangled, complicated, and subtle that even the participants are unable to see and describe clearly their own involvements. Perhaps participation in social organization is complex because it is so difficult to describe, although the inclination seems to be to maintain the reverse, that social interaction is difficult to describe because it is so complex. Social scientists have not attempted to analyze and estimate the significance of millions of grunts, sighs, inflections of voice, stances, silences, and sniffles in a husband's relationships with his wife and children. Perhaps they would be unable to do so, even if they tried. Yet it is probably the absence of analyses and estimations of this kind that make stated and recognized family problems so difficult to understand. Similarly, we cannot clearly state the importance to a prisoner or a guard of nuances in the relationships they have with each other, with other prisoners, and with other staff members. But it is these rather vague, indefinite, and subtle aspects of social participation which seem crucial to the subsequent behavior of both prisoners and guards, and, concurrently, to making the prison "work" in a way that will at least partially satisfy the members of groups having unstated and complex ideas about how it is "supposed" to work. Among these groups are administrators, guards, tradesmen, prisoners, professional personnel, and various categories of interested outsiders.

One of the most amazing things about prisons is that they "work" at all. As the various chapters of this book show, any on-going prison is made up of the synchronized actions of hundreds of people, some of whom hate and distrust each other, love each other, fight each other physically and psychologically, think of each other as stupid or mentally disturbed, "manage" and "control" each other, and vie with each other for favors, prestige, power, and money. Often the personnel involved do not know that they are in conflict, do not know with whom they are competing or cooperating, and are not sure whether they are the managers or the managed. Despite these conditions, however, the social system which is a prison does not degenerate into a chaotic mess of social relations which have no order and make no sense. Somehow the personnel, including prisoners, are bound together enough so that most conflicts and misunderstandings are not crucial—the personnel remain "organized." The organization does not disintegrate, though it may change its form and functioning from time to time, often in almost imperceptible ways. It remains an organization despite the changes and despite the personnel involved; it continues to "work" somehow.

Viewed in this way, the prison is a microcosm of the larger society which has created it and which maintains it, for this larger society also remains as a unit and continues to "work" despite numerous individual disagreements, misunderstandings, antagonism, and conflicts. The most general aim of this book is to contribute to a better understanding of the larger society through analyses of its microcosm, the prison. It should be understood, however, that all the processes occurring in a prison, or any other total institution, are not mere reflections of the larger society. There are significant differences as well as striking similarities, as Goffman shows in the first two chapters.

Like "social participation," "social organization" is an extraordinarily complex phenomenon with subtle and almost invisible aspects. A chart of a prison's administrative hierarchy, showing the lines of authority, does not begin to describe how the prison is organized, who is responsible to whom, or who influences whom. It is even difficult to draw a picture of the official parts of the organization in this way, although these are the least complex aspects of the system. In addition, there are unofficial components of institutional structure, and it is these that are complicated and, usually, unstated. In one sense, in fact, whether specific aspects of an organization are "official" or "unofficial" depends on whether or not they are clear and observable. If a prison warden can "do something about" some aspect of the institution—such as issuing an order to have a certain practice changed —he is dealing with official organization; if there is something going on, the nature of which he cannot clearly state and which, consequently, he cannot change by order, he is dealing with unofficial organization.[1]

The various chapters of this book demonstrate that both the official and unofficial aspects of social organization are important determinants of the behavior, including attitudes, opinions, and beliefs, of the persons participating. It is likely, however, that unofficial arrangements are of most significance to inmates and, at least, to lower level employees, for most of their time is spent in them. A warden who

[1] *Cf.* Alfred H. Stanton and Morris S. Schwartz, *The Mental Hospital* (New York: Basic Books, 1954), 10, 31.

controls the time budgets of inmates may officially alter their work schedules so that they have more time to participate in what is believed to be the rehabilitative program of the vocational school. At the same time, he may (perhaps unwittingly and indirectly) alter the time budgets of the vocational teachers, and the guards in the vocational school, so that they have little time for rehabilitation. The official "rehabilitation program" might, then, become a custodial program or a diagnostic program.

Such conflicts in official arrangements are, as indicated, likely to be infinitesimal in comparison with the problems arising from unofficial arrangements. Even if vocational teachers and inmates were allotted time for rehabilitative training, various conditions which they encounter during other hours might effectively block any rehabilitative effort or effect. For example, by attending school an inmate might lose a soft job given him by a guard, or he might lose his status as a "right guy" among the inmates, or he might lose his reputation as a "good inmate" among the officers assigned to guard him. The teachers, in turn, might think that they will lose prestige or will not receive salary increases unless they obtain from inmates information valuable to prediction of success on parole, or valuable to the institutional custodial force or disciplinary committee. Such arrangements would have obvious significance for both inmate rehabilitation and performance of the duties which teachers believe they are obligated to perform.

Unofficial aspects of the organization of a prison or other institution contain thousands of other, much more complex, relationships which may similarly affect the behavior of the participants. The "good feeling" or "bad feeling" between the warden and the chef, the biases of inmates, the vocabulary of the psychologists and social workers, and the sense of justice among prisoners and guards are all part of the inmate's world, and they have a powerful effect on his adjustment in the institution and on his subsequent criminality. They also are all part of the employee's world, and they have powerful effects on his behavior both inside and outside the institution.

In the chapters that follow, two principal questions will be asked and partially answered: (1) What gives these organizations the characteristics they have? and (2) What difference does the presence of these characteristics make to the behavior of staff and inmates? The answers to the two questions are closely interrelated.

The first question cannot be answered by reference to prison operations alone; as Galtung shows in Chapter 3, opinions of persons in the "outside world" also must be considered. While all the authors might not accept the following frame of reference, which has been adapted from statements by Stanton and Schwartz,[2] they all seem to be saying that any event occurring in an organization should be viewed as the resultant of three aspects of organizational pattern—the purposes of the organization, the organizational necessities, and the needs and limitations of the personnel involved. Each of these is affected by the "setting" in which the organization exists.

The purposes of a prison are protection of the community, supply of food, clothing, and shelter to convicted criminals, protection of inmates from each other and from persons in the outside community, imposition of punishment, and rehabilitation of criminals.[3] These purposes are assigned by outsiders and are shared by institutional personnel, although some of them are logically contradictory. A complex division of labor is established to attempt their achievement, and each of the purposes is achieved to some extent by the people whose institutional behavior is patterned by the roles that make up the division of labor. There are three principal sections in this division of labor—a hierarchy of custodial ranks, an industrial hierarchy, and a social welfare agency—and they are devoted to *keeping* inmates, *using* inmates, and *serving* inmates.[4]

Institutional necessities include a continuous flow of prisoners, personnel, and money; statutory permission to operate and to maintain a physical plant and program; systems for distributing rewards to staff and inmates; systems of communication, decision-making, and power; and systems for introducing changes. The internal systems are the machinery for officially assigning priority to keeping, or using, or serving inmates, as McCleery demonstrates in Chapter 4. They are used, in other words, in determining which of the institutional purposes shall be sought immediately and generally by the division of

[2] *Ibid.,* pp. 27–28.

[3] See Donald R. Cressey, "Achievement of an Unstated Organizational Goal: An Observation on Prisons," *Pacific Sociological Review,* 1 (Fall, 1958), 43–49.

[4] See Donald R. Cressey, "Limitations on Organization of Treatment in the Modern Prison," Chapter 4 in Richard A. Cloward, Donald R. Cressey, George H. Grosser, Richard McCleery, Lloyd E. Ohlin, Gresham Sykes and Sheldon L. Messinger, *Theoretical Studies in Social Organization of the Prison* (New York: Social Science Research Council, 1960), 78–80.

labor and which shall be deferred or given minimal attention. (Shall protection of the community be given priority over rehabilitation of criminals?) Further, these systems are used for clarifying alternative interpretations of the specific means to be used for attempting to accomplish each of the purposes. (Shall rehabilitation of inmates be attempted by punitive or nonpunitive measures?) They also are used for deciding which of the purposes are to be accomplished in cases of each particular inmate. (Shall "prosocial" inmates, as Schrag calls them in Chapter 8, be given the same rehabilitative and custodial attention that is given to "antisocial" inmates?) Such questions are not asked and answered solely in formal conferences and staff meetings; handling them is a part of the day-to-day activities of all personnel, including inmates.

The needs and limitations of the staff and inmates, as determined by their past experiences, reference groups, and membership groups, compose another facet of the organization. The "personalities" of the personnel affect the events in which they are involved. Yet, as indicated below, the authors are not concerned with the origins of these personalities in the sense common in psychoanalysis. Most social scientists now recognize that men are affected by their past experiences but that personalities are not easily characterized by concepts such as "sadistic," "authoritarian," or "aggressive." A person with a Ph.D. in psychology hired to give psychotherapy to inmates has needs and limitations different from those of a grammar school graduate hired to keep order and prevent escapes, or of an inmate assigned to the institution. In organizational studies, it is not necessary to ask why the psychologist is a psychologist, why the guard is a guard, or why the inmate is an inmate. However, it is relevant to observe, as Weber does in Chapter 5, that each has personal needs that must be met in the context of the institution's purposes and necessities and which, therefore, affect his involvement in institutional events. This means that institutional activities are not always carried out rationally to attain stated institutional purposes and needs; they also are carried out to meet personal needs.

If any event is determined by these three facets of organization, then there should be a patterning of similar events in the same organization at a given time, and organizations with similar purposes, necessities, and personnel should display similar patterns. Such patterning is dramatically demonstrated by McCleery, in Chapter 7. Another study has indicated that American prisons and Soviet labor camps are assigned similar purposes, with the result that the forms of organization, and unorganization, among inmates are similar.[5] Patterns of recurring events are usually recognized when they involve "problems" for administrators, but they ordinarily are given little attention when they require no direct administrative action. For example, excessive absenteeism among guards or an outbreak of fights among inmates might be viewed as a "problem" by a warden and analyzed in terms of the prison's custodial and rehabilitative purposes, the organizational hierarchies, and the personal needs of guards and inmates. It is quite likely, however, that a contemporary analysis would be made in an individualistic rather than an organizational frame of reference. Moreover, recurring events such as a tendency of tower sentries to watch lieutenants instead of inmates (in order to avoid a demerit), a tendency of guards to handle inmates as if they were children, or a tendency for inmates to behave as if guards were inferior to them, might not be even noticed, let alone analyzed in organizational terms.

Each of the following chapters analyzes, in varying degrees of detail, the effects of organization on some aspect of inmate or staff behavior. Each validates a significant point that was demonstrated but left unstated in Lloyd E. Ohlin's report on a study of staff problems in a training school: *Diagnosis and explanation of "personality disorders" and other "deviant behavior" must show concern for the organizational context in which the behavior occurs, as well as for the traits of the actor.*[6] Both social science theory and popular modes of thought have been greatly influenced by Freudian and other individualistic theories which view behavior as if it were determined by personality traits. Consequently, it has been customary to assume that such conduct as "uncooperativeness," "loyalty," "honesty," "aggressiveness," and "paranoia" are the personal property of the individuals exhibiting the behavior. In total institutions, and especially in those emphasizing "treatment," personnel policies and policies for controlling inmates are almost always based on this kind of assumption. Deviation

---

[5] Donald R. Cressey and Witold Krassowski, "Inmate Organization and Anomie in American Prisons and Soviet Labor Camps," *Social Problems*, 5 (Winter, 1957–1958), 217–230.

[6] Lloyd E. Ohlin, "The Reduction of Role Conflict in Institutional Staff," *Children*, 5 (March–April, 1958), 65–69. See also Donald R. Cressey's comments on this article in the "Readers' Exchange" section of *Children*, 5 (May–June, 1958), 119; some of these comments are repeated here.

from what is said to be expected or wanted is viewed as a consequence of something "in" the deviant. For example, a guard who deviates from what his custodial supervisors expect of him might simply be diagnosed as "lazy," "shiftless," "uncooperative," or "stupid"; and a guard who deviates from what treatment-personnel say they expect of him might be considered "neurotic," "rigid," "punitive," or even "sadistic." Such diagnoses are ordinarily followed by transfer or dismissal, or by efforts to change the deviant by punishment, education, or therapy.

The contributors to this volume use, with varying degrees of specificity, an alternative (or, at least, supplementary) theory of human conduct—a theory that views behavior as if it were determined by characteristics of the social relationships surrounding the actor. In much over-simplified form, the theory maintains, in the words of Cartwright, that

> How aggressive or cooperative a person is, how much self-respect or self-confidence he has, how energetic and productive his work is, what he aspires to, what he believes to be true and good, whom he loves or hates, and what beliefs and prejudices he holds—all these characteristics are highly determined by the individual's group membership. In a real sense, *they are properties of groups and of the relationships between people.*[7]

When this idea, or some form of it, is applied to the behavior of persons who live or work in institutions, as has been done in the chapters below, it can be observed that many traits exhibited by individual staff members and inmates are properties of the *organization,* not of the person in question. From this observation, it follows logically that if the traits are to be changed the organization, not the person, must be made the object of modification. Rather than ask how or why "sadistic" men get into police departments or institutional work, for example, we should ask what organizational conditions are present in police departments and institutions to produce conduct which we define as sadistic. The essential notion, again, is that one who participates in an organization that "owns" certain kinds of behavior will exhibit those kinds of behavior. Events occur because

---

[7] Dorwin Cartwright, "Achieving Change in People: Some Applications of Group Dynamics Theory," *Human Relations,* 4 (1951), 381–392. Emphasis added.

there is an organizational place for them to occur, and they do not recur when the place is eliminated.

To use another example, it has been customary to attribute fights between inmates to personal traits such as "aggressiveness," "latent hostility," or, simply, "hot temper." One lesson of this book is that we should also ask, "What is there about the institutional organization that produced a fight?" Once this question has been answered, we can ask, further, whether the organizational conditions can be changed and, significantly, whether it is desirable to change them. Conceivably, organizational modification to eliminate fights or other behavior that is deplored could have as its consequence the elimination or modification of other conditions which institutional administrators or interested outsiders hold dear.

In one institution we have studied, two inmates got into an argument about whether or not Mexico is governed by the United States, and shortly afterward one of them hit the other while the other was walking in a line; the second man retaliated, and there was a scuffle. Some months later, the second man was in the deputy warden's office on some unrelated business, but he was asked about the "fight" and he repeated the story above. The deputy warden remarked, "He is hot tempered, but you have a pretty hot temper yourself, you know." The inmate admitted that this was true. A subsequent check indicated that in none of the proceedings following the incident, including the hearings before the disciplinary court, was any question asked as to why the argument arose, why there was no appeal to the authority of the education department or to a knowledgeable inmate, what the statuses of the two inmates were in inmate society, who the audience was for the argument and for the scuffle, or, generally, what was the organizational context in which the argument and scuffle took place. The altercation was viewed as an affair between two "silly," "hot tempered," and "immature" men. It is this kind of relationship that is in the research domain of the social scientist, but it is also precisely this kind of relationship that has only recently been studied carefully by social scientists. The studies have not yet had a significant impact on either criminological theory or institutional administration.

We hope that the implications of the behavioral theory used here will be recognized and studied by "practical men" as well as social scientists. It has important implications for theories of delinquency and crime causation. At present, by far the most popular notion in this area is that delinquency and criminality are personal traits, "owned" by the individual deviant. The traits are usually viewed as "symptoms," to be sure, but as symptoms of something belonging to the actor's person, not to his groups (organizations). Alternatively, we might view delinquency and criminality as the property of groups, in the same way that institutional staff attitudes and conduct, and inmate attitudes and conduct, are viewed as the property of organizations. It would follow that we would use therapy designed to modify the groups owning the behavior the actor is exhibiting, rather than providing therapy of a type designed to modify individual personality characteristics. Grosser has recently made this point succinctly and well:

> Psychological and sociological research has shown that the stabler the frame of reference of an individual, the more resistant is he likely to be to a contradictory frame of reference, and that stability of a frame of reference depends not so much on the individual's own experience and reality-testing as it does on group consensus and reinforcement. This reinforcement of an existing frame of reference makes it extremely difficult for an individual to change even when he has considerable ambivalence in his feelings toward his group.[8]

We also hope that the studies reported here will have favorable effects on prison administrators and other governing bodies. In the job specifications of most wardens and governmental administrators there are no requirements for training in social science. On the contrary, administrators sometimes have strong biases against professors and social scientists. At a minimum, we hope to offset some of the bias.

There seem to be three principal reasons for administrators' lack of confidence in academic men. First, they appear to be convinced that professors—especially professors of political science, sociology, psychology, and social work—do not understand administrative problems and are not interested in understanding them; therefore, they are not of much assistance. The decisions a warden makes on a day-to-day basis are limited in scope and are attempts to solve immediate, pressing, problems; they are only remotely related to general theory or ideology. A social scientist's notions about government, about prisons, or about rehabilitation, then, are likely to be considered unrealistic or idealistic because they do not contain explicit directives

[8] George H. Grosser, "The Role of Informal Inmate Groups in Change of Values," *Children*, 5 (January–February, 1958), 26–27.

for handling a variety of daily administrative problems. We once asked a warden about the value of sociological training for prison workers, and he responded, "It is like I say around here. A man is tearing up his cell and has just attacked an officer. So I say, 'Well, let's go over here to the shelf and get one of those criminology books and find out what we should do.' There's nothing there." There never will be anything there. Nevertheless, the detailed insights by the authors of this volume show realism and concern for the practical implications of administrative decisions, and for the practical implications of social science theory for those decisions. The authors probably know more about prisons than do most wardens, and their research *can* be put to administrative use by men who are skilled in solving the day-to-day problems of government.

Second, administrators recognize that visiting social scientists, especially those doing research, have immediate access to an interested public and to the administrators' superiors. Therefore they can, through misunderstanding, create embarrassing incidents. In talking about an institutional visit by a well-known criminologist, one prison administrator said, "The only damned thing that man saw was two guys standing at attention with their arms folded. He came in here and went all through the place, and that is the only thing I heard about. We had two guys that had been in a fight and had been brought up here and were waiting in the hall. Naturally, we didn't want them to start fighting again, so we made them stand at attention. He saw it, and the Director wrote me about it the next day, saying that [the criminologist] had remarked about how we still have men standing at attention with their arms folded. That is the only thing he saw in the whole place." But the authors of this volume have seen much more than isolated incidents, and they have attempted to put them into an organizational context so that misunderstandings, even by administrators, will be minimal. Each of the chapters is based on extensive and detailed observation of prison life, plus extensive and detailed reading of social science theory.

Third, the bias against social scientists and professors also seems to stem in part from the fact that until quite recently they have not, as we indicated above, attempted actually to utilize social science theory in analyses of prisons. Social scientists have left governmental administrators pretty much "on their own." Even criminologists have traditionally concentrated on crime causation, leaving problems of correcting criminals to others; and much of such interest as they

showed in prisons was an interest in humanitarian prison reform or
in the history of imprisonment. The professor who went to prison
to do research ordinarily concentrated on interviewing a certain type
of offender, or on collecting statistics of various kinds, not on studying
the institution as an on-going social organization. But now the tremendous recent growth of social science interest and specialization in
the theory and study of organization is being both reflected and stimulated by growth of concern for study of prisons and similar institutions. The social scientists who wrote this volume are interested in
theory, but their writings also indicate their concern for "applying"
theory in such a way that their research is useful to administrators
who are interested in "keeping up." We hope the book will show
governing bodies what contemporary social scientists are thinking and
doing, just as we hope that it will show social scientists that in some
respects prisons differ significantly, if not uniquely, from other types
of organization that have been studied.

P|A|R|T| |O|N|E

SOCIETY, INMATES,

AND PRISONS

I

ERVING GOFFMAN

| | | | | | | | | |

On the Characteristics of Total
Institutions: The Inmate World[1]

Social establishments—institutions in the everyday sense of that term—are places such as rooms, suites of rooms, buildings, or plants in which activity of a particular kind regularly goes on. In sociology we do not have a very apt way of classifying them. Some establishments, like Grand Central Station, are open to anyone who is decently behaved; others, like the Union League Club of New York or the Laboratories at Los Alamos, are felt to be somewhat snippy about who is let in. Some, like shops and post offices, have a few fixed members who provide a service and a continuous flow of members who receive it. Others, like homes and factories, involve a less changing set of participants. Some institutions provide the place for the kind of pursuits from which the individual is felt to draw his social status, however enjoyable or lax these pursuits may be; other institutions, in contrast, provide a place for associations felt to be elective and unserious, calling for a contribution of time left over from more serious demands. In this chapter another category of institutions is singled out; it is claimed as a natural and fruitful one because its members appear to have so much in common—so much, in fact, that

[1] A shorter version of the discussion in Chapters 1 and 2 appears in the *Proceedings of the Symposium on Preventive and Social Psychiatry,* Walter Reed Army Institute of Research, Washington, D. C. (15–17th April, 1957), 43–84.

to learn about one of these institutions we would be well advised to look at the others.

Every institution captures something of the time and interest of its members and provides something of a world for them; in brief, every institution has encompassing tendencies. When we review the different institutions in our Western society we find some that are encompassing to a degree discontinuously greater than the ones next in line. Their encompassing or total character is symbolized by the barrier to social intercourse with the outside that is often built right into the physical plant, such as locked doors, high walls, barbed wire, cliffs, water, forests, or moors. These I am calling *total institutions,* and it is their general characteristics,[2] especially the characteristics of the inmate world and of the staff world, that I want to explore.

TOTAL INSTITUTIONS

The total institutions of our society can be listed in five rough groupings. First, there are institutions established to care for persons felt to be both incapable and harmless: these are the homes for the blind, the aged, the orphaned and the indigent. Second, there are places established to care for persons felt to be both incapable of looking after themselves and a threat to the community, albeit an unintended one: TB sanitoria, mental hospitals, and leprosoria. A third type of total institution is organized to protect the community against what are felt to be intentional dangers to it, with the welfare of the persons thus sequestered not the immediate issue: jails, penitentiaries, P.O.W. camps and concentration camps. Fourth, there are institutions purportedly established the better to pursue some work-like task, and justifying themselves only on these instrumental grounds:

[2] The category of total institutions has been pointed out from time to time in sociological literature under a variety of names, and some of the characteristics of the class have been suggested, most notably perhaps in Howard Roland's neglected paper, "Segregated Communities and Mental Health," in *Mental Health Publication of the American Association for the Advancement of Science,* No. 9, edited by F. R. Moulton, 1939. A preliminary statement of the present paper is reported in the third (1956) *Group Processes Proceedings,* Josiah Macy, Jr., Foundation, edited by Bertram Schaffner, 1957. The term "total" has also been used in its present context in Amitai Etzioni, "The Organizational Structure of 'Closed' Educational Institutions in Israel," *Harvard Educational Review,* 27 (1957), 115.

army barracks, ships, boarding schools, work camps, colonial compounds, and the servants' quarters of large mansions. Finally, there are those establishments designed as retreats from the world even while often serving also as training stations for the religious: abbeys, monasteries, convents, and other cloisters. This classification of total institutions is not neat, exhaustive, or of immediate analytical use, but it does provide a purely denotative definition of the category as a concrete starting point. By anchoring the initial definition of total institutions in this way, I hope to be able to discuss the general characteristics of the type without becoming tautological.

Before I attempt to extract a general profile from this list of establishments, I would like to mention one conceptual problem: none of the elements I will describe seems peculiar to total institutions, and none seems to be shared by every one of them; what is distinctive about total institutions is that each exhibits many items in this family of attributes to an intense degree. In speaking of "common characteristics," then, I will be using this phrase in a way that is restricted but I think logically defensible. At the same time it will become possible to exploit the method of ideal types, so that common features can be established with the hope of highlighting significant differences later.

A basic social arrangement in modern society is that we tend to sleep, play, and work in different places, in each case with a different set of co-participants, under a different authority, and without an over-all rational plan. The central feature of total institutions can be described as a breakdown of the barriers ordinarily separating these three spheres of life. First, all aspects of life are conducted in the same place and under the same single authority. Second, each phase of the member's daily activity is carried on in the immediate company of a large number of others, all of whom are treated alike and required to do the same thing together. Third, all phases of the day's activities are tightly scheduled, with one activity leading at a prearranged time into the next, and the whole sequence of activities being imposed from above through a system of explicit formal rulings and by a body of officials. Finally, the contents of the various enforced activities are brought together as parts of a single over-all rational plan purportedly designed to fulfill the official aims of the institution.

Individually, these totalistic features are found in places other than total institutions. For example, our large commercial, industrial, and educational establishments increasingly provide cafeterias and off-hour recreation for their members; use of these extended facilities remains voluntary in many particulars, however, and special care is taken to see that the ordinary line of authority does not extend to them. Similarly, housewives or farm families can find all their major spheres of life within the same fenced-in area, but these persons are not collectively regimented and do not march through the day's activities in the immediate company of many others like themselves.

The handling of many human needs by the bureaucratic organization of whole blocks of people—whether or not this is a necessary or effective means of social organization in the circumstances—can be taken, then, as the key fact of total institutions. From this follow certain important implications.

When persons are caused to move in blocks, they can be supervised by personnel whose chief activity is not guidance or periodic checking (as in many employer-employee relations) but rather surveillance— a seeing to it that everyone does what he has been clearly told is required of him, under conditions where one person's infraction is likely to stand out in relief against the visible, constantly examined, compliance of the others. Which comes first, the large blocks of managed people or the small supervisory staff, is not here at issue; the point is that each is made for the other.

In total institutions there is a basic split between the large managed group, conveniently called inmates, and the small supervisory staff. Inmates typically live in and have restricted contact with the world outside the walls; staff often operate on an eight-hour day and are socially integrated into the outside world.[3] Each grouping tends to conceive of the other in terms of narrow hostile stereotypes: staff often seeing inmates as bitter, secretive and untrustworthy, while inmates often see staff as condescending, high-handed and mean. Staff tends to feel superior and righteous; inmates tend, in some ways at least, to feel inferior, weak, blameworthy and guilty.[4]

---

[3] The binary character of total institutions was pointed out to me by Gregory Bateson, and has been noted in sociological literature. See, for example, Lloyd E. Ohlin, *Sociology and the Field of Corrections* (New York: Russell Sage Foundation, 1956), 14, 20. In situations where staff are also required to live-in, we may expect staff to feel they are suffering special hardships and to have brought home to them a status-dependency on life on the inside which they did not expect. See Jane Cassels Record, "The Marine Radioman's Struggle for Status," *American Journal of Sociology*, 52 (1957), 359.

[4] For the prison version, see S. Kirson Weinberg, "Aspects of the Prison's Social Structure," *American Journal of Sociology*, 47 (1942), 717–726.

Social mobility between the two strata is grossly restricted; social distance is typically great and often formally prescribed. Even talk across the boundaries may be conducted in a special tone of voice, as illustrated in a fictionalized record of an actual sojourn in a mental hospital:

> "I tell you what," said Miss Hart when they were crossing the dayroom. "You do everything Miss Davis says. Don't think about it, just do it. You'll get along all right."
>
> As soon as she heard the name Virginia knew what was terrible about Ward One. Miss Davis. "Is she the head nurse?"
>
> "And how," muttered Miss Hart. And then she raised her voice. The nurses had a way of acting as if the patients were unable to hear anything that was not shouted. Frequently they said things in normal voices that the ladies were not supposed to hear; if they had not been nurses you would have said they frequently talked to themselves. "A most competent and efficient person, Miss Davis," announced Miss Hart.[5]

Although some communication is necessary between inmates and the staff guarding them, one of the guard's functions is the control of communication from inmates to higher staff levels. A research study of mental hospitals provides an illustration:

> Since many of the patients are anxious to see the doctor on his rounds, the attendants must act as mediators between the patients and the physician if the latter is not to be swamped. On Ward 30, it seemed to be generally true that patients without physical symptoms who fell into the two lower privilege groups were almost never permitted to talk to the physician unless Dr. Baker himself asked for them. The persevering, nagging delusional group—who were termed "worry warts," "nuisances," "bird dogs," in the attendants' slang—often tried to break through the attendant-mediator but were always quite summarily dealt with when they tried.[6]

Just as talk across the boundary is restricted, so, too, is the passage of information, especially information about the staff's plans for inmates. An important aspect of the position from which the inmate faces staff is exclusion from knowledge of the decisions taken regarding his fate. Whether the official grounds are military, as in concealing travel destination from the ranks, or medical, as in concealing diag-

[5] Mary Jane Ward, *The Snake Pit* (New York: Signet Books, 1955), 72.
[6] Ivan Belknap, *Human Problems of a State Mental Hospital* (New York: McGraw-Hill, 1956), 177.

nosis, plan of treatment, and approximate length of stay from tuberculosis patients,[7] such exclusion gives staff a special basis of distance
from and control over inmates.

All these restrictions of contact presumably help to maintain the
antagonistic stereotypes.[8] Two different social and cultural worlds
develop, jogging alongside each other with points of official contact
but little mutual penetration. Significantly, the institutional plant and
name come to be identified by both staff and inmates as somehow
belonging to staff, so that when either grouping refers to the views or
interests of "the institution," by implication they are referring (as I
shall also) to the views and concerns of the staff.

The staff-inmate split is one major implication of the bureaucratic management of large blocks of persons; a second pertains to
work.

In the ordinary arrangements of living in our society, the authority
of the work-place stops with the worker's receipt of a money payment;
the spending of this in a domestic and recreational setting is the
private affair of the worker and a mechanism through which the
authority of the work-place is kept within strict bounds. But to say
that inmates of total institutions have their full day scheduled for
them is to say that all basic needs will have to be planned for, that
the institution must guarantee to provide everything essential. Whatever the incentive given for work, then, this incentive will not have
the structural significance it has on the outside. There will have to be
different motives for work and different attitudes toward it. Here is
a basic adjustment required of the inmates and of those who must
induce them to work.

Sometimes so little work is required that inmates, often untrained
in leisurely pursuits, suffer extremes of boredom. The work that is
required is carried on at a very slow pace and may be geared into a
system of minor, often ceremonial, payments, such as the weekly
tobacco ration and the Christmas presents that lead some mental
patients to stay on their jobs. In other cases, of course, more than a

---

[7] A very full case report on this matter is provided in a chapter titled
"Information and the Control of Treatment," in Julius A. Roth's forthcoming monograph on the tuberculosis hospital. His work promises to be a
model study of a total institution. Preliminary statements may be found in
his articles, "What is an Activity?" *Etc.*, 14 (Autumn, 1956), 54–56, and
"Ritual and Magic in the Control of Contagion," *American Sociological
Review*, 22 (June, 1957), 310–314.

[8] Suggested in Ohlin, *op. cit.*, p. 20.

full day's work is required, induced not by reward but by threat of physical punishment. In some total institutions, such as logging camps and merchant ships, the practice of forced-saving postpones buying, the usual function of money in the world; all needs are organized by the institution and payment is given only when a work season is over and the men leave the premises. In some institutions there is a kind of slavery, with the inmate's full time placed at the convenience of staff. Here the inmate's sense of self and sense of possession can become alienated from his work capacity. T. E. Lawrence gives an illustration in his record of service in a R.A.F. training depot:

> The six-weeks men we meet on fatigues shock our moral sense by their easy-going. "You're silly ——, you rookies, to sweat yourselves," they say. Is it our new keenness, or a relic of civility in us? For by the R.A.F. we shall be paid all the twenty-four hours a day, at three halfpence an hour; paid to work, paid to eat, paid to sleep: always those halfpence are adding up. Impossible, therefore, to dignify a job by doing it well. It must take as much time as it can for afterwards there is not a fireside waiting, but another job.[9]

Whether there is too much work or too little, the individual who was work-oriented on the outside tends to become demoralized by the work system of the total institution. An example of such demoralization is the practice in state mental hospitals of "bumming" or "working someone for" a nickel or dime to spend in the canteen. Persons do this—often with some defiance—who on the outside would consider such actions beneath their self-respect. (Staff members, interpreting this begging pattern in terms of their own outsider's orientation to earning, tend to see it as a symptom of mental illness and one further bit of evidence that inmates really are unwell.)

There is an incompatibility, then, between total institutions and the basic work-payment structure of our society. Total institutions are also incompatible with another crucial element of our society, the family. Family life is sometimes contrasted with solitary living, but in fact the more pertinent contrast might be with block-living, for those who eat and sleep and work with a group of fellow-workers can hardly sustain a meaningful domestic existence.[10] Correspondingly, maintaining families off the grounds often permits staff members to

---

[9] T. E. Lawrence, *The Mint* (London: Jonathan Cape, 1955), 40.

[10] An interesting marginal case here is the Israeli *kibbutz*. See Melford E. Spiro, *Kibbutz: Venture in Utopia* (Cambridge: Harvard University Press, 1956), and Etzioni, *op. cit.*

remain integrated with the outside community and to escape the encompassing tendency of the total institution.

Whether a particular total institution acts as a good or bad force in civil society, force it may well have, and this will depend on the suppression of a whole circle of actual or potential households. Conversely, the formation of households provides a structural guarantee that total institutions will not arise. The incompatibility of these two forms of social organization should tell us something about the wider social functions of them both.

The total institution, then, is a social hybrid, part residential community, part formal organization; therein lies its special sociological interest. There are other reasons for being interested in these establishments, too. They are the forcing houses for changing persons in our society; each is a natural experiment on what can be done to the self.

Some of the key features of total institutions have been suggested. I want now to consider these establishments from two perspectives— the inmate world, and the staff world—and to make some observations about contacts between the two.

THE INMATE WORLD

It is characteristic of inmates that they come to the institution with a "presenting culture" (to modify a psychiatric phrase) derived from a *home world*—a way of life and a round of activities taken for granted until the point of admission to the institution. (There is reason, then, to exclude orphanages and foundling homes from the list of total institutions, except insofar as the orphan comes to be socialized into the outside world by some process of cultural osmosis, even while this world is being systematically denied him.) Whatever the stability of the recruit's personal organization, it was part of a wider framework lodged in his civil environment—a round of experience that confirmed a tolerable conception of self, and allowed for a set of defensive maneuvers, exercised at his own discretion, for coping with conflicts, discreditings, and failures.

Now, it appears that total institutions do not substitute their own unique culture for something already formed; we deal with something more restricted than acculturation or assimilation. (If cultural change does occur, it has to do, perhaps, with the removal of certain behavior opportunities and the failure to keep pace with recent social changes on the outside. Thus if the inmate's stay is long, what has been called *disculturation*[11] may occur—that is, an "untraining" which renders him temporarily incapable of managing certain features of daily life on the outside, if and when he gets back to it.) The full meaning for the inmate of being "in" or "on the inside" does not exist apart from the special meaning to him of "getting out" or "getting on the outside." In this sense, total institutions do not really look for cultural victory. They create and sustain a particular kind of tension between the home world and the institutional world and use this persistent tension as strategic leverage in the management of men.

The recruit, then, comes into the establishment with a conception of himself made possible by certain stable social arrangements in his home world. Upon entrance, he is immediately stripped of the support provided by these arrangements. In the accurate language of some of our oldest total institutions, he begins a series of abasements, degradations, humiliations, and profanations of self. His self is systematically, if often unintentionally, mortified. He begins some radical shifts in his *moral career*, a career composed of the progressive changes that occur in the beliefs that he has concerning himself and significant others.

The Process of Mortification. The processes by which a person's self is mortified are fairly standard in total institutions.[12] Analysis of these processes can help us to see the arrangements that ordinary establishments must guarantee if members are to preserve their civilian selves.

The barrier that total institutions place between the inmate and the wider world marks the first curtailment of self. In civil life, the sequential scheduling of the individual's roles, both in the life cycle and in the repeated daily round, ensures that no one role he plays will block his performance and ties in another. In total institutions, in contrast, membership automatically disrupts role scheduling, since the inmate's separation from the wider world lasts around the clock and may continue for years. *Role dispossession* therefore occurs. In many total institutions, the privilege of visiting away from the estab-

---

[11] A term employed by Robert Sommer, "Patients Who Grow Old in a Mental Hospital," *Geriatrics,* 14 (1959), 586–587. The term "desocialization," sometimes used in this context, would seem to be too strong, implying loss of fundamental capacities to communicate and cooperate.

[12] An example of the description of these processes may be found in Gresham M. Sykes, *The Society of Captives* (Princeton: Princeton University Press, 1958), Ch. 4, "The Pains of Imprisonment," 63–83.

lishment or having visitors come to the establishment is completely withheld at first, ensuring a deep initial break with past roles and an appreciation of role dispossession. A report on cadet life in a military academy provides an illustration:

> This clean break with the past must be achieved in a relatively short period. For two months, therefore, the swab is not allowed to leave the base or to engage in social intercourse with non-cadets. This complete isolation helps to produce a unified group of swabs, rather than a heterogeneous collection of persons of high and low status. Uniforms are issued on the first day, and discussions of wealth and family background are taboo. Although the pay of the cadet is very low, he is not permitted to receive money from home. The role of cadet must supersede other roles the individual has been accustomed to play. There are few clues left which will reveal social status in the outside world.[13]

I might add that when entrance is voluntary, the recruit has already partially withdrawn from his home world: what is cleanly severed by the institution is something that had already started to decay.

While some roles can be re-established by the inmate if and when he returns to the world, it is plain that other losses are irrevocable and may be painfully experienced as such. It may not be possible to make up, at a later phase of the life cycle, the time not now spent in educational or job advancement, in courting, or in socializing one's children. A legal aspect of this permanent dispossession is found in the concept of "civil death": prison inmates may face not only a temporary loss of the rights to will money and write checks, to contest divorce or adoption proceedings, and to vote, but may have some of these rights permanently abrogated.[14]

The inmate, then, finds that certain roles are lost to him by virtue of the barrier that separates him from the outside world. The process

---

[13] Sanford M. Dornbusch, "The Military Academy as an Assimilating Institution," *Social Forces,* 33 (1955), 317. For an example of initial visiting restrictions in a mental hospital see, D. McI. Johnson and N. Dodds, eds., *The Plea for the Silent* (London: Christopher Johnson, 1957), 16. Compare the rule against having visitors which has often bound domestic servants to their total institution. See J. Jean Hecht, *The Domestic Servant Class in Eighteenth-Century England* (London: Routledge, Kegan Paul, 1956), 127–128.

[14] A useful review in the case of American prisons may be found in Paul W. Tappan, "The Legal Rights of Prisoners," *The Annals,* 293 (May, 1954), 99–111.

of entrance typically brings other kinds of loss and mortification as well. We very generally find what are called *admission procedures,* such as taking a life history, photographing, weighing, fingerprinting, number-assigning, searching, signing away of personal possessions, undressing, bathing, disinfecting, haircutting, issuing institutional clothing and instruction as to rules, and assigning to quarters.[15] Admission procedures might better be called "trimming" or "programming" because in thus being squared-away the new arrival allows himself to become shaped and coded into the kind of object that can be fed into the administrative machinery of the establishment, to be worked on smoothly by routine operations. Many of these procedures depend upon attributes such as weight or fingerprints which the individual possesses merely because he is a member of the largest and most abstract of social categories, that of the human being. Action taken on the basis of such attributes necessarily ignores most of his previous basis of self-identification.

Because a total institution deals with its inmates in so many connections, with a complex squaring away at admission, there is a special need to obtain initial cooperativeness from the recruit. Staff often feel that a recruit's readiness to be appropriately deferential in his initial face-to-face encounters with them is a sign that he will pliantly take the role of the routinely usable inmate. The occasion on which staff members first tell the inmate of his deference obligations may be structured to challenge the inmate to balk or to hold his peace forever. Thus these initial moments of socialization may involve an *obedience test* and even a *will-breaking contest*: an inmate who shows defiance receives immediate visible punishment, which increases until he openly "cries uncle" and humbles himself.

An engaging illustration is provided by Brendan Behan in his review of his contest with two warders upon his admission to Walton prison:

> "And 'old up your 'ead, when I speak to you."
>
> " 'Old up your 'ead, when Mr. Whitbread speaks to you," said Mr. Holmes.
>
> I looked round at Charlie. His eyes met mine and he quickly lowered them to the ground.

[15] See, for example, J. Kerkhoff, *How Thin the Veil: A Newspaperman's Story of His Own Mental Crackup and Recovery* (New York: Greenberg, 1952), 110; Elie A. Cohen, *Human Behaviour in the Concentration Camp,* (London: Jonathan Cape, 1954), 120; Eugen Kogon, *The Theory and Practice of Hell* (New York: Berkeley, 1950), 67.

"What are you looking round at, Behan? Look at me."
I looked at Mr. Whitbread. "I am looking at you," I said. . . .
"You are looking at Mr. Whitbread—what?" said Mr. Holmes.
"I am looking at Mr. Whitbread."
Mr. Holmes looked gravely at Mr. Whitbread, drew back his open hand, and struck me on the face, held me with his other hand and struck me again.

My head spun and burned and pained and I wondered would it happen again. I forgot and felt another smack, and forgot, and another, and moved, and was held by a steadying, almost kindly hand, and another, and my sight was a vision of red and white and pity-coloured flashes.

"You are looking at Mr. Whitbread—what, Behan?"
I gulped and got together my voice and tried again till I got it out. "I, sir, please, sir, I am looking at you, I mean, I am looking at Mr. Whitbread, sir."[16]

Admission procedures and obedience tests may be elaborated into a form of initiation that has been called *the welcome,* where staff or inmates, or both, go out of their way to give the recruit a clear notion of his plight.[17] As part of this *rite de passage* he may be called by a term, such as "fish" or "swab," which tells him that he is merely an inmate, and, what is more, that he has a special low status even in this low group.

The admission procedure may be characterized as a leaving off and a taking on, with the midpoint marked by physical nakedness. Leaving off, of course, entails a *dispossession* of property, important here because persons invest self-feelings in their possessions. Perhaps the most significant of these possessions is not physical at all, that is, one's full name; whatever one is thereafter called, loss of one's name can be a great curtailment of the self.[18]

---

[16] Brendan Behan, *Borstal Boy* (London: Hutchinson, 1958), 40. See also, Anthony Heckstall-Smith, *Eighteen Months* (London: Allan Wingate, 1954), 26.

[17] For a version of this process in concentration camps, see Cohen, *op. cit.,* p. 120, and Kogon, *op. cit.,* pp. 64–65. For a fictionalized treatment of the welcome in a girls' reformatory see, Sara Norris, *The Wayward Ones* (New York: Signet Books, 1952), 31–34. A prison version, less explicit, is found in George Dendrickson and Frederick Thomas, *The Truth About Dartmoor* (London: Gollancz, 1954), 42–57.

[18] For example, Thomas Merton, *The Seven Storey Mountain* (New York: Harcourt, Brace and Company, 1948), 290–91; Cohen, *op. cit.,* pp. 146–47.

Once the inmate is stripped of his possessions, at least some replacements must be made by the establishment, but these take the form of standard issue, uniform in character and uniformly distributed. These substitute possessions are clearly marked as really belonging to the institution and in some cases are recalled at regular intervals to be, as it were, disinfected of identifications. With objects that can be used up, for example pencils, the inmate may be required to return the remnants before obtaining a re-issue.[19] Failure to provide inmates with individual lockers, and periodic searches and confiscations of accumulated personal property[20] reinforce property dispossession. Religious orders have appreciated the implications for self of such separation from belongings. Inmates may be required to change their cells once a year so as not to become attached to them. The Benedictine Rule is explicit:

> For their bedding let a mattress, a blanket, a coverlet, and a pillow suffice. These beds must be frequently inspected by the Abbot, because of private property which may be found therein. If anyone be discovered to have what he has not received from the Abbot, let him be most severely punished. And in order that this vice of private ownership may be completely rooted out, let all things that are necessary be supplied by the Abbot: that is, cowl, tunic, stockings, shoes, girdle, knife, pen, needle, handkerchief, and tablets; so that all plea of necessity may be taken away. And let the Abbot always consider that passage in the Acts of the Apostles: "Distribution was made to each according as anyone had need."[21]

One set of the individual's possessions has a special relation to self. The individual ordinarily expects to exert some control over the guise in which he appears before others. For this he needs cosmetic and clothing supplies, tools for applying, arranging, and repairing them, and an accessible, secure place to store these supplies and tools—in short, for the management of his personal front, the individual possesses an identity kit. He also has access to services offered by barbers and clothiers.

On admission to a total institution, however, the individual is likely to be stripped of his usual appearance and of the equipment and services by which he maintains it, suffering, thus, a *personal*

[19] Dendrickson and Thomas, *op. cit.*, p. 85; also, *The Holy Rule of St. Benedict*, Ch. 55.

[20] Kogon, *op. cit.*, p. 69.

[21] *The Holy Rule of Saint Benedict*, Ch. 55.

defacement. Clothing, combs, needle and thread, cosmetics, towels soap, shaving sets, bathing facilities—all these may be taken away or denied him, although some may be kept in inaccessible storage, to be returned if and when he leaves. In the words of Saint Benedict's Holy Rule:

> Then forthwith he shall, there in the oratory, be divested of his own garments with which he is clothed and be clad in those of the monastery. Those garments of which he is divested shall be placed in the wardrobe, there to be kept, so that if, perchance, he should ever be persuaded by the devil to leave the monastery (which God forbid), he may be stripped of the monastic habit and cast forth.[22]

As suggested, the institutional issue provided as a substitute for what has been taken away is typically of a "coarse" variety, ill-suited, often old, and the same for large categories of inmates. The impact of this substitution is described in a report on imprisoned prostitutes:

> First, there is the shower officer who forces them to undress, takes their own clothes away, sees to it that they take showers and get their prison clothes—one pair of black oxfords with cuban heels, two pairs of much-mended ankle socks, three cotton dresses, two cotton slips, two pairs of panties, and a couple of bras. Practically all the bras are flat and useless. No corsets or girdles are issued.
> There is not a sadder sight than some of the obese prisoners who, if nothing else, have been managing to keep themselves looking decent on the outside, confronted by the first sight of themselves in prison issue.[23]

In addition to personal defacement that comes from being stripped of one's identity kit, there is *personal disfigurement* that comes from such direct and permanent mutilations of the body as brands or loss of limbs. Although this mortification of the self by way of the body is found in few total institutions, still, loss of a sense of personal safety is common and provides a basis for anxieties about disfigurement. Beatings, surgery, or shock therapy—whatever the intent of staff in providing these services for some inmates—may lead many

---

[22] *Ibid.,* Ch. 58.

[23] John M. Murtagh and Sara Harris, *Cast the First Stone* (New York: Pocket Books, 1958), 239–240. On mental hospitals see, for example, Kerkhoff, *op. cit.,* p. 10. Ward, *op. cit.,* p. 60 makes the reasonable suggestion that men in our society suffer less defacement in total institutions than do women.

inmates to feel that they are in an environment that does not guarantee their physical integrity.

At admission, then, loss of identity equipment can prevent the individual from presenting his usual image of himself to others. After admission, the image of himself he presents is attacked in another way.

Given the expressive idiom of a particular civil society, certain movements, postures, and stances will convey lowly images of the individual and be avoided as demeaning. Any regulation, command, or task that forces the individual to adopt these movements or postures may thus mortify the self. In total institutions, such physical indignities abound. In mental hospitals, for example, patients may be forced to eat all food with a spoon.[24] In military prisons, inmates may be required to stand at attention whenever an officer enters the compound.[25] In religious institutions, there are such classic gestures of penitence as the kissing of feet,[26] and the posture required of an erring monk—that he must

> lie prostrate at the door of the oratory in silence; and thus, with his face to the ground and his body prone, let him cast himself at the feet of all as they go forth from the oratory.[27]

In some penal institutions, we find the humiliation of bending over to receive a birching.[28]

Just as the individual can be required to hold his body in a humiliating pose, so he may have to provide humiliating verbal responses. An important instance of this is the forced deference pattern of total institutions; inmates are often required to punctuate their social intercourse with staff by verbal acts of deference, such as saying "Sir." Another instance is the necessity to beg, importune, or humbly ask for little things such as a light for a cigarette, a drink of water, or permission to use the telephone.

Corresponding to the indignities of speech and action required of the inmate are the indignities of treatment others accord him. The standard examples here are *verbal or gestural profanations*: staff or fellow inmates call the individual obscene names, curse him, point out

[24] Johnson and Dodds, *op. cit.*, p. 15; for a prison version see Alfred Hassler, *Diary of a Self-Made Convict* (Chicago: Regnery, 1954), 31.

[25] L. D. Hankoff, "Interaction Patterns Among Military Prison Personnel," *U.S. Armed Forces Medical Journal*, 10 (1959), 1419.

[26] Kathryn Hulme, *The Nun's Story* (London: Muller, 1957), 52.

[27] *The Holy Rule of St. Benedict*, Ch. 44.

[28] Dendrickson and Thomas, *op. cit.*, p. 76.

his negative attributes, tease him, or talk about him or his fellow-inmates as if he were not present.

Whatever the form or the source of these various indignities, the individual has to engage in activity whose symbolic implications are incompatible with his conception of self. A more diffuse example of this kind of mortification occurs when the individual is required to undertake a daily round of life that he considers alien to him—to undertake a *disidentifying role*. Thus in prisons denial of hetero-sexual activity can induce the fear of losing one's masculinity.[29] In military establishments, the patently useless make-work forced on fatigue details can cause men to feel their time and effort are worthless.[30] In religious institutions, there are special arrangements to ensure that all inmates take a turn performing the more menial aspects of the servant role.[31] An extreme is the concentration camp practice requiring prisoners to administer whippings to other prisoners.[32]

There is another form of mortification in total institutions; beginning with admission, a kind of *contaminative exposure* occurs. On the outside, the individual can hold objects of self-feeling—such as his body, his immediate actions, his thoughts, and some of his possessions—clear of contact with alien and contaminating things. But in total institutions these territories of the self are violated: the boundary that the individual places between his being and the environment is invaded and the embodiments of self profaned.

There is, first, a violation of one's informational preserve regarding self. During admission, facts about the inmate's social statuses and past behavior—especially discreditable facts—are collected and recorded in a dossier available to staff. Later, insofar as the establishment officially expects to alter the self-regulating inner-tendencies of the inmate, there may be dyadic or group confession—psychiatric, political, military or religious—according to the type of institution. On these occasions the inmate has to expose facts and feelings about self to new kinds of audiences. The most spectacular examples of such exposure come to us from Communist confession camps and from the *culpa* sessions that form part of the routine of Catholic religious institutions.[33] The dynamics of the process have been explicitly considered by those engaged in so-called milieu therapy.

[29] Sykes, *op. cit.*, pp. 70–72.
[30] For example, Lawrence, *op. cit.*, pp. 34–35.
[31] *The Holy Rule of St. Benedict*, Ch. 35.
[32] Kogon, *op. cit.*, p. 102.
[33] Hume, *op. cit.*, pp. 48–51.

Not only do new audiences learn discreditable facts about oneself that are ordinarily concealed, but they are also in a position to perceive some of these facts directly. Thus prisoners and mental patients cannot prevent their visitors from seeing them in humiliating circumstances.[34] Another example is the shoulder-patch of ethnic identification worn by concentration camp inmates.[35] Medical and security examinations often expose the inmate physically, sometimes to persons of both sexes. Collective sleeping arrangements cause a similar exposure, as do doorless toilets.[36] An extreme here, perhaps, is the situation of the mental patient who is stripped naked for what is felt to be his own protection and placed in a constantly-lit seclusion room, into whose judas-window any person passing on the ward can peer. In general, of course, the inmate is never fully alone; he is always within sight and often within earshot of someone, if only his fellow-inmates.[37] Prison cages with bars for walls fully realize such exposure.

Perhaps the most obvious type of contaminative exposure is the directly physical kind—the besmearing and defiling of the body or of other objects closely identified with the self. Sometimes this involves a breakdown of the usual environmental arrangements for insulating oneself from one's own source of contamination, as in having to empty one's own slops[38] or having to subject one's evacuation to regimentation, as reported in Chinese political prisons:

> An aspect of their isolation regimen which is especially onerous to Western prisoners is the arrangement for the elimination of urine and feces. The "slop jar" that is usually present in Russian cells is often absent in China. It is a Chinese custom to allow defecation and urination only at one or two specified times each day—usually in the morning after breakfast. The prisoner is hustled from his cell

[34] Wider communities in Western society, of course, have employed this technique too, in the form of public floggings and public hangings, the pillory and stocks. Functionally correlated with the public emphasis on mortifications in total institutions is the commonly found strict ruling that staff is not to be humiliated by staff in the presence of inmates.

[35] Kogon, *op. cit.*, pp. 41–42.

[36] Behan, *op. cit.*, p. 23.

[37] For example, Kogon, *op. cit.*, p. 128; Hassler, *op. cit.*, p. 16. For the situation in a religious institution, see Hulme, *op. cit.*, p. 48. She also describes a lack of aural privacy: thin cotton hangings are used as the only door closing off the individual sleeping cells (p. 20).

[38] Heckstall-Smith, *op. cit.*, p. 21; Dendrickson and Thomas, *op. cit.*, p. 53.

by a guard, double-timed down a long corridor, and given approximately two minutes to squat over an open Chinese latrine and attend to all of his wants. The haste and the public scrutiny are especially difficult for women to tolerate. If the prisoners cannot complete their action in about two minutes, they are abruptly dragged away and back to their cells.[39]

A very common form of physical contamination is reflected in complaints about unclean food, messy quarters, soiled towels, shoes and clothing impregnated with previous users' sweat, toilets without seats, and dirty bath facilities.[40] Orwell's comments on his boarding school may be taken as illustrative:

For example, there were the pewter bowls out of which we had our porridge. They had overhanging rims, and under the rims there were accumulations of sour porridge, which could be flaked off in long strips. The porridge itself, too, contained more lumps, hairs and unexplained black things than one would have thought possible, unless someone were putting them there on purpose. It was never safe to start on that porridge without investigating it first. And there was the slimy water of the plunge bath—it was twelve or fifteen feet long, the whole school was supposed to go into it every morning, and I doubt whether the water was changed at all frequently—and the always-damp towels with their cheesy smell. . . . And the sweaty smell of the changing room with its greasy basins, and, given on this, the row of filthy, dilapidated lavatories, which had no fastenings of any kind on the doors, so that whenever you were sitting there someone was sure to come crashing in. It is not easy for me to think of my school days without seeming to breathe in a whiff of something cold and evil-smelling—a sort of compound of sweaty stockings, dirty towels, fecal smells blowing along corridors, forks with old food between the prongs, neck-of-mutton stew, and the banging doors of the lavatories and the echoing chamber-pots in the dormitories.[41]

[39] L. E. Hinkle and H. G. Wolff, "Communist Interrogation and Indoctrination of 'Enemies of the State,' " *A.M.A. Archives of Neurology and Psychiatry*, 76 (1956), 154. An extremely useful report on the profanizing role of fecal matter, and the social necessity of personal control as well as environmental control, is provided in C. E. Orbach, et al., "Fears and Defensive Adaptations to the Loss of Anal Sphincter Control," *The Psychoanalytical Review*, 44 (1957), 121–175.

[40] For example, Johnson and Dodds, *op. cit.*, p. 75; Heckstall-Smith, *op. cit.*, p. 15.

[41] George Orwell, "Such, Such Were the Joys," *Partisan Review*, 19 (Sept.–Oct., 1952), 523.

There are still other sources of physical contamination, as an interviewee suggests in describing a concentration camp hospital:

> We were lying two in each bed. And it was very unpleasant. For example, if a man died he would not be removed before twenty-four hours had elapsed because the block trusty wanted, of course, to get the bread ration and the soup which was allotted to this person. For this reason the dead person would be reported dead twenty-four hours later so that his ration would still be allotted. And so we had to lie all that time in bed together with the dead person.[42]

> We were on the middle level. And that was a very gruesome situation, especially at night. First of all, the dead men were badly emaciated and they looked terrible. In most cases they would soil themselves at the moment of death and that was not a very esthetic event. I saw such cases very frequently in the lager, in the sick people's barracks. People who died from phlegmonous, suppurative wounds, with their beds overflowing from pus would be lying together with somebody whose illness was possibly more benign, who had possibly just a small wound which now would become infected.[43]

The contamination of lying near the dying has also been reported in mental hospital reports,[44] and surgical contamination has been cited in prison documents:

> Surgical instruments and bandages in the dressing-room lie exposed to the air and dust. George, attending for the treatment, by a medical orderly, of a boil on his neck, had it lanced with a scalpel that had been used a moment before on a man's foot, and had not been sterilised in the meantime.[45]

Finally, in some total institutions the inmate is obliged to take oral or intravenous medications, whether desired or not, and to eat his food, however unpalatable. When an inmate refuses to eat, there may be forcible contamination of his insides by "forced-feeding."

I have suggested that the inmate undergoes mortification of the self by contaminative exposure of a physical or surface kind, but this must be amplified: for when the agency of contamination is another human being, then the inmate is in addition contaminated by forced

---

[42] David P. Boder, *I Did Not Interview the Dead* (Urbana: University of Illinois Press, 1949), 50.

[43] *Ibid.*

[44] Johnson and Dodds, *op. cit.*, p. 16.

[45] Dendrickson and Thomas, *op. cit.*, p. 122.

interpersonal contact and, in consequence, a forced social relation-ship. Similarly, when the inmate loses control over who observes him in his predicament, or who knows about his past, he is being con-taminated by a forced relationship to these people—for it is through such perception and knowledge that relations are expressed.

The model for interpersonal contamination in our society is pre-sumably rape, but, while sexual molestation certainly occurs in total institutions, there are many other less dramatic examples. Upon ad-mission, one's on-person possessions are pawed and fingered by an official as he itemizes and prepares them for storage. The inmate himself may be frisked and searched to the extent—often reported in the literature—of a rectal examination.[46] Later in his stay he may be required to undergo searchings of his person and of his sleeping-quarters, either routinely or when trouble arises. In all these cases it is the searcher as well as the search that penetrates the private reserve of the individual and violates the territories of his self. Even routine inspections can have this effect, as Lawrence suggests:

> In the old days men had weekly to strip off boots and socks, and expose their feet for an officer's inspection. An ex-boy'd kick you in the mouth, as you bent down to look. So with the bath-rolls, a certificate from your N.C.O. that you'd had a bath during the week. One bath! And with the kit inspections, and room inspections, and equipment inspections, all excuses for the dogmatists among the officers to blunder, and for the nosy-parkers to make beasts of themselves. Oh, you require the gentlest touch to interfere with a poor man's person, and not give offence.[47]

Further, the practice of mixing age, ethnic, and racial groups in prisons and mental hospitals can lead an inmate to feel he is being contaminated by contact with undesirable fellow-inmates. A prisoner, describing his admission to prison, provides an example:

> Another warder came up with a pair of handcuffs and coupled me to the little Jew, who moaned softly to himself in Yiddish.[48]

---

[46] For example, Murtagh and Harris, *op. cit.,* p. 240; Lowell Naeve, *A Field of Broken Stones* (Glen Gardner: Libertarian Press, 1950), 17; Kogon, *op. cit.,* p. 67; Holley Cantine and Dachine Rainer, Eds., *Prison Etiquette* (Bearsville, N.Y.: Retort Press, 1950), 46.

[47] Lawrence, *op. cit.,* p. 196.

[48] Heckstall-Smith, *op. cit.,* p. 14.

> Suddenly, the awful thought occurred to me that I might have to share a cell with the little Jew and I was seized with panic. The thought obsessed me to the exclusion of all else.[49]

Obviously, group-living will necessitate mutual contact and exposure among inmates. At the extreme, as in cells for Chinese political prisoners, mutual contact may be very great:

> At some stage in his imprisonment the prisoner can expect to find himself placed in a cell with about eight other prisoners. If he was initially isolated and interrogated, this may be shortly after his first "confession" is accepted; but many prisoners are placed in group cells from the outset of their imprisonment. The cell is usually barren, and scarcely large enough to hold the group it contains. There may be a sleeping platform, but all of the prisoners sleep on the floor; and when all lie down, every inch of floor space may be taken up. The atmosphere is extremely intimate. Privacy is entirely nonexistent.[50]

Lawrence provides a military illustration in discussing his difficulties in merging with fellow-airmen in the barracks hut:

> You see, I cannot play at anything with anyone: and a native shyness shuts me out from their freemasonry of —— and blinding, pinching, borrowing, and talking dirty: this despite my sympathy for the abandon of functional frankness in which they wallow. Inevitably, in our crowded lodging, we must communicate just those physical modesties which polite life keeps veiled. Sexual activity's a naive boast, and any abnormalities of appetite or organ are curiously displayed. The Powers encourage this behaviour. All latrines in camp have lost their doors. "Make the little ——s sleep and —— and eat together," grinned old Jock Mackay, senior instructor, "and we'll have 'em drilling together, naturally."[51]

One routine instance of this contaminative contact is the naming system for inmates. Staff and fellow-inmates automatically assume the right to employ an intimate form of address or a truncated formal one: for a middle class person, at least, this denies the right to hold himself off from others through a formal style of address.[52] When the

---

[49] *Ibid.,* p. 17.
[50] Hinkle and Wolff, *op. cit.,* p. 42.
[51] Lawrence, *op. cit.,* p. 91.
[52] For example, see Hassler, *op. cit.,* p. 104.

individual has to eat food he considers alien and polluted, this contamination sometimes derives from other persons' connection with the food, as is nicely illustrated in the penance of "begging soup" practiced in some nunneries:

> . . . she placed her pottery bowl on the left of the Mother Superior, knelt, clasped her hands and waited until two spoonfuls of soup had been put into her beggar's bowl, then on to the next oldest and the next, until the bowl was filled. . . . When at last her bowl was filled, she returned to her place and swallowed the soup, as she knew she must, down to the last drop. She tried not to think how it had been tossed into her bowl from a dozen other bowls that had already been eaten from.[53]

Another kind of contaminative exposure is that which brings an outsider into contact with the individual's close relationship to significant others. For example, an inmate may have his personal mail read and censored, and even made fun of to his face.[54] Another example is the enforced public character of visits, as reports from prisons suggest:

> But what a sadistic kind of arrangement they have for these visits! One hour a month—or two half-hours—in a big room with perhaps a score of other couples, with guards prowling about to make sure you exchange neither the plans nor the implements of escape! We met across a six-foot-wide table, down the middle of which a sort of bundling-board six inches high presumably prevents even our germs from intermingling. We were permitted one sanitary handshake at the beginning of the visit and one at the end; for the rest of the time we could only sit and look at each other while we called across that vast expanse![55]

> Visits take place in a room by the main gate. There is a wooden table, at one side of which sits the prisoner and at the other side his visitors. The warder sits at the head; he hears every word that is spoken, watches every gesture and nuance of expression. There is no privacy at all—and this when a man is meeting his wife whom he may not have seen for years. Nor is any contact allowed between prisoner and visitor, and, of course, no articles are allowed to change hands.[56]

[53] Hulme, *op. cit.,* pp. 52–53.
[54] Dendrickson and Thomas, *op. cit.,* p. 28.
[55] Hassler, *op. cit.,* pp. 62–63.
[56] Dendrickson and Thomas, *op. cit.,* p. 175.

A more thoroughgoing version of this type of contaminative exposure occurs in institutionally-arranged confessions. When a significant other must be denounced, and especially when this other is physically present, confession of the relationship to outsiders can mean an intense exposure and contamination of self. A description of practices in a nunnery provides an illustration:

> The bravest of the emotionally vulnerable were the sisters who stood up together in the culpa and proclaimed each other—for having gone out of their way to be near to one another, or perhaps for having talked together in recreation in a way that excluded others. Their tormented but clearly spoken disclosures of a nascent affinity gave it the *coup de grâce* which they themselves might not have been able to do, for the entire community would henceforth see to it that these two would be kept far apart. The pair would be helped to detach themselves from one of those spontaneous personal attachments which often sprang to life in the body of the community as unexpectedly as wildflowers appeared, now and again, in the formal geometric patterns of the cloister gardens.[57]

A parallel example can be found in highly professionalized mental hospitals devoted to intensive milieu therapy, where patient-pairs conducting an affair may be obliged to discuss their relationship during group meetings.

In total institutions, exposure of one's relationships can occur in even more drastic forms, for there may be occasions when an individual must witness a physical assault upon someone to whom he has ties, and suffer the permanent mortification of having taken no action. Thus we learn of a mental hospital:

> This knowledge [of shock therapy] is based on the fact that some of the patients in Ward 30 have assisted the shock team in the administration of therapy to patients, holding them down, and helping to strap them in bed, or watching them after they have quieted. The administration of shock on the ward is often carried out in full sight of a group of interested onlookers. The patient's convulsions often resemble those of an accident victim in death agony and are accompanied by choking gasps and at times by a foaming overflow of saliva from the mouth. The patient slowly recovers without memory of the occurrence, but he has served the others as a frightful spectacle of what may be done to them.[58]

[57] Hulme, *op. cit.*, pp. 50–51.
[58] Belknap, *op. cit.*, p. 194.

Melville's report on flogging aboard a nineteenth century man-of-war provides another example:

> However much you may desire to absent yourself from the scene that ensues, yet behold it you must; or, at least, stand near it you must; for the regulations enjoin the attendance of almost the entire ship's company, from the corpulent captain himself to the smallest boy who strikes the bell.[59]

And the inevitableness of his own presence at the scene: the strong arm that drags him in view of the scourge, and holds him there till all is over: forcing upon his loathing eye and soul the sufferings and groans of men who have familiarly consorted with him, eaten with him, battled out watches with him—men of his own type and badge —all this conveys a terrible hint of the omnipotent authority under which he lives.[60]

Lawrence offers a military example:

> Tonight's crash of the stick on the hut door at roll call was terrific; and the door slammed back nearly off its hinges. Into the light strode Baker, V.C., a corporal who assumed great licence in the camp because of his war decoration. He marched down my side of the hut, checking the beds. Little Nobby, taken by surprise, had one boot on and another off. Corporal Baker stopped. "What's the matter with you?" "I was knocking out a nail which hurts my foot." "Put your boot on at once. Your name?" He passed on to the end door and there whirled around, snorting, "Clarke." Nobby properly cried, "Corporal," and limped down the alley at a run (we must always run when called) to bring up stiffly at attention before him. A pause, and then curtly, "Get back to your bed."
>
> Still the Corporal waited and so must we, lined up by our beds. Again, sharply, "Clarke." The performance was repeated, over and over, while the four files of us looked on, bound fast by shame and discipline. We were men, and a man over there was degrading himself and his species, in degrading another. Baker was lusting for trouble and hoped to provoke one of us into some act or word on which to base a charge.[61]

The extreme of this kind of *experiential mortification* is found of course in the concentration camp literature:

> A Jew from Breslau named Silbermann had to stand by idly as SS Sergeant Hoppe brutally tortured his brother to death. Silber-

---

[59] Herman Melville, *White Jacket* (New York: Grove Press, n.d.), 135.
[60] *Ibid.*
[61] Lawrence, *op. cit.*, p. 62.

mann went mad at the sight, and late at night he precipitated a
panic with his frantic cries that the barracks was on fire.[62]

I have considered some of the more elementary and direct assaults
upon the self—various forms of disfigurement and defilement through
which the symbolic meaning of events in the inmate's immediate
presence dramatically fails to corroborate his prior conception of self.
I would like now to consider a source of mortification that is less
direct in its effect, with a significance for the individual that is less
easy to assess: a disruption of the usual relationship between the
individual actor and his acts.

The first disruption to consider here is *looping*: an agency
that creates a defensive response on the part of the inmate takes
this very response as the target of its next attack. The individual finds
that his protective response to an assault upon self is collapsed into
the situation; he cannot defend himself in the usual way by establishing distance between the mortifying situation and himself.

Deference patterns in total institutions provide one illustration of
the looping effect. In civil society, when an individual must accept
circumstances and commands that affront his conception of self, he
is allowed a margin of face-saving reactive expression—sullenness,
failure to offer usual signs of deference, *sotto voce* profaning asides,
or fugitive expressions of contempt, irony, and derision. Compliance,
then, is likely to be associated with an expressed attitude to one's
compliance which is not itself subject to the same degree of pressure
for conformity. Although such self-protective expressive response to
humiliating demands does occur in total institutions, staff may
directly penalize inmates for such expressive activity, citing sullenness
or insolence explicitly as grounds for further punishment. Thus, in
describing the contamination of self resulting from having to drink
soup from a beggar's bowl, Kathryn Hulme says that she:

> . . . blanked out from her facial expression the revolt that rose up
> in her fastidious soul as she drank her dregs. One look of rebellion,
> she knew, would be enough to invite a repetition of the awful abase-
> ment which she was sure she could never go through again, not
> even for the sake of the Blessed Lord Himself.[63]

The desegregating process in total institutions creates other instances of looping. In the normal course of affairs in civil society,
audience and role segregation keep one's avowals and implicit claims

[62] Kogon, *op. cit.*, p. 160.
[63] Hulme, *op. cit.*, p. 53.

regarding self, made in one physical scene of activity, from being tested against conduct in other settings.[64] In total institutions, spheres of life are desegregated, so that an inmate's conduct in one scene of activity is thrown up to him by staff as a comment and check upon his conduct in another context. Thus a mental patient, in an effort to present himself in a well-oriented, unantagonistic manner during a diagnostic or treatment conference may be directly embarrassed by evidence introduced concerning his apathy during recreation, or by showing him the bitter comments he made in a letter to a sibling—a letter which the recipient has forwarded to the hospital administrator, to be added to the patient's dossier and brought along to the conference.

Psychiatric establishments of the advanced type play a special role in looping, since didactic feedback may there be erected into a basic therapeutic doctrine. A "permissive" atmosphere is felt to encourage the inmate to "project" or "act out" his typical difficulties in living, which can then be brought to his attention during group therapy sessions.[65]

Through the process of looping, then, the inmate's reaction to his own situation is collapsed back into this situation itself, and he is not allowed to retain the usual segregation of these phases of action. A second assault upon the inmate's status as an actor may now be cited, one that has been loosely described under the categories of regimentation and tyrannization.

In civil society, by the time the individual is an adult he has incorporated socially acceptable standards for the performance of most of his activity so that the issue of the correctness of his action arises only at certain points, as when his productivity is judged. Beyond this, he is allowed to go at his own pace.[66] He need not con-

---

[64] In civil society, crimes and certain other forms of deviance affect the way in which the offender is received in all areas of life, but this breakdown of spheres applies mainly to offenders rather than to the bulk of the population that does not offend in these ways or offends without being caught.

[65] A clear statement may be found in R. Rapoport and E. Skellern, "Some Therapeutic Functions of Administrative Disturbance," *Administrative Science Quarterly*, 2 (1957), 84–85.

[66] The span of time over which an employee works at his own discretion without supervision can in fact be taken as a measure of his pay and status in an organization. See, Elliot Jacques, *The Measurement of Responsibility: A Study of Work, Payment, and Individual Capacity* (Cambridge: Harvard University Press, 1956). And just as "time-span of responsibility" is an index of position, so a long span of freedom from inspection is a reward of position.

stantly look over his shoulder to see if criticism and other sanctions are coming. In addition, many actions will be defined as matters of personal taste, with choice from a range of possibilities specifically allowed. For much activity, then, the judgment and action of authority is held off and one is on one's own. Under such circumstances, one can schedule activity so as to fit actions into one another to one's over-all profit—a kind of "personal economy of action," as when an individual postpones eating for a few minutes in order to finish a task, or lays aside a task a little early in order to join a friend for dinner, or maintains a side-activity while focusing on a main one. For a person who joins a total institution, however, minute segments of his line of activity may be subjected to regulations and judgment by staff; the individual's life is penetrated by the constant, sanctioning interaction with staff, especially during the initial period of stay before the inmate accepts the regulations unthinkingly. Each specification robs the individual of an opportunity to balance his needs and objectives in a personally efficient way, and opens up his line of action to sanctions. Thus the autonomy of the act itself is violated.

Although this process of social control is in effect in all organized society, we tend to forget how detailed and act-controlling it can become in total institutions. The routine reported for one jail for youthful offenders provides a striking example:

> At 5:30 we were wakened and had to jump out of bed and stand at attention. When the guard shouted "One!" you removed your night shirt; at "Two!" you folded it; at "Three!" you made your bed. (Only two minutes to make the bed in a difficult and complicated manner.) All the while three monitors would shout at us: "Hurry it up!" and "Make it snappy!"
>
> We also dressed by numbers: shirts on at "One!"; pants at "Two!"; socks at "Three!"; shoes at "Four!" Any noise, like dropping a shoe or even scraping it along the floor, was enough to send you to the line.
>
> . . . Once downstairs everyone faced the wall at strict attention, hands at side, thumbs even with trouser seams, head up, shoulders back, stomach in, heels together, eyes straight ahead, no scratching or putting hands to face or head, no moving even the fingers.[67]

A jail for adults provides another example:

> The silence system was enforced. No talking outside the cell, at meals or at work.

[67] Hassler, *op. cit.*, p. 155.

No pictures were allowed in the cell. No gazing about at meals. Bread crusts were allowed to be left only on the left side of the plate. Inmates were required to stand at attention, cap in hand, until any official, visitor or guard moved beyond sight.[68]

And a concentration camp:

In the barracks a wealth of new and confusing impressions overwhelmed the prisoners. Making up beds was a particular source of SS chicanery. Shapeless and matted straw pallets had to be made as even as a board, the pattern of the sheets parallel to the edges, head bolsters set up at right angles.[69]

The SS seized on the most trifling offenses as occasions for punishment: keeping hands in pockets in cold weather; turning up the coat collar in rain or wind; missing buttons; the tiniest tear or speck of dirt on the clothing; unshined shoes . . . ; shoes that were too well shined—indicating that the wearer was shirking work; failure to salute, including so-called "sloppy posture"; . . . The slightest deviation in dressing ranks and files, or arranging the prisoners in the order of size, or any swaying, coughing, sneezing—any of these might provoke a savage outburst from the SS.[70]

From the military comes an example of the specifications possible in kit-laying:

Now the tunic, so folded that the belt made it a straight edge. Covering it, the breeches, squared to the exact area of the tunic, with four concertina-folds facing forward. Towels were doubled once, twice, thrice, and flanked the blue tower. In front of the blue sat a rectangular cardigan. To each side a rolled puttee. Shirts were packed and laid in pairs like flannel bricks. Before them, pants. Between them, neat balls of socks, wedged in. Our holdalls were stretched wide, with knife, fork, spoon, razor, comb, toothbrush, lather brush, button-stick, in that order, ranged across them.[71]

Similarly, an ex-nun speaks of having to learn to keep her hands still and hidden and to accept the fact that only six specified items were

[68] T. E. Gaddis, *Birdman of Alcatraz* (New York: Signet Books, 1958), 25. For a similar rule of silence in a British prison, see Frank Norman, *Bang to Rights* (London: Secker and Warburg, 1958), 27.

[69] Kogon, *op. cit.,* p. 68.

[70] *Ibid.,* pp. 99–100.

[71] Lawrence, *op. cit.,* p. 83. In this connection see the comments by M. Brewster Smith on the concept of "chicken," p. 390, Vol. 1, S. Stouffer, et al., *The American Soldier* (Princeton: Princeton University Press, 1949).

permitted in one's pockets.[72] An ex-mental patient speaks of the humiliation of being doled out limited toilet paper at each request.[73]

As suggested earlier, one of the most telling ways in which one's economy of action can be disrupted is the obligation to request permission or supplies for minor activities that one can execute on one's own on the outside, such as smoking, shaving, going to the toilet, telephoning, spending money, or mailing letters. This obligation not only puts the individual in a submissive or suppliant role "unnatural" for an adult but also opens up his line of action to interceptions by staff. Instead of having his request immediately and automatically granted, the inmate may be teased, denied, questioned at length, not noticed, or, as an ex-mental patient suggests, merely put off:

> Probably anyone who has never been in a similarly helpless position cannot realize the humiliation to anyone able-bodied yet lacking authority to do the simplest offices for herself of having to beg repeatedly for even such small necessities as clean linen or a light for her cigarette from nurses who constantly brush her aside with, "I'll give it to you in a minute, dear," and go off leaving her unsupplied. Even the canteen staff seemed to share the opinion that civility was wasted upon lunatics, and would keep a patient waiting indefinitely, while they gossiped with their friends.[74]

I have suggested that authority in total institutions is directed to a multitude of items of conduct—dress, deportment, manners—that constantly occur and constantly come up for judgment. The inmate cannot easily escape from the press of judgmental officials and from the enveloping tissue of constraint. A total institution, then, is like a finishing school, but one that has many refinements and is little refined.

I would like to comment on two aspects of this tendency toward a multiplication of actively enforced rulings. First, these rulings are often geared in with an obligation to perform the regulated activity in unison with blocks of fellow-inmates. This is what is sometimes called regimentation.

Secondly, these diffuse rulings occur in an authority system of the *echelon* kind; *any* member of the staff class has certain rights to discipline *any* member of the inmate class, thereby markedly increas-

[72] Hulme, *op. cit.*, pp. 3, 39.
[73] Ward, *op. cit.*, p. 23.
[74] Johnson and Dodds, *op. cit.*, p. 39.

ing the probability of sanction. (This arrangement, it may be noted, is similar to the one that gives any adult in some small American towns certain rights to correct, and demand small services from, any child not in the immediate presence of his parents.) On the outside, the adult in our society is typically under the authority of a *single* immediate superior in connection with his work, or under authority of one spouse in connection with domestic duties; the only echelon authority he must face—the police—is typically not constantly or relevantly present, except perhaps in the case of traffic-law enforcement.

Given echelon authority and regulations that are diffuse, novel, and strictly enforced, we may expect inmates, especially new ones, to live with chronic anxiety about breaking the rules and in fear of the consequence of breaking them—physical injury or death in a concentration camp, being "washed out" in an officer's training camp, or merely demotion in a mental hospital:

> Yet, even in the apparent liberty and friendliness of an "open" ward, I still found a background of threats that made me feel something between a prisoner and a pauper. The smallest offence, from a nervous symptom to displeasing a sister personally, was met by the suggestion of removing the offender to a closed ward. The idea of a return to "J" ward, if I did not eat my food, was brandished at me so constantly that it became an obsession and even such meals as I was able to swallow disagreed with me physically, while other patients were impelled to do unnecessary or uncongenial work by a similar fear.[75]

In total institutions, then, staying out of trouble is likely to require persistent conscious effort. The inmate may therefore forego certain levels of sociability with his fellows to avoid possible incidents.

In concluding this description of the processes of mortification, three general issues must be raised.

First, total institutions disrupt or defile precisely those actions that in civil society seem to have the special role of attesting to the actor and to those in his presence that he has some command over his world—that he is a person with "adult" self-determination, autonomy, and freedom of action. A failure to retain this kind of adult executive competency, or at least the symbols of it, can produce in the inmate the terror of feeling radically demoted in the age-grading system.[76]

[75] *Ibid.*, p. 36.
[76] *Cf.* Sykes, *op. cit.*, pp. 73–76, "The Deprivation of Autonomy."

A margin of self-selected expressive behavior—whether of antagonism, affection, or unconcern—is one symbol of self-determination.
This evidence of one's autonomy is weakened by such specific obligations as having to write one letter home a week, or having to refrain
from expressing sullenness. It is further weakened when this margin
of behavior is used as evidence concerning the state of one's psychiatric, religious, or political conscience.

There are certain bodily comforts significant to the individual
that tend to be lost upon entrance into a total institution—for example, a soft bed,[77] or quietness at night.[78] Loss of this set of comforts
is apt to reflect a loss of self-determination, too, for the individual
tends to ensure these comforts the moment he has resources to
expend.[79]

Loss of self-determination seems to have been ceremonialized in
concentration camps; thus we have atrocity tales of prisoners being
forced to roll in the mud,[80] stand on their heads in the snow, work
at ludicrously useless tasks, swear at themselves[81] or, in the case of
Jewish prisoners, sing anti-Semitic songs.[82] A milder version is found
in mental hospitals where attendants have been observed forcing a
patient who wanted a cigarette to say "pretty please," or to jump
for it. In all such cases the inmate is made to display a giving up of
his will. Less ceremonialized, but just as extreme, is the embarrassment to one's autonomy that comes from being locked in a ward,
placed in a tight wet-pack, or tied up in a camisole, and thereby
denied the liberty of making small adjustive movements.

Another clear-cut expression of personal inefficacy in total institutions has to do with inmates' use of speech. One implication of
using words to convey decisions about action is that the recipient of
an order is seen capable of receiving a message and acting under his
own power to complete the suggestion or command. Executing the
act himself, he can sustain some vestige of the notion that he is self-
determining. Responding to the question in his own words, he can
sustain the notion that he is somebody to be considered, however

[77] Hulme, *op. cit.,* p. 18; Orwell, *op. cit.,* p. 521.

[78] Hassler, *op. cit.,* p. 78; Johnson, *op. cit.,* p. 17.

[79] This is one source of mortification that civilians practice on themselves during camping vacations, perhaps on the assumption that a new sense
of self can be obtained by voluntarily foregoing some of one's previous self-
impregnated comforts.

[80] Kogon, *op. cit.,* p. 66.

[81] *Ibid.,* p. 61.

[82] *Ibid.,* p. 78.

slightly. And since it is only words that pass between himself and the others, he succeeds in retaining at least physical distance from them, however unpalatable the command or statement.

The inmate in a total institution can find himself denied this kind of protective distance and self-action. Especially in mental hospitals and political training prisons, the statements he makes may be discounted as mere symptoms, and the non-verbal aspects of his reply attended to.[83] Often he is considered to be of insufficient ritual weight to be given even minor greetings, let alone listened to.[84] Or the inmate may find that a kind of rhetorical use of language occurs: questions such as, "Have you washed yet?" or "Have you got both socks on?" may be accompanied by a simultaneous searching action by staff which physically discloses the facts, making their verbal questions superfluous. And instead of being told to move in a particular direction at a particular rate, he may find himself pushed along by the guard, or pulled (in the case of overalled mental patients), or frog-marched. And finally, as will be discussed later, the inmate may find that a dual language exists, with the disciplinary facts of his life given a translated ideal-phrasing by staff that mocks the normal use of language.

The second general consideration is the rationale that is employed for assaults upon the self. This issue tends to place total institutions and their inmates into three different groupings.

In religious institutions, the implications environmental arrangements have for self are explicitly recognized:

> That is the meaning of the contemplative life, and the sense of all the apparently meaningless little rules and observances and fasts and obediences and penances and humiliations and labors that go to make up the routine of existence in a contemplative monastery: they all serve to remind us of what we are and Who God is—that we may get sick of the sight of ourselves and turn to Him: and in the end, we will find Him in ourselves, in our own purified natures which have become the mirror of His tremendous Goodness and of His endless love . . .[85]

The inmates, as well as the staff, actively seek out these curtailments of the self, so that mortification is complemented by self-mortification,

---

[83] See A. Stanton and M. Schwartz, *The Mental Hospital* (New York: Basic Books, 1954), 200, 203, 205–206.

[84] For an example of this non-person treatment see Johnson and Dodds, *op. cit.*, p. 122.

[85] Merton, *op. cit.*, p. 372.

restrictions by renunciations, beatings by self-flagellations, inquisition by confession. Because religious establishments are explicitly concerned with the processes of mortification, they have a special value for sociological study.

In concentration camps, and to a lesser extent, prisons, some mortifications seem to be arranged solely or mainly for their mortifying power, as when a prisoner is urinated on, but here the inmate does not embrace and facilitate his own destruction of self.

In many of the remaining total institutions, mortifications are officially rationalized on other grounds, such as sanitation in connection with latrine duty, responsibility for life in connection with forced pill-taking, combat capacity in connection with Army rules for personal appearance, "security" in connection with restrictive prison regulations.

In total institutions of all three varieties, however, the various rationales for mortifying the self are very often merely rationalizations, generated by efforts to manage the daily activity of a large number of persons in a small space with a small expenditure of resources. Further, curtailments of the self occur in all three, even in the case where the inmate is willing and the management has ideal concerns for his well-being.

Two issues have been considered: the inmate's sense of personal inefficacy, and the relation of his own desires to the ideal interests of the establishment. The connection between these two issues is variable. Persons can voluntarily elect to enter a total institution and cease thereafter, to their regret, to be able to make such important decisions; in other cases, notably the religious, inmates may begin with and sustain a willful desire to be stripped and cleansed of personal will. Total institutions are fateful for the inmate's civilian self, although the attachment of the inmate to this civilian self can vary considerably.

The processes of mortification I have been considering have to do with the implications for self that persons oriented to a particular expressive idiom might draw from an individual's appearance, conduct, and general situation. In this context I want to consider a third and final issue: the relation between this symbolic-interaction framework for considering the fate of the self and the conventional psycho-physiological one centered around the concept of stress.

The basic facts about self in this report are phrased in a sociological perspective, always leading back to a description of the institutional arrangements which directly delineate the personal prerogatives of a member. Of course, a psychological assumption is also implied; cognitive processes are invariably involved, for the social arrangements must be "read" by the individual and by others for the image of himself that they imply. But, as I have argued, the relation of this cognitive process to other psychological processes is quite variable: according to the general expressive idiom of our society, having one's head shaved is easily perceived as a curtailment of the self, but while this mortification may enrage a mental patient, it may please a monk.

Mortification or curtailment of the self is very likely to involve acute psychological stress for the individual; but for an individual sick with his world or guilt-ridden in it, mortification may bring psychological relief. Further, the psychological stress often created by assaults on the self can also be produced by matters perceived as unrelated to the territories of the self—such as loss of sleep, insufficient food, or protracted decision-making. So, too, a high level of anxiety or the unavailability of fantasy materials, such as movies and books, may greatly increase the psychological effect of a violation of the self-boundaries; but in themselves these facilitating factors have nothing to do with the mortification of the self. Empirically, then, the study of stress and of encroachments on the self seem to be tied together; but analytically, two different frameworks are involved.

The Privilege System. While the process of mortification goes on, the inmate begins to receive formal and informal instruction in what will here be called the *privilege system.* Insofar as the inmate's attachment to his civilian self has been shaken by the stripping processes of the institution, it is largely the privilege system that provides a framework for personal reorganization. Three basic elements of the system may be mentioned.

First, there are the *house rules,* a relatively explicit and formal set of prescriptions and proscriptions that lay out the main requirements of inmate conduct. These rules spell out the austere round of life of the inmate. Admission procedures, which strip the recruit of his past supports, can be seen as the institution's way of getting him ready to start living by the house rules.

Secondly, against this stark background, a small number of clearly defined rewards or *privileges* are held out in exchange for obedience to staff in action and spirit. It is important to see that many of these potential gratifications are carved out of the flow of support that the inmate had previously taken for granted. On the outside, for example the inmate probably could unthinkingly decide how he wanted his coffee, whether to light a cigarette, or when to talk; on the inside, such rights may become problematic, a matter of a great deal of desire, fantasy, and conscious concern. Held up to the inmate as possibilities, these few recapturings seem to have a reintegrative effect, re-establishing relationships with the whole lost world and assuaging withdrawal symptoms from it and from one's lost self. The inmate's attention then, especially at first, comes to be fixed on these supplies and obsessed with them. He can spend the day, like a fanatic, in devoted thoughts about the possibility of acquiring these gratifications or in contemplation of the approaching hour at which they are scheduled to be granted. Melville's report on navy life contains a typical example:

> In the American Navy the law allows one gill of spirits per day to every seaman. In two portions, it is served out just previous to breakfast and dinner. At the roll of the drum, the sailors assemble round a large tub, or cask, filled with the liquid; and, as their names are called off by a midshipman, they step up and regale themselves from a little tin measure called a "tot." No high-liver helping himself to Tokay off a well-polished sideboard smacks his lips with more mighty satisfaction than the sailor does over his tot. To many of them, indeed, the thought of their daily tots forms a perpetual perspective of ravishing landscapes, indefinitely receding in the distance. It is their great "prospect in life." Take away their grog, and life possesses no further charms for them.[86]

> It is one of the most common punishments for very trivial offences in the Navy, to "stop" a seaman's grog for a day or a week. And as most seamen so cling to their grog, the loss of it is generally deemed by them a very serious penalty. You will sometimes hear them say, "I would rather have my wind *stopped* than my grog!"[87]

The building of a world around these minor privileges is perhaps the most important feature of inmate culture and yet is something that cannot easily be appreciated by an outsider, even one who has previously lived through the experience himself. This situation sometimes leads to generous sharing; it almost always leads to a willingness to beg for such things as cigarettes, candy, and news-

[86] Melville, *op. cit.*, pp. 62–63.

[87] *Ibid.*, p. 140. For examples of the same process in P.O.W. camps, see, Edgar H. Schein, "The Chinese Indoctrination Program for Prisoners of War," *Psychiatry*, 19 (1956), 160–61.

papers. Understandably, then, inmate conversation often revolves around a *release-binge fantasy,* namely, a recital of what one will do during leave or upon release from the institution. This fantasy is related to a feeling that civilians do not appreciate how wonderful their life is.[88]

The third element in the privilege system is *punishments*. These are designated as the consequence of breaking the rules. One set of punishments consists of the temporary or permanent withdrawal of privileges, or abrogation of the right to try to earn them. In general, the punishments meted out in total institutions are more severe than anything encountered by the inmate in his home world. In any case, conditions in which a few easily-controlled privileges are so important are the same conditions in which their withdrawal has a terrible significance.

There are some special features of the privilege system which should be noted.

First, punishments and privileges are themselves modes of organization peculiar to total institutions. Whatever their severity, punishments are largely known in the inmate's home world as something applied to animals and children. For adults, this conditioning, behavioristic model is actually not widely applied, since failure to maintain required standards typically leads to indirect disadvantageous consequences and not to specific immediate punishment at all.[89] And privileges in the total institution, it should be emphasized, are not the same as perquisites, indulgences, or values, but are merely the absence of deprivations one ordinarily expects one would not have to sustain. The very notions, then, of punishments and privileges, are not ones that are cut from civilian cloth.

Second, it is important to see that the question of release from the total institution is elaborated into the privilege system. Some acts will become known as ones that mean an increase or no decrease in length of stay, while others become known as means for lessening the sentence.

Third, punishments and privileges come to be geared into a resi-

[88] Interestingly enough, there is sometimes a corresponding pre-entrance binge, during which the inmate-to-be indulges grandly in activity he feels will soon be quite unavailable to him. For an example regarding nuns, see Hulme, *op. cit.,* p. 7.

[89] See S. F. Nadel, "Social Control and Self-regulation," *Social Forces,* 31 (1953), 265–273.

dential-work system. Places to work and places to sleep become clearly defined as places where certain kinds and levels of privilege obtain, and inmates are shifted very frequently and visibly from one place to another as the administrative device for giving them the punishment or reward their cooperativeness warrants. The inmates are moved, the system is not. We can therefore expect some spatial specialization, with one ward or hut acquiring the reputation of a punishment place for especially recalcitrant inmates, while certain guard assignments become recognized as punishments for staff.

The privilege system, then, consists of a relatively few components, put together with some rational intent, and clearly proclaimed to the participants. The over-all consequence is that cooperativeness is obtained from persons who often have cause to be uncooperative.[90] An illustration of this model universe may be taken from a recent study of a state mental hospital:

> The authority of the attendant in the operation of his control system is backed up by both positive and negative power. This power is an essential element in his control of the ward. He can give the patient privileges, and he can punish the patient. The privileges consist of having the best job, better rooms and beds, minor luxuries like coffee on the ward, a little more privacy than the average patient, going outside the ward without supervision, having more access than the average patient to the attendant's companionship or to professional personnel like the physicians, and enjoying such intangible but vital things as being treated with personal kindness and respect.
>
> The punishments which can be applied by the ward attendant are suspension of all privileges, psychological mistreatment, . . . locking up the patient in an isolated room, denial or distortion of access to the professional personnel, threatening to put or putting the patient on the list for electroshock therapy, transfer of the

---

[90] As a qualification, it has been argued that in some cases this system is either not very effective or not much relied upon. In some prisons, the rewards that are carved out of usual expectations are granted upon entrance, and little official betterment of position is apparently possible—the only change in status possible involving a loss of privileges (Sykes, *op. cit.*, pp. 51–52). It has been further argued that if the inmate is stripped of enough, then instead of cherishing what remains he can come to see little remaining difference between this and complete expropriation, and so cease to be subject to the power of staff to motivate him to obedience, especially when disobedience may bring prestige among the inmate group (*Ibia.*).

patient to undesirable wards, and regular assignment of the patient to unpleasant tasks such as cleaning up after the soilers.[91]

A parallel may be found in British prisons in which the "four stage system" is employed, with an increase at each stage of payment for labor, "association" time with other prisoners, access to newspapers, group-eating, and recreation periods.[92]

Associated with the privilege system are certain processes important in the life of total institutions.

An *institutional lingo* develops through which inmates express the events that are crucial in their particular world. Staff, especially its lower levels, will know this language too, and use it when talking to inmates, reverting to more standardized speech when talking to superiors and outsiders. Along with a lingo, inmates acquire knowledge of the various ranks and officials, an accumulation of lore about the establishment, and some comparative information about life in other similar total institutions.

Furthermore, staff and inmates will be clearly aware of what, in mental hospitals, prisons, and barracks, is called *messing up*. Messing up involves a complex process of engaging in forbidden activity (including sometimes an effort at escape), getting caught, and receiving something like the full punishment accorded this. There is usually an alteration in privilege status, categorized by a phrase such as "getting busted." Typical infractions involved in messing up are: fights, drunkenness, attempted suicide, failure at examinations, gambling, insubordination, homosexuality, improper leave-taking, and participation in collective riots. While these infractions are typically ascribed to the offender's cussedness, villainy, or "sickness," they do in fact constitute a vocabulary of institutionalized actions, but a limited one, so that the same messing up may occur for quite different reasons. Inmates and staff may informally agree, for example, that a given messing up is a way for inmates to show resentment against a situation felt to be unjust in terms of the informal agreements between staff and inmates,[93] or a way of postponing release without having to admit to one's fellow-inmates that one does not really want to go. Whatever their given meaning, messings up have some impor-

[91] Belknap, *op. cit.,* p. 164.

[92] See Dendrickson and Thomas, *op. cit.,* pp. 99–100.

[93] For example, see, Morris G. Caldwell, "Group Dynamics in the Prison Community," *Journal of Criminal Law, Criminology and Police Science,* 46 (1956), 656.

tant social functions for the institution. They tend to limit rigidities which would occur were seniority the only means of mobility in the privilege system; further, demotion through messing up brings old-time inmates into contact with new inmates in unprivileged positions, assuring a flow of information concerning the system and the people in it.

In total institutions there will also be a system of what might be called *secondary adjustments,* namely, practices that do not directly challenge staff but allow inmates to obtain forbidden satisfactions or to obtain permitted ones by forbidden means. These practices are variously referred to as angles, knowing the ropes, conniving, gimmicks, deals, or ins. Such adaptations apparently reach their finest flower in prisons, but of course other total institutions are overrun with them too.[94] Secondary adjustments provide the inmate with important evidence that he is still his own man, with some control of his environment; sometimes a secondary adjustment becomes almost a kind of lodgement for the self, a *churinga* in which the soul is felt to reside.[95]

We can predict from the presence of secondary adjustments that the inmate group will have evolved some kind of code and some means of informal social control to prevent one inmate from informing staff about the secondary adjustments of another. On the same ground, we can expect that one dimension of social-typing of and among inmates will be this question of security, leading to definitions of persons as "squealers," "finks," "rats," or "stoolies" on one hand, and definitions of persons as "right guys" on the other.[96] When new inmates can play a role in the system of secondary adjustments, either by providing new faction members or new sexual objects, then their "welcome" may indeed be a sequence of initial indulgences and enticements instead of exaggerated deprivations.[97] Because of sec-

[94] For example, see, Norman S. Hayner and Ellis Ash, "The Prisoner Community as a Social Group," *American Sociological Review,* 4 (1939), 364 *ff.* under "Conniving Processes"; also, Caldwell, *op. cit.,* pp. 650–651.

[95] See, for example, Melville's extended description of the fight his fellow seamen put up to prevent the clipping of their beards, the clipping being in accordance with full Navy regulations. Melville, *op. cit.,* pp. 333–347.

[96] See, for example, Donald Clemmer, "Leadership Phenomena in a Prison Community," *Journal of Criminal Law, Criminology and Police Science,* 28 (1938), 868.

[97] See, for example, Ida Ann Harper, "The Role of the 'Fringer' in a State Prison for Women," *Social Forces,* 31 (1952), 53–60.

ondary adjustments we also find *kitchen strata,* a kind of rudimentary, largely informal, stratification of inmates differentiated on the basis of each one's access to disposable illicit commodities; again, too, we find social-typing to designate the powerful persons in the informal market system.[98]

The privilege system seems to provide the chief framework within which re-assembly of the self takes place. There are other factors that characteristically lead by different routes in the same general direction. Relief from economic and social responsibilities—much touted as part of the therapy of mental hospitals—is one, although in many cases it seems that the disorganizing effect of this moratorium is more significant than its organizing effect. More important as a reorganizing influence is the *fraternalization process,* through which socially distant persons find themselves developing mutual support and common *counter-mores* in opposition to a system that has forced them into intimacy and into a single, equalitarian, community of fate.[99] The new recruit frequently starts out with something like the staff's popular misconceptions of the character of the inmates; he comes to find that most of his fellows have all the properties of ordinary, occasionally decent human beings worthy of solidarity and support. The offenses that inmates are known to have committed on the outside cease to provide an effective means for judging their personal qualities—a lesson that conscientious objectors, for example, seem to have learned in prison.[100] Further, if the inmates are persons who are accused of having committed a crime of some kind against society, then the new inmate, even though sometimes in fact quite guiltless, may come to share both the guilty feelings of his fellows and their well-elaborated defenses against these feelings. A sense of common injustice and a sense of bitterness against the outside world tends to

[98] For concentration camps, see the discussion of "Prominents" throughout Cohen, *op. cit.;* for mental hospitals, see Belknap, *op. cit.,* p. 189; for prisons, see the discussion of "Politicians" in Donald Clemmer, *The Prison Community,* New Edition (New York: Rinehart, 1959), pp. 277–279 and 298–309; also Hayner, *op. cit.,* p. 367, and Caldwell, *op. cit.,* pp. 651–653.

[99] For the version of this inmate solidarity to be found in military academies, see, Dornbusch, *op. cit.,* p. 318.

[100] An interesting example of this re-evaluation may be found in a conscientious objector's experience with non-political prisoners; see Hassler, *op. cit.,* pp. 74, 117. In mental hospitals, of course, the patient's antagonism to staff obtains one of its supports from the discovery that, like himself, many other patients are more like ordinary persons than like anything else.

develop, marking an important development in the inmate's moral career. This response to felt guilt and massive deprivation is most clearly illustrated perhaps in prison life:

> By their reasoning, after an offender has been subjected to unfair or excessive punishment and treatment more degrading than that prescribed by law, he comes to justify his act which he could not have justified when he committed it. He decides to "get even" for his unjust treatment in prison and take reprisals through further crime at the first opportunity. *With that decision he becomes a criminal.*[101]

An imprisoned conscientious objector provides a similar statement from his own experience:

> A point I want to record here is the curious difficulty I have in feeling innocent, myself. I find it very easy to accept the notion that I am paying for the same kind of misdeeds as those charged to the other men in here, and I must remind myself from time to time that a government that actually believes in freedom of conscience should not put men in prison for practicing it. Consequently, what indignation I feel toward prison practices is not the indignation of the persecuted innocent or the martyr, but of the guilty who feels his punishment to be beyond his deserts and *inflicted by those who are not themselves free of guilt*. This latter point is one that all the inmates feel strongly, and is the source of the deep cynicism that pervades the prison.[102]

A more general statement may be taken from two other students of the same kind of total institution:

> In many ways, the inmate social system may be viewed as providing a way of life which enables the inmate to avoid the devastating psychological effects of internalizing and converting social rejection into self-rejection. In effect, it permits the inmate to reject his rejectors rather than himself.[103]

[101] Richard McCleery, *The Strange Journey* (Chapel Hill: University of North Carolina Extension Bulletin, 1953), 24, italics in the original. Brewster Smith (in Stouffer, *op. cit.*,) suggests that with the decision that officer training camp has "earned" him rights over enlisted men, the officer trainee becomes an officer. The pain suffered in camp can be used as a justification for the pleasures of command.

[102] Hassler, *op. cit.*, p. 97. (Stress in the original.)

[103] Lloyd W. McCorkle and Richard Korn, "Resocialization Within Walls," *The Annals*, 293 (May, 1954), 88.

Here of course is one irony of a somewhat therapeutic and permissive policy—the inmate becomes less able to protect his ego by directing hostility to external targets.

There is one secondary adjustment that very clearly reflects the fraternalization process and the rejection of staff, namely, *collective teasing*. Although the punishment-reward system can deal with individual infractions that are identifiable as to source, inmate solidarity may be strong enough to support brief gestures of anonymous or mass defiance. Examples are: slogan shouting,[104] booing,[105] tray thumping, mass food rejection, and minor sabotage.[106] These actions tend to take the form of "rise-getting"; a warder, guard, or attendant—or even the staff as a whole—is teased, mocked, or accorded other forms of minor abuse until he loses some self-control and engages in ineffective counteraction.

In addition to fraternalization among all inmates, there is likely to be bond formation of a more differentiating kind. Sometimes special solidarities extend throughout a physically closed region, such as a ward or cottage, whose inhabitants perceive they are being administered as a single unit and hence have a lively sense of common fate. Lawrence provides an illustrative statement concerning air force "administrated groups":

> There lies a golden mist of laughter—even if silly laughter—over our hut. Shake together fifty-odd fellows, strangers of every class, in a close room for twenty days: subject them to a new and arbitrary discipline: weary them with dirty, senseless, uncalled for yet arduous fatigues . . . but there has not been a sharp word between any two of us. Such liberality of body and spirit, such active vigour, cleanliness and good temper would hardly have persisted save in the conditions of common servitude.[107]

And of course still smaller units are found too: cliques; more or less stable sexual ties;[108] and, most importantly perhaps, "buddy-forma-

[104] Cantine and Rainer, *op. cit.,* p. 59; see also Norman, *op. cit.,* pp. 56–57.

[105] Cantine and Rainer, *op. cit.,* p. 40.

[106] Chapter One, "Resistance in Prison," by Clif Bennett, in Cantine and Rainer, *op. cit.,* provides a useful review of techniques for collective teasing.

[107] Lawrence, *op. cit.,* p. 59.

[108] The classic treatment still seems to be Clemmer's, "Sexual Patterns in the Prison Community," *op. cit.,* Chap. X.

tion" whereby a pair of inmates come to be recognized by other inmates as "buddies" or "mates" and come to rely on each other for a wide range of assistance and emotional support.[109] Although these friendship pairs may be given quasi-official recognition, as when a boatswain on board ship arranges for buddies to take a watch together,[110] deep involvement in the relationship may also meet with a kind of institutional incest taboo functioning to prevent dyads from creating their own world in the institution. In fact, in some total institutions, staff feel that solidarity among sets of inmates can provide the base for concerted activity forbidden by the rules, and they may consciously try to hinder primary group formation when its presence is detected.

Although there are solidarizing tendencies such as fraternalization and clique formation, they are limited. Constraints which place inmates in a position to sympathize and communicate with each other do not necessarily lead to high group morale and solidarity. In some concentration camps and prisoner of war installations, the inmate cannot rely on his fellows, who may steal from him, assault him, and squeal on him, leading to what some sources have referred to as "anomie."[111] In mental hospitals, dyads and triads may keep secrets from the authorities, but anything known to a whole ward of patients is likely to get to the ear of the staff. (In prisons, of course, inmate organization has sometimes been strong enough to run strikes and short-lived insurrections; in prisoner of war camps, it has sometimes been possible to organize sections of the prisoners to operate escape channels;[112] in concentration camps there have been periods of thoroughgoing underground organization;[113] and on ships there have been mutinies; but these concerted actions seem to be the exception, not the rule.) Even though there often is little group loyalty in total

[109] For example, Heckstall-Smith, *op. cit.*, p. 30. Behan, *op. cit.*, provides much material throughout on the buddy or mate relation.

[110] S. A. Richardson, *The Social Organization of British and United States Merchant Ships* (Unpublished monograph available at The New York School of Industrial and Labor Relations, Cornell University, 1954), 17.

[111] A full statement of this theme may be found in Donald R. Cressey and W. Krassowski, "Inmate Organization and Anomie in American Prisons and Soviet Labor Camps," *Social Problems*, 5 (Winter-1957-1958), 217-230.

[112] See, for example, P. R. Reid, *Escape from Colditz* (New York: Berkeley, 1956).

[113] See Paul Foreman, "Buchenwald and Modern Prisoner-of-War Detention Policy," *Social Forces*, 37 (1959), 289–298.

institutions, the expectation that group loyalty should prevail forms part of the inmate culture and underlies the hostility accorded those who break inmate solidarity.

Some Lines of Adaptation. The privilege system and the mortifying processes that have been discussed represent the conditions to which the inmate must adapt. These conditions allow for different individualistic ways of meeting them—apart from any effort at collective subversive action. The same inmate will employ different personal lines of adaptation at different phases in his moral career and may even fluctuate between different tacks at the same time.

First, there is the tack of *situational withdrawal.* The inmate withdraws apparent attention from everything except events immediately around his body and sees these in a perspective not employed by others present.[114] This drastic curtailment of involvement in interactional events is best known, of course, in mental hospitals, under the title of "regression." Aspects of "prison psychosis" or going "stir simple" represent the same adjustment, as do some forms of "acute depersonalization" described in concentration camps. I do not think it is known whether this line of adaptation forms a single continuum of varying degrees of withdrawal or whether there are standard plateaus of disinvolvement. Given the pressures apparently required to dislodge an inmate from this status, as well as the currently limited facilities for doing so, this line of adaptation is effectively irreversible.

Second, there is the *intransigeant line*: the inmate intentionally challenges the institution by flagrantly refusing to cooperate with staff.[115] The result is a constantly communicated intransigeancy and sometimes high individual morale. Many large mental hospitals, for example, have wards where this spirit prevails. Sustained rejection of a total institution often requires sustained orientation to its formal organization, and hence, paradoxically, a deep kind of involvement in the establishment. Similarly, when staff take the line that the intransigeant inmate must be broken (as they sometimes do in the case of hospital psychiatrists prescribing lobotomy[116] or military tribunals prescribing the stockade), then the institutions show as much special devotion to the rebel as he has shown to them. Finally, al-

[114] See the discussion in Chapter 7, pp. 286–290, below.
[115] See, for example, the discussion of "The Resisters," in Schein, *op. cit.,* pp. 166–167.
[116] Belknap, *op. cit.,* p. 192.

though some prisoners of war have been known to take a staunchly intransigeant stand throughout their incarceration, intransigeance is typically a temporary and initial phase of reaction, with the inmate shifting to situational withdrawal or some other line of adaptation.

A third standard alignment in the institutional world is *colonization*: the sampling of outside world provided by the establishment is taken by the inmate as the whole, and a stable, relatively contented existence is built up out of the maximum satisfactions procurable within the institution.[117] Experience of the outside world is used as a point of reference to demonstrate the desirability of life on the inside, and the usual tension between the two worlds collapses, thwarting the motivational scheme based upon this felt discrepancy. Characteristically, the individual who too obviously takes this line may be accused by his fellow-inmates of "having found a home" or of "never having had it so good." Staff itself may become vaguely embarrassed by this use that is being made of the institution, sensing that the benign possibilities in the situation are somehow being misused. Colonizers themselves may feel obliged to deny their satisfaction with the institution, if only to sustain the counter-mores supporting inmate solidarity. They may find it necessary to mess up just prior to their slated discharge, thereby providing themselves with an apparently involuntary basis for continued incarceration. Significantly, staff who try to make life in total institutions more bearable must face the possibility that doing so may increase the attractiveness and likelihood of colonization.

A fourth mode of adaptation to the setting of a total institution is that of *conversion*: the inmate appears to take over the official or staff view of himself and tries to act out the role of the perfect inmate. While the colonized inmate builds as much of a free community for himself as possible by using the limited facilities available, the convert takes a more disciplined, moralistic, monochromatic line, presenting himself as someone whose institutional enthusiasm is always at the disposal of the staff. In Chinese POW camps, we find Americans who became "Pros" and fully espoused the communist view of the world.[118] In army barracks there are enlisted men who give the impression that they are always "sucking around" and always

---

[117] In the case of mental hospitals, those who take this line are sometimes called "institutional cures" or are said to suffer from "hospitalitis."

[118] Schein, *op. cit.*, pp. 167–169.

"bucking for promotion." In prisons there are "Square Johns." In German concentration camps, longtime prisoners sometimes came to adapt the vocabulary, recreation, posture, expressions of aggression, and clothing style of the Gestapo, executing their role of straw-boss with military strictness.[119] Some mental hospitals have the distinction of providing two quite different conversion possibilities—one for the new admission who can see the light after an appropriate inner struggle and adapt the psychiatric view of himself, and another for the chronic patient who adopts the manner and dress of attendants while helping them to manage the other ward patients with a stringency sometimes excelling that of the attendants themselves. And of course in officer training camps we find trainees who quickly become "G.I.," espousing a torment of themselves that they will soon be able to inflict on others.[120]

Total institutions differ in a significant way: many, like progressive mental hospitals, merchant ships, TB sanitaria, and brainwashing camps, offer the inmate an opportunity to live up to a model of conduct that is at once ideal and staff-sponsored—a model felt by its advocates to be in the best interests of the very persons to whom it is applied. Other total institutions, like some concentration camps and some prisons, do not officially sponsor an ideal that the inmate is expected to incorporate.

The alignments that have been mentioned represent coherent courses to pursue, but few inmates seem to pursue any one of them very far. In most total institutions, most inmates take the tack of what they call *playing it cool*. This involves a somewhat opportunistic combination of secondary adjustments, conversion, colonization, and loyalty to the inmate group, so that the inmate will have a maximum chance in the particular circumstances of eventually getting out physically and psychologically undamaged.[121] Typically, when an inmate is with fellow-inmates he will support the counter-mores and conceal

[119] See Bruno Bettelheim, "Individual and Mass Behavior in Extreme Situations," *Journal of Abnormal and Social Psychology,* 38 (1943), 447–451. It should be added that in concentration camps, colonization and conversion often seemed to go together. See Cohen, *op. cit.,* pp. 200–203, where the role of the "Kapo" is discussed.

[120] Smith, *op. cit.,* p. 390.

[121] See the discussion in Schein, *op. cit.,* pp. 165–166, of the "Get-Alongers," and Robert J. Lifton, "Home by Ship: Reaction Patterns of American Prisoners of War Repatriated from North Korea," *American Journal of Psychiatry,* 110 (1954), 734.

from them how tractably he acts when alone with staff.[122] Inmates who play it cool tend to subordinate contacts with their fellows to the higher claim of "keeping out of trouble"; they tend to volunteer for nothing; and they may learn to cut their ties to the outside world just enough to give cultural reality to the world inside but not enough to lead to colonization.

I have suggested some of the lines of adaptation that inmates can take to the pressures present in total institutions. Each tack represents a way of managing the tension between the home world and the institutional world. Sometimes, however, the home world of the inmate has been, in fact, such as to *immunize* him against the bleak world on the inside, and for these persons no particular scheme of adaptation need be carried very far. Thus some lower-class mental hospital patients who have lived all their previous life in orphanages, reformatories, and jails, tend to see the hospital as just another total institution, to which they can apply the adaptive techniques learned and perfected in other total institutions. Playing it cool does not represent for these persons a shift in their moral career but an alignment that is already second nature. Similarly, Shetland youths recruited into the British merchant service are apparently not much threatened by the cramped, arduous life on board, because Island life is even more stunted; they make uncomplaining sailors because from their point of view they have little to complain about.

An effect similar to immunization is achieved by inmates who have special compensations inside the institution or special means of being impervious to its assaults. In the early period of German concentration camps, criminals apparently derived compensative satisfaction from living with middle-class political prisoners.[123] Similarly, the middle-class vocabulary of group psychotherapy and the classless ideology of "psychodynamics" give to some socially ambitious and

---

[122] This two-facedness is very commonly found in total institutions. In the state type mental hospital studied by the writer, even the few elite patients selected for individual psychotherapy, and hence in the best position for espousal of the psychiatric approach to self, tended to present their favorable view of psychotherapy only to the members of their intimate cliques. For a report on the way in which army prisoners concealed from fellow offenders their interest in "restoration" to the army, see the comments by Richard Cloward in Session 4 of *New Perspectives for Research on Juvenile Delinquency,* ed. by Helen L. Witmer and Ruth Kotinsky, U.S. Dept. of H.E.W., Children's Bureau Bulletin, 1955, especially p. 90.

[123] Bettelheim, *op. cit.,* p. 425.

socially frustrated lower-class mental patients the closest contact with
the polite world that they have ever had. Strong religious and political
convictions have served to insulate the true believer against the assaults
of a total institution. Even a failure to speak the language of the staff
may cause the staff to give up its efforts at reformation, freeing the
nonspeaker from certain pressures.[124]

The Inmate Culture.   Let us consider now some of the dominant
themes of inmate culture.

First, it seems that in many total institutions a peculiar kind and
level of self-concern is engendered. The low position of inmates relative to their station on the outside, established initially through the
stripping processes, creates a milieu of personal failure in which one's
fall from grace is continuously pressed home. In response, the inmate
tends to develop a story, a line, a sad tale—a kind of lamentation
and apologia—which he constantly tells to his fellows as a means of
creditably accounting for his present low estate. (In consequence, the
inmate's self may become even more a focus of his conversation and
concern than it does on the outside, leading to much self-pity.[125])
Although staff constantly discredit these stories, inmate audiences
tend to be tactful, suppressing at least some of the disbelief and boredom engendered by these recitations. Thus, an ex-prisoner writes:

> Even more impressive is the almost universal delicacy when it comes
> to inquiring into another man's misdeeds, and the refusal to de-
> termine one's relations with another convict on the basis of his
> record.[126]

Similarly, in American state mental hospitals, inmate etiquette allows
one patient to ask another what ward and service he is on, and how
long he has been in the hospital; but questions about why one is in
are not quickly asked, and, when asked, the biased version almost
inevitably given tends to be accepted.

Secondly, among inmates in many total institutions there is a
strong feeling that time spent in the establishment is time wasted or
destroyed or taken from one's life; it is time that must be written off;

---

[124] Thus, Schein, *op. cit.*, p. 165 fn. suggests that Puerto Ricans and other
non-English-speaking prisoners of war in China were given up on and allowed
to work out a viable routine of menial chores.

[125] For prison examples, see Hassler, *op. cit.*, p. 18; Heckstall-Smith, *op.
cit.*, pp. 29–30.

[126] Hassler, *op. cit.*, p. 116.

it is something that must be "done" or "marked" or "put in" or "pulled." (Thus, in prisons and mental hospitals, a general statement of how well one is adapting to the institution may be phrased in terms of how one is doing time, whether easily or hard.[127]) This time is something its doers have bracketed off as such for constant conscious consideration in a way not quite found on the outside. And as a result, the inmate tends to feel that for the duration of his required stay—his sentence—he has been totally exiled from living.[128] It is in this context that we can appreciate something of the demoralizing influence of an indefinite sentence or a very long one.[129]

However harsh the conditions of life in total institutions, harshness alone cannot account for this quality of life wasted; rather we must look to the social disconnections caused by entrance and to the usual failure to acquire within the institution gains that can be transferred to outside life—gains such as money earned, or marital relations resolved, or certified training received. One of the virtues of the doctrine that insane asylums are treatment hospitals for sick people is that inmates who have given up three or four years of their life to this kind of exile can try to convince themselves they have been busily working on their cure and that, once cured, the time spent getting cured will have been a reasonable and profitable investment.

This sense of dead and heavy-hanging time probably explains the premium placed on what might be called *removal activities,* namely, voluntary unserious pursuits which are sufficiently engrossing and exciting to lift the participant out of himself, making him oblivious for the time to his actual situation. If the ordinary activities in total institutions can be said to torture time, these activities mercifully kill it.

Some removal activities are collective, such as field games, dances, instrument playing, choral singing, lectures, art classes[130] or wood-

[127] Much material on the conception of time in total institutions may be found in Maurice L. Farber, "Suffering and Time Perspective of the Prisoner," *University of Iowa Studies in Child Welfare,* 20 (1944), 155–227.

[128] The best description that I know of this feeling of not-living is Freud's paper, "Mourning and Melancholia," where the state is said to come about as a consequence of losing a loved object. See, *Collected Papers of Sigmund Freud* (London: Hogarth Press, 1953), Vol. 4, 152–170.

[129] See, for example, Cohen, *op. cit.,* p. 128; and Galtung's discussion in Chapter 3 below, pp. 112–122.

[130] A good prison illustration is provided by Norman, *op. cit.,* p. 71.

working classes, and cardplaying; some are individual but rely on public materials, such as reading[131] and solitary TV-watching.[132] No doubt private fantasy ought to be included, too, as Clemmer suggests in his description of the prisoner's "reverie-plus."[133] Some of these activities may be officially sponsored by staff; some, not officially sponsored, will constitute secondary adjustments—for example, gambling, homosexuality, or "highs" and "jags" achieved with industrial alcohol, nutmeg, or ginger.[134] Whether officially sponsored or not, whenever any of these removal activities become too engrossing or too continuous, staff is likely to object—as they often do, for example, to liquor, sex, and gambling—since in their eyes the institution, not some other kind of social entity enclosed within the institution, must possess the inmate.

Every total institution, then, can be seen as a kind of dead sea in which appear little islands of vivid, encapturing activity. Such activity can help the individual withstand the psychological stress usually engendered by assaults upon the self. Yet it is precisely in the insufficiency of these activities that an important deprivational effect of total institutions can be found. Thus, in civil society, an individual pushed to the wall in one of his social roles usually has an opportunity to crawl into some protected place where he can indulge in commercialized fantasy—movies, TV, radio, reading—or employ narcotics such as cigarettes or drink. In total institutions, however, especially right after admission, these materials may be unavailable. At a time, then, when these resting points are most needed, they may be most difficult to obtain.[135]

---

[131] See, for example, the fine description by Behan, *op. cit.*, pp. 72–75 of the delights of reading in bed in one's cell, and the consequent precaution of rationing one's reading supply.

[132] Such activity is, of course, not restricted to total institutions. Thus, we find the classic case of the bored and weary housewife who "takes a few minutes for herself" to "put her feet up," removing herself from home by reading the morning paper over a cup of coffee and a cigarette.

[133] Clemmer, *op. cit.*, pp. 244–247.

[134] Cantine and Rainer, *op. cit.*, pp. 59–60, provide an example.

[135] For example, Cantine and Rainer, *op. cit.*, p. 59:

"I missed the drinks even more than the women and a number of guys agreed with me. When you get the blues on the outside you can always kill them with a couple of drinks. But in jail you just have to wait until the blues wear off and that may take a long while."

Return to the Outside. In this discussion of the inmate world, I have commented on the mortification processes, the reorganizing influences, the lines of response inmates take, and the cultural milieu that develops. I would like to add a concluding comment on the processes that generally occur if and when the inmate is released and sent back into the wider society.

Although inmates do plan release-binges and may keep an hourly count of the time until their release, those about to be released very often become anxious at the thought, and, as suggested, some mess up or re-enlist to avoid the issue. The inmate's anxiety about release often seems to take the form of a question put to himself and his friends: "Can I make it on the outside?" This question brackets all of civil life as something to have conceptions and concerns about. What for outsiders is usually an unperceived ground for perceived figures, is for the inmate a figure on a larger ground. Perhaps such a perspective is demoralizing, providing one reason why ex-inmates often think about the possibility of "going back in" and one reason why an appreciable number do return.

Total institutions frequently claim to be concerned with rehabilitation, that is, with resetting the inmate's self-regulatory mechanisms so that after he leaves he will maintain the standards of the establishment of his own accord. (Staff is expected to be properly self-regulating upon first coming to the total institution, sharing with members of other kinds of establishments the ideal of needing merely to learn procedure.) In fact, it seems this claim of change is seldom realized, and, even when permanent alteration occurs, the changes are often not of the kind intended by the staff. Except in some religious institutions, neither the stripping processes nor the reorganizing processes seem to have a lasting effect,[136] partly because of the availability of secondary adjustments, the presence of counter-mores, and the tendency for inmates to combine all strategies and play it cool.

Of course, immediately upon release the inmate is likely to be marvelously alive to the liberties and pleasures of civil status that civilians ordinarily do not see as events at all—the sharp smell of fresh air, talking when you want to, using a whole match to light

[136] Important evidence for this comes from our knowledge of the re-adjustment of repatriated brainwashed prisoners of war. See Hinkle, *op. cit.*, p. 174.

a cigarette, having a snack at a table set for only four people.[137] Thus a mental patient, back at the hospital after a week-end visit home, describes her experience to a circle of closely listening friends:

> I got up in the morning, and I went into the kitchen, and I fixed coffee; it was wonderful. And in the evening we had a couple of beers and went and had chili; it was terrific, really delicious. I didn't forget one minute that I was free.[138]

And yet it seems that shortly after release, the ex-inmate will forget a great deal of what life was like on the inside, and will once again begin to take for granted the privileges around which life in the institution was organized. The sense of injustice, bitterness, and alienation, so typically engendered by the inmate's experience and so commonly marking a stage in his moral career, seems to weaken upon graduation.

But what the ex-inmate does retain of his institutional experience tells us important things about total institutions. Very often, entrance will mean for the recruit that he has taken on what might be called a *proactive status*: not only is his relative social position within the walls radically different from what it was on the outside, but, as he comes to learn, if and when he gets out his social position on the outside will never again be quite what it was prior to entrance. Where the proactive status is a relatively favorable one—as it is for those who graduate from officers' training schools, elite boarding schools, ranking monasteries, etc.—then jubilant official reunions, announcing pride in one's "school," can be expected. When the proactive status is unfavorable, as it is for those who graduate from prisons or mental hospitals, we can employ the term *stigmatization* and expect that the ex-inmate may make an effort to conceal his past and try to "pass."

As one writer has implied,[139] an important kind of leverage possessed by staff is their power to give the kind of discharge that reduces stigmatization. Army prison officials can hold out the possibility of the inmate's restoration to active duty and, potentially, an honorable discharge; mental hospital administrators can hold out the possibility of a "clean bill of health" (discharged as cured) and also personal recommendations. Here we have one reason why inmates, when with

[137] Lawrence, *op. cit.*, p. 48.
[138] Writer's field notes.
[139] Cloward, *op. cit.*, pp. 80–83.

staff, sometimes affect enthusiasm for what the institution is doing for them.

We can now return to a consideration of release-anxiety. One explanation offered for it is that the individual is unwilling or too "sick" to reassume the responsibility from which the total institution freed him. My own experience in the study of one type of total institution, mental hospitals, tends to minimize this factor. One factor likely to be more important is disculturation, the loss or failure to acquire some of the habits currently required in the wider society. Another is stigmatization. Where the individual has taken on a low proactive status by becoming an inmate, he is likely to find a cool reception in the wider world—and is likely to experience this at a moment, hard even for those without his stigma, when he must apply to someone for a job and a place to live. Furthermore, release is likely to come just when the inmate has finally learned the ropes on the inside and won privileges that he has painfully learned are very important. In brief, he may find that release means moving from the top of a small world to the bottom of a large one. In addition, when the inmate returns to the free community, he may leave with some limits on his freedom. Some concentration camps required the inmate to sign a release, attesting that he had been treated fairly; he was warned of the consequences of telling tales out of school.[140] In some mental hospitals and prisons an inmate being prepared for discharge is interviewed a final time to discover whether or not he harbors resentment against the institution and those who arranged his entrance into it, and he is warned against causing trouble to the latter. Further, the departing inmate must often promise to seek help should he again find himself "getting sick" or "getting in trouble," and often he learns his kin and employer have been advised to get in touch with the hospital should trouble again arise. For the man who leaves prison, there may be formal parole, with the obligation to report regularly and to keep away from the circles from which he originally entered the institution.

Despite these several ways in which the total institution casts a shadow on its graduates, release to the outside tends to transmute bad times into bad memories, and another reality comes to take hold, the civil reality that is able to hold us firmly without our feeling it.

[140] Cohen, *op. cit.*, p. 7; Kogon, *op. cit.*, p. 72.

2

ERVING GOFFMAN

| | | | | | | | | |

On the Characteristics of Total Institutions: Staff - Inmate Relations

THE WORK-WORLD OF STAFF

Most total institutions, most of the time, seem to function merely as storage dumps for inmates. Nevertheless, these establishments present themselves to the public as rational organizations designed consciously, through and through, as effective machines for producing a few officially avowed and officially approved ends: one frequent official objective being the re-formation of inmates in the direction of some ideal standard. The contradiction between what the institution does and what its officials must say it does forms the basic context of this chapter.

Perhaps the first thing to say about staff is that their work, and hence their world, has uniquely to do with people. This people-work is not quite like personnel work or the work of those involved in service relationships; although staff have objects and products to work upon, not relationships, these objects and products are people.

As material upon which to work, people can take on somewhat the same characteristics as inanimate objects. Surgeons prefer to operate on slender patients rather than on fat ones because with fat ones the instruments get slippery and there is extra blubber to cut through. Morticians in mental hospitals sometimes favor thin females over fat men because heavy stiffs are difficult to move and male stiffs must be dressed in jackets that are hard to pull over stiffened arms and entangling fingers. Also, mismanagement of animate and inanimate objects alike leave telltale marks for supervisors to see. And just as an article being processed through an industrial plant must be followed by a paper shadow showing what has been done by whom and what remains to be done and who last had responsibility for its being done, so a human object moving through a prison system must be followed by a chain of informative receipts detailing what has been done to-and-by the prisoner and who had most recent responsibility for him. Even the presence or absence of a particular inmate at a given meal or for a given night may have to be recorded so that a cost accounting can be maintained and appropriate adjustments rendered in billing. In the inmate's career from admission room to burial plot, many different kinds of staff will add their official note to his case file as he temporarily passes under their jurisdiction; and long after he is dead physically, his marked remains will survive as an actionable entity in the prison's bureaucratic system. It is further true that just as tin mines, paint factories, or chemical plants involve special work hazards for employees, there are (staffs believe, at least) special dangers specific to some kinds of people-work. In mental hospitals, staffs believe that patients may strike out "for no reason" and injure an official, and some attendants feel that prolonged exposure to mental patients can have a contagious effect; in TB sanitoria and in leprosaria, staff feel they are being specially exposed to dangerous diseases.

While there are these similarities between people-work and object-work, the crucial determinant of the work-world of staff derives from the unique aspect of people as material to work upon.

Some Problems of People-Work. Confronted with the physiological characteristics of the human organism, it is obvious that certain requirements must be met if any continued use is to be made of people. But this, of course, is the case with inanimate objects too; the temperature of any storehouse must be regulated, regardless of whether people or things are present or are stored therein. However, persons are nearly always considered to be ends in themselves—according to the broad moral principles of a total institution's environing society—and almost always, then, we find that some technically unnecessary standards of handling must be maintained with human materials. This maintenance of what we call humane standards comes to be defined as part of the "responsibility" of the institution and presumably is one of the things the institution guarantees the inmate in exchange for his liberty. Thus prison officials are obliged to thwart suicidal efforts of a prisoner and to give him full medical attention, even though this may sometimes require postponement of his execution. Similar instances have been reported in German concentration camps, where inmates were sometimes given medical attention although destined for the gas chamber.

A second special contingency in the work-world of staff is that inmates typically have statuses and relationships in the outside world that must be taken into consideration. (This is, of course, related to the previously mentioned fact that the institution must respect some of the rights of inmates *qua* persons.) Even in the case of the committed mental patient, whose civil rights are largely taken from him, a large amount of paper work will be involved. The rights that are so denied, of course, are usually transferred to a relation, to a committee, or to the superintendent of the hospital itself, who then becomes the legal person whose authorization must be obtained for the many matters originating outside the institution: social security benefits; income taxes; upkeep of properties; insurance payments; old age pensions; stock dividends; dental bills; legal obligations incurred prior to commitment; permission to release psychiatric case records to insurance companies or attorneys; permission for special visits from persons other than next of kin; etc. All of these issues have to be dealt with by the institution, even if only to pass the decisions on to those legally empowered to make them.

Staff is reminded of their obligations in these matters of standards and rights not only by their own internal superordinates but also by various watchdog agencies in the wider society and often by the kin of inmates. The material of work itself can command a role. Thus some attendants in mental hospitals prefer to work on regressed wards because patients there tend to make fewer time-consuming requests than do patients on better wards who are in good contact. And there are even phrases employed by staff, such as the navy term "sea lawyer," for denoting an inmate who demands treatment "by the book." Kin, as critics, present a special problem, because while inmates can be educated about the price they will pay for making demands on their own behalf, relations receive less tutoring in this regard and rush in with requests for inmates that inmates would blush to make for themselves.

The multiplicity of ways in which inmates must be considered ends in themselves, and the multiplicity of inmates themselves, forces upon staff some of the classic dilemmas that must be faced by those who govern men. Since a total institution functions somewhat as a state, its staff must suffer somewhat from the tribulations that beset governors.[1]

In the case of any single inmate, the assurance that certain standards will be maintained in his own interests may require sacrifice of other standards; implied in this is a difficult weighing of ends. For example, if a suicidal inmate is to be kept alive, staff may feel it necessary to keep him under constant deprivatizing surveillance or even tied to a chair in a small locked room. If a mental patient is to be kept from tearing at grossly irritated sores and repeating time and again a cycle of curing and disorder, staff may feel it necessary to curtail the freedom of his hands. A patient who refuses to eat may have to be humiliated by forced-feeding. If inmates of TB sanitaria are to be given an opportunity to recover, it will be necessary to curtail freedom of recreation.

The standards of treatment that one inmate has a right to expect may conflict, of course, with the standards desired by another, giving rise to another set of governmental problems. Thus, in mental hospitals, if the grounds' gate is to be kept open out of respect for those with town parole, then some other patients who otherwise could have been trusted on the grounds may have to be kept on locked wards. And if a canteen and mailbox are to be freely available to those on the grounds, then patients on a strict diet, or those who write threatening and obscene letters, will have to be denied liberty of the grounds.

The obligation of staff to maintain certain humane standards of treatment for inmates presents problems in itself, but a further set of characteristic problems is found in the constant conflict between humane standards on one hand and institutional efficiency on the other. I will cite only one example. The personal possessions of an individual are an important part of the materials out of which he builds a self, but as an inmate, the ease with which he can be managed by staff is likely to increase with the degree to which he is dispossessed. Thus, the remarkable efficiency with which a mental hospital ward can adjust to a daily shift in number of resident patients is related to the fact that the comers and leavers do not come or

[1] See the detailed discussion of this theme by McCleery in Chapter 4, page 149.

leave with any properties but themselves and do not have any right to choose where they will be located. Further, the efficiency with which the clothes of these patients can be kept clean and fresh is related to the fact that everyone's soiled clothing can be indiscriminately placed in one bundle, and laundered clothing can be redistributed not according to ownership but according to approximate size. Similarly, the quickest assurance that patients going on the grounds will be warmly dressed is to march them past a pile of the ward's allotment of coats, requiring them for the same purposes of health to throw off these collectivized garments on returning to the ward.

Just as personal possessions may interfere with the smooth running of an institutional operation, and be removed for this reason, so parts of the body may conflict with efficient management and the conflict may be resolved in favor of efficiency. If the heads of inmates are to be kept clean, and the possessor easily identified, then a complete head shave is efficacious, regardless of the damage this does to appearance. On similar grounds, some mental hospitals have found it useful to extract the teeth of "biters," give hysterectomies to promiscuous female patients, and perform lobotomies on chronic fighters. Flogging on men-of-war, as a form of punishment, expressed the same issue between organizational and humane interests:

> One of the arguments advanced by officers of the Navy in favour of corporal punishment is this: it can be inflicted in a moment; it consumes no valuable time; and when the prisoner's shirt is put on, *that* is the last of it. Whereas, if another punishment were substituted, it would probably occasion a great waste of time and trouble, besides thereby begetting in the sailor an undue idea of his importance.[2]

I have suggested that people-work differs from other kinds of work because of the tangle of statuses and relationships which each inmate brings with him to the institution and because of the humane standards that must be maintained with respect to him. Another difference occurs when inmates have rights to visit off the grounds, for then the mischief they may do in civil society becomes something for which the institution has some responsibility. Given this responsibility, it is understandable that total institutions tend to view off-grounds leave unfavorably. Still another type of difference between

---

[2] Herman Melville, *White Jacket* (New York: Grove Press, n.d.), 139.

people-work and other kinds of work (and perhaps the most important difference of all) is that by the exercise of threat, reward, or persuasion, human objects can be given instructions and relied upon to carry them out on their own. The span of time during which these objects can be trusted to carry out planned actions without supervision will of course vary a great deal, but, as the social organization of the back wards in mental hospitals teaches us, even in the limiting case of catatonic schizophrenics a considerable amount of such reliance is possible. Only the most complicated electronic equipment shares this capacity.

While human materials can never be as refractory as inanimate ones, their very capacity to perceive and follow out the plans of staff ensures that they can hinder the staff more effectively than inanimate objects can. Inanimate objects cannot purposely and intelligently thwart our plans (although we may momentarily react to them as if they had this capacity). Hence, in prisons and on "better" wards of mental hospitals, guards have to be ready for organized efforts at escape and they must constantly deal with attempts by the inmate to bait them, "frame" them, and otherwise get them into trouble; the guard's consequent anxiety is not alleviated by knowledge that the inmate may do these things merely to gain self-respect or to relieve boredom.[3] Even an old, weak, mental patient has tremendous power in this regard; for example, by the simple expedient of locking his thumbs in his trouser pockets he can remarkably frustrate the efforts of an attendant to undress him. This is one reason why staff members tend to conceal decisions taken regarding the fate of inmates, for were the inmate to know the worst of what was planned for him, he might purposely and openly obstruct the smooth realization of his fate—so, for example, mental patients being prepared for shock treatment may be told kindly tales and sometimes kept from seeing the room in which they will be treated.

A third general way in which human materials differ from other materials (and hence present unique problems) is that however distant staff tries to stay from these materials, such materials can become objects of fellow-feeling and even affection. There is always the danger that an inmate will appear human; if what are felt to be hardships

[3] For comments on the very difficult role of guard, see Lloyd W. McCorkle and Richard Korn, "Resocialization Within Walls," *The Annals*, 293 (May, 1954), 93–94; and Gresham M. Sykes, "The Corruption of Authority and Rehabilitation," *Social Forces*, 34 (1956), 257–262.

must be inflicted on the inmate, then sympathetic staff will suffer. (This, after all, is one rationale officers give for keeping social distance from enlisted men.) And, on the other hand, if an inmate breaks a rule, staff's conception of him as a human being may increase their sense that injury has been done to their moral world: expecting a "reasonable" response from a reasonable creature, staff may feel incensed, affronted, and challenged when the inmate does not conduct himself properly.

The capacity of inmates to become objects of staff's sympathetic concern is linked to what might be called the *involvement cycle* that is sometimes recorded in total institutions. Starting at a point of social distance from inmates (a point from which massive deprivation and institutional trouble cannot easily be seen), the staff person finds he has no reason to refrain from building up a warm interest in some inmates. This involvement, however, brings the staff member into a position to be hurt by what inmates do and what they suffer, and also brings him to a position from which he is likely to threaten the distant stand from inmates taken by his fellow staff members. In response, the sympathizing staff member may feel he has been "burnt," and he will retreat into paper work, committee work, or other staff-enclosed routine. Once removed from the dangers of inmate contact, however, he may gradually cease to feel he has reason to be wary and thus the cycle of contact and withdrawal may be repeated again.

When we combine the fact that staff are obliged to maintain certain standards of humane treatment for inmates with the fact that they may come to view inmates as reasonable, responsible creatures who are fitting objects for emotional involvement, we have the background for some of the quite special difficulties of people-work. In mental hospitals, for example, there always seem to be some patients who dramatically act against their own obvious self-interest: they drink water they have themselves first polluted; overstuff on Thanksgiving and Christmas so that on these days there are bound to be a few ruptured ulcers and clogged esophagi; rush headfirst against a wall; tear out their own sutures after a minor operation; flush down the toilet false teeth, without which they cannot eat and which take months to obtain; or smash glasses, without which they cannot see. In an effort to frustrate these visibly self-destructive acts, staff members may find themselves forced to manhandle these patients, creating an image of themselves as harsh and coercive just at the moment that they are attempting to prevent someone from doing to himself what no human being is expected to do to anyone. At such times, understandably, it is extremely difficult for staff to keep their own emotions in control.

INSTITUTIONAL GOALS AND PERSPECTIVES

The special requirements of people-work establish the day's job for staff; the job itself is carried out in a special moral climate. The staff is charged with meeting the hostility and demands of the inmates, and what they have to meet the inmate with, in general, is the rational perspective espoused by the institution. We must therefore look at these perspectives.

The avowed goals of total institutions are not great in number: accomplishment of some economic goal; education and training; medical and psychiatric treatment; religious purification; protection of the wider community from pollution; and, as one study of prisons suggests, "incapacitation, retribution, deterrence, and reformation."[4] It is widely appreciated that total institutions typically fall considerably short of their official aims. It is less well appreciated that each of these official goals or charters seems admirably suited to provide a key to meaning—a language of explanation that staff, and sometimes inmates, can bring to every crevice of action in the institution. Thus, a medical frame of reference is not merely a perspective through which a decision concerning dosage can be determined and made meaningful; it is a perspective ready to account for all manner of decisions, such as the hours that hospital meals are served or the manner in which hospital linen is folded.

Each official goal, then, lets loose a doctrine, with its own inquisitors and its own martyrs, and within institutions there seems to be no natural check on the license of easy interpretation that results. Thus every institution must not only make some effort to realize its official aims but must also be protected, somehow, from the tyranny of a diffuse pursuit of them, lest the exercise of authority be turned into a witch hunt. The phantom of "security" in prisons and the staff actions justified in its name are instances of these dangers. Paradoxically, then, while total institutions seem the least intellectual of

---

[4] Donald R. Cressey, "Achievement of an Unstated Organizational Goal: An Observation on Prisons," *Pacific Sociological Review,* 1 (1958), 43.

places, nevertheless it is here, at least recently, that concern about words and verbalized perspectives has come to play a central and often feverish role.

The interpretative scheme of the total institution begins automatically to operate as soon as the inmate enters, staff having the notion that entrance is *prima facie* evidence that one must be the kind of person the institution was set up to handle. A man in a political prison must be traitorous; a man in a prison must be a lawbreaker; a man in a mental hospital must be sick. If not traitorous, criminal, or sick, why else would he be there?

This automatic identification of the inmate is not merely name-calling; it is at the center of a basic means of social control. An illustration is provided in an early community study of a mental hospital.

> The chief aim of this attendant culture is to bring about the control of patients—a control which must be maintained irrespective of patient welfare. This aim is sharply illuminated with respect to expressed desires or requests of patients. All such desires and requests, no matter how reasonable, how calmly expressed, or how politely stated, are regarded as evidence of mental disorder. Normality is never recognized by the attendant in a milieu where abnormality is the normal expectancy. Even though most of these behavioral manifestations are reported to the doctors, they, in most cases, merely support the judgments of the attendants. In this way, the doctors themselves help to perpetuate the notion that the essential feature of dealing with mental patients is in their control.[5]

When inmates are allowed to have face-to-face contact with staff, the contact will often take the form of "gripes" or requests on the part of the inmate and justification for the prevailing restrictive treatment on the part of staff; such, for example, is the general structure of staff-patient interaction in mental hospitals. Having to control inmates and to defend the institution in the name of its avowed aims, staff resort to the kind of all-embracing identification of the inmates that will make this possible. The staff problem here is to find a crime that will fit the punishment.

Further, the privileges and punishments staff mete out are often phrased in a language that reflects the legitimated objectives of the institution, as when solitary confinement in prisons is called "con-

---

[5] J. Bateman and H. Dunham, "The State Mental Hospital as a Specialized Community Experience," *American Journal of Psychiatry*, 105 (1948), 446.

structive meditation." Inmates or low-level staff will have the special job of translating these ideological phrasings into the simple language of the privilege system. Belknap's discussion of what happens when a mental patient breaks a rule and is punished provides an illustration:

> In the usual case of this kind, such things as impudence, insubordination, and excessive familiarity are translated into more or less professional terms, such as "disturbed" or "excited," and presented by the attendant to the physician as a medical status report. The doctor must then officially revoke or modify the patient's privileges on the ward or work out a transfer to another ward where the patient has to begin all over to work up from the lowest group. A "good" doctor in the attendants' culture is one who does not raise too many questions about these translated medical terms.[6]

The institutional perspective is also applied to actions not clearly or usually subject to discipline. Thus Orwell reports that in his boarding school bed-wetting was seen as a sign of "dirtiness" and wickedness,[7] and that a similar perspective applied to disorders even more clearly physical.

> I had defective bronchial tubes and a lesion in one lung which was not discovered till many years later. Hence I not only had a chronic cough, but running was a torment to me. In those days, however, "wheeziness," or "chestiness," as it was called, was either diagnosed as imagination or was looked on as essentially a moral disorder, caused by overeating. "You wheeze like a concertina," Sim [the headmaster] would say disapprovingly as he stood behind my chair; "You're perpetually stuffing yourself with food, that's why."[8]

And of course Chinese "thought-reform" camps are claimed to have carried this interpretative process to the extreme, translating the innocuous daily events of the prisoner's past into symptoms of counterrevolutionary action.[9]

Although there is a psychiatric view of mental disorder and an environmental view of crime and counterrevolutionary activity, both

[6] Ivan Belknap, *Human Problems of a State Mental Hospital* (New York: McGraw-Hill, 1956), 170.

[7] George Orwell, "Such, Such Were the Joys," *Partisan Review*, 19 (September–October, 1952), 506–509.

[8] *Ibid.*, p. 521.

[9] See, for example, R. Lifton, " 'Thought Reform' of Western Civilians in Chinese Communist Prisons," *Psychiatry*, 19 (1956), esp. pp. 182–184.

of which free the offender of moral responsibility for his offense, total institutions can little afford this particular kind of determinism. Inmates must be caused to *self-direct* themselves in a manageable way, and for this to be promoted, desired and undesired conduct must be defined as springing from the personal will and character of the individual inmate himself, and defined as something worthy or blameworthy he can himself do something about. In short, each institutional perspective must contain a personal morality, and in each total institution we can see in miniature the development of something akin to a functionalist version of morality.

The translation of inmate behavior into moralistic terms suited to the institution's avowed perspective will necessarily contain some broad presuppositions as to the character of human beings. Given the inmates of whom they have charge, and the processing that must be done to these objects, staff tends to evolve what may be thought of as a *theory of human nature*. As an implicit part of institutional perspective, this theory rationalizes the scene, provides a subtle means of maintaining social distance from inmates and a stereotyped view of them, and gives sanction to the treatment accorded them.[10] Typically, the theory covers the "good" and "bad" possibilities of inmate conduct, the forms that messing up take, the instructional value of privileges and punishments, and the "essential" difference between staff and inmates. In armies, officers will have a theory about the relation between discipline and the obedience of men under fire; the qualities proper to men; the "breaking point" of men; and the difference between mental sickness and malingering. And they will be trained into a particular conception of their own natures, as one ex-Guardsman suggests in listing the moral qualities expected of officers:

> While much of the training was inevitably designed to promote physical fitness, there was nevertheless a strongly held belief

[10] I derive this from Everett C. Hughes' review of Leopold von Wies's *Spätlese,* in *American Journal of Sociology,* LXI, (1955), 182. A similar area is covered under the current anthropological term "ethnopsychology," except that the unit to which it applies is a culture, not an institution. It should be added that inmates, too, acquire a theory of human nature, partly taking over the one employed by staff and partly developing a countering one of their own. In this connection see the very interesting description of the concept of "rat" as evolved by prisoners, in Richard McCleery, *The Strange Journey* (Chapel Hill: University of North Carolina Extension Bulletin, 1953), 14–15; and in McCleery's Chapters 4 and 7, below.

that an Officer, whether fit or not, should always have so much in the way of pride (or "guts") that he would never admit to physical inadequacy until he dropped dead or unconscious. This belief, a very significant one, was mystical both in its nature and intensity. During a crippling exercise at the end of the course two or three Officers fell out complaining of blisters or other mild indispositions. The Chief Instructor, himself a civilized and self-indulgent man, denounced them in round terms. An Officer, he said, simply could not and did not fall out. Will-power, if nothing else, should keep him going forever. It was all a matter of "guts." There was an unspoken implication that, since other ranks could and did fall out, even though they were often physically tougher, the Officer belonged to a superior caste. I found it an accepted belief among Officers later on that they could perform physical feats or endure physical discomforts without it being in the least necessary for them to train or prepare for such things in the manner required of the private soldier. Officers, for example, just did not do P.T.: they did not need it; they were Officers and would endure to the very end, had they stepped straight on to the field from a sanitorium or a brothel.[11]

In prisons, we find a current conflict between the psychiatric and the moral-weakness theories of crime. In convents, we find theories about the ways in which the spirit can be weak and strong and the ways in which its defects can be combatted. Mental hospitals stand out here because staff pointedly establish themselves as specialists in the knowledge of human nature, who must diagnose and prescribe on the basis of this intelligence. Hence in the standard psychiatric text-books there are chapters on "psychodynamics" and "psychopathology" which provide charmingly explicit formulations of the "nature" of human nature.[12]

An important part of the theory of human nature in many total institutions is the belief that if the new inmate can be made to show extreme deference to staff immediately he will thereafter be manageable—that in submitting to these initial demands his "resistance" or

[11] Simon Raven, "Perish by the Sword," *Encounter*, XII (1959), 38–39.

[12] The engulfing character of an institution's theory of human nature is nicely expressed currently in progressive psychiatric establishments. The theories originally developed to deal with inmates are being applied more and more in these places to the staff as well, so that low-level staff must do its penance in group psychotherapy, and high-level staff in individual psychoanalysis. There is even some movement to bring in consulting sociological therapists for the institution as a whole.

"spirit" is somehow broken. (This is one reason for the will-breaking ceremonies and welcoming practices discussed in Chapter 1.) Of course, if inmates adhere to the same theory of human nature, then staff views of character will be confirmed. Recent studies of the conduct of American army personnel taken prisoner in the Korean war provide an example. In America there is a current belief that once a man is brought to the "breaking point," he will thereafter be unable to show any resistance at all. Apparently this view of human nature, reinforced by training injunctions about the danger of any weakening at all, led some prisoners to give up all resistance once they had made a minor admission.[13]

A theory of human nature is of course only one implication of the interpretative scheme offered by a total institution. One further area covered by institutional perspectives is work. Since on the outside, work is ordinarily done for pay, profit, or prestige, the withdrawal of these motives means a withdrawal of certain interpretations of action and an introduction of new interpretations. Thus in mental hospitals there is what are officially known as "industrial therapy" and "work therapy"; patients are put to tasks, typically mean ones, such as raking leaves, waiting on tables, working in the laundry, and washing floors. Although the nature of these tasks derives from the working needs of the establishment, the claim presented to the patient is that these tasks will help him to relearn to live in society and that his capacity and willingness to handle them will be taken as diagnostic evidence of improvement.[14] The patient may himself perceive work in this light. A similar process of redefining the meaning of work is found in religious institutions, as the comments of a Poor Clare suggest:

> This is another of the marvels of living in obedience. No one is ever doing anything more important than you are, if you are obeying. A broom, a pen, a needle are all the same to God. The

[13] See the useful paper by Albert Biderman, "Social-Psychological Needs and 'Involuntary' Behavior as Illustrated by Compliance in Interrogation," *Sociometry*, 23 (1960), 120–145.

[14] It would be quite wrong to view these "therapies" too cynically. Work such as that in a laundry or shoe repair shop has its own rhythm and is managed often by individuals more closely connected with their trade than with the hospital; hence very often time spent at these tasks is much more pleasant than time spent on a dark silent ward. Further, the notion of putting patients to "useful" work seems so captivating a possibility in our society, that operations such as shoe-repair shops or mattress-making shops may come to be maintained, at least for a time, at an actual cost to the institution.

obedience of the hand that plies them and the love in the heart of the nun who holds them are what make an eternal difference to God, to the nuns, and to all the world.[15]

People in the world are forced to obey manmade laws and workaday restrictions. Contemplative nuns freely elect to obey a monastic Rule inspired by God. The girl pounding her typewriter may be pounding for nothing but dollars' sake and wishing she could stop. The Poor Clare sweeping the monastery cloisters is doing it for God's sake and prefers sweeping, at that particular hour, to any other occupation in the world.[16]

An implication here is that although heavily institutionalized motives such as profit or economy may become excessively proliferated in commercial establishments,[17] these frames of reference may nevertheless function to restrain other types of interpretation. When the usual rationales of the wider society cannot be invoked, the field becomes dangerously clear for all kinds of interpretative flights and excesses, and, in consequence, for new kinds of tyranny.

I would like to add a final point about institutional perspectives. The management of inmates is typically rationalized in terms of the ideal aims or functions of the establishment, which entail humane technical services. Professionals are usually hired to perform these services, if only to save management the necessity of sending the inmates out of the institution for servicing, it being unwise "for monks to go abroad, for this is not at all healthful for their souls."[18] Professionals joining the establishment on this basis are likely to become dissatisfied, feeling that they cannot here properly practice their calling and are being used as "captives" to add professional sanction to the privilege system. This seems to be a classic cry.[19] In many mental hospitals there is a record of disgruntled psychiatrists

---

[15] Sister Mary Francis, P.C., *A Right to be Merry* (New York: Sheed and Ward, 1956), 108.

[16] *Ibid.*, p. 99. The application of an alternate meaning to poverty is of course a basic strategy in the religious life. Ideals of spartan simplicity have also been used by radical political and military groups; currently, beatniks impute a special meaning to a show of poverty.

[17] A good representation of this interpretative spread and thickness is given in Bernard Malamud's novel about management problems in a small grocery store: *The Assistant* (New York: Signet Books, 1958).

[18] *The Holy Rule of Saint Benedict*, Ch. 66.

[19] See, for example, Harvey Powelson and Reinhard Bendix, "Psychiatry in Prison," *Psychiatry*, 14 (1951), 73–86; and Waldo W. Burchard, "Role Conflicts of Military Chaplains," *American Sociological Review*, 19 (1954), 528–535.

asserting they are leaving so that they can do psychotherapy. Often a special psychiatric service, such as group psychotherapy, psychodrama, or art therapy, is introduced with great support from higher hospital management; then slowly interest is transferred elsewhere, and the professional in charge finds that gradually his job has been changed into a species of public relations work—his therapy given only token support except when visitors come to the institution and higher management is concerned to show how modern and complete the facilities are.

Professionals, of course, are not the only staff group standing in a somewhat difficult relation to the official goals of the establishment. Those members of staff who are in continuous contact with inmates may feel that they too are being set a contradictory task, having to coerce inmates into obedience while at the same time giving the impression that humane standards are being maintained and the rational goals of the institution realized.

INSTITUTIONAL CEREMONIES

I have described total institutions from the point of view of inmates and, briefly, from the point of view of staff. Each point of view has as a crucial element an image of the other grouping. Although there is this image-of-the-other, it is seldom of the kind that leads to sympathetic identification—except perhaps on the part of those inmates who take a trusty role and seriously "identify with the aggressor." When unusual intimacies and relationships do occur across the staff-inmate line, we know that involvement cycles may follow, and all kinds of awkward reverberations are likely to occur,[20] with a subversion of authority and social distance that again gives one the impression of an incest taboo operating within total institutions.

In addition to illicit or questionable "personal" ties that cross the staff-inmate line, a second irregular type of contact between staff and inmate occurs. Staff, unlike inmates, hold some aspects of their life separate from the institution—even though these may be located on or near the grounds. At the same time, it is understood that inmates'

[20] See Erving Goffman, *The Presentation of Self in Everyday Life* (New York: Anchor Books, 1959), 200–204; McCorkle and Korn, *op. cit.*, pp. 93–94.

work time is of little value to inmates themselves and is subject to the discretion of staff. Under these circumstances, role segregation seems difficult to maintain, and inmates find themselves led into performing menial personal services for staff—such as gardening, house-painting, house-cleaning, and baby-sitting. Because these services are not part of the official frame of reference of the institution, staff members are forced to give some consideration to their servants and are unable to maintain the usual distance from them. The ordinary restrictions of institutional life make inmates usually quite happy to break through staff-inmate alignments in this manner. Lawrence provides a military example:

> The Sergeant Major set an example of misuse, when he led the last fatigue man in the rank to his wife's house, and had him black the grate and mind the children, while she shopped. "Gave me a slab of jam-tart, she did," boasted Garner, lightly forgiving the crying infant because of the belly-full he'd won.[21]

But in addition to these ways of crossing the line, every total institution seems to develop a set of institutionalized practices— whether spontaneously or by imitation—through which staff and inmates come close enough together to get a somewhat favorable image of the other and to identify sympathetically with the other's situation. These practices express unity, solidarity, and joint commitment to the institution rather than differences between the two levels.

In form, these institutionalized get-togethers are characterized by a release from the formalities and task-orientation that govern inmate-staff contacts, and by a softening of the usual chain of command. Often, participation is relatively voluntary. Given the usual roles, then, these activities represent "role releases";[22] of course, given the pervasive effect of inmate-staff distance, any alteration in the direction of expressing solidarity automatically represents a role release. It is possible to speculate on the many functions of these comings-

[21] T. E. Lawrence, *The Mint* (London: Jonathan Cape, 1955), 40. For a concentration camp version, see Eugen Kogon, *The Theory and Practice of Hell* (New York: Berkeley, 1950), 84–86. As a qualification, it should be added that in some total institutions, notably ships, these personal services may be legitimated as part of the proper duties of one of the ratings; the same is true of the role of batman in the British army. But in these exceptions, staff may have little life that is not official.

[22] This term was suggested by Everett C. Hughes and is employed in an unpublished paper on institutional catharsis by Joseph Gusfield.

together, but the explanations so far suggested seem far less impressive than the singular way in which these practices keep cropping up in every kind of total institution, and in what would seem to be the poorest possible soil. One is led to feel that there must be very good reasons for these practices, even though these have not yet been found.

One of the most common forms of institutional ceremony is the *house organ*—typically a weekly newspaper or a monthly magazine. Usually all the contributors are recruited from within inmate ranks, resulting in a kind of mock hierarchy of those so engaged, while supervision and censorship are provided by a member of the staff who is relatively congenial to inmates, yet reliably loyal to his fellow-officials. The printed content is such as to draw a circle around the institution and to give the accent of public reality to the world within.

Two kinds of material that appear in the house organ may be mentioned. First, there is "local news." This includes reports on all recent institutional ceremonies, as well as reference to "personal" events such as birthdays, promotions, trips, and deaths, occurring to members of the institution, especially to high-placed or well-known members of staff. This content is of a congratulatory or condolence-offering character, presumably expressing for the whole institution its sympathetic concern for the lives of the individual members. Here is an interesting aspect of role segregation: since the institutionally-relevant roles of a member tend to set him off against whole categories of other members, these roles cannot be used as a vehicle for the expression of institutional solidarity; instead, use must be made of nonrelevant roles, especially those such as parent and spouse that are imaginable, if not possible, for all categories.

Secondly, there is material that can reflect an editorial view. This includes news from the outside world bearing on the social and legal status of inmates and ex-inmates, accompanied by appropriate comment; original essays, short stories, and poetry; editorials. This material is written by inmates but expresses the official view of the functions of the institution, the staff's theory of human nature, an idealized version of inmate-staff relationships, and the views an ideal convert ought to take. In short, this material presents the institutional line.

The house organ, however, survives in the delicacy of a nice balance. Staff allows itself to be interviewed, written about, and read about by inmates, thus coming under some slight control of the writers and readers; at the same time inmates are given an opportunity to show that they are high enough on the human scale to handle the official language and the official line with educated competence.[23] Contributors, on the other hand, guarantee to follow the official ideology, presenting it for inmates by inmates. Interestingly enough, inmates who make this compact with staff often do not cease to affirm the counter-mores. They introduce whatever open criticism of the institution that the censors will permit; they add to this by means of oblique or veiled writing or pointed cartoons; and, among their cronies, they may take a cynical view of their contribution, claiming that they write because this provides a "soft" job setting or a good route for release recommendations.

While house organs have been customary for some time, it is only recently that a somewhat similar form of role-release has appeared in total institutions. I refer here to the several forms of "self-government" and "group therapy." Typically, the inmates speak the lines and a congenial member of staff performs the supervision. Again, a kind of compact between inmates and staff is found. The inmates are given the privilege of spending some time in a relatively "unstructured" or equalitarian milieu and even the right to voice complaints. In return they are expected to become less loyal to the counter-mores and more receptive to the ideal-for-self that the staff defines for them.

Inmate use of the official staff language and staff philosophy in discussing or publishing gripes is a mixed blessing for staff. Inmates can manipulate staff's own rationalization of the institution, and through this threaten the social distance between the two groupings. Hence in mental hospitals we find the engaging phenomenon of staff using stereotyped psychiatric terminology in talking to each other or to patients but chiding patients for being "intellectualistic" and for avoiding the issues when they use this language too. Perhaps the distinctive thing about the group therapy form of institutional role release is that a group of academically oriented professionals are interested in it, and so there is already more literature on this aspect of total institutions than on most other aspects combined.

A somewhat different type of institutional ceremony is found in the *annual party* (sometimes held more than once a year) at which staff and inmates "mix" through standard forms of sociability such as commensualism, party-games, or dancing. At such times staff and

[23] The scholarly legal petitions which circulate in many prisons and mental hospitals, and which are written by inmates, seem to serve the same function.

inmates will have the license to "take liberties" across the caste line, and social reachings may be expressed through sexual ones.[24] In some cases this liberty may be extended to the point of ritual role-reversal, during which staff wait table for inmates and perform other menial services for them.[25]

Often linked with the annual party in total institutions, is the Christmas-New Year celebration. Once a year inmates will decorate the establishment with easily removable decorations partly supplied by staff, in this way banishing from the living quarters what an extra-special meal will then banish from the table. Small gifts and indulgences will be distributed among the inmates; some work duties will be cancelled; visitor time may be increased and restrictions on leave-taking decreased. In general, the rigors of institutional life for the inmates will be relaxed for a day. A British prison version may be cited:

> The authorities did their best to cheer us. On Christmas morning we sat down to a breakfast of cornflakes, sausages, bacon, beans, fried bread, margarine and bread and marmalade. At midday we were given roast pork, Christmas pudding and coffee, and at supper, mince pies and coffee, instead of the nightly mug of cocoa.
>
> The halls were decorated with paper streamers, balloons and bells, and each had its Christmas tree. There were extra cinema shows in the gymnasium. Two of the officers each presented me with a cigar. I was allowed to send and receive some greeting telegrams, and for the first time since I had been in prison, I had enough cigarettes to smoke.[26]

[24] Of course, the "office parties" found in establishments not of the total kind have similar dynamics, and were the first no doubt to give rise to comment. See, for example, Gusfield, *op. cit.* The best reports on these events are still to be found in fiction. See, for example, Nigel Balchin's description of a factory party in *Private Interests* (Boston: Houghton-Mifflin, 1953), 47–71; Angus Wilson's description of a hotel staff-guest party in his short story "Saturnalia" in *The Wrong Set* (New York: William Morrow, 1950), 68–89; and J. Kerkhoff's version of the annual party in a mental hospital in *How Thin the Veil: A Newspaperman's Story of His Own Mental Crackup and Recovery* (New York: Greenberg, 1952), 224–225.

[25] See Max Gluckman, *Custom and Conflict in Africa*, Ch. V "The License in Ritual," (Glencoe: Free Press, 1955), 109–136.

[26] Anthony Heckstall-Smith, *Eighteen Months* (London: Allan Wingate, 1954), 199. See also Alfred Hassler, *Diary of a Self-Made Convict* (Chicago: Regnery, 1954), 157. For Christmas license in a mental hospital see Kerkhoff, *op. cit.*, pp. 185 and 256. The same on a man-of-war is presented by Melville, *op. cit.*, pp. 95–96.

An interesting institutional ceremony, often connected with the annual party and the Christmas celebration, is the *institutional theatrical*.[27] Typically, the players are inmates and the directors of the production are staff, but sometimes "mixed" casts are found. The writers are usually members of the institution, whether staff or inmate, and hence the production can be full of local references, imparting through the private use of this public form a special sense of the reality of events internal to the institution. Very frequently the offering will consist of satirical skits which lampoon well-known members of the institution, especially high-placed staff members.[28] If, as is frequent, the inmate community is one-sexed, then some of the players are likely to perform in the costume and burlesqued role of members of the other sex. Limits of license are often tested, the humor being a little more broad than some members of the staff would like to see tolerated. Melville, in commenting on the relaxation of discipline during and immediately after a theatrical on board ship, has the following to say:

> And here White Jacket must moralize a bit. The unwonted spectacle of the role of gun-room officers mingling with *the people* in applauding a mere seaman like Jack Chase filled me at the time with the most pleasurable emotions. It is a sweet thing, thought I, to see these officers confess a human brotherhood with us, after all; a sweet thing to mark their cordial appreciation of the manly merits of my matchless Jack. Ah! they are noble fellows all round, and I do not know but I have wronged them sometimes in my thoughts.[29]

In addition to satirical sketches, there may be dramatic presentations recounting the bad historical past of like total institutions, as a contrast to the presumably better present.[30] The audience for the

[27] See, for example, the prison version in Frank Norman, *Bang to Rights* (London: Secker and Warburg, 1958), pp. 69–70.

[28] For an example of prisoners lampooning guards and the Prison Governor, see George Dendrickson and Frederick Thomas, *The Truth About Dartmoor* (London: Gollancz, 1954), 110–111.

[29] Melville, *op. cit.*, p. 101. (Stress in the original.) Melville proceeds then to comment bitterly that soon after this role-release, the officers seemed to have a capacity to "ship their quarter-deck faces," reverting fully to their usual strictness. See also Kerkhoff, *op. cit.*, p. 229, and Heckstall-Smith, *op. cit.*, pp. 195–99.

[30] Neither the "before" nor "after" need have much relation to the facts, since each version is meant to clarify a situation, not to measure it, and in any case the "past" may be slyly presented because of its similarity to the present.

production will pointedly contain both inmate and staff, although often ecologically segregated, and in some cases even outsiders may be permitted to come.

The fact that the institutional theatrical is sometimes presented before an outside audience no doubt provides inmate and staff with a contrasting background against which to sense their unity. Other kinds of institutional ceremony fulfill this function too, often more directly. Increasingly there is the practice of the annual *open house*, during which the kinfolk of members, or even the public at large, may be invited to inspect the premises. They can then see for themselves that high humane standards are being maintained. At such times, staff and inmates tend to be on visibly good terms with one another, and the usual price for this is some tempering of ordinary stringencies.

Open house is a likely success because it occurs in the context of an institutional front or *institutional display*. Sometimes this display is directed to an internal audience, especially high staff members, as an ex-mental patient illustrates:

> Breakfast over, some of the patients dressed and left the ward, reappearing shortly afterwards armed with mops and brushes with which they began, in a queer mechanical way, to clean the floors; like robots that had just been wound up. This sudden activity surprised me. The probationers rushed about bringing bright new rugs to spread on the polished boards. As if by magic, one or two lockers made a belated appearance and the flowers of midsummer blossomed unexpectedly around. The ward was unrecognizable, so different did it seem. I wondered if the doctors ever saw it in its usual bareness, and was equally surprised when, after their visit, all this glory departed as swiftly as it had appeared.[31]

In the main, institutional display seems to be addressed to visitors. Sometimes the focus of concern is the visit of a particular inmate

---

I have seen mental patients from good wards give a stage performance of conditions which presumably used to prevail in backward mental hospitals. Victorian costumes were used. The audience consisted of psychiatrically enlightened well-wishers from the environing city. A few buildings away from where the audience sat, equally bad conditions could be observed in the flesh. In their performance, the performers knew their roles well because they had played them.

[31] D. McI. Johnson and N. Dodds, Eds., *The Plea for the Silent* (London: Christopher Johnson, 1957), 92.

by a particular outsider. Often, outsiders are little broken to the ways of the hospital and, as earlier suggested, can make embarrassing demands. Here the inmate himself may play a heavy role in the institution's presentation. A physician's report on mental hospitals provides an example:

> The situation can be clarified by asking what happened when such a patient received a visitor. First the visitor was announced by telephone from the central office of the hospital. Then the patient concerned was taken out of restraint, bathed, and dressed. When ready for display the patient was taken to a "visiting room" from which the ward could not be seen. If too intelligent to be trusted the patient was never left alone with the visitor. In spite of such precaution, however, suspicions were sometimes aroused, and it then became the duty of all the ward attendants to keep the situation under control.[32]

The visiting room in some total institutions is important here. Both decor and conduct in these places are typically much closer to outside standards than are those that prevail in the inmate's actual living quarters. The view of inmates that outsiders get thus functions to decrease the pressure these outsiders might otherwise bring to bear on the institution. It is a melancholy human fact that after a time all three parties—inmate, visitor, and staff—realize that the visiting room presents a dressed-up view, realize that the other parties realize this too, and yet all tacitly agree to continue the fiction.

Institutional display may also be directed to visitors in general, and function to tell them what kind of image of the establishment is appropriate—this image being one calculated to allay their vague dread about involuntary establishments. In the guise of being shown all, the visitors are of course likely to be shown only the more prepossesing, cooperative inmates and the more prepossessing parts of the establishment.[33] In large mental hospitals, in fact, modern treatment such as psychodrama or dance therapy may come to play a special role in this regard, as already suggested, with the therapist and his crew of regular patients developing the kind of capacity to perform before strangers that comes from constant experience. Furthermore, a small group of pet inmates may for years handle the task of escorting visitors around the institution's Potemkin village. Visitors can easily

[32] J. M. Grimes, M.D., *When Minds Go Wrong* (Chicago: Author, 1951), 81.

[33] For a prison example, see Holley Cantine and Dachine Rainer, Eds., *Prison Etiquette* (Bearsville, N. Y.: Retort Press, 1950), 62.

take the loyalty and social skills of these receptionists as a sample
of the character of the entire inmate group. The right of staff to
limit, inspect, and censor outgoing mail, and the frequent rule against
writing anything negative about the institution, help to maintain the
visitors' view of the establishment—and also alienate inmates from
those on the outside to whom they cannot write frankly. Often the
physical remoteness of the establishment from the homes of the
inmates' kin functions not only to conceal "conditions" on the inside
but also to transform a family visit into something of a festive
excursion, for which it will be feasible for staff to make ample
preparation.

It is possible, of course, for a visitor to be an official one, part
of the institutional connection between the highest staff officer and
an agency responsible for controlling a whole class of institutions;
and then we can expect display and its preparation to be especially
elaborate. An example from British prison life (in the writer's spelling
and prison lingo) may be cited:

> Every now and a gain this nick like all other nicks in the
> country, would get a visit from the commistioner. Now this is a
> very big day in the life of screws and the governors, the day
> before he is due to arrive they start haveing a big clean up, all
> the floors are scrubed and the brasses are polished, also the
> recesses are give a good clean out. The exersize yard is swept and
> the flower beds are weeded and we are told to make sure our
> peters are clean and tiedy.
>
> At last the great day is here. The Commissioner usualy wears
> a black over coat and black Antoney Edden hat even in the
> summer., he also quite often carrys an umbreler. I don't realy
> know why they make such a fuss of him as all he does is come
> and have lunch with the governor have a little look around the
> nick get in his big car and drive off again. Some times he comes
> round just as we are being fed, and may pick on some one and
> say. "What's the food like? any complaints?"
>
> You look at the governor and the chief in turn (for they are
> his constant companions while he is in the nick) you then answer.
> "No complaints; sir."[34]

It may be added that whatever such visits do for everyday standards,
they do seem to serve as a reminder to everyone in the establishment
that the institution is not completely a world of its own, but bears

[34] Norman, *op. cit.*, p. 103.

some connection, bureaucratic and subordinative, to structures in the wider world. Institutional display, whatever its audience, can also convey to inmates that they are connected with what is the best institution of its kind. Inmates seem surprisingly ready to believe this of their institution. Through such a belief, of course, they can feel they have a status in the wider world, even through the very condition that exiles them from it.

The development of institutional display teaches us something in general about the symbolization process. First, the displayed part of the institution is likely to be the new, up-to-date part of the institution, which will change as new practices or equipment are added. Thus, when a new ward building is commissioned for use in a mental hospital, the staff of the previously "new" building may relax in the knowledge that their role as model staff persons and official greeters has been passed along to someone else. Secondly, display certainly need not be connected with frankly ceremonial aspects of the institution, such as flower beds and starched curtains, but often stresses utilitarian objects such as the latest kitchen equipment, or an elaborate surgical suite; in fact the display function of the equipment may be part of the reason for acquiring it. Finally, each item of display will necessarily have substantive implications; although these can hardly equal the impression the item creates as display, they can none the less be significant. The display of photographs in the lobbies of total establishments, showing the cycle the ideal inmate goes through in connection with the ideal staff, often has extremely little to do with the facts of institutional life, but at least a few inmates spent a pleasant morning posing for the pictures. The inmate-painted mural that prisons, mental hospitals, and other establishments pridefully display in a conspicuous space is not evidence that inmates as a whole were encouraged in art work, or felt creatively inspired in the setting, but it does provide evidence that at least one inmate was allowed to throw himself into his work.[35] The food served on inspection and open house days can provide at least a day's respite from

[35] Perhaps the classic case of an inmate exploiting the public relations value of his hobby is the ornithological laboratory assembled by prisoner Robert Stroud at Leavenworth. See T. E. Gaddis, *Birdman of Alcatraz* (New York: Signet Books, 1958). As one might expect, artist inmates have sometimes refused to cooperate, declining to accept liberty to paint in exchange for producing something that could be used by staff as evidence of the over-all character of the establishment. See Lowell Naeve, *A Field of Broken Stones* (Glen Gardner: Libertarian Press, 1950), 51–55.

the usual fare.[36] The favorable view of the establishment conveyed in
the house organ and the theatricals at least carries some validity in
terms of the round of life of the small fraction of inmates who participate in fabricating these ceremonies. And a prize admission building containing several comfortable admission wards can provide visitors
with an impression that is correct for an appreciable fraction of the
inmate population.

It might be added that the dynamics of appearance involve more
than merely display and reality. In many total institutions, punishments are meted out that are not legitimated by the rulings. These
penalities are typically administered in a closed cell or in some other
place away from the attention of most of the inmates and most of the
staff. And although these actions may not be frequent, they do tend
to occur in a structured way, as a known or hinted consequence of
certain types of transgression. These events are to the daily round in
the institution what the daily round is to the display put on for
outsiders, and all three aspects of reality—that which is concealed
from inmates, that which is revealed to inmates, and that which is
shown to visitors—must be considered together as three closely connected and differently functioning parts of the whole.

I have suggested that individual visits, open house, and inspections
allow outsiders to see that everything is all right on the inside. Some
other institutional practices offer the same opportunity. For example,
there is an interesting arrangement between total institutions and
stage performers who are amateurs or ex-professionals. The institution
provides a stage and guarantees an appreciative audience; the performers contribute a free show. There can be such a compelling need
of each for the services of the other, that the relationship may pass
beyond the matter of personal taste and become almost symbiotic.[37]
In any case, while the members of the institution are watching the

[36] See, for example, Cantine and Rainer, *op. cit.*, p. 61; Dendrickson and
Thomas, *op. cit.*, p. 70.

[37] We appreciate how needful total institutions are of entertainment
charity, but we tend to be less aware of how desperately nonprofessional en-
tertainers need audiences for whom to be charitable. For example, the mental
hospital I studied apparently had the only stage in the vicinity large enough
for all the members of a particular dancing school to perform on at once.
Some of the parents of the students did not particularly like coming onto the
hospital grounds, but if the school was to have any ensemble numbers, the
hospital stage had to be used. In addition, fee-paying parents expected their
child to appear in the annual school show, regardless of how much training
the child had had, or even in fact whether she was old enough to absorb

performers, the performers can see that staff-inmate relations are sufficiently harmonious for staff and inmates to assemble together for what looks like a voluntary evening of unregimented recreation.

Institutional ceremonies that occur through such media as the house organ, group meetings, open house, and charitable performances presumably fulfill latent social functions; some of these seem relatively clear in another kind of institutional ceremony, *intermural sports*.[38] The inside team tends to be a group of all-stars chosen by intramural contest among all the inmates. By competing well with outsiders, the all-stars take roles that palpably fall outside the stereotype of what an inmate is—since team sport requires such qualities as intelligence, skill, perseverance, cooperativeness, and even honor—and these roles are taken right in the teeth of outsiders and staff observers. In addition, the outsider team, and any supporters it manages to bring into the grounds, are forced to see that there are natural places on the inside where natural things go on. In exchange for being allowed to demonstrate these things about themselves, inmates through their intermural team convey some things about the institution. In pursuing what is defined as an uncoercible endeavor, the inmate team demonstrates to outsiders and observing inmates that the staff, in this setting at least, is not tyrannical, and that a team of inmates is ready to take on the role of representing the whole institution and allowed to do so. By vocal support of the home team, both staff and inmates show a mutual and similar involvement in the institutional entity. Incidentally, staff may not only coach these inmate teams but also participate on them occasionally, opening themselves up for the period of the game to the remarkable forgetfulness of social differences that can be generated in sports. Where intermural sports are not held, intramural competition may be substituted, with visitors coming in from the outside as a kind of symbolic team to watch, referee, and present the prizes.[39]

Sunday services and Sunday amusements are sometimes set in

---

training. Some numbers in the show, then, required an extremely indulgent audience. Patients can supply this since most patients in the audience are marched to the auditorium under the discipline of an attendant; once there, they will watch anything, under the same discipline, since infraction of rules may lead to cancellation of the privilege of leaving the ward on such occasions. The same kind of desperate bond tied the hospital audience to a group of mild office workers who belonged to a bell-ringing choir.

[38] See, for example, the comments on prison sports by Brendan Behan, *Borstal Boy* (London: Hutchinson, 1958), 327–329.

[39] For a prison example, see Norman, *op. cit.*, pp. 119–20.

opposition to each other; in total institutions this can partly be understood in terms of an unnecessary duplication of function. Like sports and charity performances, a service is a time when the unity of staff and inmates can be demonstrated by showing that in certain nonrelevant roles both are members of the same audience vis-à-vis the same outside performer.

In all instances of unified ceremonial life that I have mentioned, staff is likely to play more than a supervisory role. Often a high-ranking officer attends as a symbol of management and (it is hoped) of the whole establishment. He dresses well, is moved by the occasion, and gives smiles, speeches, and handshakes. He dedicates new buildings on the grounds, gives his blessing to new equipment, judges contests, and hands out awards. When acting in this capacity, his interaction with inmates will take a special benign form; inmates are likely to show embarrassment and respect, and he is likely to display an avuncular interest in them. (Interestingly enough, one of the functions of well-known inmates is to provide ranking members of staff with subjects whom they know enough about to use as reciprocals for the avuncular role.) In the case of our very large and very benevolently oriented mental hospitals, executive officers may be required to spend a goodly portion of their time putting in an appearance at these ceremonial occasions, providing us with some of the last occasions in modern society in which to observe a lord-of-the-manor gentry role. The gentry aspects of these ceremonies, incidentally, should not be taken lightly, since the model for some of them seems to derive from the "annual fête" which joined tenants, servants, and masters associated with a "great house"—joining them in competitive flower shows, sports, and even dances with "mixing" of some kind.[40]

Some final comments should be added about these institutional ceremonies. They tend to occur with well-spaced periodicity and to give rise to some social excitement. All the groupings in the establishment join in, regardless of rank or position, but are given a place that expresses their position. These ceremonial practices could bear strong witness to the value of a Durkheimian analysis: a society

[40] For a recent statement, complete with a report of skits put on by servants in mockery of masters, see, M. Astor, "Childhood at Clivedon," *Encounter*, 13 (1959), 27–28. Fêtes involving a whole village and sets of local gentry are, of course, described in many English novels, for example, L. P. Hartley's, *The Go-Between* (New York: Knopf, 1954).

dangerously split into inmates and staff can through these ceremonies hold itself together. The content itself of these ceremonies supports this same kind of functionalist interpretation. For example, there is often a hint or a splash of rebellion in the role that inmates take in the ceremonies. Whether through a sly article, a satirical sketch, or overfamiliarity during a dance, the subordinate in some way profanes the superordinate. Here we can follow Max Gluckman's analysis and argue that the very toleration of this skittishness is a sign of the strength of the establishment-state.

> Hence to act the conflicts, whether directly or by inversion or in other symbolic forms, emphasizes the social cohesion within which the conflicts exist.[41]

To act out one's rebellion before the authorities at a time legitimated for this is to exchange conspiracy for expression.

But a simply functionalist analysis of institutional rituals is not wholly convincing, except in the effect that apparently results occasionally from group therapy. In many cases it is a nice question whether these role releases create any staff-inmate solidarity at all. Staff typically complain to each other of their boredom with the ceremonies and their obligation to participate because of their own *noblesse oblige* or, worse still, because of that of their superiors. Inmates often participate because, wherever the ceremony is held, they will be more comfortable and less restricted there than where they otherwise would be. Further, inmates sometimes participate to gain the eye of the staff and to earn an early release. A total institution perhaps needs collective ceremonies because it is something more than a formal organization; but its ceremonies are often pious and flat, perhaps because it is something less than a community.

Whatever a ceremony offers a total institution, it offers something appreciable to students of these organizations. In temporarily modifying the usual relation between staff and inmate, ceremony demonstrates that the difference in character between the two groupings is not inevitable and unalterable. However flat (and however functional), ceremony does mark a putting aside and even a reversal of the usual social drama, and so reminds us that what was put aside has a dramaturgical, not concrete character. Intransigeance, collective

[41] Gluckman, *op. cit.*, p. 125. See also his "Rituals of Rebellion in South-West Africa," *The Frazer Lecture, 1952,* (Manchester: Manchester University Press, 1954).

teasing of staff, and personal involvements that cross the staff-inmate line all similarly suggest the social reality in a total institution is precarious. I think we should not be surprised by these weaknesses in the staging of grim social distance but rather wonder that more faults do not appear.

Starting with aims, regulations, offices, and roles, establishments of any kind seem to end up by adding depth and color to these arrangements. Duties and economic rewards are allocated, but so, at the same time, are character and being. In total establishments the self-defining aspects of office seem to be carried to an extreme. In becoming a member, one becomes thought of as possessing certain essential traits and qualities of character; moreover, these traits will differ radically, depending on whether one has joined staff or inmates.

The role of staff and the role of inmate cover every aspect of life. But these fully rounded characterizations must be played by civilians already deeply trained in other roles and other possibilities of relationship. The more the institution encourages the assumption that staff and inmate are of profoundly different human types (as, for example, by rules prohibiting informal social intercourse across the staff-inmate line), in short, the more profound the drama of difference between staff and inmate, the more incompatible the show becomes with the civilian repertoire of the players, and the more vulnerable to it.

There are grounds, then, for claiming that one of the main accomplishments of total institutions is staging a difference between two constructed categories of persons—a difference in social quality and moral character, a difference in perceptions of self and other. Thus every social arrangement in a mental hospital seems to point to the profound difference between a staff doctor and a mental patient; in a prison, between an official and a convict; and in military units (especially elite ones), between officers and men. Here, surely, is a magnificent social achievement, even though the similarity of the players, to which institutional ceremonies attest, can be expected to create some staging problems and therefore some personal strain.

I would like to mention one symptom of these staging problems. In total institutions, we characteristically obtain *identity anecdotes.* Inmates tell of times they were mistaken for staff members and carried off the misidentification for a while, or of times they mistook a staff member for an inmate. And staff persons similarly recount times when they were mistaken for inmates. We find *identity joking,* where a member of one group briefly acts like a member of the other, or briefly treats a co-member as someone of the other category, for the avowed purpose of amusement. Annual skits satirizing staff are one source of this joking; uneventful moments of horseplay during the day are another. And we also find *identity scandals,* a dwelling on cases where a person started out as a member of the staff, was disgraced in some way, and became a member of the inmate group in the same (or same kind of) institution. I assume these identity concerns point to the difficulty of sustaining a drama of difference between persons who could in many cases reverse roles and play on the other side. (In fact, these persons do engage in playful role-reversal.) It is not clear what problems these ceremonies solve, but it is clear what problems they point to.

INSTITUTIONAL DIFFERENCES

In this chapter, as in Chapter 1, total institutions have been considered in terms of a single basic articulation: inmates and staff. Having done this, we are in a position to ask what this view leaves out and what it distorts.

In a closer study of total institutions it would be important to ask about the typical differentiation of role that occurs *within* each of the two main groups,[42] and to ask about the institutional function of these more specialized postions. Some of these special roles have been mentioned in discussing special institutional tasks: someone on the staff will have to represent officially the institution in the councils of the wider society and will have to develop a non-institutional polish in order to do this effectively; someone on staff will have to deal with visitors and other connections of the inmates; someone will have to offer professional services; and someone will have to spend time in relatively close contact with inmates. Someone may even have to provide a personal symbol of the institution for the inmates—

[42] A treatment of role differentiation among prisoners may be found in Gresham M. Sykes, *The Society of Captives* (Princeton: Princeton University Press, 1958), Ch. 5. "Argot Roles," 84–108, and his "Men, Merchants, and Toughs; a Study of Reactions to Imprisonment," *Journal of Social Problems,* 4 (1956), 130–138. For staff-defined types among mental hospital patients see, Otto von Mering and S. H. King, *Remotivating the Mental Patient,* (New York: Russell Sage Foundation, 1957), esp. pp. 27–47, "A Social Classification of Patients."

a symbol on which they may project many different kinds of emotion.[43]
A close treatment of total institutions should give systematic attention
to these intra-category differences.

There are two aspects of intra-group role differentiation that I
would like to consider, both having to do with the dynamics of the
lowest level of staff. One special characteristic of this group is that
they are likely to be the long-term employees and hence the tradition-
carriers, while higher staff, and even inmates, may have a high rate
of turnover.[44] In addition, it is this group that must personally
present the demands of the institution to the inmates. They can
come, then, to deflect the hate of inmates from higher staff persons,
and at the same time make it feasible, should an inmate break
through to contact with a higher staff person, for this person to grant
avuncular kindness and even dispensations.[45] These acts of clemency
are possible simply because like all uncles, higher staff do not have
the immediate task of disciplining inmates, and their contacts with
inmates are so few that this leniency does not disrupt general discipline. I think that inmates very generally obtain some sense of
security from the feeling, however illusory, that although most staff
persons are bad, the man at the top is really good—but perhaps
merely hoodwinked by those under him. (An expression of this
appears in popular stories and movies involving police: the bottom
levels may be sadistic, prejudiced, or corrupt, but the man at the top
of the organization is "O.K.") Here we have a nice example of what
Hughes refers to as "the moral division of labor," for here a difference
in task performed by the individual clearly entails a difference in
moral attributes imputed to him.

The second aspect of role differentiation among staff that I want
to consider has to do with deference patterns. In civil society, the
interpersonal rituals that persons accord one another while in each
other's immediate physical presence have a crucial component of

[43] The dynamics of this process are outlined in Freud's well-known, *Group
Psychology and the Analysis of the Ego* (London: Hogarth Press, 1948). For
one application, see Amiai Etzioni, "The Organizational Structure of 'Closed'
Educational Institutions in Israel," *Harvard Educational Review*, XXVII
(1957), 123. There are other such targets of projection (for example, the
team mascot) and perhaps they should all be considered together.

[44] See, for example, Belknap, *op. cit.*, p. 110.

[45] See, for example, Elliott Jaques, "Social Systems as a Defence against
Persecutory and Depressive Anxiety," in Melanie Klein *et al.*, *New Directions
in Psycho-Analysis* (London: Tavistock, 1955), 483.

spontaneity. The giver is obliged to perform the ritual in an uncalculated, immediate, unthinking fashion if it is to be a valid expression of his presumed regard for the recipient, else how could these acts "express" inward feelings? The giver can manage this because he learned the quite standardized deference rituals of his society so early in his life that by adult years they are second nature. Now since the deference the giver shows a recipient is supposed to be a direct and free expression, the recipient can hardly demand proper deference should it not be forthcoming. Action can be coerced, but a coerced show of feeling is only a show. An affronted recipient can take action against the person who is insufficiently deferential, but typically must disguise the specific reason for this corrective action. Only children, presumably, can be openly sanctioned by the recipient for showing improper deference; this is one sign that we hold children to be not-yet-persons.

It seems characteristic of every establishment, and especially of total institutions, that some forms of deference will be specific to it, with inmates as givers and staff as recipient. For this to occur, those who are to receive spontaneous expressions of regard must be the very ones to teach the ruling and to enforce it. It follows that in total institutions one crucial difference from civil life is that deference is placed on a formal footing, with specific demands being made and specific negative sanctions accorded for infractions. Feeling-tones such as insolence will be explicitly penalized. Not only will acts be required, but also the outward show of inward feelings.

Staff partially protect themselves from this altered relation to deference by some standard devices. First, to the degree that the inmates are defined as not-fully-adults, staff need not feel a loss by coercing deference from their charges. Secondly, we sometimes find, especially in the Military, the notion that it is the uniform, not the man, that is saluted (so that the man is not demanding deference for himself); linked with this we find the notion that "it does not matter what you feel as long as you don't show it." Thirdly, the lowest level of staff can perform the training, thus leaving the higher levels free to receive personally uncoerced grants of deference. As Gregory Bateson suggests:

> Essentially, the function of the middle member is to instruct and discipline the third member in the forms of behavior which he should adopt in his contacts with the first. The nurse teaches the child how to behave towards its parents, just as the N.C.O. teaches

and disciplines the private in how he should behave towards officers.[46]

I have commented on some intra-group differences. Just as we must see that neither the staff nor the inmate group is homogenous, so we must see that sometimes a simple division between staff and inmate groups can conceal important facts. In some establishments, the trusty or straw-boss of inmate rank is not too far away in function and prerogatives from the lowest staff level, the guards; and in some cases the highest man in the lower stratum has more power and authority than the lowest man in the higher stratum.[47] Further, there are some establishments that oblige *all* members to share some basic deprivations, a kind of collective hardship-ceremony that might be considered (in its effects) along with the annual Christmas party and other institutional ceremonies. Good examples are recorded in the literature on nunneries:

> Every member of the community including the Superior General was housed here regardless of age, rank or function. Choir nuns, artists, doctors of medicine and the humanities, cooks, laundresses, shoemaker nuns and the peasant sisters who worked the truck gardens lived in those boxlike cells, each one identical in form and content, in arrangement of bed, table and chair and thrice-folded coverlets over each chair.[48]

> St. Clare has legislated that the abbess and vicaress are to conform to the common life in all things. So, how much more the others! St. Clare's idea of the prerogatives of a superior was entirely novel in her century. A Poor Clare abbess boasts neither staff nor train. She wears no pectoral cross, but the same little wedding-ring ($2.50 net) as her daughters. Our abbess is currently resplendent in a large patch across the front of her habit. It was put there by her own hands, the same hands that quarter

[46] Gregory Bateson, in M. Mead and R. Métraux, Eds., *The Study of Culture at a Distance* (Chicago: University of Chicago Press, 1953), 372.

[47] See, for example, the discussion of the boatswain's role in S. A. Richardson, *The Social Organization of British and United States Merchant Ships,* (unpublished monograph available at the New York School of Industrial and Labor Relations, Cornell University, 1954), 15–18. The Regimental and Battalion Sergeant Major compared to the platoon lieutenant provides other examples.

[48] Kathryn Hulme, *The Nun's Story* (London: Muller, 1957), 20.

and de-worm apples with the best of them, the same hands that wield a dish towel like a professional.[49]

For some of these religious institutions the notion of a staff-inmate division is not fruitful; one apparently finds, rather, a single collegial group, internally stratified in terms of a single finely-graded rank order. Further, in total institutions such as boarding schools, it may be useful to add to the strata of teachers and students a third one, comprising housekeeping staff.

Total institutions vary considerably in the amount of role differentiation found within the staff and the inmate groupings, and in the clarity of the line between the two strata. There are other important differences that have been only incidentally mentioned; one of these I would like to consider further here.

Recruits enter total institutions in different spirits. At one extreme we find the quite involuntary entrance of those who are sentenced to prison, committed to a mental hospital, or pressed into the crew of a ship. It is perhaps in such cases that staff's version of the ideal inmate has least chance of taking hold. At the other extreme, we find religious institutions which deal only with those who feel they have gotten the call, and of these volunteers, take only those who seem to be the most suitable and the most serious in their intentions. In such cases, conversion seems already to have taken place, and it only remains to show the neophyte along what lines he can best discipline himself. Midway between these two extremes, we find institutions like the Army where inmates are required to serve but are given much opportunity to feel that this service is a justifiable one required in their own ultimate interests. Obviously, significant differences in tone will appear in total institutions, depending on whether recruitment is voluntary, semi-voluntary, or involuntary.

Along with the variable of mode of recruitment there is another variable—the degree to which a self-regulating change in the inmate is explicitly striven for by staff. In custodial and work institutions, presumably, the inmate need only comply with action standards; the

---

[49] Francis, *op. cit.*, pp. 179–80. The rule in Anglo-American military tradition that officers should undergo all the risks they set their men and be concerned for the food and comforts of their men before their own during battle provides a subtle variation on these hardship ceremonies; by showing *more* concern for their men than for themselves, officers can at the same time reinforce ties with their men and maintain distance.

spirit and inward feeling with which he goes about his assignment would not seem to be an official concern. In brainwashing camps, religious establishments, and institutions for intensive psychotherapy, the inmate's private feelings are presumably at issue. Mere compliance with work rulings would not here seem to be enough, and the inmate's incorporation of staff standards is an active aim as well as an incidental consequence.

Another dimension of variation among total institutions is what might be called their *permeability,* that is, the degree to which the social standards maintained within the institution and the social standards maintained in the environing society have influenced each other, the consequence being to minimize differences. This issue, incidentally, gives us an opportunity to consider some of the dynamic relations between a total institution and the wider society that supports it or tolerates it.

In examining the admission procedures of total institutions, one tends to be struck by the impermeable aspects of the establishment, since the stripping and leveling processes which occur at this time directly cut across the various social distinctions with which the recruits enter. St. Benedict's advice to the abbot tends to be followed:

> Let him make no distinction of persons in the monastery. Let not one be loved more than another, unless he be found to excel in good works or in obedience. Let not one of noble birth be raised above him who was formerly a slave, unless some other reasonable cause intervene.[50]

Thus, the new cadet in a military school finds that discussions "of wealth and family background are taboo," and that, "Although the pay of the cadet is very low, he is not permitted to receive money from home."[51] Even the age-grading system of the wider society may be stopped at the gates, as illustrated, in the extreme, in some religious institutions:

> Gabrielle moved to the place that would ever be hers, third in the line of forty postulants. She was third oldest in the group because she had been third to register on that day less than a week ago

[50] *The Holy Rule of St. Benedict,* Ch. 2.

[51] Sanford M. Dornbusch, "The Military Academy as an Assimilating Institution," *Social Forces,* 33 (1955), 317. The classic case of this kind of echelon-leveling is found perhaps in the fagging system in British public schools.

when the Order had opened its doors to new entrants. From that moment, her chronological age had ceased and the only age she would henceforth have, her age in the religious life, had started.[52]

(Milder examples of the same process can be seen in Air Forces and university science departments, where, during periods of national crisis, very young men may be tolerated in very high ranks.) And just as age dates may be suppressed, so, in some quite radical total institutions, the names of members may be changed upon entrance, the better (presumably) to symbolize a break with the past and an embrace of the life of the establishment.

It seems that some impermeability in an establishment is necessary if morale and stability is to be maintained. It is by suppressing external social distinctions that a total institutions can build up an orientation to its own scheme of honor. Thus, the few mental patients of high socio-economic status in a state mental hospital can provide everyone assurance that there is a distinctive mental patient role, that the institution is not merely a disposal station for some oddments from the lower classes, and that the fate of the inmate is not one he suffers merely because of his general social background; the same can be said of the role of "toffs" in British prisons and nuns of noble lineage in French nunneries. Further, if the institution has a militant mission, as in the case of some religious, military, and political units, then a partial reversal on the inside of external status arrangements can act as a constant reminder of the difference and enmity between the institution and its environing society. It should be noted that in thus suppressing externally valid differences the harshest total institution may be the most democratic, and in fact the inmate's assurance of being treated no worse than any other of his fellows can be a source of support as well as a deprivation.[53] But there are some limits to the value of impermeability for these institutions.

I have already described the role of representative that topmost members of staff may be obliged to perform. If they are to move with grace and effectiveness in the wider community, then it may be advantageous for them to have been recruited from the same small social grouping as leaders of other social units in the wider society.

[52] Hulme, *op. cit.*, pp. 22–23. The Benedictine view of dis-aging may be found in Ch. 63 of The Rule.

[53] Here of course is a drawback to the medical management of mental hospitals and prisons that would tailor treatment specifically to individual diagnosis.

Further, if staff persons are uniformly recruited from a stratum in the wider society that has a legitimated and firm-standing higher ranking than the stratum from which inmates are uniformly recruited, then the cleavage in the wider society will presumably lend support and stability to the rule of the staff. The Military in Britain up to the first world war seemed to have illustrated this, with all ranks speaking in "common" accents and all officers speaking public school English derived from what was called "a good education." So, too, since the crafts, trades and professions of those who become inmates are often required within the institution, staff will understandably allow and even encourage some role carry-over.[54]

The permeability of a total institution can have, then, a variable consequence for its internal workings and cohesion. This is nicely illustrated by the precarious position of the lowest staff level. If the institution is appreciably permeable to the wider community, then these staff members may have the same, or even lower, social origins as the inmates. Sharing the culture of the inmates' home-world, they can serve as a natural communication channel between high staff and inmates (albeit a channel that is often blocked to upward communication). But, on the same ground, they will have difficulty maintaining social distance from their charges. As a student of prisons has recently argued, this may merely complicate the warder's role, further opening him up to inmate derision and to inmate expectation that he will be decent, reasonable, and corruptible.[55]

Whatever the utilities and disutilities of impermeability, and regardless of how radical and militant a total institution appears to be, there will always be some limits to its reshuffling tendencies and some use made of social distinctions already established in the environing society, if only so the institution can conduct necessary affairs with this society and be tolerated by it. Thus, there does not seem to be

---

[54] Even in concentration camps. See, for example, Elie A. Cohen, *Human Behavior in the Concentration Camp* (London: Jonathan Cape, 1954), 154. St. Benedict (ch. 57), sagely notes the danger of this practice:

"Should there be craftsmen in the monastery, let them exercise their crafts with all humility and reverence, if the Abbot so command. But if one of them grow proud because of the knowledge of his craft, in that he seem to confer some benefit on the monastery, let such a one be taken away from this craft and not practice it again, unless perchance, after he has humbled himself, the Abbot may bid him resume it."

[55] Sykes, "The Corruption of Authority and Rehabilitation," *op. cit.* See also Cantine and Rainer, *op. cit.*, pp. 96–97.

a total institution in Western society which provides block-living completely independent of sex; and ones like convents that appear to be impervious to socio-economic gradings, in fact tend to apportion domestic roles to converts of rural peasant background, just as the patient garbage crews in our prize integrated mental hospitals tend to be wholly Negro.[56] Similarly, in some British boarding schools it is found that boys of noble lineage may be allowed extra infractions of the house rules.[57]

One of the most interesting differences among total institutions is to be found in the social fate of their graduates. Typically, these become geographically dispersed; the difference is found in the degree to which structural ties are maintained in spite of this distance. At one end of the scale are the year's graduates of a particular Benedictine Abbey, who not only keep in touch informally, but find that for the rest of their life their occupation and location has been determined by their original membership. At the same end of the scale are ex-cons whose stay in prison orients them to the calling and to the nationwide underworld community that will comprise their life thereafter. At the other end of the scale, we find enlisted men from the same barracks who melt into private life immediately upon demobilization, and even refrain from congregating for regimental reunions. Here, too, are ex-mental patients who studiously avoid all persons and events that might connect them with the hospital. Midway between these extremes we find "old-boy" systems in private schools and graduate universities, which function as optional communities for the distribution of life-chances among sets of fellow-graduates.

CONCLUSION

I have defined total institutions denotatively by listing them, and then have tried to suggest some of their common characteristics. We now have a sizeable literature on these establishments and should be in a position to supplant mere suggestion with a solid framework bearing on the anatomy and functioning of this kind of social animal.

---

[56] It seems to be true that within any given establishment the topmost and bottom-most roles tend to be relatively permeable to wider community standards, while the impermeable tendencies seem to be focused in the middle ranges of the institution's hierarchy.

[57] Orwell, *op. cit.*, pp. 510 and 525.

Certainly the similarities obtrude so glaringly and persistently that we have a right to suspect that these features have good functional reasons for being present, and that it will be possible to fit these features together and grasp them by means of a functional explanation. When we have done this, I feel we will then give less praise and blame to particular superintendents, commandants, wardens, and abbots and tend more to understand the social problems and issues in total institutions by appealing to the underlying structural design common to all of them.

3

JOHAN GALTUNG

Prison: The Organization of Dilemma[1]

THE PRISON AS A DEFENSE MECHANISM

Anyone reading penological literature is likely to gain the distinct impression that the prison is not only among the least successful social institutions found in modern societies, but that it has an air of *irrelevance* which is shared by few other institutions. By "irrelevance" we do not mean the extent to which the structures that make up the institution fail to contribute to the manifest functions so often stated for the prison. Manifest functions may be the product of more or less wise afterthought; they may be more or less conscious efforts to make functional what seems utterly dysfunctional or non-func-

[1] During the winter 1954–1955 the author served a six month sentence in Norway's largest prison, *Olso Kretsfengsel,* in connection with conscientious objection. (He had refused to perform alternative conscientious objection service for longer than twelve months, the period of regular military service required of conscripts.) After some months in prison, the idea of using the stay for systematic observations occurred, interview data were added later, and the outcome was a thesis, *Fengselssamfunnet* (The Prison Community), Oslo University Press, 1959 (1st edition mimeoed, 1957). This chapter is to a large extent based on ideas developed in the book, some of which have been presented in an article, "The Social Functions of a Prison," *Social Problems,* 6 (Fall, 1958), 127–140. It should be kept in mind that Norwegian prisons differ from American prisons in at least three major respects: they are much *smaller* (the "large" one we observed had only about 300 inmates), the *interaction is more restricted* (almost all of the inmates are completely iso-

tional.[2] Three manifest functions of the prison today are *retribution*, *social sanitation* (decrease in visibility of the violator and his deviant acts), and the relatively uncomplicated function of old standing—*confinement*. These seem to be performed quite satisfactorily by most prison systems, but this does not mean that they can be performed only by prisons. The fact that a violator is made innocuous by means of physical constraints does not imply that the same docility could not be induced by drugs or other bio-chemical constraints. In the long run, there should be no reason to prefer physical restraint to chemical restraint, ethical considerations notwithstanding. Similarly, the range of alternatives for exacting retribution is so great that the method practiced in prisons—deprivation of liberty—looks like a very special, almost randomly-selected device. The ubiquity of prisons, as we know them, probably is accounted for by the fact that the prison serves so many functions at the same time that it gets an air of relevance from its multifunctionality.

But there remains a degree of irrelevance in respect to what Sorokin calls "logico-meaningful integration."[3] We do not know that there is a logico-meaningful integration of the basis for admission to the prison as a sentenced convict, on the one hand, and the stay in it as an inmate, on the other. On a common-sense level, the lack of relevance of this kind is well-expressed by prisoners who say something like: "I do not say that this prison is good or bad; I just don't see what it has to do at all with my crime." Prisoners using such expressions may, at the same time, agree in principle that "something must be done" when an act defined as a crime is committed. "Society must have its rules." But the "something" that is done may not have obvious relevance for either the society or the offender.

When *A* deprives *B* of some valued thing—such as a possession, physical health, virtue, dignity, or reputation—the immediate problem

---

lated for two-thirds of the 168 hours of the week), and the criminals seem considerably *less dangerous* than those confined in United States' prisons.

The following discussion should be regarded as reflections and speculations based on intimate knowledge of one prison only, but possibly with some general applicability. The author wants to express his gratitude to several of those he met in prison, on both sides of the bar, who have contributed through conversations and discussions. But the author alone is responsible for the views expressed.

[2] See Galtung, *op. cit.*

[3] Pitirim Sorokin, *Social and Cultural Dynamics* (Boston: Porter Sargent, 1957), 7 *ff.*

could be one of restoring the value. When the valued thing is of such a nature that it cannot be restored (like life, the virtue of a raped virgin, or some very personal possession destroyed by arson), then the problem could be one of insuring that the victim or some collectivity in which he is a member gets at least some kind of approximate functional equivalent of the value lost. Thus, one positive, constructive, and well-integrated consequence of a criminal act seems to be restoration of the value lost by that act. Yet such a consequence is remarkably infrequent in current institutionalized reactions to crime. Insurance against theft, for instance, is a rather impersonal device with a latent function of facilitating a complete break in interaction between A and B after the crime. More generally, criminals are held "responsible" for their crimes, but only infrequently are they held responsible for restoring deprived values to victims.

Despite the fact that there seems to be a trend toward an increasing frequency of court orders stipulating that restitution be made, as in cases in which offenders are granted probation providing they agree to pay for the property stolen, a general penal system based on value-compensation would be extraordinarily difficult to establish. For example, it would be necessary to define the value-equivalents of some rather vaguely-defined values. And even if value-compensation were institutionalized there might not be any necessary interaction between the criminal and his victim after the crime. Perhaps the system whereby probationers make restitution payments to a *court* and the court passes the money on to the victim was invented to insure that the victim neither forgives the criminal nor exacts retribution from him. Similarly, the present system of criminal justice that impersonally incarcerates the criminal, rather than seeking value-compensation, protects the victim from being reminded of the offense and the person who has wrought him so much wrong. Very negative feelings toward criminals are often postulated on behalf of victims. Yet such feelings might not be present. At least they are highly dependent on cultural variations in the extent to which, for example, a distinction is made between the criminal as an *individual* and the criminal act as an *event*.

The current system of criminal justice does not make a clear distinction between crimes in which the victim is randomly selected by the criminal from among persons possessing some value (such as an automobile), and crimes which are directed against one particular person, with no possible substitutions. Further, sociologists and others

have conducted very few studies directed at understanding the situation of the victim and the relationship between criminal and victim.[4]
The usual theory of social conflict, with a paradigm of two actors
competing for a value, does not apply too well to *universalistic crime*[5]
—crime in which victims are randomly selected. Yet it is likely that
most random victims will so define themselves only with some difficulty. On the contrary, they might ask themselves, "Why exactly
should *I* be selected? What wrong have *I* done?" Accompanying such
a search for the meaning of their selection as a target, will be, perhaps, an effort to personalize the relation to the criminal, so that he
may better serve as an object for the hostility and even retributive
action. To the extent this is true, prisons may be said to be functional
in protecting both criminals and their victims from further extensive
interaction with each other.[6]

This condition presents us with a first basic dilemma. If the
tendency among victims to particularize universalistic crime is an
empirical fact, then mere personal restraint may not be enough if
the victim is not only brought into the judiciary process as a witness,
but also into the penal process as a kind of creditor. On the other
hand, if the penal process permits almost complete indifference to
both the victim and the value taken from him, then simple pedagog-
ical principles about the importance of uniting learning methods with
learning ends can be used to predict that any case of social learning
(resocialization) occurring within prison walls will be almost miracu-
lous. It may be argued that in many cases the kind of crime, as well
as the victim, is randomly selected from a large assortment of deviant
acts. *L'uomo delinquente* was said to have an innate propensity
toward *crime,* and a member of a delinquent gang subsisting on the
periphery of society is also believed to have a propensity toward
crime; biological determinants have been exchanged for sociological
ones. Nevertheless, a criminal is apprehended and convicted of *a*
crime, not crime generally, and this specific crime will in most cases

[4] For a preliminary analysis, see Hans von Hentig, *The Criminal and His
Victim* (New Haven: Yale University Press, 1948), 383–450.

[5] *Cf.* Talcott Parsons, *The Social System* (Glencoe: The Free Press,
1951), 46–51.

[6] Cressey has shown that an important goal of modern prisons is protection
of inmates from society and that this goal supplements the goal of protecting
society from inmates. Donald R. Cressey, "Achievement of an Unstated
Organizational Goal: An Observation on Prisons," *Pacific Sociological Review,* 1 (Fall 1958), 43–49.

play a dominant role in affecting the judicial process. And of this particular crime only the sentence, measured in time, remains after the incarceration. The special circumstances surrounding the crime, whether biological or social, are to be suppressed by the prisoner.

In the current system, a third party, the state, intervenes as soon as the crime is brought to its attention. Though the state's functions and statuses are highly specialized (detection, trial, and confinement), it probably presents itself as a whole to the criminal—whether he calls it "they," "the state," "courts-and-prison," "the upper-class," or something else. To a prisoner, "they" and other criminals become the predominant interactors. Life starts revolving around the structure provided by these two role partners. This does not mean that criminality in a general sense disappears: on the contrary, much is done to keep it alive in the prisoners' mind. But in this situation the idea that there is value to be restored and that a victim does exist may gradually wane and give away completely to the notion that the incarcerated criminal is a loser in a conflict with *society*.[7]

At this point, a simple dichotomy may be useful. Any human being in a socio-cultural setting can be described by means of a huge number of variables and attributes. Some of these may be regarded in the culture as *essential*, others as *incidental* to the human being concerned. For example, in our culture it seems that bodily characteristics are often perceived as incidental, while mental characteristics contribute to form the "I" of the person concerned and are considered more important. This dichotomy also is expressed as a difference in *internal* and *external* characteristics.

One principal insight into the present prison system may now be formulated: The criminal who is incarcerated loses, but he does not lose everything. Incarceration, based on a transformation of the conflict between criminal and victim to one between criminal and state, is focused on external characteristics like bodily movements, not on internal ones like motives. Instead of any restoration of value to victims, a deprivation of value from the criminal becomes the goal.

This, of course, is the idea of punishment. Some *external* (mainly somatic) attributes are not left at what the criminal defines as their "natural" values—such as those he is accustomed to or has as his goal. It is well known that this change has consequences for the mental state of prisoners as well, but these internal consequences seem not

---

[7] For a normative system expressing prisoner culture on this point see Galtung, *op. cit.*, p. 133.

to be intended. What is called "treatment" of criminals is usually considered very different from bodily constraint or punishment. "Treatment" can be identified as measures changing values of certain *internal* variables, so that a new human being is turned out. But if change in psychic identity of the criminal is not desired by the criminal, what then? And if modification of external attributes has consequences for internal characteristics, then what makes a reaction to a crime a treatment, and what makes it a punishment? The intention of those who react? The effect on recidivist rates? The *predominance* of external vs. internal variables as focus of the reaction? The degree of immediate suffering reported by the criminal? Or all of these, taken together?

Even "treatment" might not change criminals in a desired direction. When the victim was excluded from the judicial process, the possibility of focusing the reaction on internal characteristics was greatly diminished. It is this condition that produces the second basic dilemma of the present prison systems: If there is direct and intentional interference with the prisoner's self, a higher degree of resocialization may be possible; on the other hand, *the prisoner who loses some of his pre-crime identity, loses completely.* If one does not interfere or tamper too much with internal variables, identity, for good or for bad, is preserved. Thus the present system, aimed at resocialization but dealing almost exclusively with external variables can very well be regarded a huge *institutionalized defense mechanism for convicts.*[8]

INSTITUTIONALIZED UNCERTAINTY

It is difficult to state in one formula what is essential in prison as a means of value-deprivation—"essential" in the sense that it is a *conditio sine qua non* for a prison, not in the sense that it is experienced as a "worst" by a majority of prisoners. Prisoners are excluded from the rest of social life for some time against their will, but this applies to other categories of persons as well—people in isolated regions

---

[8] Of 35 prisoners interviewed in our prison, 27 (77%) felt that they were innocent. As an estimate of the prisoner population as a whole, this is probably too high. Yet the proportion is valuable as an indicator of the compatibility of incarceration with refusal to admit what has happened.

of the country, adolescents at school, and an unknown proportion of religious devotees (they need not be in monasteries to exclude themselves from most of society), to mention some. Even the "total institution" aspect is present in many cases such as mental hospitals, ships, and military establishments.[9] Enforced value-deprivation is ubiquitous, although its character of being enforced or not being enforced may be ideologically determined (in Marxist theory, the state of being dispossessed).

But the prison seems to be the only case in which value deprivation takes place within a total institution, is perceived as enforced, and has both a minimum *and* maximum duration (the two may coincide). Leaving the institution is not voluntary, as in the case of some isolated work-place, and imprisonment is not necessarily institutionalization for life, as it may be in a concentration-camp or a monastery. Thus, the prisoner is precluded from changing his fate in an essential way through any act of his own. The minimum time to be served is perceived as unchangeable, yet only those prisoners whose minimum sentence exceeds a probable lifetime, can, like the nun, adapt themselves fully to the internal structure of the institution. Most prisoners are conscious of the fact that they are citizens of two worlds, within and outside walls, and the relation between the two may seem obscure and incompatible to them. They also are painfully aware of the necessity of preserving an identity relevant for life outside when release comes, while at the same time playing a role in prison however high or low its degree of relevance for life outside may be.

Thus, time becomes essential and so important that it is almost considered a thing, concrete and materialized. The *extent* to which time becomes a concern of all prisoners, except some of the most adjusted, is surprising to nonprisoners. Detailed calculations as to amount of time left, and meditation on how that time could have been spent with the other identity, certainly are not bed-time reflections only or once-an-hour thoughts. Concern for time seems to be an almost constant and painful *state-of-mind.*

Two consequences follow from this, neither of which have attracted the attention it deserves. The first is the individual prisoner's *time-perspective,* which both incorporates and is affected by individual

⁶ See Chapters 1 and 2, above.

psychological variables as well as by social and cultural variables.[10] Much has been written about the difference between objective and subjective time. First, how much of a *time-span* forward into the future represents reality to the prisoner? Some prisoners seem to live in the present, which means that even the near future is in a kind of fog, with no mileposts except those provided by the official calendar. Other prisoners have the future lined up in their plans and dreams. *Time is structured,* far ahead. Second, how do prisoners equalize *time intervals*? A month may be an ocean of time and a lost experience for one prisoner but not for others. Probably equalization depends, for any given interval, on how many events, pleasant or unpleasant, an individual is accustomed to packing together in a limited amount of time. If we assume that these two aspects of time-perspective are correlated so that the person who is able to see far ahead, by and large, is also the one who can attach value to the smallest interval of time, then it seems that one and the same sentence punishes the person with a high score on both dimensions much more than it does the man with low scores on both dimensions. Perhaps "reformation" should appear with greater frequency among persons with high scores than among those whose scores are low. Corporal, but not lethal, punishment was often adjusted to the ability of the criminal to withstand pain, even if age were the only indicator of this ability. But in the system of imprisonment, deprivation of valued time is not explicitly adjusted to the convict's ability to cherish time.[11]

[10] The following quotation illustrates the cultural relativity of *time*: "A spirit of restlessness began to pervade life towards the end of the Middle Ages. The concept of time in the modern sense began to develop. Minutes became valuable; a symptom of this new sense of time is the fact that in Nürnberg the clocks have been striking the quarter hours since the sixteenth century. Too many holidays began to appear as a misfortune. Time was so valuable that one felt one should never spend it for any purpose which was not useful." Erich Fromm, *The Fear of Freedom* (London: Routledge and Kegan Paul, 1942), 49.

[11] Many desires are subordinated to the value of release from prison. Until 1958, Norwegian prisoners could obtain permission to convert 60 days of ordinary prison to 20 days "bread-and-water," that is, prison with the food restricted to water, bread, cod liver oil and vitamin pills; in addition to this deprivation, no smoking and no admission to the work-shops (work was permitted in the cells). Among 35 prisoners interviewed, 25 said they would prefer the shorter term if given the permission to do so; 16 would like to convert even more than 60 days; and 26 could well imagine some other kind

The second consequence of the importance of time is in the realm of *predictability*. Little is known about the importance of predictability to the psychological welfare of human beings. If time is viewed as a road with illuminated signposts in the distance, then prison time is always a highway with small signposts set at regular intervals along it, each inscribed with some of the regularities and technicalities of prison routine. In addition, the highway is characterized by special, movable signposts with the significant events for the prisoner written on them—a meeting of the parole board, a decision concerning transfer from one penal institution to another, etc. In this situation, extreme regularity will prevail unless effectively counteracted. Prisons provide us with highly conclusive evidence that regularity that is perceived as enforced will be counteracted by irregularity. As one prisoner put it: "I guess they are going to start with movies in the prison now. If they do, they will probably pick one day, *movie-day*. But that is not the way I like to go to the movies. I like to decide for myself, on the spur of the moment." He could have said: "I like to decide for myself, and not know in advance when I have to decide for myself."

There is little doubt, from the point of view of bureaucratic efficiency as well as from the point of view of universalistic patterns of correctional treatment, that administration of prison routines at regular intervals as well as on a collective basis is preferable, if not necessary. But this pattern has some important and non-trivial consequences. First of all, it provides time with its signposts *and thus stretches out time in the future*. A prisoner with a short time-perspective before incarceration finds himself in a situation where the perspective is elongated, thus, we presume, bringing the reality of the duration of the sentence to his constant awareness. Secondly, the future becomes uniformly like the present, which again becomes a copy of the past. *Regularity means predictability*, and predictability has two sides to it. It leaves out, after an initial training period, the possibility that situations filled with ambiguity, uncertainty, and threat may arise. It also leaves out the possibility of new challenges, and unknown and unexplored possibilities. Even the illusion of *auto-causation* (effects concerning oneself with perceived causes in oneself) may be eradicated. Though we have no real evidence, it appears that the

of value-deprivation (no radio, no letters or visits, no bed) which they would exchange for early release. Only six prisoners answered "no" to all these possibilities, saying "It is bad enough as it is."

pleasantness and unpleasantness of routine events are of relatively minor significance if the events are predictable and planned by an external agency. The *visita conyugal* and even sexual orgies combined with the use of narcotics might lose some of their intrinsic attractiveness to many prisoners if they occurred "every second Wednesday for prisoners in Wing *A*, every second Thursday for . . . ," etc.

We postulate that all disturbances brought into the regularity of the prison have, in addition to possible other effects, the effect of decreasing predictability and, hence, altering the time scale of the inmate until order is restored. If there is "wish for new experience,"[12] it is probably a wish for unpredictable experience more than a wish for pleasant experience. Disturbances are not entirely negative from the point of view of the guards, either. Guards probably are not conscious instigators of irregularities, for they can, in principle, experience irregularities in their periods outside the walls, though on a limited scale because of low salaries and low prestige.[13] Yet if one looks at the "itinerary" of guards in the prison studied by Gresham Sykes[14] and in other prisons, it seems reasonable to conclude that there is an accumulated need for change. Further, irregularities are always dangerous, by definition, thus making the tougher of the guards functional. So much of the prison structure is based on the doctrine of the dangerousness of inmates that the mechanism of the self-fulfilling prophecy is difficult to halt.[15]

Irregularities call for action, for deeds which will provide lower-ranking guards with chances to distinguish themselves. Among employees in many organizations there is a compensatory ideology to the effect that the bosses or leaders or foremen are "theoreticians," "stamp-lickers," "pencil-pushers," or other kinds of persons who must depend on the underlings in real emergencies when practicality is needed, and this ideology flourished in the prison we knew. Even in the informal ranking among guards, irregularities may provide an

[12] W. I. Thomas and F. Znaniecki, *The Polish Peasant* (New York: Dover, 1958), 73.

[13] Why this low social status? Probably not only because so little training is involved, but also because the low status serves the function of preventing a status connected with so much collective guilt-feeling from coming into the limelight. Compare the rank given the executioner.

[14] Gresham M. Sykes, *The Society of Captives* (Princeton: Princeton University Press, 1958), 137 *ff*.

[15] Robert K. Merton, *Social Theory and Social Structure,* Revised Edition (Glencoe: Free Press, 1957), Ch. XI.

individual guard with an opportunity of changing his position upward —he may get a chance to show in a highly visible way that his quiet appearance hides a real lion. Thus, a periodic outburst of "irregularities" seems to be a predictable consequence of the prison structure, and particularly of its predictability.[16]

In the prison we knew, there were two principal systems for manipulating time. First, prisoners tried to *change the signposts already there* by conscious interference with prison routines, especially by infractions of the rules and by conscious or unconscious provocation of illness. Second, they tried to *introduce new and private signposts* by interaction with the prison officials and by exploring all possible or impossible avenues to new statuses in the penal system— through pardon, conditional release, transfer within or between institutions, etc. Both systems give the effect that auto-causation is occurring, although the first is preferable in this respect because of the relative immediacy of effects.[17]

A frequent sequence involved actions of the second kind followed by actions of the first kind, especially when the second kind of system did not produce the desired irregularity. The high frequency of requested and granted interaction with prison officials indicated that the second system was frequently tried. We suggest that this occurred because a pattern of *institutionalized uncertainty,* originated in the behavior of the officials in response to the strain created by extreme

[16] Sykes mentions another function of these outbursts: "Disturbances within the walls must often be viewed as highly dramatic efforts to communicate with the outside world, efforts in which confined criminals pass over the heads of their captors to appeal to a new audience." *Op. cit.,* p. 8.

[17] The lifer is a special case. In principle, the lifer's prison time-road is an endless row of signposts disappearing in the distance. Nevertheless, few lifers accept the full implication of the life sentence. They do not believe they will be in prison literally for life, they do not think the number of years they will serve is completely unpredictable, and they do not think they will die in prison. They all set a rough target date for their release and then begin to accept it, as they could never accept an unqualified life sentence with its diabolically unpredictable length and uncertain future. Lifers will give statistics, case comparisons, and so on, to support the term-of-years sentence they have invented to avoid the complete hopelessness of their life sentence, but they will seldom publicly admit that it is just a little trick they are playing on themselves, a dream they have made up to give their lives a dimension, a direction, and a purpose which a life sentence, squarely faced, would preclude. See J. M. Yeager, "The Lifer: A Peaceful Rebel," *The Keystone* (prison paper of the Western State Penitentiary, Pennsylvania), (Autumn, 1959), 6.

regularity, was a fundamental structural component of the prison system. Perhaps it is a characteristic of all prisons. The official may give the prisoner hope or he may not. If his power to grant or deny inmate requests is absolute, his prediction can be a probability prediction, saying that the probability is low that the desired change of status for the given prisoner will occur. He knows that this probability statement will be magnified in the mind of the prisoner. More important is the fact that the degree of probability *is not a lasting property of any individual prisoner, but of a collective of prisoners with some special characteristics* (for example, prisoners who are "doing time" for the first time in their lives, and have impeccable prison careers). For the individual prisoner whose request is denied, it is a question of all or none, and there is no comfort in knowing that for the collective, $p = .10$. But for the collective it is a question of degrees of probability.

There are numerous alternative answers to the question, "How much of a hope shall a prison official offer a prisoner?" At least the following arguments concerning possible over- or understatement of p by the officer are relevant:

Consequences of giving the prisoner no hope

The *prisoner* must someday return to the time perspective he formerly used. He is deprived of a positive signpost and may aggress against himself or against other parts of the system.

The *official* will have to witness the disappointment and even aggression of the prisoner. To minimize this possibility, the unhappy message may be sent through a guard who then becomes the immediate object of aggression, or the act of denial may be blamed on authorities higher up in the hierarchy of the prison or the prison system.

Consequences of giving the prisoner hope

The *prisoner* gets a chance to restructure his time perspective and hence to adapt better to the situation, which may mean a temporary tension release both for him and for the system as a whole.

The *official* will be saved from witnessing the disappointment and aggression of the prisoner, and may even be the object of gratitude and affection. A given official can call the prisoner to his office when happy messages are to be given, and inmates have no way of testing statements to the effect that the happy consequence was all due to the official's intervention.

Consequences of giving the prisoner no hope

The *official* saves himself work, provided the prisoner accepts the situation as hopeless. The importance of this argument depends on the ratio of officials to prisoners.

The *official* presents an image of himself as a person with almost unlimited power over the prisoner, *but also as a person with no power over those who control him* ("I would like to help you, you know, but those higher up. . . .")

The *prisoner* is given the best basis for prediction (provided p is less than $\frac{1}{2}$) in the same sense that one who is told that a roulette wheel is ever so slightly biased toward red is given a sound basis for prediction. And any mistake he might make will be to his advantage in the long run.

Consequences of giving the prisoner hope

The *official* enters into a chain of time-consuming interaction, especially if the prisoner believes the official must often be reminded of the situation or if he must often get additional information from the official.

The *official* presents an image of himself as a person with some power over higher levels in the hierarchy but also as a person who can be manipulated by the prisoner, at least to some extent.

The *prisoner* is given, or gives himself, a poor basis for prediction in the same sense as one who plays red $\frac{3}{4}$ of the time and black $\frac{1}{4}$ of the time on a roulette known to give red $\frac{3}{4}$ of the time. Any mistake will be to his disadvantage.

Of these two patterns, a pattern of institutionalized uncertainty seems desirable because, by and large, the arguments favoring an increase in the hopes of prisoners seem strongest. Actually, no comparisons of weights or frequencies are needed, for *any* hope fed into the individual or collective inmate system will immediately contribute to uncertainty. The fact that change in status for a prisoner is defined as a possibility with a probability different from zero, however small, is always evidence of the *existence of a decision-mechanism which does not always yield the same decision.* If the mechanism always yielded the same decision, the functional basis of the status of the decision-maker would be seriously threatened. It would look as though there was no decision to be made. Even a chance device that yielded a long sequence of "no's" or "yes's" would very soon be turned in for inspection.

What we have called "arguments" above might better be termed "functions." Whether they are manifest or latent functions is an empirical (and perhaps not very interesting) question; whether they are negative or positive depends upon evaluation of short-term and long-term consequences. Since the present trend in penology is toward increased interaction between prisoners and personnel, dysfunctional consequences for the prisoners of either course of action will probably become of greater concern. Let us imagine for a moment a rather drastic change in the prison structure, from the highly predictable structure of mid-twentieth century efficiency, to a highly efficient impredictability based on a chance device so complex that a human mind would not suffice to grasp the regularity inherent in it.

We are thinking of a prison where most prison activities occur at irregular intervals—an electronic computer rings a bell or flashes a light and feeding, or exercise, or movies, or whatever kind of event prison life may offer, starts. In order not to make the illustration completely unrealistic, we shall have to feed the computer with a few restraints, like "not more than four, nor less than two meals a day; at not more than four, nor less than two hour intervals." What will be the consequences? Assume further that the prison bureaucracy would be able to carry out the directives given according to the whims of the electronic tube. What would be the consequences if, for example, a prisoner were transferred from one status in the system to another whenever his private little lamp started twinkling?

In a very real sense, such a system would provide prisoners with a more realistic model of social life than does the existing system. At least the model would more closely resemble that of persons whose degree of auto-causation and whose ability to predict both seem low, as for large categories of low-status people. The chance system might provide prisoners with good training for the capriciousness of real life where events may look exactly like chance events, and at the same time do away with some of the time-perspective difficulties mentioned earlier. On the other hand, the system might immediately break down completely for lack of predictability. Inability to predict might be added punishment, and if this were true, prisoners might ask for a little institutionalized certainty, for the one certain "yes" or "no" they could use as a basis for orientation in prison life. Probably, they would devote most of their time in trying to find the hidden key, the hidden regularity, and in guessing at its rationale.[18]

It might be argued that a system in which routines occurred by chance would be inferior to the present one because there could be no learning; there could be no possibility of inferring relations between sanctions and past behavior and then using this inference to predict the consequences of present behavior. This may be true for the negative sanctions, but it is not a very valid argument because the positive sanctions the present prison has to offer are greatly limited. Moreover, such positive sanctions as are available come to be regarded by prisoners as something granted, so that the absence of a positive sanction is defined as a negative one. Also, in the present system there is, from the point of view of the prisoner, low probability of a change to the better, an enormous complexity of factors relevant to one's fate, and opportunities for cheating and pretense. All these contribute to making any selection for a better status in the penal system seem like a random one.

However, the present system remains quite different from a prison which would use a mechanical chance device, where one might pass days and nights watching The Lamp. Again, to preserve some realism, the chance device for individual prisoners might be adjusted to preserve, in a probabilistic sense, the *proportionality axiom* ("the more evil *A* has inflicted on *B*, the more evil will *C* inflict on *A*") in penal theory. We are not arguing that prisons be reformed by the introduction of the chance system, though such a system might be as effective at rehabilitation as the present one based on extreme regularity. The Lamp would make everything about crime a gamble, even the confinement. A non-zero probability would be assigned so that, for example, a petty thief might get a longer and tougher stay than the professional murderer, thus doing away with a tremendous bureaucracy.

Which is worse: perfect predictability or perfect chance? Probably the latter, yet we do not know what degree of uncertainty is equivalent to perfect certainty in negative value, and what degree of uncer-

---

[18] Something like this occurred in concentration camps during World War II and in Chinese camps holding American prisoners of war during the Korean conflict. See Bruno Bettelheim, "Individual and Mass Behavior in Extreme Situations," *Journal of Abnormal and Social Psychology,* 38 (October, 1943), 417–458; and Edgar H. Schein, "The Chinese Indoctrination Program for Prisoners of war," *Psychiatry,* 19 (1956), 160–161.

tainty is optimal for the welfare of the prisoners. The dilemma is clear enough: justice and efficiency both point in the direction of perfect certainty, but this is contrary to the basic needs of the prisoners. Certainty may perhaps also be contrary to resocialization, but that remains to be proved.

FUNCTIONAL UNITY AND FUNCTIONAL PLURALITY

Probably the most frequently contemplated topic in the entire field of penological theory is the functional incompatibility of such ends as, for example, retribution and therapy.[19] The list of alleged inherent contradictions in an institution where both ends are attempted can easily be made quite long and convincing. *You cannot at the same time:*

(1) *have punishment orienta-* AND *have treatment orientation;*
tion;

(2) have an *ideology* concerning prison and prisoners such that external, exculpatory causes are *only necessary* AND *causes,* not sufficient causes of criminal acts by reason of the fact that individual free will and auto-causation are assumed;
have an *ideology* concerning prison and prisoners such that external exculpatory causes (social, mental, biological, and physical determinants) are seen as *both necessary and sufficient causes of crime;*

(3) portray the prison to society in negative terms, so that AND it functions as a collective deterrent and as a general reference for negative sanctions;
portray the prison to society in terms such that it stands as a neutral or positive symbol;

(4) put the inmate into the institution against his own AND wishes;
expect the inmate to adopt an attitude of willingness to undergo therapy;

[19] See, for example, Donald R. Cressey, "Professional Correctional Work and Professional Work in Correction," *National Probation and Parole Association Journal,* 5 (January, 1959), 1–15; and Donald R. Cressey, "Contradictory Directives in Complex Organizations: The Case of the Prison," *Administrative Science Quarterly,* 4 (June, 1959), 1–19. See also Chapter 5, below.

(5) intentionally (and with the inmate knowing that the action is intentional) inflict evils on the inmate or deprive him of positive values during his stay in prison; AND expect the inmate to believe what is done is done for his own good, and to cooperate in his own treatment and therapy;

(6) institutionalize secondary relations between inmates and personnel in an effort to assure equality in treatment and to prevent formation of personal ties that may endanger operative efficiency in emergencies; AND institutionalize primary relations between inmates and personnel in an effort to assure or facilitate a transfer of values to inmates;

(7) train personnel to orient themselves only to simple, consensual and highly visible variables like age, crime committed, criminal career and sentence; AND train personnel to orient themselves to subtle, dissensual and latent characteristics of the inmates;

(8) release the inmates after time periods which are mainly a function of their behavior *before* they were institutionalized. AND release inmates after time periods which are mainly a function of their behavior *after* they were institutionalized.

Although many points could be added, the list is sufficiently long for the present purpose. It should be noted that the decision to include an item in the list is based upon the extent to which there is a real *incompatibility* between the two horns of the dilemma and on the extent to which the two "horns" are really *necessary conditions* for the fulfillment of the goals of punishment or treatment, respectively. These two conditions will form one point of departure for our discussion of the idea that "you cannot have both," but two preliminary points must be made.

However much one might argue about details in this or similar lists, an institution that attempts to maximize both goals will clearly be ridden by internal conflicts. Yet it does not follow logically that this will be an institution which is *ipso facto* unfit for the supreme goal of rehabilitating criminals, whether by the punishment or the treatment method. A smooth, streamlined organization where intra-status as well as inter-status conflicts have been engineered away will no necessarily serve as the working model of the living society which shall receive the released inmate. An organization with no structural strain (which is a fiction, but a useful one) will, if adequate social-ization has taken place, be a kind of Utopian organization with a very high degree of predictability, as we have indicated in the pre-vious section. The kind of confusing, and often very disturbing, conflicts on different levels between the two goals in contemporary prison systems may not be desirable, but nevertheless some functional plurality and incompatibility may be useful in development in inmates of general social skills, particularly in role relations.

More important, perhaps, is the notion that there may be some-thing basically false in the dichotomy, "punishment *or* treatment." When viewed from the perspective of officials, the two reactions differ significantly, both in the *definition* of the criminal (including the feelings toward him) and in the *methodology* adapted for his re-habilitation. But there are also important similarities when the two reactions are seen from the prisoners' point of view, and these simi-larities make the dichotomy less sharp.

Both "punishment" and "treatment" refer to *reactions*, control, and efforts to change people. To what extent criminals in various categories, consciously or unconsciously, may want to undergo a change toward conformity and adaptation to society, we do not know. More often than not, criminals who are incarcerated are underdogs who live in the periphery or even outside of society, whereas those who "react" are recruited from the center of society. As prisons grad-ually shift in emphasis toward "treatment" and, hence, to more selected and trained personnel, this will become even more apparent. Transferring an individual from "periphery" to "center" involves a drastic change of identity unless the process incorporates the gradual (if whimsical) adjustments that occur when the transfer is not against the wishes of the inmate.

It is difficult to foretell what the reactions of the resocializees will be when they have to face *treatment* which has rehabilitation as its goal, and which has a degree of efficiency close to the efficiency encountered in, say, surgery. In Norway, reactions of the prisoners to what is called "treatment" may be extremely negative, but this is probably due in part to the fact that whatever happens to them is evaluated in terms of how time-consuming it is and how highly inefficient the treatment is. Separate categories of offenders—the juvenile delinquents, loiterers, and the mentally retarded—are controlled by means of patterns often referred to as "treatment" or at least "not punishment."[20] The vehemence of inmates' negative reactions may be due to the duration of enforced institutionalization (two years, three years, five years are very frequent for the respective categories). But there is another factor, well-expressed by one inmate in the last category:

> When you get regular punishment, it is an evil, but when you are through, you have a new deal . . . People may think of you as an ex-criminal, but if they do, they still think of you as a kind of normal being, because crime is something they understand. But if you at long last are let out of this — institution you'll be carrying a poster "not normal" on you the rest of your life. People may not blame you—they may even pity you—but they will never think of you as one of their own kind. You are outside for life, and the institution has probably made you worse.

Thus, three conditions contribute to the aggression of the patient-prisoner toward "treatment": (1) lack of positive effects, and even obvious cases of negative effects, (2) the duration of the reaction, and (3) the definition of the convict as somehow abnormal in a direction not controlled by his will, hence abnormal in a latent, subtle, and even mystical sense. It should be remembered that the more highly-trained and "expert" the personnel used in treating criminals, the higher the probability that whatever prisoners think is ailing them will be thought of as threatening, and experienced as anxiety-provoking. The model of the highly-respected and highly-trained surgeon with his knife does not apply too well, as it is so easy to identify with the surgeon's patient. It is hardly likely that an identification with the criminal will be complete, as so many important and tenacious norms and values cluster around the negative identification with him.

Let us for a moment eliminate two of the three conditions which seem to contribute to the negative reaction of the prisoner. To do this, we need only assume that an anti-crime drug or technique that works quickly and effectively, even when forced upon the criminal, has been invented. In fact, the technical invention might even be some social-psychological technique—like a particularly intense com-

[20] See Vilhelm Aubert, "Legal Justice and Mental Health," *Psychiatry,* 21 (1958), 107.

bination of sociodrama, group therapy, and training in specific kinds of important role relations. If one could convince public opinion that treatment with such a technique is completely successful and that there are no harmful after effects, even the "lifers" might be released. If such a technique is invented (and there is little reason to believe that man is barred from ever inventing such a thing, although it might have the effect of provoking some new criminal acts in efforts to "beat" the cure) it probably will be welcomed by penologists while disapproved of by people who feel that there are great dangers for the integrity of the personality involved. When there is identification with the criminal rather than with the administrators of the technique, devices of this kind will be called "brain-washing," not "treatment." Most prisoners would, then, have to postulate two values as valid: a return to society as soon as possible, and protection of the prisoner's identity against the rehabilitative device. We would guess that even in the current system, prisoners participating in psychotherapy sessions on a voluntary basis are recruited mainly from three categories of prisoners: those who seriously want a new identity; those who see that a new identity for them is what is intended, but do not want it to happen and think they are clever enough to cheat the psychologist; and those who do not see what is going on at all. Most deliberate attempts to change prisoners now produce change so slowly that the prisoner who wants to fight against efforts to change him can do so successfully. But with a sudden change in this rate of change, the prisoner would have to face a terrible choice between freedom for the unknown future and identity with the well-known past. This conflict would be made worse by a structural arrangement arising in penal institutions—the personnel would be split between adherents of the "doing-time-and-quit" and "taking-chemical-or-social-drug-and-change" methods.[21]

[21] Cressey discusses an important difficulty encountered by the guard in a treatment-oriented institution: "Although inmate rehabilitation was an explicit goal of the organization, it was impossible to measure the institution's success in this regard. Numerous pre-institutional and post-institutional conditions affect recidivism rates, making it impossible to correlate either high or low recidivism rates with institutional activities. More specfically the *contribution of any one guard* to the rehabilitation or recidivism of inmates could not be measured. In judgment of guard competence, emphasis was placed on the production of a desired end-result, rehabilitated inmates, rather than adherence to specific procedures for achieving this goal. But because rehabilitative effectiveness of a guard could not be measured, the guard in associa-

With these points in mind, we can move on to discussion of the notion that a prison cannot have both punishment and treatment. The extent to which the alternative statements on pp. 122-123 are real dilemmas, in the sense that they are contradictory, depends on the interpretation of the crucial expression "at the same time." Real dilemmas will show up as contradictory role expectations for one or more of the statuses in the system. But apparent contradictions can be handled without neglecting or suppressing one of the alternatives, and in a manner which preserves a certain degree of institutional unity. Many such mechanisms are forms of "compartmentalization."

The most extreme kind of compartmentalization is a combination of temporal and spatial segregation, and it involves institutional sequences, within the same general administrative framework. In dealing with prisoners, punishment might have priority in time, with a subsequent transfer to a treatment-oriented institution as a last step before the final release.[22] This institution tries to undo any harmful effects of the punishment, and then, after the prisoner is brought to the pre-incarceration level, to control by various therapeutic devices his lack of conformity. The opposite institutional sequence would also do away with all the problems listed, but it would at least create conflict between the personnel of the two institutions. This is not an unusual solution, for similar conflicts are found at other places in society where institutions compete for the opportunity to inculcate their values in the same individuals (between school, church, and family).

Less drastic, but also less efficient, is compartmentalization in time only or in space only. These methods include strict division within the same institution, so that parts are devoted to punishment and other parts to treatment; or so that the inmates are exposed to punishment at some periods of time and to treatment during others.

---

tion with inmates who became rehabilitated could not be given higher ratings than a guard who had supervised inmates who became recidivists." "Contradictory Directives in Complex Organizations: The Case of the Prison," *op. cit.*, p. 15. (Italics added.)

Although the last sentence seems to be an overstatement of the case (however wrong it may be as an implication of causal factors, the fact that "my former inmate" was rehabilitated, if known in the institution, will always be significant), the statement points out how tempting it must be to withdraw to the concreteness of custodial roles.

[22] *Cf.* Richard R. Korn and Lloyd W. McCorkle, *Criminology and Penology* (New York: Henry Holt, 1959), 542–552.

This is the solution used in many larger prisons in the world today, under the impact of the present slow and tentative change toward treatment orientation. Perhaps separate rooms or buildings within a prison, and separate hours or days of the week devoted to "treatment," facilitate *dropping of one role and taking a new role* for the inmate. Somehow, he has to shift from the role of prisoner to the role of patient, which, according to Parsons, involves (1) exemption from *normal social role responsibilities,* (2) institutionalized definition that the sick person cannot be expected by "pulling himself together" to get well by an act of decision or will, (3) definition of the state of being ill as itself undesirable with its obligation to want to "get well," and (4) an expectation that the person will seek *technically competent* help and will *cooperate* with his helper in the process of trying to get well.[23]

Thus, in our society, taking the role of patient may be a difficult, even hazardous step for people who are only dropping for a period ordinary family and vocational roles. And, most importantly, this is more often than not done by people who possess ordinary skills in social relations in general and in role-taking in particular. The prisoner is handicapped in three ways relative to the normal man outside the walls, who has fallen ill. He has much further to go when he changes his role to that of patient; he probably has less general ability in changing roles; and he has to undertake the change often, perhaps more than once a week, or even more than once every day. The first handicap involves problems relating to the distance between the two roles, which we shall call *role distance,* meaning something like "average discrepancy between comparable role expectations."

Both inmates who are being punished and inmates who are being treated are exempted from normal social role responsibilities by the fact of their institutionalization. But the basis of recruitment to a prison differs from the basis of recruitment to a hospital in the crucial question of the role of free will. "Free will" is supposed to contribute when the law-abiding citizen becomes a criminal, but is not supposed to contribute when the healthy person becomes an ill person. A necessary internal cause is postulated for crime, but not for illness. This theoretical difference may be made to shrink if or when our knowledge of internal, sufficient causes of illness increases, but at the present

---

[23] Parsons, *op. cit.,* p. 436 *ff.*

stage in our thinking, the dichotomy has several important social consequences. First is the differential importance attributed to "pulling oneself together." If free will has made a criminal, then free will can make a noncriminal; if a person has become ill in spite of free will, then he must become healthy without reliance upon free will also. This simple philosophy may be incorrect in a causal sense, but not in a social sense—treatment enters as an automatic effect for the patient (although he must want to get well), but not so for the prisoner.

Second, it is one thing to define a prisoner's stay in prison as undesirable, another to define the status of a criminal as undesirable per se, regardless of its social consequences. It seems unlikely that therapy can proceed if the prisoner's definition of the situation does not transcend the "here and now" of the prison, at least if reliance is placed on interactional techniques. It is easy to imagine a world, very different from ours, where the definitions of "moral health" (legality, morality, law-obedience) are highly consensual, with very low dispersion on a continuum of moral behavior, whereas the definitions of "somatic health" are highly dissensual. If we invoke the theory of cognitive dissonance, it seems reasonable to assume that a deviant along any dimension will try to "take his definition of health with him," if the social pressure is not too overwhelming. That is, a very consensual definition of health will facilitate a definition of one's own deviance as undesirable, but the less consensus there is, the greater the chance of constructing around oneself a social milieu such that a definition of one's own condition as "normal" becomes possible. This is perhaps the fundamental and fatal importance of social interaction among prisoners. Such interaction and consequent definition of one's self as "normal" reflects a difference in moral philosophy between those at the center and those at the periphery of the society. More important, however, is the fact that the interaction produces a collectively-upheld redefinition of the situation that serves as a mutual insurance and common mechanism of defense.

Third, "technically competent help" is sought by prisoners, as well as by patients, only if the experts can legitimate their competence. One source of legitimation in our empirically-minded society would be evidence that the help is effective, and such evidence is indeed not overabundant. Charismatic powers are always useful as a source of legitimation, but charisma becomes bureaucratized; and the more

so, the more bureaucratic the bureaucracy is. Since prison administrations can easily be shown to rank high in most dimensions used
to describe bureaucracies, charisma is not effective except in isolated
instances. Even religious or other ideological means of legitimation
do not furnish the prison with a general key to authority, for there is
little consensus on religious and ideological propositions.

One technique of legitimation was effectively used in the prison
we knew, and it seems to be used in many other prisons as well.
This was an attempt to merge efforts to control the criminal for his
aberrances with treatment for somatic diseases, thus drawing on the
deeply-institutionalized authority of the somatic physician. It is not
necessary that one person be an expert at treatment of both crime
and somatic disorders, though this may be a good solution of the
legitimation problem if such rare persons can be found and given
appointments in prisons. Alternatively, a more "spatial" kind of solution is used. Suitable rooms and facilities for group therapy, work
therapy, psychological counseling, role-playing, etc., are set up in
the prison hospital. The hospital serving our prison was in a separate
building located between Norway's two largest prisons, and transition
from the role of prisoner to the role of patient was manifested and
mirrored in the transition from one building to another. Closeness to
the prison hospital implies both a transfer of authority and the
presence of role models in the persons of bona fide somatic patients.
But there is always the danger that the transfer might work the other
way, although this is probably less likely, due to the difference in
consensus about the two definitions of "health."

It should be pointed out that, despite role distance, there are
prisoners who declare themselves willing to "try" any kind of therapy.
We have already hinted at explanation of this phenomenon: treatment does something to the time-structure of the prisoner, and it may
be a way out of the prison: Who knows, in the treatment-game there
may be a hidden key to the prison gate. But the odds seem to be
against *successful* treatment unless there is the extreme kind of compartmentalization mentioned earlier, and in establishing such a
condition there always is the danger of streamlining the organization,
or the sequence of organizations, too much. Though we are in want
of any empirical evidence, our guess is that the more equal the
time-distribution for the individual prisoner between efforts to take
the role of the patient and efforts to take the role of the prisoner, the
more harmful the consequences of frequent shuttling back and forth

between the roles.²⁴ It is possible that rapid movement from one role to the other produces a social shock that is comparable to electric shock treatment, and that it has some kind of unknown, and unanticipated, therapeutic effect. This is unlikely, however, when we remember that it is considered therapeutic for patients to remain in the role of patient during the entire stay in the hospital and, as a matter of fact, that patients are often discouraged from expeditions out of the hospital, too frequent visits, and efforts to take up work in bed.

Let us follow the idea of compartmentalization further. We have mentioned some possibilities of mitosis of the prison, wholly or partly, with specialization resulting. But mitosis does not necessarily stop at the first division; it continues in the two new parts. Thus, there will be structural provision for the function of treatment within the punishment-oriented part, and structural provision for the function of punishment within the treatment-oriented part. It would appear that the closer organizationally the two parts of the original institution, the more "mutual contamination" and the less necessary specific structural arrangements in the two new parts. But whenever there is mitosis there are conflicts between personnel: "Everything we achieve by means of therapy is wasted as soon as prisoners go back to those brutes, the guards," and "Just as soon as we have managed to get a little discipline into the inmates, the psychologist puts some nonsense into their heads and they come back worse than ever." Loyalties to personnel in the other division are important in breaking down these conflicts. The two groups need each other, just as a warden planning anti-escape measures needs the chief of police in the prison town. A custodial prison needs treatment personnel to help maintain security, and a prison hospital needs custodians to guard the sick, but nevertheless dangerous, criminals.

This is the dilemma: On the one hand, there is a functional necessity for some of the skills of the other division; on the other hand, there is a functional necessity for keeping the divisions as separate as possible so that the creation of specific statuses "for the opposite purpose" will not blur a distinction that looks useful. A simple, if not at all perfect, solution to this problem in our prison

²⁴ This correlation is not predicted for any and all conditions. It probably would not appear if the time intervals were so short that there could be no real internalization of role behavior before time for the next change, and it probably would not appear if the intervals were long enough to permit real adjustment in one role before shifting to the other.

was *self-selection within the ranks of the ordinary personnel*. In the prison hospital, a few male nurses constituted a self-appointed, but tacitly acknowledged, bodyguard for the rest. These men could in most cases contain rebellious attempts until reinforcements—chosen also on a partly self-selected basis—arrived from the prison itself. In the prison, a less clear structuring of informal roles took place, but it appeared that some of the "softer" guards got a reputation for being good at talking a prisoner into calming down, and these guards often abstained from the use of physical or personal violence. They could do so because of the presence of self-selected guards for the tougher roles.[25]

Role conflict is one of the main sources of role differentiation. In a prison, one is almost daily a witness to this fact as he observes that treatment roles become more and more clearly defined and distinct from the punishment or custodial roles. Yet the differentiation may not be apparent on organizational charts. It sometimes is organizationally unwise to avoid codification of obvious role differentiation. If the two distinct roles are not formalized and named, it is easier to define the institution as either treatment-oriented or punishment-oriented. Further, codification would produce manifest conflicts. On all levels in the hierarchy there is conflict between the orientations of punishment and treatment—ideological conflict, structural conflict, conflict between personality types, etc. For example, one part of a prison may be predominantly geared toward punishment although latent ideological disagreement is present among the interacting guards. If to this group is added a manifestly very treatment-oriented or very punishment-oriented person, there probably will be some kind of point counter-point effect, which can be interpreted as an equilibrating mechanism. Someone probably will feel called upon to

[25] Prisoners also may be soft or tough, but in this prison there was little possibility for prisoners to select their own role partners among the guards, for pairing of guard and prisoner was done by administrators. Custodially-oriented guards in effect encouraged new arrivals to play the role of prisoner, and a few treatment-oriented guards in effect provoked an orientation toward the role of the patient. Similarly, prisoners had some power to provoke custodial or treatment role-playing among guards. Although interaction was minimal (complementarity in roles did not mean much, and the inconsistencies were gross) there was a tendency for conflict among the guards to be mirrored in corresponding conflict among the prisoners. Thus at the prison hospital, inmates held lively discussions as to what was preferred, soft treatment or tough custody.

make very explicit his ideology of the opposite kind. Others will follow, the latent issue will be turned into a manifest debate, and almost inevitably there will be polarization into two camps with differential interaction frequency.

If, in addition, the original status, "guard," is formally split into two statuses, then the conflict will become formalized and frozen. It may be argued that with formalization the conflict will become less bitter because of less internal conflict due to role conflict, less feeling of personal threat due to doubts concerning the status, and more social distance due to the occupational dissimilarity. But communication barriers accompany formalized role differentiation, and with them come decreased possibilities of adopting a prison colleague with a slightly different orientation as a role model, and organizational conflict continues.

In short, if efforts are made to carry out the two discrepant functions within the same micro-unit—such as role, status, or ward— the difficulties look rather insurmountable. They do not seem so insurmountable if a suitable space-time separation is found, but even this sequential solution is fraught with problems. Harsh punishment will not be tolerated if it is not mellowed by the softer overtones of treatment—or at least by some intended treatment—and treatment administered with little concern for custody and punishment is likely to be considered "too soft." Thus to drop one of the two reactions, even sequentially, seems impossible at present, for both are deeply ingrained in our culture. Yet we should beware of the self-fulfilling prophecy. Efforts to find solutions need not be postponed because sociologists or others declare something to harbor an incompatibility. Descriptive laws tend to acquire a normative character, but it may well be that research, skill, and administrative insight may bring forth a new reality, or at least a new perspective, such that incompatibility is dissolved.

DIFFERENTIAL DEFINITIONS OF THE PRISONER

Whatever philosophical point of view we may choose with regard to the meaning of "justice," it seems that we shall be at variance with common-sense conceptions if we do not include something about "persons with the same characteristics being treated alike." Somehow, prisoners who are equivalent in terms of *the basic variables* are to be given equivalent "treatment," or at least what is *intended* to be equivalent treatment. But it has not been decided which characteristics of the prisoner are relevant. There are at least three principal structural constraints that tend to reduce the number of equivalence-classes both of prisoners and of treatments.

First, the definitions of the prisoner have to be protected by a certain amount of *consensus*. The prison is a community where the most minute amount of injustice, nepotism, and difference in treatment is perceived, commented on, and magnified until it takes on the correct dimensions as defined by the prisoner. Gross differences are grossly magnified. Thus, consensus among personnel is not enough; somehow prisoners' opinions must also be respected. The need for consensus means that many possible characteristics of prisoners will be eliminated as not relevant. Those remaining become the nuclei of prison interaction, and they are indisputable *physical characteristics*— such as age, sex, race and other ascribed statuses—on which everyone agrees.

Second, definitions and classifications made by *other institutions* must be respected. Thus, for example, a prisoner's sentence becomes an important characteristic. The inference from evidence to sentence may be highly dissensual, but the sentence as a datum is indisputable even at a low level of administrative efficiency.

Third, there must be acknowledgement of *consensus due to authority*. How the authority is legitimized is of minor importance. It may be the religious authority of a minister passing his verdict about an inmate's religious status or it may be the scientific authority of a physician who makes a statement about somatic health. The external paraphernalia of this authority—ritual, aloofness, and expert statements that are at least partially incomprehensible to laymen—are important, for the moment the characteristics of prisoners defined by such authority lose their awe-inspiring qualities, *discussion* may begin, and the likely result is a dissensus highly dysfunctional for the system.

The main function of selecting consensual variables is that of providing a basis for "just" interaction which at the same time is smooth. Perhaps it is hoped that the prisoner will accept consensual definitions more readily than definitions supporting his own deviant definition of himself. There always is a possibility that the individual prisoner who does not find any adherents of his own definition of himself will become completely isolated if that definition differs from the official one in the prison. But lack of adherents does certainly not mean that he will accept the official definition; it may even imply that he will accept no definition at all for lack of evidence of consensus among fellow-inmates. Once definitions of prisoners are brought into the prison, interaction begins, and with this interaction comes derivative definitions and new foci of interaction. If the original conception views prisoners simply as human beings who must be stored for a prescribed amount of time—beings who essentially have to feed, sleep, get a little fresh air, and work, and excrete—the derivative definitions and foci probably will center on the rules of the prison. The main focus will be on the dangerousness of prisoners. If the guards act on the assumption that all prisoners are dangerous, but define no prisoner as more dangerous than another until a high degree of dangerousness has been exhibited, then a consensual definition is present among them. And if guards postpone their judgment of an individual inmate until something has happened, then see to it that inmates know how dangerous the offending person is, they may have the tacit support of the inmates in their definition of the offender as exceptionally dangerous.

But consensus is never enough. *Relevance* of the characteristic in question is also needed. Relevance for what? An answer consistent with common-sense observations of daily prison routines is: Relevance to the goals of maintaining a *constant level of deprivation* (constant from day to day and from prisoner to prisoner), while at the same time avoiding obviously harmful effects and obvious and avoidable interference with rehabilitation. The necessary minimum of external constancy is achieved by means of the consensus already discussed and by patterns of visibility. Guards and prisoners can know how one guard treats one prisoner, so gross and continued inconstancies are rare but also important if they are detected. Prison architecture is important in maintaining a constant level of deprivation. In our prison, the occupants of each of the five wards could see and hear the activities in other wards. Cells equipped with a grid instead of a door (not found in Norwegian prisons) have a similar effect in preventing particularistic role definitions.

While both consensus and relevance are necessary to the definitions of prisoners, one of the tragedies of prisons arises from the inverse relation between easily-achieved consensus and relevance for the goals of the institution. As one prison official asked, "Does one treat the prisoners alike by giving all of them shoes of the same size?" There may be consensus among the givers as to the equivalence of things

passing from guard to prisoner, but it is difficult to achieve this consensus among the receivers. If the prisoners were more interested in
cooperation with the institution, their descriptions of iniquities in
treatment might be taken as bona fide data, but at present that is
hardly possible. In everyday life, we probably rely upon some complex
combination of projection and empathy when we try to evaluate the
effect something has on others. However, projection does not extend
very far over the gulf separating prisoners and guards, and empathy
seems to presuppose either a particularistic relationship (a sensitive
kind of primary relation), or a universalistic relationship based on
expertness of the kind some psychologists seem to possess. Men who
are not experts in any formal sense, and who do not stand in a
particularistic relationship to the prisoners can be right most of the
time in their judgment as to the effect on a given individual of a
treatment designed to be a manifestation of justice. But in prisons,
such men are not given authority sufficient for consensus to ensue,
and their nebulous kind of expertness cannot easily be institutionalized.
In our prison, establishing particularistic relationships was quite explicitly ruled out by the personnel regulations. On the contrary, it
was easy to see the patterns of universalism, specificity, achievement,
affective neutrality, and collectivism in the rules, as one might have
predicted.[26] The guard-prisoner ratio was high enough to permit quite
a lot of interaction, but only universalistic interaction was permitted.
Perhaps this was wise, for the almost inevitable consequence of particularism—some kind of favoritism—would have had very upsetting
consequences in the prison, with its great emphasis on justice.

But it is one thing to rule out particularistic relations by regulation; another, to curb the propensity toward such relations. In fact,
one can argue *for* particularistic relationships. A particularistic orientation is by definition subjective ("it is my own definition of my own
prisoner that counts") and this subjectivity implies a certain independence from persons higher up in the hierarchy, and from other
guards as well. As long as a guard sticks to a minimum of general
prison regulations, he and his prisoner are the only ones who know
the rules of *their* private game, and the only ones who have the right
to know them in detail. Such relationship between guard and prisoner
are the natural outcome of interaction through months, during
which time even the least socially-perceptive guard will be forced to

---

[26] See Parsons, *op. cit.*, p. 459.

differentiate between the prisoners entrusted to his custody. This particularistic role has the advantage that it *can*, if played by a skillful guard, fit the prisoner like a tailor-made suit, and its effects can be adjusted to the changing moods of the prisoner. Further, in a particularistic relation less drastic sanctions should have higher efficiency than they have in a universalistic relationship, for greater sensitivity to subtleness will be cultivated.

On the other hand, there are more arguments against particularism than the favoritism already mentioned. Particularism may lead to a trivialization of a profession, to reducing professional, expert conduct to a level such that there is almost nothing left to set it apart from the common-sense conduct of men with no training at all. A sense of professional unity was rather undeveloped among the guards in the prison we knew, and a change in the direction of particularism would have been considered one more step toward degradation. "Just *talking* to them, like women, what is that?" Further, in a system of particularism, guards would have to differentiate between prisoners much more than at present. Such differentiation is not difficult for the trained expert, but it would place enormous strain on the guard who many times a day must shift relationships from one prisoner to another. Also, it cannot be expected that there will be more than a minimum of particularistic interaction institutionalized when one of the actors, the prisoner, does not necessarily feel obliged to follow the subtler rules and has the power to let the guard down at any time by simple withdrawal. Particularistic relations also make it difficult to apply extreme negative sanctions unless there is skillful role differentiation.[27]

All these arguments or indicators of them were heard over and over again in our prison and they gave a clue to the principal dilemma of the guards—the oscillation between primary and secondary relations, between contact and withdrawal, *in the same social setting*. This kind of oscillation is experienced by most people many times during a single day, as when, for example, they move from work relations to family relations. When the oscillations are frequent, and especially when they occur in the same social setting (the secretary

[27] See Donald R. Cressey, "Organizational Limitations on Treatment in the Modern Prison," Chapter IV in Richard A. Cloward, Donald R. Cressey, George H. Grosser, Richard McCleery, Lloyd E. Ohlin, Gresham Sykes and Sheldon Messinger, *Theoretical Studies in Social Organization of the Prison* (New York: Social Science Research Council, 1960), 107–109.

and boss who are in love, the worker and foreman who are personally obnoxious to each other, etc.), they become "problems." Guards are almost constantly in such a "problem" situation. In our prison, "nervous breakdowns" were frequent among the guards, and some of them surely can be attributed to unsuccessful attempts to resolve the dilemma. Both the mechanism of complete withdrawal into secondary relations and the mechanism of violating prison rules to enter into particularistic relations with inmates were unsatisfactory to many guards.[28]

In principle, there is a solution to the guard's dilemma, but it seems to lie far in the future. The relation of a nurse to a patient may also be described as both universalistic and particularistic, but it differs from the role of the guard in that more consensual variables are taken into account, and a high degree of *relevance* obtains for these variables. Thus, the nurse does not necessarily have a dilemma to resolve. But at present only a tiny segment of the prisoner is left to the discretion of the guard. In the future, this segment may broaden, more training will be required to make the knowledge truly relevant to whatever goal the prison might have, and a dilemma in the status of the guard may be resolved.[29] At present, there seems to be a polarization among the guards between those who play primary and those who play secondary roles with prisoners, and this cleavage seems to be correlated with the one between punishment-oriented and treatment-oriented guards.[30]

[28] See the discussion of the defense-mechanisms used by one institution's employees, in Chapter 5, below.

[29] One student of prisons has said, "What is needed is a correctional technique which is explicitly based on a theory of behavior *and* of criminality and which can be routinely administered by a rather unskilled worker in the framework of the eight-hour shift. Caution is needed, however. Insulin and electric shock treatment is more popular in state mental hospitals than is individual psychotherapy, but this greater popularity is not necessarily attributable to the fact that shock therapy is more effective or more consistent with behavioral theory. Rather, it probably is popular because it can be both routinely and cheaply administered." (Italics added.) Donald R. Cressey, "The Nature and Effectiveness of Correctional Techniques," *Law and Contemporary Problems,* 23 (Autumn, 1958), 754–771.

[30] Such a cleavage means decrease in interaction and hence decrease in communication. For a discussion of the crucial role of communication patterns, see Richard McCleery, *Policy Change in Prison Management* (East Lansing: Michigan State University Government Research Bureau, 1957). A case in this connection is reported in Oscar Grusky, "Role Conflict in Organi-

We now return to the problem of establishing equivalence-classes among the prisoners, known as *differential treatment*. There is one immediate argument against any extensive division of this kind: the short-term costs are higher (separate buildings or wards are needed, cells and living quarters must be specialized, and trained specialists must be hired), and convincing proofs of long-term gains are difficult to obtain. The variables to be used in making the division are not important to our general argument, but let us assume that division of inmates into categories for differential treatment is based on both consensual and relevant variables, rather than on variables that could be used to classify any group, such as sex, age, and I.Q. The variables might be kind of crime, degree of recidivism, length of sentence, or psychological characteristics held to be etiologically important. But no matter what the basis, even the most trivial differentiation will probably tend to have overtones of evaluation in the penal community. One reason for this lies, as mentioned, in the practice of magnifying all nuances in a world where differences are otherwise flattened out. Another reason can perhaps be found in the tendency of underdogs not to unite, but rather to emphasize differences and rank them in such a way that someone is interposed between themselves and the bottom of the scale.

In our prison, there was ample evidence that evaluation of categories of prisoners was commonplace. We asked prisoners, "With what kind of prisoner would you prefer to share a cell, and with what kind would you rather not be together?" The following ranking of a list of offenses was made: driving while drunk, embezzlement, car-theft, fraud, loitering, treason, safe-cracking, and robbery. From the comments, we got the impression that two factors were of importance in determining the relative ranks. These were positive or negative

zation: A Study of Prison Camp Officials," *Administrative Science Quarterly*, 3 (1958) 466. A new prison supervisor strongly committed to custody arrived. "Once the supervisor had initiated his strongly custodially-oriented policies, little informal interaction occurred between him and the treatment-oriented guards. This in turn resulted in an even greater decrease in the influence of treatment criteria on camp policies and also promoted a general lack of substantive knowledge on the part of the supervisor as to the impact of his policies on the inmates. Since the treatment-oriented guards had interacted more often with the inmates, they had functioned as a major source of information—information to which the former supervisor, because of his neutrality, had had access but which was unavailable to the new man because of his custodial-orientation."

identification with the kind of *people* the respondent believed would be most likely to commit the kind of crime, and evaluation of the *kind of crime.* There also seemed to be pronounced differences between evaluations expressed privately and the collective evaluations expressed by groups of prisoners. The ranking mentioned above was by private individuals and is highly correlated with the white-collar/ blue-collar variable, at least as perceived by the respondents. The only exception involved men sentenced for treason (namely, collaborators with the Germans or the Quisling party during World War II). The few collaborators still left in Norwegian prisons as late as ten years after the capitulation were almost all of relatively high social rank but they were ranked near the bottom of the scale. Officials reported that shortly after the war ordinary prisoners objected strenuously whenever new "quislings" arrived. By so doing, and by giving traitors a low rank on our scale, conventional criminals could raise their own rank within walls and identify with their compatriots outside the walls.

It appears, then, that prisoners privately ranked crimes according to a scale of "crimeness" and expressed a desire to avoid personal association with persons perpetrating the crimes on the lower ranks on this scale. From this, one can be tempted to draw the conclusion that administrative differentiation on the basis of "crimeness" might serve as a stimulus to identification with higher ranks. This seems incorrect. A prisoner cannot change the crime for which he is doing time, and other crimes, detected or not, tend to be forgotten, *so there would be no objective base for mobility along the scale.* Further, it must be remembered that any differential evaluation in the prisoner's behalf assumes that he has at least some experiential background, however slight, for making the evaluation himself. In a prison highly differentiated on the basis of evaluations prisoners seem to make of each other, there is no reason to believe that there will be correspondence between "crimeness" and avoidance of association, a phenomena that would be conducive to reformation. On the contrary, the very fact that a category has been placed high by the archenemy, the prison authorities, might be sufficient reason for its debasement by prisoners, so that "crimeness" becomes a characteristic of *desirable* associates.

Differential treatment means segregated treatment and will always be a two-edged sword. A person arguing that some prisoners must be protected from the harmful influences of others easily forgets that when the sheep are divided from the goats, the goats as well as the sheep become a special group. Social behavior is never a psychological characteristic "owned" by an individual alone (as, for instance, he owns the color of his hair). On the contrary, it is "owned" by groups to a large extent and is, thus, dependent on the social milieu. Hence, some sheep might turn into goats when left alone, whereas they might have been protected from this role behavior if some goats had been let in with them to take care of some of the functional needs of the group. ("Bad" prisoners who express aggression against guards may be doing so on behalf of "good" prisoners even if both groups are unaware of this fact.) Similarly, it may be argued that when the sheep are removed, some of the goats are given an opportunity to express their sheep-like character.[31]

Sykes has shown that positive sanctions in prisons have two important aspects. First, because of the extreme paucity of such sanctions and the overabundance of negative sanctions, positive sanctions tend to be merely the absence of negative sanctions.[32] Not sticking

[31] Ohlin and Lawrence comment on the rare inmate who openly proclaims his commitment to official values, and particularly to the demands of clinical experience. "He may capitulate to in-group pressures for conformity, or he may openly rebel against them. In the latter instance, the individual invites social isolation within the inmate system. In-group hostility often has the further consequence of intensifying allegiance to out-group values. This process, by which some inmates become detached from in-group values and oriented to out-group values may be called "rehabilitation by rejection." Lloyd E. Ohlin and William C. Lawrence, "Social Interaction among Clients as a Treatment Problem," *Social Work* (April, 1959), 10.

This effect was observed in our prison among some isolated criminals who perhaps perceived more rejection than was really the case. It seems wise to include in the calculations of the possible effects of segregated treatment that in-group pressure among the "sheep" may decrease because of the absence of goats.

Another observation to this effect has been made by McCleery, who says, "The processes by which the formal hierarchy is sustained create the conditions for a parallel hierarchy in the inmate community. Exploitive and authoritarian inmate leaders may be removed to segregation, but others rise to fill their place because their role is necessary in the situation." Richard H. McCleery, unpublished paper read at a meeting of the SSRC Conference on Research in Correctional Organization, December, 1955. Quoted by Donald R. Cressey and Witold Krassowski, "Inmate Organization and Anomie in American Prisons and Soviet Labor Camps," *Social Problems*, 5 (Winter, 1957–58), 219.

[32] Gresham M. Sykes, *Crime and Society* (New York: Random House, 1956), 105 *ff.*

strictly to the rules emphasizes the relativity of values, as illustrated by a guard who (by postponing the locking of cell doors some minutes) gave prisoners a small taste of liberty, even if it was only an illusion that they were at liberty to walk in the corridors if they chose. The gratitude was enormous and deeply felt, "Our guard is more humane," the rumor went.

The other aspect mentioned by Sykes has to do with the definition of the zero-point from which the prisoner starts the day he enters prison.[33] Any social system must have both positive and negative sanctions. But in prisons there is a tendency for positive sanctions to disappear as rewards and to take on the appearance of negative sanctions, punishments, when they are not granted fully or automatically. For example, a positive sanction would be the literal granting of "time-off for good behavior." The tendency, however, is to deduct a certain part of the sentence (in Norwegian prisons this fraction is one-third) at the time the inmate enters the prison and then to add pieces of this deducted time to the reduced sentence whenever the prisoner misbehaves. This practice may be considered a consequence of penal philosophy: Everyone is innocent until proved guilty; everyone behaves well unless, in fact, he behaves badly. The practice also may be considered a step toward general reduction of sentences by administrative fiat rather than through cumbersome revision of the penal code. However, we suspect that even if these two considerations were eliminated the practice would continue, for the following reasons.

Sanctions within walls can be divided in two categories, depending on whether they refer to prison life (transfer, better kind of work or cell) or have relevance for life outside walls. A punishment administered to the prisoner within walls can be contained within walls and may have no easily detectable aftereffects, provided it is not the addition of a fraction or fixed amount of time to his sentence. The latter kind of punishment is brought to the attention of everyone who is relevant to the prisoner; he has no way of defending himself against dissemination of this information, as the time of release is so visible. Further, literally granting "time-off for good behavior" in individual cases might arouse criticism, especially among the police. Under such conditions, neither the prison nor the prisoner is protected against the reactions of the outside world. By granting all inmates, auto-

[33] *The Society of Captives, op. cit.*, pp. 28, 51.

matically, a reduction in sentence for good behavior two important things are achieved. The *decision is simplified* because a given inmate who behaves well will not appear to be released early, and an apparatus devoted to the detection and filing of *negative* behavior (rather than a more complicated device for measuring positive behavior) can be developed.[34]

When trying to understand decision-making, it is always useful to ask what will happen if it becomes known that the decisions are wrong. If a prisoner loses good time but later is released and behaves very well, the conclusion will probably be that he has benefited and learned from his negative experience. If he behaves badly, the conclusion may be that this is the proof of what a hardened criminal he is. If he gets time-off for good behavior, and subsequently behaves well, the conclusion may be that the prison has reformed him. But, this is the crucial point, if he receives time-off for good behavior and then behaves badly by committing a highly conspicuous crime, the prison administration may be severely criticized by the press, the police, and certain parts of the public.[35] Thus, it is profitable to make arrangements such that early release for good behavior appears to be both statutory and automatic, rather than due to a deliberate decision for which prison officials are responsible.

Again, the dilemma is clear. Undifferentiated and unsegregated treatment may produce a rich variety of experience and the necessity for rapid adjustment—as in social life outside the walls—but it is probably more true that the over-all effects of life in an undifferentiated prison are detrimental to rehabilitation. On the other hand, segregated treatment will always imply some sort of ranking, and probably will have dysfunctionl effects if there are no built-in oppor-

[34] In connection with this, an important feature of most prison systems should be noted. It is recognized that imprisonment is a frustrating experience, and that this frustration may be turned into aggressive acts. If this aggression is outwardly directed, against fellow inmates or against the personnel, reactions will follow. But aggression turned inward may be even more significant, but not controlled, for the apparatus tuned to the detection of this kind of aberrance is almost undeveloped.

[35] For an account of the effects of such public criticism, see Lloyd E. Ohlin, "The Routinization of Correctional Change," *The Journal of Criminal Law, Criminology and Police Science*, 45 (1955), 403; and Lloyd E. Ohlin, "Conflicting Interests in Correctional Objectives," Chapter V in Cloward, Cressey, Grosser, McCleery, Ohlin, Sykes and Messinger, *op. cit.*, pp. 111–129.

tunities for mobility in the system. Significantly, it seems very difficult to construct mobility criteria that are relevant for behavior after the release and that are not primarily relevant only to orderliness within walls.

CONCLUSION

There are numerous other dilemmas connected with prison life, but the four we have described seem to be of particular pertinence. They are connected with each other in a simple way: The latter three fill prisons with an overabundance of built-in structural problems that contribute to the enigmatic and strange character of prison life, and the first one makes this picture complete by removing the victim from the judicial process, particularly as it operates in prisons. Many prison practices, then, are irrelevant, in the sense that putting sick people in a total institution other than a hospital would be irrelevant even if it served the social function of removal of the sick.

We are back to the point of departure. The irrelevance of the prison is a social dilemma in a peculiar kind of vacuum, for it attracts the serious attention of few people only, except when extraordinary circumstances are reported in the prison. The dilemma is difficult precisely because it is publicly considered only at intervals—after cases of corruption or fraud, dramatic escapes, mutinies, or intramural felonies have become public. The reaction usually is in the direction of security measures, for these have immediate effects and are easily understood and administered. Continuous struggle with the problems is necessary if there are to be constructive solutions, and perhaps a prolific division of labor between expert and layman also is needed. Ambivalence about prisons may perhaps be traced to the fact that we recognize the necessary character of the functions that prisons, military organizations, and certain aspects of the police force serve, but at the same time detest some of the dysfunctional consequences of such organizations. Serving time in prison has a flare of obvious necessity, but as a permanent job it may willingly be left to others. Similarly, the secrecy surrounding prisons and the indifference to them both contribute to the enormous attention given to conspicuous prison events. The hidden world is revealed; just as when the former nun writes her story. Somehow prisons do not belong to social reality.

Thus, it may be that one dilemma lies at the base of all the others: On the one hand, there is a necessity for letting the prison benefit from public initiative and public acceptance; on the other hand, there is a necessity for retaining the prison as a negative symbol that is rejected by the public. Unless the whole idea of formal, negative sanctions is abandoned (and it is difficult to imagine a society possessing positive sanctions only), a total institution with punishment as one of its objectives cannot possibly be the object of positive identification. But from this none of the four dilemmas follows as a logical consequence; each is only a probable consequence in the present socio-cultural setting. This makes the construction of a total institution, where membership is a relevant and meaningful consequence of crime, a most fascinating endeavor; although such an institution probably will be witnessed only by generations still far in the future.

P|A|R|T| |T|W|O

SOME CONSEQUENCES

OF ADMINISTRATIVE

STABILITY AND CHANGE

4

RICHARD H. MCCLEERY

| | | | | | | | | |

The Governmental Process and Informal Social Control

An analysis of prison government must distinguish, in its areas of study, elements which may have dramatic or intrinsic interest from those attaining dimensions of theoretical significance. The institutional processes constituting the foci of this chapter are not significant by reason of being exotic or unique. On the contrary, these processes are significant because they are the commonplace processes of change, adjustment, and accommodation to new goals which are part of the natural history of any social institution. The problems of prison government are those of formulation of rational policy, enforcement, and maintenance of the compliance, discipline, and morale crucial to the survival of any institution. The prison studied, like many others, was an administrative agency engaged in a redefinition of traditional goals and in the reconciliation of conflicting purposes. The series of dangerous and costly prison riots elsewhere in recent years testifies to a general failure of penal administration to provide an effective blueprint for institutional change. The particular prison studied, however, was distinctive mainly because it was able to keep the consequences of change within reasonably manageable limits during a decade of transition.

The distinctive quality of the prison as a setting for research lies in the unique opportunity provided by its relatively self-contained social system for the examination of those commonplace characteristics of social order. The prison provides exceptionally controlled conditions for the study of relationships among the elements of social control. The object of this study is not a set of universal propositions descriptive of prisons or social institutions in general. The object is, rather, to assert relationships between events and the conditions of their occurrence. Thus, it is asserted that violence marks interpersonal relations under conditions in which the system of communication fails to transmit common definitions of the situation to elements of the community. Study of the prison may concentrate on those conditions which have a distinctive prominence in that social system and on the consequences which follow change in those conditions.

It can be noted that the prison illustrates a high degree of conformity to norms with a rather low degree of internalization of those norms. Conformity, for the new inmate at least, is associated with very little of the habit, tradition, affection, and loyalty associated with social control in the free society. As a power structure, the prison relies on and permits concentration on the processes of formulation, communication, and reinforcement of norms in its system of social control. The consequences for conformity which attend change in those processes of social control can be observed with unique clarity over a period of time.

The data for this report were drawn mainly from the examination of changes in Oahu Prison, the maximum security institution of the, then, Territory of Hawaii. In 1946, the starting point of these observations, the old prison was a tightly knit, static, and traditional institution, dominated by the values of security and control. Those values were expressed in its militantly disciplined and sharply defined custodial hierarchy and in its detailed procedures of operation. The same values were reflected as clearly in the complex maze of role definitions, ritual behaviors, and patterns of informal contact which characterized the prison as a social system. The control orientation, accent on power, and centralization of authority in the prison suggest an analogy to the authoritarian society in which the abstract interests of the "state" supersede all claims for the will, the welfare, or the dignity of the subjects.

The authoritarian quality of the system sharpened the problem of executive succession at the death of the warden in 1946. His replacement did not assume office with a commitment to alter the policy or personnel of the agency, yet much of the institutional revolution which followed may be traced in origin to the personality and administrative behavior of the new warden and his lack of prior penal experience. His easy availability to everyone in the institution brought information to the policy level which custodial control of formal communications had suppressed in the past. With other inexperienced men whom he added to the staff, he injected patterns of behavior which were inconsistent with traditional patterns; and he expressed outrage at irregular practices which years of toleration had incorporated into the system of custodial control.

In the formal pronouncements of the prison, rehabilitation had long stood as a goal equivalent to custody. The dominant role of the custodial hierarchy, expressed in its command of institutional communications, had permitted custodians to qualify the goal of rehabilitation in practice and to define it in terms consistent with custodial procedures. Men assigned to treatment functions had been drawn from the custodial ranks and charged with the orientation dominant there. The substance of an administrative revolution began when the new warden appointed a small group of inexperienced men to carry out treatment functions. By taking advantage of its access to the warden, the new group formalized its position as a policy committee, restructured organizational lines, and published a policy and philosophy manual for personnel. Their central tactics involved circumvention and reconstruction of formal communication channels so that information on individual inmate needs was included in administrative decision-making processes.

In general analyses of changes in governments, the emergence of a liberal group that drafts a new "constitution" and dominates the new policy-making centers thus created signifies completion of a revolution. In the prison, the revolution had barely begun at this stage. Implementation of new concepts required effective control over both employees and prisoners, but control at all levels was institutionalized in every detail of operating procedure by which traditional definitions of the situation had been communicated. The contest between rehabilitative and custodial concepts became a contest for the means by which such concepts could be communicated and reinforced, and it affected the status definitions, roles, values, and social structure of both inmate and official groups in the prison society.

The types of duties, responsibilities, and forms of organization in a prison stimulate a conservative position there. Some statuses seem to require the characteristics of the "authoritarian personality" quite apart from the inclinations of their occupants, and to cast their occupants automatically into opposition to liberal change. As the contest for control of the prison developed, a substantial portion of the "old guard" was forced into a position of resistance and outright rebellion. Although the tradition of disciplined obedience in the guard force suggests that the "old guard" might readily accept new official policy, the tradition actually worked to produce resistance to change of even small details. The guard force was driven, in violation of its own basic code, to search for alliances both outside and within the institution. At the same time, as inmate society arrived at the verge of riot, contacts across staff-inmate lines developed, despite the fact that such contacts violated the norms of both groups.

The disintegrating institutional revolution ended with compromise and with the reconciliation of many issues in practice which defied reconciliation in theory. The heightened tensions generated by change provided the motive for a merging of conservative and liberal positions in procedures developed for the adjustment of conflict. However, the fact that significant changes did occur is indicated in distinctive differences in the old and new social systems by which inmates adapt to the conditions of institutional life.

The following analysis of this institutional transition and crisis directs attention to the relationship between power and the processes by which influence is communicated to the centers of agency decision-making. However, it also focuses attention on the notion that the decisions involved in any system of social control are decisions of compliance as well as of command—of consent as well as of coercion. Our general propositions border on truisms: the status of an element within a social system is determined by its capacity to impose its definitions of the situation as premises on the behavior of others; decisions reflect the interests which are communicated most effectively on the organizational level at which they are made. The analysis traces the implications of these principles throughout the details of a complex social organization. Finally, by pointing out the manner in which values and definitions become intrenched in the conventional procedures of an institution, the analysis demonstrates the problems and limits of institutional change. Any social institution is more than a pattern of lines and boxes on a chart. It is a potentially explosive system of human energies in delicate balance, and ill-considered change may generate tensions which even a prison cannot contain.

ORIENTING CONCEPTS

There are several rather low-level propositions, useful in analysis of any social system, which can serve as orienting concepts for studies of prisons. Such propositions tend to be ignored in both analyses and administration of penal institutions. As our description of one prison will indicate, when these propositions are obscured by certain overt but incidental characteristics of the prison community, conceptual and administrative errors are apt to result. Study of change in the prison community through a period of time will underline propositions about relationships associated with order and stability in any social system. Four such orienting propositions are discussed below.

The existence of a stable system of authority testifies to the existence of a common community, shared definitions, and relatively continuous patterns of interaction.

This proposition is another form of the observation that all government rests on consent. Systems of power differ most significantly in the type and intensity of means employed to extract the consent of the governed. The illusion, fostered by certain physical appearances in the prison, that control rests on the instruments of force rather than the procedures for creating consensus is a rich source of error for inexperienced scholars or officials. Constant administrative emphasis on distinctions of rank, status, privilege and uniform—on overt distinctions between staff and inmate—creates the superficial impression that an official society is superimposed on a community of inmates. This appearance of two separate societies is an inevitable administrative reaction to continuous internal processes which tend to make the prison community a single social entity.

Every order or duty imposed by rule is as much an obligation on the official as upon the inmate. The role of the inmate in acquiescence and the role of the official in communicating commands are inseparable parts of the system of authority, and the official policies of distinguishing status, restricting fraternization, or brandishing the instruments of force represent a modestly effective effort to minimize the reversal of those roles and avoid compromise with values originating in the inmate population. Just as responsible democratic government rests on freedom of communication and open access to officials, an authoritarian system of power requires procedures which retain initiative for the ruling class, minimize reciprocity, and prevent the communication of popular values to the ruling elite. Authoritarian control does not rest basically on the imposition of punitive sanctions. It rests, instead, on the definition, in a system of authority, of a role for the ruler which makes use of punitive sanctions superfluous. Thus, the heart of custodial controls in traditional prisons lies in the daily regimentation, routines, and rituals of domination which bend the subjects into a customary posture of silent awe and unthinking acceptance.

The exercise of authority involves the formulation of definitions of the situation, their communication, and their acceptance—perhaps in consequence of procedures for their re-enforcement.[1]

Authority is a relationship among individuals and not the property of a particular person. In the effort to "rationalize" and, hence, to restrict the exercise of authority to administrators, the principal form of communication of definitions is signed orders and personal commands. No matter how much such commands simply serve to legitimize the obvious or endorse the inevitable, and such is their normal character, they create an appearance that authority inheres in the will of individuals formally entitled to exercise discretion. Such a system, rigidly reinforced with procedures, may inhibit the flow of definitions up the chain of command and the compromise of formal values with those of the population. But the brute fact remains that an organizational structure designed to control subordinates constrains the initiative of every participant in the system. The apparent autocrat of a militant, penal bureaucracy will confess an inability to initiate changes in routine—an inability that would discredit his counterpart in any liberal organization.

By assigning information a disproportionate scarcity value through censorship and restriction of communication, the authoritarian system makes any informational channel a significant factor in the analysis of authority, and it makes any effort to equip initiative with information an anarchic factor within the system. The concept of authority as a structured pattern of interaction—as a system of communication—serves to explain two paradoxical characteristics of the prison com-

---

[1] Chester Barnard has defined authority as "the character of any communication (order) in formal organization by virtue of which it is accepted by a . . . member of the organization as governing the action he contributes." *The Functions of the Executive*, Rev. Ed. (Cambridge: Harvard University Press, 1954), 163.

munity. First, the most militantly disciplined and normally responsive elements of the community, the custodial force and senior inmates, are the most completely resistant to changes in routine. Second, the details of a most dramatic reform can normally be found in the archives of a prior decade. The tendency toward restoration of the customs and values of a conventional status quo seems to exist as a characteristic of the system itself and apart from conscious will or deliberate intent of any particular individual. A generally shared, fundamental definition of the situation works to "filter out" inconsistent orders and to "authorize" those orders which are consistent with it.

Because the structure of authority in any social group inheres in the pattern of communication by which definitions are transmitted in that group, some degree of conflict between treatment and custodial elements seems to be inevitable and a standard characteristic of modern prisons. Those who equate authority with an act of will tend to see that conflict as a conscious philosophical antagonism and charge their opponents with a subversive intent. While such may be the case in some extreme and aggravated situation, explanation does not require that the contest be elevated to cosmic proportions. The patterns of communication involved in a process of education and counseling are inconsistent with those required for authoritarian control.[2] Since any administrative unit seeks control over the means essential to fulfill its responsibilities—which are the means for imposing its definitions as the premises of behavior—the elements of conflict are present in the situation even if not present in the motives of the participants.

There are structural, procedural, and operational differences between a system of domination and a system of leadership—between a system which suppresses the initiative of the subject and one which directs that initiative.

Even in analyses of free communities, there is an unfortunate tendency to examine *power* in terms of the concepts of Marx and

[2] See Donald R. Cressey, "Contradictory Directives in Complex Organizations: The Case of the Prison," *Administrative Science Quarterly*, 4 (June, 1959), 1–19; and "Limitations on Organization of Treatment in the Modern Prison," in Richard A. Cloward, Donald R. Cressey, George H. Grosser, Richard McCleery, Lloyd E. Ohlin, Gresham M. Sykes and Sheldon Messinger, *Theoretical Studies in Social Organization of the Prison* (New York: Social Science Research Council, 1960), 78–110.

Gumplowicz and to equate it with the capacity of one class to restrain, suppress and constrain the aspirations of another. In a purely custodial institution like a traditional prison, the power to inhibit the initiative of the subjects may, then, be the most prominent aspect appearing for analysis. However, a more significant dimension of power lies in the capacity exhibited by some individuals to generate and mobilize the energies of the community against an external object. That type of power is a capacity to arouse and direct the human resources of the system against fire, flood, social problems and external enemies, and not against a scapegoat class. Failure to appreciate the operational differences between the authority of domination and the authority of leadership may lead to an underestimation of the ability of an undisciplined, liberal group to contest power with a dictatorial group as well as to misconceptions of what the contest between those groups involves in behavioral terms.

Demonstrations of the authority of leadership in prison communities are provided by cases in which inmates have been employed against the hazards of flood and forest fire. The heroism of inmates in such crises has moved some commentators to assert that convicts are quite like other people, when, in fact, other people were probably retreating in panic. The "moral equivalent of war" in such cases is present in the situation rather than in the personalities involved. Such mobilizations of energy are marked by the fact that both the object of action and the means to the object are communicated with dramatic clarity by the situation itself. The problem of leadership is one of communicating a definition of the situation which will initiate a desired course of action.

Domination and suppression of initiative both involve suppressing information on which discretion and discontent can be based and limiting perceived alternatives. Hence, authoritarian domination is inevitably associated with secrecy and institutionalized in censorship. Leadership and generation of initiative, on the other hand, involve transmission of data on which initiative can be based. The more abstract a problem is—the more its solution depends upon the acceptance of concepts as premises in the decision of individuals—the greater the active or positive function of communication becomes. The authority of domination fails in the task of mobilizing the energies of prison inmates toward rehabilitation. Domination may have a deterrent effect, but it cannot achieve positive rehabilitation in the sense of moving the individual to meet new situations with new concepts and techniques. The development of rehabilitative programs in the prison involves generation of patterns of interaction and communication inconsistent with custodial patterns of constraint.

The distinctive characteristic of bureaucracy is institutionalization of rationality and value, in contrast with the internalization of those properties in the personality of individuals.

The norms, goals, and values of a bureaucracy become incorporated in rules, routines, and records which permit the rational prediction of individual patterns of behavior. Decisions made on the basis of a record reflect the values incorporated in the data transmitted to the point of decision, and particular decision-makers can be treated as interchangeable parts. By structuring the premises of administrative decision from the level of policy to that of compliance, bureaucracy inhibits the impact of private passion or personal ideals on the functioning of a larger social system. The power that inheres in a capacity to impose the premises of decision is the power to predict and control the behavior of others. Change in the processes by which the premises of decision are defined and transmitted detracts from the probability of rational prediction. In more commonplace terms, such change corrupts authority, generates anarchy, and produces social disorganization quite apart from the motives of individuals or anyone's conscious intent.

Although the ideal bureaucracy of rules, records, and procedures makes internalized norms superfluous and particular individuals dispensable, it cannot avoid certain human failings of its participants. The administrative system achieves rationality in limited spheres of action by specialization, by limiting the premises and alternatives for action in prescribed situations. Guards may be instructed to report inmates moving out of a given area. Treatment officers may be required to act on all inmates falling within a defined category. But individuals tend to internalize the instrumental values of their function and confuse means—the observance of particular rules—with the ends of treatment or custody which the means were designed to achieve. Officers may make the enforcement of some petty ordinance an end in itself and its violation a moral evil. The enforcement of norms by means of punitive sanctions is one supplement or alternative to reinforcement by other means. However, as individuals internalize specialized rules and elevate them to the status of absolute values, alternative means are made inconsistent, and effective enforcement of norms collapses in the conscious conflict between advocates of alternative means.

THE TRADITIONAL PRISON COMMUNITY

Currently, the majority of penal institutions, and especially those most accessible to examination, stand at some intermediate point in the process of transition to be outlined later. The traditional penal patterns from which that transition departed may exist today mainly in the time-dimmed recollections of senior inmates and staff of the progressive institution. Based largely on the study of Oahu Prison prior to 1947 and the Central Prison of North Carolina in 1953,[3] this passage will emphasize distinctive qualities of the "good old days" and what made them good.

As senior inmates recall the traditional custodial institution, they praise it as a system in which "every man knew exactly where he stood." There was a certain security in that relationship even when the inmate stood in the most subordinate status that the wit of the custodians could impose. The old prison stood as a monolithic system of power governed by the homogeneous values of custodial control, while the social and belief systems of the inmate society reflected a similar simplicity. Whatever the public relations material of the old prison may have implied, its internal operations betrayed no confusion of custodial and rehabilitative purposes, its structure of authority exhibited no uncertain division of power between treatment officials and the guard force, and its inmate society was not disorganized by competing claims of *politicians* and *hard cons*. Inmates were caustic critics of an administration which provided no rehabilitative treatment; but the wall of official solidarity (like the concrete physical constraints) offered few cracks which the inmate could exploit to his own advantage.

The Official Staff. The old prison contained embryonic elements of treatment and industrial programs, but promotion through the custodial ranks was the avenue by which positions in these programs were filled and their values defined. The foundation of custodial control was custodial management of all records and communication in the prison. The custodial values of discipline and order determined the content of records and, in consequence, the decisions based upon the records. Although the formal status of the industrial supervisors was equal to that of guards, supervisors communicated through the custodial hierarchy, and they were perceived as ranking below the

[3] See Richard McCleery, *The Strange Journey* (Chapel Hill: University of North Carolina Extension Bulletin, 1953).

guards, from whom they received orders and addressed requests. Requests for such professional services as existed, medical and psychological treatment, moved through the office of the captain, reinforcing the impression that such services were also adjuncts of custody. The guard force had influence in administrative decisions far out of proportion to its rank in the formal hierarchy of published, institutional values. The warden retained initiative in general policy as a result of strict control of communication with the outside world, but the day-to-day management of the prison centered in the office of the Captain of the Yard. In signing orders for internal administration, the warden could do nothing but endorse the obvious as that was defined by the custodial force. In summary, non-custodial activities took place, but the custodial force had asserted the predominance of its own function and monopolized the means by which its own norms could be imposed as definitive for the behavior of all.

The function of the custodial force was to deprive the inmates of freedom. In order to understand the impact of custodial control on the society of the prison, it is necessary to examine in detail what that function implied. It was something vastly more complex than the task of watching the walls or shooting the men who attempted escape. As a matter of fact, any extensive outburst of shooting would have called down the wrath of outside society which was, even then, vastly more ambivalent about the purposes of prison than the prison staff. Because deprivation of freedom was executed efficiently, the old prison could dispense with the practice of shooting inmates and, very nearly, dispense with the practice of watching walls. There have been prisons which restricted the guard force to perimeter control, but an arrangement of this kind is possible only if effective control of inmate society has been delegated either to inmates or to a special staff. Ordinarily, it is only when detailed control of the prosaic and ordinary aspects of inmate society collapses, a condition illustrated by riot, that reinforcement of the wall guards with state troopers and militia is required. It is the contrast between such exceptional circumstances and ordinary conditions in which a few aged and dozing custodians keep the peace that testifies to the vital significance of internal and indirect security measures—the social controls institutionalized in the drab details of routine activity and interaction.

In its full and detailed sense, deprivation of inmate freedom required control of inmate initiative. More than restriction of physical opportunities for action was required. The conditions of exact physical security had long since been compromised by the advent of prison industries. Effective denial of freedom involved control over *perception* of such opportunities to act as inevitably exist, control over the *means* and instruments of action, control over the *premises* of action, and control over the *will* to act. Thus, the complex processes employed in depriving the subjects of initiative went far beyond the punishment of observed misbehaviors. The use of punitive sanctions for exemplary reinforcement was the last resort of custodial control, as of any other system of control, and such use amounted to a confession that the primary means of control had failed.

When the prison later moved into its period of change, many of the rituals of custody were criticized because they bore no apparent relationship to physical security. The significance of those rituals becomes clear only when they are viewed as part of the ruling class's effort to monopolize initiative. By censorship and control over association within the walls, inmate activity and social intercourse were closely regimented so that any expressions of discontent could not enlist an active audience. While no amount of regimentation could suppress the actual circulation of discontent ("the time to worry is when they stop griping"), regulation denied legitimacy to the premises of action transmitted by "grapevine" means. Because every detail of the situation combined to declare his authority, the bull-voiced captain could smash smoldering rebellion with verbal commands alone.

No active social system can keep its subjects in a permanent posture of silent obeisance, but stable attitudes of subordination were imposed by periodic shake-downs, formations, and counts. Such ritual formations created precise roles for the communicants and thus habitual behaviors appeared. For example, the start of evening count-down waited until absolute silence had prevailed in the assembly for long moments. The captain mounted a lighted platform and intoned the roll with level voice, syllables rolling together without regard for persons; the incantation seemed like a devotion to power, the meaning of which had long been forgotten though the form preserved. Any interruption was treated as a sacrilege. At the conclusion of the ceremony, locking bars were dropped across the cell tier with a crash like that of a temple gong, and the gradually rising murmur of voices added to the sense that a sacred moment had passed. By such means, custodial supremacy was imposed as a fundamental definition of the situation.

Another important element in the denial of initiative was denial of individual personality. The prison haircut, the drab denim uniform issued in a single size, and the denial of other details by which persons differentiate themselves in free society struck at the roots of inmate initiative. This is not to say that inmate society was an undifferentiated mass or that no inmates had positions that enabled them to initiate action. Just the reverse was true, for the prison ostensibly prohibited far more than it intended to prevent. Differentiating marks of status existed by official tolerance and consequently were instruments by which officials could influence inmate social structure. By multiplying the system of deprivations far beyond the denial of escape—the one deprivation which could not be compromised—the guards equipped themselves with an arsenal of sanctions to be dispensed and incentives to be exchanged for conformity. Guards could not create inmate leadership directly. Nevertheless, they could license a wider sphere of movement, access to physical goods, initiative in petty things, distinctions in dress and appearance, and advance knowledge of official action—all the symbols of high status in inmate society—to those inmates who accepted the essential custodial values of peace and order.

The principal foundation of custodial order was the custodians' monopoly on information. General censorship, requiring silence in assemblies, isolating inmate agitators, refusal to formulate formal orienting principles, and restricting contact between inmates and guards were critical administrative practices. Such practices denied meaning, purpose, and the capacity to criticize, anticipate, or control to the inmates. They gave the appearance of arbitrariness, the quality of a "reign of terror," to an administrative system which, in fact, made a ritual of regularity. Unlike the situation said to characterize some traditional prisons, control did not rest on a mass of published rules.[4] Only twenty-six rules, as wide in their import as the guard's sense of insubordination, constituted the body of regulation. The publication of rules establishes a government of law and provides a basis of appeal from men—a principle as old as the revolt of the Plebes in Rome and the law of the twelve tables. The authority of the old prison was that of rank and not that of principle.

The monopoly of information established the guards (some of whom had little natural advantage over inmates) as a relatively intellectual elite, and thus gave legitimacy to their authority. Further,

---

[4] For description of a prison in which enforcement of a host of detailed rules was a major custodial aim, see Cressey, "Contradictory Directives in Complex Organizations," *op. cit.;* and Chapter 5, below.

each higher step in the official hierarchy buttressed its authority with a somewhat wider sphere of movement and access to information so that each superior was, in fact, better informed and better able to define issues in conflict than his subordinate. This differential allocation of information through the official hierarchy solved the eternal paradox of control in authoritarian systems. It kept the initiative of guards within tolerable limits and hence permitted aboslute and unqualified endorsement of actions taken by guards. Only by restricting initiative (and the informational basis of initiative) in the inmate body still further, could the administration institutionalize the authority of the guards over their subjects. Control of information saps the very will to resist. It removes from the universe of discourse the premises of criticism, and gains fatalistic conformity. Inmates regarded authority in the old prison as mean, arbitrary, abusive, and unjust; but, more important, they regarded it as inevitable.

In the period prior to the administrative revolution in the old prison, the ideal structure of custodial authority had been gradually compromised. The under-manned guard force had delegated much of the task of imposing the norms of peace and order to a group of senior inmates, and it had exempted those inmates from the incidental deprivations of the prison. The incidence of escape and reported violence remained low, but a large degree of initiative had been given to inmate leaders. This initiative was symbolized in licensed freedom of movement, access to goods, and distinctions of dress. It influenced inmate transfers, job assignments, and penalities imposed within the institution. Especially in situations where administrative needs for inmate labor compromised physical security, where technical maintenance tasks required initiative on the part of inmate workers, large elements of authority fell to the inmates.

For example, the inmate electrician and hospital orderly held court in the prison yard wearing non-regulation clothing, sharing gossip and bits of pilfered food with a circle of friends, and exchanging banter with the guards. Their favored position compelled them to express attitudes of contempt for officials and to lead the condemnation of others who would win favor by ratting on their fellows. The position of such inmate leaders, men enjoying an exceptionally wide range of physical movement and ideally placed to arbitrate social conflict and guide inmate opinion, seemed to exemplify the ideal of a self-regulating inmate society independent of custodial control and fulfill the convict dream of "running the joint." For the most part, however, inmate leaders were exponents of adjustment within an order which guaranteed their own position. They gave expression and interpretation to adaptive norms which were shared by guards and inmates alike: "Do your own time and don't bring on the heat!" These are norms of adjustment to the prison world and not rebellion against it. Their internalization permitted inmate society to treasure a sense of independence and contempt for the custodians without anarchic consequences in behavior. However, the custodial processes which thus served so efficiently to restrain disorder were ripe for the charges raised later that prohibitions were violated and values compromised in the inmate community. Values that governed behavior in the system were originating in the lower reaches and being transmitted up rather than down the corrupted hierarchy of authority.[5]

Inmate Society. The prison supplied basic physical needs for food and shelter, thus eliminating industry or productivity as avenues to personal recognition and simplifying the structure of social process. The system of relationships among inmates was principally a response to the complex system of deprivations involved in custodial control. Like the hope of heaven among some groups, a desire for ultimate freedom was an orienting force in social affairs, but the main dimensions of social action emerged in relation to needs generated or exaggerated by the deprivational system. The structure of social action was governed by needs to achieve what the processes of custodial control denied: personal identity, meaning, and purpose for behavior, independence from official sanctions, space for free movement in both the physical and psychological sense, and physical symbols by which integrity could be displayed.

Officials asserted and inmates demanded, as a fundamental premise of prison life, that all inmates be treated equally; yet the basic interpersonal relationship in inmate society was dominance and subordination. This apparent inconsistency has led some analysts to suggest that the highest personal value in prison society is placed on the exercise of coercive power.[6] In the old prison, however, where custodial control was the dominant official goal, *independence* was

[5] For similar analyses, see Gresham M. Sykes, "The Corruption of Authority and Rehabilitation," *Social Forces*, 34 (March, 1956), 257–269; and Richard A. Cloward, "Social Control in the Prison," in Cloward, Cressey, Grosser, McCleery, Ohlin, Sykes and Messinger, *op. cit.*, pp. 41–48.

[6] See, for example, Lloyd McCorkle and Richard Korn, "Resocialization Within Walls," *The Annals*, 293 (May, 1954), 88–98.

the dominant personal value among inmates. The abuse of others was one means by which initiative and independence might be demonstrated, but abusiveness alone was not an avenue to status, and irresponsible abuses were regulated by informal social controls. High status was accorded inmates who exercised power, those who mediated successfully with official power or rationalized its apparently arbitrary exercise, and those who demonstrated through time a capacity to bear the most severe sanctions bravely and without breaking. The man who retained his initiative and his capacity to do his own time in the face of the most savage punishments, maintained a standing in inmate society equivalent to that of the "bull of the yard," even in periods when he was helplessly isolated in a punishment cell. New inmates were abused on admission, but this was as much a test of their courage, a formalized rite of initiation, as it was an exploitation of their helplessness.

The procedures of custodial regimentation, the atmosphere of uncertainty and suspicion created by official secrecy and the fear of "rats," and, perhaps, the social characteristics of inmates prevented all but a minimum of cohesion and integration in the inmate social system. The only approach to a unifying goal that provided a focus for the inmate community was independence from official control and deliverance from the perils of arbitrary, official action. In order to win this degree of freedom, inmates enforced conformity by sanctions more severe than those permitted the guards, and inmate society thus maintained peace and order with a minimum of official interference. The demand for equality of treatment from officials did not imply equality of status, and it was addressed to inmates rather than to officials. It was a demand that inmates refrain from seeking official intervention in the affairs of the yard so that issues in conflict could be settled by inmates alone.

As long as the inmate social system helped men adjust to the conditions of life within the walls, it supplemented official custodial goals. The old guard force was not notably restrained in its use of punitive sanctions, but there are fatal limits on the capacity of punitive sanctions alone to maintain control. No amount of naked force can substitute for peer-group formulation and enforcement of norms. The silent treatment, the signs of social disapproval, and the prolonged physical harassment by inmate gangs were sanctions which the custodial force could neither employ nor ignore. So that informal sanctions would be used in support of the goal of adjustment within the prison, custodians delegated a large share in management of internal disorder to inmate society and clothed its leaders with authority by the simple expedient of looking the other way. If such an alliance seems strange, it should be noted that the delegation of internal management to inmates has marked the administration of even the most savage, totalitarian, death camps.[7]

The social order which emerged in response to inmate needs and the deprivations of custodial control exhibited a status hierarchy closely related to seniority, although the demands of leadership were more than seniority alone could fill. Custodial practice made admission to the prison a harsh, demoralizing and depersonalizing experience, but it included no positive preparation for life in the yard. The absence of official orientation or published regulations, the secrecy and arbitrariness of discipline, the shocking unfamiliarity of prison life and the demands imposed by regimentation combined to make the new inmate helplessly dependent on experienced men. Old inmates knew the limits of official tolerance in a system which, of necessity, prohibited more than it punished, and they could share on their own terms the physical goods and adaptive myths which made prison life tolerable. This control over the rites and tests of initiation gave senior inmates the power to assign new men a subordinate status and hold them there until they accepted the norms of inmate culture.

Men just admitted, along with those homosexuals whose role symbolized abject submission to force, occupied the lowest place on the social scale. Prison society, like other authoritarian societies, treated the weak with contempt, hatred, and fear. Completing the lower classes were men whose prison jobs, attitudes, and ties with the outside world or transparent longing for freedom gave rise to fears that they might conspire with officials to betray the community of inmates. Like a primitive tribe in an environment of seemingly arbitrary power, inmate-thinking was obsessed with a devil theory which attributed every act of official force to "rats" or informers. This fear of "rats" dominated all social intercourse and led to isolation or abuse of all who had not proved their dependability under pressure. The low status and isolation of nonconformists, in turn, protected the adjustive processes and adaptive myths of inmate society from challenge or criticism.

Although men with heavy sentences for serious crimes predom-

[7] Eugen Kogon, *The Theory and Practice of Hell* (New York: Berkeley Publishing Company, 1950). See also Donald R. Cressey and Witold Krassowski, "Inmate Organization and Anomie in American Prisons and Soviet Labor Camps," *Social Problems,* 5 (Winter, 1957–58), 217–230.

inated at the top of the social ladder, even those with notorious criminal reputations started with little advantage over their fellows. Former prisoners and reform school graduates began their sentences with a greater fund of skills in adjustment than the most dangerous first-offenders. The road to "old con" status was long, and a capacity to "do time" could not be demonstrated overnight. To ascribe status on the basis of newspaper reputations, apart from the capacity to do time and adjust to prison life, would have had anarchic consequences in the stable, inmate society. Hence, the new man was admitted gradually into the mysteries of the inmate tribe as he bore its tests without violating its norms.

In time, a majority of new inmates gained at least marginal acceptance in some primary group and a degree of protection against the abuses of psychotic, aggressive isolates. Adding zest or comfort to the conditions of prison life required an element of concerted action, and small groups formed around such activities as smuggling, pilfering supplies, gambling pools, and circulation of gossip. The atmosphere of suspicion normally prevented a rational combination of such primary groups, but men who gradually earned recognition and proved their dependability in several such groups emerged as opinion leaders for the community as a whole. Their network of contacts enabled them to manage a substantial commerce in goods, manipulate cell and job transfers, mediate conflicts, and supply advance warning of official action. The customary avenues to status, the required apprenticeship, and the requirement of high standing in a primary group constrained the influence of very young and violently aggressive men; leadership roles were reserved for those with long experience in adjustment to prison life. Such senior leadership initiated the norms and definitions which structured activity in the prison yard, for inmates respected definitions made by their own leaders, definitions which they would have rejected had these taken the form of orders from guards.

The set of deprivations to which inmate society adapted was as much psychological as physical, and the needs met by the inmate social structure were largely those for rationalizations which asserted the inmates' own value and integrity, depreciated the officials, provided self-justifying accounts of events, and blamed every calamity on the "rats." Guards mocked the inmate "grapevine" for its inaccuracy, but its value lay in that very inaccuracy—in the adaptive distortions which made prison life psychologically tolerable. The elders of the inmate tribe who created satisfying myths in a vacuum of official explanation manipulated those myths to their own advantage, but they performed a vital function in stabilizing the society and hence served as a crucial adjunct to custodial control.

Stability in any social system depends on the acceptance by individuals of certain common definitions as the premises of their behavior. The ideal definition is one that is self-enforcing. Its publication is sufficient to provide for its observance, and its character is more of an announcement than a threat. "Dinner is served at eight," is a member of a class of propositions that is at the core of a system of uniformity, social order, rationally predictable behavior, and hence civilization. A problem of rule enforcement arises in connection with a different class of propositions—those that are not adequate in themselves to insure predictable compliance. Rational, deliberate, social control begins when another element is added to the definition of the situation: "The dining hall will be closed at nine." Enforcement problems become obvious when the message changes still further: "You will be at the dining hall on time or you will wish you were!" Use of punitive sanctions is a poor and rather minor means of gaining compliance with a given order, for punitive sanctions can be employed only when there is acceptance of more general assumptions about the legitimacy of punishment.[8] It begins when verbal communication fails to define the situation in a manner adequate to the demands for predictable conformity. The old prison counted its men at the mess-hall door, and the tolerable limits of nonconformity there were most narrow. Failure to appear provoked sanctions in addition to simple hunger. However, without straining the conceptual model unduly, even exemplary punishment can be considered as a part of the process of communicating definitions—"*See* what will happen to you if you don't appear on time!" Rule enforcement involves complex processes of formulation, transmission, and acceptance of norms, and the imposition of sanctions is the last resort, not the first element of that complex.

The new inmate, and often the new custodial officer, tended to misconceive the total prison social system because they saw the prison in its relation to the larger society. The convict had exhausted the patience of the larger society, and he therefore normally assumed that the prison's controls rested directly on force and physical abuse. Such assumptions, as parts of the definition of the situation, tended to fulfill themselves. By refusing to "listen to reason," the new inmate

[8] See the general discussion in Alvin W. Gouldner, *Patterns of Industrial Bureaucracy* (Glencoe: The Free Press, 1954).

was apt to seek out the limits of toleration and to provoke punitive sanctions which ordinarily were initiated by the newer guards. To avoid such anarchic consequences, the entire prison society conspired to limit the initiative of new men until they learned that force was a last resort and that norms are reinforced in prison, as elsewhere, principally by repetition, exhortation, habituation, authoritative transmission, and by myths which give coherence to diverse demands.

In sum, the old prison achieved highly-controlled patterns of behavior by limiting the communication of premises on which behavior was based. A vast majority of the definitions that kept deviant behavior within tolerable limits were communicated by senior inmates (who had no idea that they were serving custodial ends) and accepted by others on the authority of that source. Although the effective definitions were not cast in language which officials would have used, the resulting behavior was no less subject to prediction and control. Some judicious use of force by inmate society often avoided the necessity of official action, but the peace and order of the prison community was maintained with a surprisingly minimal use of punitive sanctions by either inmates or officials.

THE ADMINISTRATIVE REVOLUTION

The administrative revolution in the old prison was initiated in 1946 on the death of the old Warden and his replacement with a man of limited penal experience and no background in maximum security institutions. There were no corresponding changes in the higher ranks of the Department of Institutions, and there is little evidence to suggest that the consequences which followed were related to conscious change in major policy commitments there. As we indicated earlier, the bases of the revolution were the new attitudes and behavioral patterns injected into the institution by the new warden and a few equally inexperienced appointees who acted without any deliberate intent to subvert custodial control. Except as it introduced attitudes, habits, and interpersonal relations familiar in the free community, it began as a revolution without a theory.

The first kind of change was directed toward reestablishing and reaffirming the official custodial norms of the traditional institution. Because of his "open door" policies and easy accessibility to all within the institution, and because of his need for and willingness to hear advice from all quarters, the new warden soon became aware of the corruptions of authority that characterized the custodial system. Information on tolerated abuses, commerce with the inmates, and the dispensation of privileges multiplied until the warden called in outside investigators (a move that was necessary because the "old guard" controlled formal communication channels) and dismissed a number of the guards. At about the same time, the warden's newly appointed deputy refused to endorse custodial punishment orders pro forma and established a disciplinary committee to examine complaints against inmates. The disciplinary committee, manned in part by treatment officials, began to apply a concept of "justice" rather than the concept of exemplary punishment to the cases before it. These two developments began to remove arbitrariness and the ability to manipulate incentives and sanctions from the arsenal of custodial control devices. They were followed by a significant rise in disciplinary problems.

The second kind of change involved a significant reconstruction and enlargement of official communication patterns. Two new staff members were appointed to reinstitute the largely defunct rehabilitation program, and they came to their position without the customary, long-term indoctrination in custodial values. Immediately sensitive to the absence of records which would permit classification or treatment on the basis of inmate needs, they sponsored an enlargement of the records, established direct channels of communication with work supervisors, and accumulated a body of information in their own hands. Armed with the newly gained data, the treatment officials were able to claim a place in the making of many decisions. They instituted a committee system of decision-making which modified the once uncompromised claims of custodial security.

The reconstruction of communication patterns had even more significant consequences for inmate society. The treatment function required open communication and interaction patterns with inmates. Although guards attempted to suppress inmate requests and applications which they regarded as improper, it was no longer possible for them to completely block the transmission of definitions up and down the official hierarchy, and it was soon clear to the inmates that inconsistent conceptions of propriety existed within the official staff. There were cracks in the once solid front of officialdom, and opportunities for expression became available to an element of inmate society that had been silenced by the nature of the old order. As treatment officials began to assert a voice in a wide variety of institutional decisions and to sponsor a variety of activities in the yard, new and relatively unincumbered channels of influence on decision-makers were opened to the inmates. Treatment officials operated within the prison yard itself and in face-to-face, informal contacts. The traditional inmate prohibition against talking to the "screws" hardly seemed to apply in such situations, and it was honored only by the old-inmate elite. The "outcast" element of inmate society was the first to exploit the new avenues to influence.

The third and final kind of change was incorporation of the patterns outlined above in the formal structure of the agency and legitimation of them in a manual of administrative policy and philosophy. Unlike the custodial force whose own disciplined and militant tradition barred it from considerations of high-level policy, the newly-appointed treatment and industrial heads took advantage of the availability of the warden to raise policy questions, and joined themselves in an informal policy council. By 1949, two treatment officials and the heads of the industrial and maintenance programs were members of a regular staff conference which exercised significant powers in the formulation of prison policy. The custodial force, always the largest numerical element of the staff by far, had only an ineffective, minority representation on the committee.

There was little difference between the formal statement of policy in the traditional prison and the descriptive "wake them—work them—and lock them up" of the guards. An authoritarian system is necessarily weak in operational ideology because it must resolve issues by an appeal to the superior official rather than by appeal to principle. However, the new policy committee set out to define the policy of the institution in a Manual which asserted "rehabilitation through treatment and constructive industry" (note the alliance of organizational units) as the primary institutional purpose. It stated that the democratic approach to the management of men was the soundest, and it contained commitments to:

> The delegation to lower management levels of all possible responsibility and authority commensurate with sound management. A practice of constant consultation, dissemination of information, and discussion of problems up and down the management chain.

Such concepts were directly inconsistent with authoritarian hierarchy and control. Unable to communicate effectively in the new policy forum, suspicious and on the defensive, the guard force withdrew from the area of general policy and fell back on its control over the operations, communications, and society of the prison yard. It was not until late in 1950, when principles and theory became conscious and the guards were faced with specific changes inconsistent with traditional values, that evident conflict came to mark relationships between elements of the staff and to promise disorders in the inmate community. Inconsistent definitions of the situation had been established, and control turned on the issue of which definition was to be accepted as the premises of behavior. Guards saw inmate access to the decision-makers as more direct than their own, and, operating on their own quite explicit communication theory of power, rejected the new definition as inmate inspired.

In 1950 and 1951, the treatment staff was engaged in developing an educational program and in expanding the areas of constructive activity available to the inmates. The addition of new activities did not impinge immediately on the social structure of the inmate community, and its existing leadership was able to claim credit for the sunshine. Even an inmate council, established with unusually broad responsibilities and direct access to the warden on policy matters, did not at first disturb the social order of the prison community, for old inmate leaders gained election to a majority of its seats. This extension of privileges, for each new chance for activity and self-expression was a privilege in the prison, produced an atmosphere of good feeling and relaxation in the community and the lowest rate of internal disorder in its recent history. That condition was short lived, however, for it led to the stage, familiar in the government of any suppressed population, in which the granting of one privilege leads to redoubled demands.

Analysis of this "multiplying ingratitude" reveals its internal dynamics. The power structure of the inmate community reflected an adaptation to the old, custodial regime. Leaders were men equipped to function within custodial limits. Although they dominated some of the newly-permitted activities, they lacked either the talent or the inclination to monopolize all or the most constructive of these. Accordingly, other elements of the inmate body, often from its lowest caste, sought access to these activities, caused the old cons to withdraw in disgust, and reaped both status and privileges from participation in the programs sponsored by treatment personnel. As these outcasts gained a hearing in their society, old leaders found it necessary to seek additional prestige symbols to sustain their relative status, the alternative being abdication of traditional functions. The guards supported the old cons by harassing treatment-oriented inmates who got "out of their place" and by entering into a competition with treatment for the power to distribute incentives. Such competition could not continue without creating the "country club" which some guards foresaw.

When the custodial force administered all activities, such matters as inmate recreation, letter writing, job assignment, promotion in grade, movement within the walls, and craft shop privileges were manipulated as incentives to conformity and as measures to insure the stability of inmate society. Treatment officials, acting on the basis of their records of individuals and attempting to concentrate all incentives in support of their own goals, invaded these areas of operational decision without being aware of their past significance. The majority of incentives were concentrated behind treatment objectives, and the custodial force and senior inmates then had little but habit and the threat of force left for insuring orderliness and their own prestige. The values of peace and order dissipated in a rising wave of violence, disorder, and anarchy within the institution. Senior custodial officers, honestly outraged at the administrative revolution they were no longer able to resist or contain, entered into alliance with inmates and groups outside the prison to discredit the administration.

When the contest reached the level of a legislative investigation, in 1953, the old custodial officers had retreated to defending an archaic penal philosophy by questionable methods. The full weight of progressive, professional, penal theory was on the side of the administration, and the protests of the "old guard" were repudiated with little regard for the considerable evidence on which they were based—inmate disorder and rising recidivism. Several events worked together to reduce the tensions which followed: the resignation of several defeated, old custodians, the recruitment and special training of several new guards who were additions to the custodial force, the transfer of several inmates to other prisons, and an enhanced appreciation of the custodial position, despite its defeat by the administration. Of major significance among these factors, however, was the legislature's endorsement to interested inmates of what was essentially the treatment personnel's position in the conflict of definitions.

SOCIAL DISORGANIZATION

The dependent variables in this study of administrative change were the structure, degree of integration, discipline, and pattern of adaptive behaviors of inmate society. Examination of such variables involves one in an extremely complex set of interrelationships through which elements of the inmate community play a part in the communication of premises of behavior. An illustration of the complexity is provided by one instance of inmate reaction to the first stages of administrative change. Emergence of identifiable standards in discipline and the practice of making treatment officials available to all inmates tended to reduce the dependence of new men on old inmates. Increased violence during this period suggests that positions previously justified by the functions they performed were being challenged and defended by force. However, in a pattern which has been repeated through the years, the old inmates utilized new means to communicate their own position and the values on which it was based. The warden supported freedom of expression and encouraged it in the inmates' magazine. One of the old inmates used this vehicle to contradict the new philosophy and the accent on cooperation which challenged the traditional dominance of his group:

> Apropos to many "speeches" we've heard for the benefit of the new man who may wish to fit in easily and smoothly, we call attention to the fact that each man should "do his own time." By that we mean—attend to your own business, keep your affairs from men who are by necessity forced to live with you. Keep your ideas and suggestions to yourself—as no thinking-man cares to become involved in any of them. Voice your opinions only when you are asked, and be careful then.[9]

An atmosphere of fairness and freedom of expression was quickly seen as a threat to the inmate social order and attacked by the very means which the administration provided to achieve its own goals.

Social Structure at Midpoint.   In 1951 when the inmate council was initiated in the yard, several diverse elements were emerging within the inmate community. Inmate society was still dominated by senior inmates who had served under one or more previous administrations, who had expressed skepticism of the treatment program and preference for the old days, and who had provided guidance, orientation, and interpretation for the majority of inmates. Under the influence of this group were less experienced recidivists and the more criminalistic of the older first offenders. At the third level of this traditional hierarchy were the majority of young, first-offenders, attracted by the successful adjustment and "wise" attitude of their elders. This element was more distinct than had been the case in the

[9] Editorial, *Paahao Press* (March, 1948), p. 2.

past, however, and less dependent on the advice or subject to the exploitation of the older groups. It had come to have a certain focus and identity of its own in the recreational activities of the prison, and, while not committed to formal, rehabilitative programs, it was not averse to enjoying such as were pleasant.

Another and more distinctive element of the population consisted of reform-school graduates. In the old prison, such young men immediately fell under the domination of senior leaders and willingly accepted a place in one of the power groups of the community. There was no identifiable reform school group. These young men saw prison society as tough and masculine—values which they had come to prize most highly in their reform school backgrounds. By 1950, midpoint in the period of transition, the reform school element had repudiated the leadership of prison society and embarked on a course which the guards defined as calculated to "make it tough on themselves." A decline in the capacity of senior inmates to manipulate power and its symbols had cost them the allegiance of the reform school group. Implicit also in the revolt of the younger men and the emergence of an organization incorporating their own values was a decline in the "toughness" of the prison society as a whole.

Another distinctive change in inmate society was the emergence of an identifiable group, consisting mainly of middle-aged, first-offenders, oriented to the treatment and industrial activities of the institution. With the gradual extension of treatment unit activities into a number of areas of operating decision and the concurrent dispersion of energy of treatment officials, increasing responsibilities and opportunities for manipulation of privileges fell into the hands of inmates associated with the unit. The enlarged sphere of activity under the sponsorship of the treatment unit had created a new community of interest and the core of a functional leadership of its own. Formalization of disciplinary procedures had done much to abolish the myth that undesirable official actions were prompted by reports from "rats," and the resultant decline in hostility permitted the elevation of administration-oriented men from outcast status. The middle-aged group of first-offenders had gained a standing in the society which permitted it to attract to its association other prisoners who were not dramatically inclined toward crime. It had gained an audience for the substantial body of information and definition which its contact with treatment officials enabled it to communicate.

It was establishing the inmate council as an activity conducted in the prison yard which finally gave the group of treatment-oriented inmates its channel of communication to the population as a whole. Prior to that time, there may have been other elements of the community with something to say and a potential audience to hear them, but senior inmates and guards had monopolized effective channels of communication. The idea of inmate-staff cooperation as legitimate behavior and as a means of earning status had been expressed before by both inmates and staff, but only with the conduct of council meetings in the yard itself was that idea provided with a forum in which it could be transmitted with effect. Some measure of its effectiveness is indicated by the fact that the number of assaults reported in the population reached the highest level in a decade during the first month of the council's establishment, although the rate of disciplinary infractions and major offenses for the year had been relatively low.

Moral Disorganization. While the social and economic aspects of disorganization are subject to more direct empirical measurement, moral disorganization remains an inseparable part of the complex and interrelated process. The concepts or definitions which establish the range of alternatives for behavior must be measured indirectly by testimony or implied from the behaviors themselves, but they cannot be ignored in research. Because the integrating concepts which constitute the moral basis of the inmate community differ from those of the penologist, they tend to be ignored or attacked. Because the inmate code is no more descriptive of actual behavior than are the ten commandments in the "good" society, the penal official tends to dismiss the significance of the code. However, the function of a code is not to describe behavior; its function is to provide a norm by which consensus assigns status or applies sanctions to the behavior of others. The consequence of demoralization in a community—whatever its mores may be—is to remove the consensual basis on which status is ascribed and to deteriorate the status positions which serve to communicate premises of behavior for the whole.

Any attrition of the ideal that the good convict never "talks to a screw" tends to remove a vital conceptual basis for social hierarchy in inmate society. Any communication of the rehabilitative ideal constitutes an attack on the status of the old, prison-adjusted convict as the model man. The circulation of the idea of cooperation as an avenue to success undercuts the concept that the good man is the man who "does his own time." The operation of the inmate council and the activities of treatment officials in the prison yard thus involved communication of disintegrating definitions as premises of inmate behavior. The authority of those inmates who had monopolized communication and held high status was threatened as much by the new process of communication as by its content. As the theoretical revolution became a behavioral, procedural revolution, it went to the foundations of authority and consent in all the interpersonal relationships in the institution. The first loss was the ability of the inmate community to govern itself—to resolve issues in conflict—through its own leaders. The collapse of that large part of the total system of social control which had rested within inmate society is reflected in the sharp increase in the work load of the official disciplinary committee.

The first part of the dramatic increase in disciplinary infractions which marks the record of 1952 and 1953 did not represent inmate rebellion against the officials or the institution. It represents official adjustment of conflicts among inmates which could no longer be accommodated informally. The capacity to resolve interpersonal conflicts is the first and most fundamental function of any government, and a failure to perform that function discredits government and the governors in any social system. Although older guards tried to resolve as many conflicts as possible in the cell block rather than in the disciplinary committee, and became the most effective advocates of the old order in the process, the social and conceptual basis of functional, inmate self-government atrophied from the very hour the formal apparatus of the inmate council appeared. By the ordinary standards of prison administration, the inmate council exercised an exceptional amount of delegated discretion and responsibility in a wide range of activities, but its powers could not substitute for the judicial functions of the old inmate society as an instrument of social control. As the authority of the old inmate leaders narrowed to their immediate circle of associates, the inmate body ceased to be a community in any meaningful sense of that term and became a set of conflicting factions confined by all too narrow walls.

Social Disintegration. A description of the factions within the prison by 1953 cannot imply a commonly-perceived order of status. Force had replaced shared definitions as the arbiter of conflict. The disciplinary record, showing the increasing frequency and intensity of official sanctions applied, indicates that force was necessarily being met with force. The origin of violence was in the inmate body, largely in the group of young, reform-school graduates for whom violence was a positive virtue. In retrospect, both inmates and officials were convinced that there was a large increase in the number of reform school graduates in the population, but that common impression is contradicted by the record. The impact of the reform-school group on the prison lies in the fact that this element, which earlier had been subordinated within a structure of inmate society, was quite out of control. Although other groups were emerging, the common background and attitudes of the reform-school group gave it a cohesiveness all out of proportion to its size. This group turned for its leadership (and established as its heroes) to two types of men whose status had been restricted by the traditional structure of the prison community: the most powerful and aggressive of older inmates, and new inmates who reached the prison with newspaper reputations for violent criminality. Those men, now cast in leadership roles, competed to oblige the expectations of their followers with aggression against the administration, as well as against other elements of inmate society. The second phase of the increase in disciplinary cases reflects a wave of escapes and other aspects of rebellion against the institution.

The old inmate leaders retained a narrow circle of influence, strengthened by their increasingly overt alliance with custodial officers and an ability to provide some support for their adherents against the depredations of the younger group. As custodians of the myth of the "good old days," they served to slow down the pace of transition and minimize the social impact of new activities wherever possible. Unlike any other element of the population, they were moved by a sense that the prison was their home and by a sincere concern for the consequences of disorder. Although they shared with the guard force a conviction that treatment officials and the rehabilitative programs were underlying causes of anarchy, they worked to contain the rebellious activities of the younger group and came to tolerate the expanding circle of men oriented to the treatment program.

The group that centered around treatment activities was heterogeneous in character and age. Some were drawn by the opportunity to enjoy or manipulate privileges, some by a desire to withdraw from the tensions of the yard and some were moved by a sincere devotion to the rehabilitative ideal. In the course of time it became increasingly apparent that administrative influence was shifting to the hands of the treatment staff—that its definitions were being accepted as the premises of administrative decision. Access, or the appearance of access, to these influential officials enhanced the status of inmates employed in the treatment program, and the institutional structure of the inmate council and its committees provided a focus for the activities of the treatment-oriented group. Official support of treatment programs and the council was indistinguishable in effect from support for that group among other factions of the inmate body. Leaders of the treatment-oriented group assumed the status of "politicians" rather than the standing of outcast or isolate which they occupied in an earlier period.

In addition to these three principal elements, other social groups of inmates formed around industrial activities or as defensive alliances against the hazards of yard life. The aggressions of the younger group and a decline in the type of insecurities once reflected in the "rat" concept reduced the number of entirely unaffiliated men in the society. However, the three groups had the significant influence in inmate society, and each group represented a different conceptual basis of authority. For the young group, the basis was force. For the old cons, the basis was rank or status ascribed in terms of adjustment within the prison. For the treatment-oriented group, the basis was a concept borrowed from the treatment staff, the authority of function. Treatment officials had disrupted the conventional administrative hierarchy of rank by claiming authority on the basis of functions they performed, and the same diversified structure of influence characterized the inmate group that formed around the treatment program.

The treatment-oriented and old con groups both had a certain amount of official sanction and an institutional base of activity. The reform-school gangs and their adherents had neither of these resources, and their bid for power had a surprising degree of coherence under the circumstances. The young men conceived of themselves as a "syndicate" and took that label proudly as a badge of criminal sophistication. Their organization and its tactics bear a strong resemblance to a fascist movement, and the syndicate as a social force combined elements of idealism with instruments of violence.[10] A concentrated

---

[10] The idea of the prison as a laboratory for the study of general principles of social organization is strikingly reinforced by the ideological character of the syndicate as a totalitarian movement. Alexander Leighton formulates the principle which applies here from his study of a war-time relocation center: "Out of the confusion of a community under stress there is likely to arise a single radical system of belief which may or may not bring a stability, but which will bring to a large section of the population a sense of at least temporary relief from stress." *The Governing of Men* (Princeton: Princeton University Press, 1945), 310. For a theoretical conception of wide generality and precise application here, see William Kornhauser, *The Politics of Mass Society* (Glencoe: The Free Press, 1959), Part II, "Social Sources of Mass Movements."

campaign of argument and intimidation was directed toward capturing the inmate council and the inmate craft shop which had been placed under council management. The production of craft articles for public sale was the core of economic life in the inmate society, and control of the craft shop had once been a prized prerogative of senior inmate leaders. The move of the syndicate to take over the craft shop involved elements of simple exploitation, the grasp for a status symbol, and an aspect of economic reform. In 1953, the young group won a majority of seats on the council and placed its own man as inmate, craft-shop supervisor. This success is one measure of the disorganization of the traditional inmate community. As another measure, the same year saw 57 attacks and assaults reported on the formal disciplinary record, 13 escapes, and a total of 148 major violations of prison rules, or a 400 percent increase in major disciplinary infractions over a base period prior to administrative change. These statistics do not reflect the numerous conflicts, unresolved by either official or informal adjudication, which added to increasing tension within the prison.

Economic Disorganization. The combining of economic disorganization with social and moral disintegration in inmate society emerges from a study of the society's economic records. The personal cash accounts of inmates, kept by the business office of the institution, provides an index of the economic life of the community. Prior to 1949, the craft shop was located outside the main prison enclosure and access to it was granted to only a few senior inmates. Those men, in turn, put out tasks of finishing craft products to other members of the inmate body at rates which exploited cheap and available labor. In 1948 and 1949, which may be taken as normal years for the traditional inmate society, the total amount of cash in 375 inmate accounts was $11,500 or an average of about $30 per account. The concentration of economic control is indicated by four accounts which stood at over $1,000, but wealth was rather widely distributed in spite of the monopolistic economic and social structure.

In 1950 the craft shop was closed and economic opportunities were withdrawn from the privileged few who had enjoyed access to it. Although a relatively small amount of the total inmate enterprise had been conducted in that shop, the wealth of the community dropped to $4,300 in 300 accounts, an average of approximately $14.00 per account. At the end of 1951, the shop was reestablished within the walls under the supervision of the inmate council, and the economic depression was partially reversed. The balance of inmate accounts rose by the end of 1952 to $9,800, the number of accounts rose to 325, and the average account again stood at the "normal" level of $30. Responsible management by early inmate councils had equalized craft shop opportunities, limited exploitation and established a loan fund by which new inmates could begin their work. This was the economic aspect of inmate life which the syndicate set out to control and promised to manage more effectively. The period of syndicate domination was brief but its impact was dramatic. Records of inmate income in 1953 indicate an $8,000 increase in receipts, but the cash balance at year's end had fallen to $5,700, the number of accounts to 300, and the average account to $19.00. Indications are that the syndicate leadership had turned a handsome profit for itself and had brought the inmate society close to economic collapse as well as anarchy.

The syndicate's following dropped away as rapidly as it had emerged. Some of its own more responsible membership repudiated the movement and fragmented the original group. Under syndicate domination, the inmate council lost almost all of the respect that it had gained earlier, and the leader of the young men resigned his chairmanship. As the leadership of the young group began to wither away under the contempt of the general inmate population and the sanctions of the disciplinary committee, its radical following became even more aggressive and uncontrolled in its rebellious behavior. Groups within the yard organized for outright gang warfare, and forewarnings of a planned riot led the administration to mount machine guns on the cell block roof at one crucial moment of rising tension. These were the conditions in which the disgruntled element of old guards carried its complaints against the administration to a legislative hearing; the complaints were rejected.

To summarize the process of disorganization, a number of administrative changes had combined to undermine the structure by which a common definition of the situation was transmitted, reducing prison society to a set of conflicting factions. The nature of bureaucratic society tends to perpetuate the fiction that all behavior is the result of will or intention. Inmates with their "rat" concept and officials with their endless orders agree that events occur because they are willed. That tendency leads to a disposition on all levels of the prison community to see misadventures as evidence of conspiracy and to fix blame on persons for every unfortunate situation. The hostilities that multiplied in inmate society had their counterparts in the attitudes of officials. Analysis suggests, however, that the chain of consequences, once started for the best of motives, continues of its own momentum. Resort to force had little impact against the waves of anarchy. Increased official sanctions against misbehavior did not reverse the trend, and the intensification of security measures with the enlargement of the guard force had little identifiable impact. When the internal functions of social control once performed within inmate society were abdicated to official processes, force did not serve to insure their performance. By the same token, the attempt of the syndicate to reestablish social control within inmate society on the principle of force only compounded the problem. The evidence suggests that force is not really a principle of human organization at all but, rather, an instrument by which some commonly shared principle may be sustained.

RECONSTRUCTION

Anarchy is its own best answer, and the tensions generated by anomie can make even the prison inmate and his keeper into "political animals." The core of politics is compromise, and the prison was pregnant with the spirit of compromise by the end of 1953. In inmate society, the need for some type of integrating idea, which had been manifest in the acceptance given to the radical ideals of the syndicate, increased in strength. Old inmate leaders and the treatment-oriented group joined in a search for some basis of order. In the hour of their public defeat, the old-guard officers gained a more generous hearing from the staff than they had received in years. Two death-row heroes, ex-leaders of the syndicate, made declarations in support of the warden and his administrative philosophy to the legislative hearing. The warden, in turn, held a series of open meetings with the entire inmate body, speaking directly to problems raised by the men and eloquently restating his liberal penal philosophy. The resignation of some of the extremists in the custodial force further opened the channels of communication and eased the path to compromise.

The legislative inquiry served as a vital step in the process of reconstruction. Discussion there reduced some issues from the level of philosophical generalization and raised others from the context of petty, divisional bickering to which they had fallen. In the debate on institutional management the issue was not one of theoretical conflict between rehabilitative and custodial aims but of the practical necessity of integrating both functions within the institution. The custodial theory that treatment officials were illegitimately turning the institution over to the inmates was aired and rejected. The notion that the guard force constituted a conspiracy to block "progress" was also exploded. The principle which emerged was that each institutional unit exercised a legitimate authority which rested on and was bounded by the function it performed.

The pluralistic principle of authority, although inconsistent with the structure of authority in the traditional institution, was not new to top officials. For them, it was the reaffirmation of concepts which had been submerged in the conflict of unit loyalties and divisional responsibilities. However, clear formulation of the principle was new to inmate society, an attentive audience for newspaper reports of the hearings. The social processes by which inmate society formulated and transmitted its own orienting definitions had dissolved while the needs for orientation had increased, creating a condition in which the legislative pronouncements served an important social function. While the issues in the legislative hearing remained in doubt, tension was high. Legislative endorsement of the administrative position and the rehabilitative theory was followed by a significant decline in tension and disorder.

Communication of new orienting concepts did not stop with legislative announcements and newspaper circulation within the walls. The warden instituted a series of Warden's Nights, formal meetings with the entire inmate body. In prison management, there is no official substitute for pronouncements by the warden, for such pronouncements are perceived as transcending the narrow perspective and interests of particular administrative units. In the most dramatic of his meetings with the men, the warden came to the platform equipped with the verbatim questions and complaints of men in the cell block, and he announced these in the precise inflections of yard argot. (He had been coached for that role by two, tough, long-term convicts who conspired in this effort to restore order.) The warden's direct and eloquent answers to those issues are credited by inmates and staff alike with breaking the back of institutional tension. The crucial issue for analysis lies in the fact that, with that dramatic performance, the warden assumed precisely the definitional role in resolving conflict once performed by inmate leadership in the yard.

A third element in the restoration of orienting concepts was an inmate-written newspaper, established as a means of internal communication. This paper had none of the functions and none of the restrictions which had characterized the public-relations oriented, inmate magazine of old. It assumed the practical functions of distributing news and interpretation, which had been the province of senior inmates. Its circulation removed insecurities and uncertainties which had prevailed in the absence of any generally respected voice in the community, and its biases reflected an acceptable distortion of the values which prevailed in the treatment office where it was published. Guards, industrial supervisors, the reform-school gang, and even treatment officials took frequent exception to the content of the paper, but they read it and were exposed to the concepts it reflected.

On these foundations, a new pattern of order began to emerge. Escape, assault, and major infractions declined sharply. The incidence of minor infractions dealt with by the disciplinary committee remained high, however, suggesting some general acceptance of the committee as a means for resolving issues in the community. Voluntary attendance in classes and rehabilitative activities increased, enlarging the opportunities for official communication to inmate society and indicating inmate acceptance of such communication. Indices of economic activity returned to normal and above. Instances of inmates volunteering for extra work assignments, a novelty produced by the early era of good feeling and creation of the inmate council, became more frequent. Yet reduction of conflict in inmate society, indicated by the decline of violence and the capacity of diverse individuals to work together in economic activity, was not matched by a return to the rigid structure and homogeneous value pattern of the traditional community. The new structure indicated pluralistic organization of functional groups, increased tolerance for diverse patterns of individual behavior, and substantially less ostracism or abuse as pressures for conformity. The functions once performed by an elite had been institutionalized in a more open social structure.

The new order of inmate society is potentially more explosive than the old. There has been an instance in recent times of inmates attempting to dynamite the room in which the staff conference was held. The potential instability of the new social order rests in large part on the increased range of initiative allowed to the inmates, an initiative essential to the operation of rehabilitative programs. The dangers of this situation, still evident to the custodial force, may be outweighed by inmate creativity and increased industrial production. The energy and imagination of officials, never sufficient to the tasks which face prison management, are supplemented by a substantial input of inmate effort and initiative in the new order. It should not be implied that all elements of the inmate population fall within the new order of its society. The youngest and more aggressive members refuse to listen to reason or to conform to officially formulated norms. Other elements of the inmate population gained enough cohesion and stability by 1954, however, to resist the aggressions of the younger group and add the force of informal constraints to the weight of official sanctions in the contest with young rebels. During 1954 and 1955, the end of the decade of change, it was apparent that a system of informal social controls was emerging to supplement official control within the prison. With the combination of those two elements, it was possible to say that the situation was under control again. Indeed, the luxury of security and good morale suggested the prospect of a new cycle of conflict among elements within the prison community.*

ANALYSIS

Examination of administrative and social change has been guided by and has tended to support the broad and commonplace propositions advanced at the start of this chapter. On one hand, this validates the idea that the prison can be used as a laboratory for examination of general propositions in a theory of social control. On the other hand, it endorses the notion that general concepts can be applied to problems of prison management. There is little place for a special theory of penal administration as such, and a significant number of problems in prison administration grow from the failure to treat the prison as a social and political community.

A fundamental principle that seems to guide much penal administration, and which is generally confirmed by our study, is the notion that any significant change is dangerous and disorganizing. It must be agreed that the structure of interpersonal relationships and communication in any society imposes limits on the amount and type of

* Editor's note: In late summer 1960, about six months after this chapter was written, Oahu prison witnessed a most destructive riot, complete with arson, hand-to-hand fighting, and the National Guard. Professor McCleery went to Honolulu to make a follow-up analysis, but prior to the riot the Prison System had been shifted into a Department of Social Services, and the new Director of this Department denied McCleery access to the institution.

change that can be accommodated without violence. Prison government, no less than any other, rests essentially on a basis of compliance and consent—on what has been called the authority of the situation or the acceptance of definitions of the situation which legitimize a system of controls. Change which transcends boundaries of legitimacy institutionalized in the process of social definition generates violence which normally serves to reinforce the status quo. Failure to recognize the function of inmate society in the circulation of adjustive definitions, or the force of those social controls which operate within it, leaves the limits of institutional change extremely narrow. On the other hand, recognition of those variables in compliance might enlarge the limits of orderly change to a substantial degree.

A common attitude on the part of custodial officers and a constant annoyance to staff members of a rehabilitative persuasion is the declaration of the guard, "We don't have to explain what we do to inmates." Descriptively, this is quite true. Inmate society has its own explanations which would make custodial efforts superfluous. However, if institutional change is to proceed on the basis of new orienting concepts, the function of formulating and communicating those concepts has to be assumed by the staff and, more difficult, that element of the community which has performed the function before must be superceded or convinced. Either alternative is difficult. The inmate elite is not easy to convince, and its institutional alliances are normally with the traditional hierarchy of official power in the custodial ranks. Yet if the elite is to be superceded as a source of definition, the staff must be prepared to assume the tasks of social control previously borne by it.

The limits of administrative change are usually narrowed by the inability of prison officers to recognize the substantial part of the total system of social control which lies within the structure of inmate society. The myth of authority, *will*, which dominates any militant bureaucracy and makes "morale" such a mystery to officials, generates misconceptions about what can be accomplished by orders. The same myth of authority leads to the interpretation of all disorder as malicious, to a conspiracy theory of failure, and to the assumption that, behind all trouble, there is a "trouble maker." This habit of thought accounts for much of the high level of psychological tension and interpersonal hostility which normally accompanies administrative change. It disposes individuals at all levels of the social system to an immediate but ineffective resort to punitive sanctions. It usually re-

inforces the definition of the situation implicit in a given structure
of social relationships and consigns efforts at administrative change
to insignificance. When change has gone so far as to fragment the
conventional structure of social relationships, however, force becomes
an instrument of anarchy. After inmate society had been disorganized
in the present case, there is no evidence that increased official use of
force served any more practical purpose than inmate violence in restoration of order.

To review the evidence in terms of the propositions advanced, the
prison in both its stable periods must be regarded as a single community with relatively continuous patterns of interaction and communication. Despite the fact that the prison *seemed* to contain two distinct
societies in its traditional period, integration of its inmate elite with
the custodial hierarchy and their sharing of common functions and
attitudes is clear. Instability began with the circulation of an inconsistent definition by treatment officials and with removal from custodial
control of means by which its definition was reinforced. In the period
of maximum conflict and disorganization among inmates, the major
conflicting factions corresponded to major factions in the administration. A maximum of conflict and tension followed the failure of any
element in inmate society to achieve a status from which it could
define the situation for the whole, and the reduction of conflict
followed when the warden assumed the function of providing the
needed definition.

The equation of authority and the communication of a common
definition is supported by the location of rebellion in both inmate and
official ranks. That element of the guard force which was isolated by
its own disciplined traditions from the more open communication
patterns of the new administration served as a center of resistance to
change. The problem of transmitting and reinforcing new concepts
to the guard force, in the absence of applicable sanctions, constituted
one of the most serious limits on administrative change. The only
problem of equivalent weight was that of communicating to the young
reform-school graduates. These young men were subordinated and
substantially controlled at a time when their values were affirmed by
the traditional inmate culture, and they remain more sensitive to
peer-group enforcement and informal social norms than to official
sanctions. Their potential for disorder gives them a veto on further
liberal amendments in the institutional order.

Differences between the institutional structures of leadership and of domination mark out the line on which the conflict between re-habilitative and custodial elements was fought. The rehabilitative institution must permit a degree of initiative to its inmates that the purely custodial institution denies, and it is this fact that brings treatment officials into conflict with custody in a thousand details. Where domination constrains the initiative of subjects, leadership involves supplying the subjects with a body of information on which initiative can be rationally based and constructively directed. But a rehabilitative program which subverts the system of domination tends to stop short, in conflict with custodial interests, of providing sufficient information and a system of active leadership in its place. This failure generates the conditions of anarchy. Active leadership in the formulation and communication of premises for behavior avoided anarchy at one point in the institution studied. The question remains whether or not the enlarged patterns of institutional communication can serve to maintain an acceptable reconstruction of the social order in the future. An under-staffed guard force in early days abdicated a large part of its authority to an inmate elite. The future will tell whether or not the understaffed treatment office will sustain its authority or abdicate it to an inmate group. The warden's meetings with the inmates were suspended at the end of the crisis, but the inmate-written newspaper continues.

The institutionalization of rationality by formalizing the premises of action in specialized areas of behavior is an inevitable characteristic of bureaucracy. It serves to extract the maximum of predictable performance from limited human resources and constitutes the only efficient way to accomplish complex and difficult social tasks. Yet bureaucracy has notable limitations as a device for the governing of men. The institutionalization of rationality in a system can only to a limited degree substitute for the internalization of rationality in individuals. At some point, specialization becomes narrowness of perspective, and predictability becomes inflexibility. The capacity to change and accommodate to new conditions is lost, and any change in the premises of decision becomes the basis of conflict.

The guard whose institutional purpose is to shoot escaping inmates will come to define inmates as people who should be shot. An agency unit with the special task of balancing the books will elevate that task into a cosmic philosophy and an ultimate purpose. A disposition of men to find meaning and purpose in what they do leads the bureaucrat to elevate specialized means into absolute ends. This disposition and the conflict it generates among administrative units constitutes another significant limit to institutional change. Treatment, custodial and industrial units of a prison staff stand jealous guard on the premises of their own behavior and the means of their communication. They contest every implication of change, and those discontinuities between official units correspond to potentially conflicting fragments of inmate society which take their own orienting definitions of the situation from the units in which they work. It is this fragmentation of the social system in a complex, multi-purpose institution that poses the most difficult problem for executive leadership. Perhaps the easiest and most natural course of action is to elevate the purpose of one conflicting administrative unit as the dominant purpose of the institution and subordinate other ends. This conforms to the administrative principle of hierarchy and simplifies the problems of social control.

It is easy to read the conflicts between specialized administrative units as an inconsistency of institutional goals, an insoluble problem of contradictory purposes. It is vastly more difficult to define treatment, custody and industry as equally legitimate, alternative means to the end of protecting society and correcting the individual. The challenge to the executive in the progressive institution is one of formulating and communicating for the entire community a definition which transcends narrow divisional lines and perspectives. By assuming the burden of imposing his own definition of the situation, the executive avoids the impact of radical alternatives emerging from below and retains in official hands the keys of social control. The limits of administrative change are narrow, but they can be enlarged by an awareness of the nature of authority and the functions of communication in social control.

5

GEORGE H. WEBER

| | | | | | | | | |

Emotional and Defensive Reactions of Cottage Parents[1]

The major purpose of this chapter is to call attention to and document the emotional and defensive reactions of cottage parents to the behavior of delinquents and to the process of change in an institutional treatment program. This aspect of the treatment of delinquent children in institutions has been overlooked and neglected. The reasons for this neglect are not clear but several factors seem to be involved: (1) the general lag in studying correctional institutions, particularly in studying the personnel involved in the treatment aspects

[1] At the time of Dr. Ralph Coltharp's death in 1951, he and the writer were revising a paper entitled "Emotional Reactions of People Working with Disturbed Children," which they had presented at a meeting of the Midcontinent Psychiatric Association in Kansas City, Missouri, in 1950. The present paper is a revision and enlargement of this earlier paper. Its material is taken from two sources: (1) those aspects of the original paper which pertained to the emotional and defensive reactions of the cottage parents to the behavior of the delinquents, as well as to certain impacts of the changing institution on the cottage parents, and (2) the notes of Dr. Coltharp and the writer about a) their conversations and interviews with cottage parents, and their observations of them and b) their observations of a training school's changing organization. These notes were recorded over a period of approximately two and one-half years, and they varied from detailed descriptions to brief notations. Some cottage parents were studied carefully over the entire time of the project; others were observed less intensively over shorter periods of time. Most of the observations, conversations, and interviews took place in the

of such institutions,[2] (2) the lack of time and opportunity for people working in institutions to study the feelings and reactions of their colleagues and themselves, (3) the reluctance or inability of these workers to communicate their feelings and discuss their reactions when they do recognize them. In addition to these points, there also may be some reluctance to acknowledge and publish this type of material because of the "public-relations" orientation of some administrators. The material presented here also may serve to raise pertinent questions about how the work of cottage parents can be changed so that effective treatment roles are involved, how the work of cottage parents can be related to the work of others in the institutional programs, and how it can be changed so that less strain is experienced by cottage parents. Perhaps the material will also stimulate thought about the organizational structure of an institution and its importance in changing a program.

Currently, there are approximately 219 public and 78 private institutions that care and provide some measure of treatment for delinquent children. These institutions employ about 10,000 persons whose duties are essentially the same as those of cottage parents, though the personnel have titles such as houseparent, supervisor, and counselor. In recent years, most of the institutions have been attempting to change their programs,[3] and the attempts at change have posed

---

regular course of work, in which Dr. Coltharp and the writer worked as institutional psychiatrist and clinical psychologist, respectively. The lack of uniform data does not allow any qualifications of the material, and no claim is made for the representiveness of the cottage parents. The opinions and statements advanced herein are those of the author and are not necessarily to be regarded as those of the Children's Bureau, U.S. Department of Health, Education, and Welfare.

[2] See Lloyd E. Ohlin, *Sociology and the Field of Corrections* (New York: Russell Sage Foundation, 1956).

[3] This movement is reflected in various standard-setting documents that have been published in the last several years: American Psychiatric Association (1785 Mass. Ave., N.W., Washington 6, D.C.), *Training Schools for Delinquent Children* (1952); Children's Bureau (U.S. Department of Health, Education and Welfare), *Institutions Serving Delinquent Children—Guides and Goals* (Washington: Government Printing Office, 1957); and Martin Gula, *Child-Caring Institutions* (Washington: Government Printing Office, 1958).

The institutional movement is closely related to developments in the juvenile court field. The juvenile court developments are reflected in several documents: Children's Bureau (U.S. Department of Health, Education,

THE COTTAGE PARENTS' REACTIONS
IN A PROCESS OF INSTITUTIONAL CHANGE

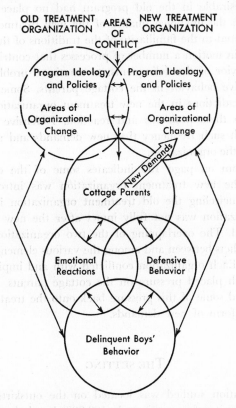

serious problems for cottage parents, whose work has become more complex and whose duties, in some instances, have become conflicting and contradictory. The report that follows describes the introduction of a new treatment-orientation, complete with philosophy, goals, means, and values, into a custodial and punitive organization that had been operating quite smoothly for several years.

The new treatment organization placed emphasis on diagnostic studies of the delinquent's personality and social background, individ-

and Welfare), *Standards for Specialized Courts Dealing with Children* (Washington: Government Printing Office, 1954); Committee on the Standard Family Court Act, "Standard Family Court Act," *National Probation and Parole Association Journal,* 5 (April, 1959), 105–160.

ual and group therapy, and a cottage program regulated to meet the individual needs of the children. In many respects, that which was useful and desirable in the old program had no place in the new program. Also, the unknown quality of the new treatment organization, as compared to the familiarity of the traditions of the established programs, set in motion a number of processes that contributed, along with the behavior of the delinquents, to emotional problems and extensive defensive behavior in the cottage parents. Some inconsistencies and contradictions in the new treatment organization itself also contributed to these problems and reaction. Defensive mechanisms were used with such frequency that new demands and modifications were made on the organization.

The diagram on page 191 indicates some of the changes that occurred as the new treatment organization was introduced. The broken lines encircling the old treatment organization indicate that the old organization was not fully intact after the new organization was introduced. The overlapping of the two organizations is shown, as are the conflicts between and among the various elements of the two organizations. Each organization conflicted with and impinged on the other, and each placed pressure on the cottage parents. The cottage parents directed some of this pressure back onto the treatment organization in the form of new demands.

THE SETTING

The institution studied was located on the outskirts of a midwestern community of approximately 100,000. Proximity to this community made it relatively easy for the institution to recruit personnel, obtain specialized services for its youth, and develop opportunities for the boys to participate in some community activities. The population of the institution usually numbered approximately 150 boys, who lived in five cottages. Three of the cottages usually had a population of approximately 35 to 40 boys; the other two had populations of about half that size. Sixteen years was the maximum age at the time of commitment, and the average age of the boys in the institution was approximately 14½ years. Although there was no minimum age for commitment, there were few boys under twelve years of age. Administrators tried to group the boys in cottages according to similarity of age and maturity, but each cottage usually had an age range of several years. The boys slept in their cottages, and much of their recreation and free time activities centered in them.

Two senior cottage parents, usually husband and wife, were responsible for the boys in each cottage. They were assisted by two relief cottage parents, one of whom worked when there was a heavy concentration of boys in the cottage and when the senior cottage parents were off duty. The senior cottage parents' positions were almost always filled by the longer-term employees and the relief positions by the younger, less experienced people. The senior cottage parents were supervised directly by the superintendent during the time of this study.

In addition to its cottage program, the institution had an active educational program and psychological, social work, psychiatric, and religious services. Five social workers, two psychologists, one psychiatrist, one clinically-trained chaplain, and ten teachers were usually on the staff. A psychological interne, a social work student on field placement, several psychiatric residents, and from one to six ministerial students or ministers on their clinical field placement, all of whom were on temporary or rotating placement, were also in the setting.

THE COTTAGE PARENTS

The forty-six cottage parents employed during the period of our observations were, with a few exceptions, from midwestern farms or small communities. The majority had completed high school; about a fifth had attended college. A core of middle-aged married couples and widows had been at the institution for five years or more, and this group made up the largest number of cottage parents in the institution at any one time. However, the turnover rate in this group was low, as compared to the rate among younger employees, so that a total of fourteen middle-aged persons and thirty-two younger unmarried and married young men were studied.

The occupational histories of the cottage parents varied. Jobs such as carpentry, farming, barbering, sales work, baking, law enforcement work, secretarial work, armed services, and housekeeping were represented. Frequent job changes were common in the occupational histories. Many of the older people apparently began working at the institution because of the security the job offered and because of the more general protection the institution afforded. For some, this search for security was combined with a genuine desire to help children in trouble. The younger cottage parents took the institutional jobs for a variety of additional reasons: to earn money to pay their expenses at a local university, as a second job and a supplement to their income, or as an exploratory experience to help them decide whether or not to pursue graduate work in psychology, sociology, or social work.

The institution made a consistent effort to employ only mature persons who were interested in children and their welfare. Most of the people who were employed measured up quite well to this standard, but there were occasions when pressures to cover shifts of work and lack of applicants forced the institution to hire people who did not meet the standard.

AREAS OF ORGANIZATIONAL CHANGE

About two years before this study was initiated, the institution started to change its program from one with a suppressive, militaristic emphasis to one that included the more "progressive" practices aimed at treatment, rehabilitation, and correction. This change was guided by a conviction that a suitable program for each delinquent, based on a diagnostic evaluation of his particular needs, should be developed. The previous program had tried to establish acceptable habits in the boys by teaching them vocational skills and enforcing the rules of both the school and the society. The new program was to include diagnoses by the clinical staff of the causes of each boy's delinquency, and a program designed to implement the "prescriptions" based on such diagnoses. Groups outside the institution had precipitated and helped initiate the change. They continued to support it. As a result, the treatment program was irrevocable; there could be no turning back to a custodial program.

Introduction of the new program was accompanied by a permissive attitude about the behavior of the boys on the part of administrators. The basic notion here was that the boys needed opportunities to express themselves. It was assumed that the disturbances that were involved in causing the boys' delinquencies would be expressed in various institutional activities and that this expression would give the staff something concrete on which to work in helping the boys change.

The program was guided by the belief that the boys would assume greater individual responsibility for their behavior.

The permissive attitude about the boys called for changes in the routines of the cottages. Cottage parents were called upon to handle constructively many kinds of behavior that they had previously suppressed. Some aggressive and impulsive boys began acting out hostilities. Some of the seriously maladjusted began expressing bizarre ideas. Some of those who were withdrawn withdrew still further. Other boys began to test the limits of the cottage rules in their newfound freedom. Since the number of institutional cottages was limited, each cottage had boys with each of these characteristics. Working with a group of boys manifesting any one of these problems is difficult; attempting to manage a heterogeneous group was a tremendous undertaking and placed stress on the cottage parents.

Conflicts in Authority Patterns. The change in the institution's function from one of custody toward one of treatment had far-reaching implications. Initially, it was implemented by a change in superintendents, and then specialized personnel were hired to carry out clinical services and program activities. At the same time, the total institutional environment began to change. By the time our study began, the systems of authority and supervision had changed radically, particularly as conceived and practiced by the superintendent and the heads of the major departments.

The previous superintendent's administration had been firm if not absolute. He had made all the major decisions affecting the institution and had followed their application down to the routine matters of the cottages. The current superintendent's pattern was considerably different. Though he made the major decisions affecting the institution, he involved the staff in the process and encouraged them to use their initiative in carrying out the decisions. He usually followed departmental and organizational lines in working with the staff; however, he did not hesitate to go around various levels of the institution's hierarchy if he thought that by doing so he could be helpful or if he believed a matter needed his personal attention. This was considerably different from the previous superintendent, who emphasized his status by administration through official organizational lines. The previous superintendent had provided the cottage parents with a precise and detailed set of rules for governing the boys' behavior; the current superintendent tried to impart a point of view about delinquent behavior and its treatment to the cottage parents. He asked them in a general way to study the problems the boys faced and to deal with them individually. He tried to teach them principles and techniques for coping with individual problems.[4]

The institution's new system of authority and supervision was confusing to the cottage parents because it was so different from the previous system. The situation was further complicated by the tendency of cottage parents to interpret the "consulations" by the social work and clinical staff as "directives" and "orders." Previously, authority had been ascribed to the cottage parents as part of their employment. This traditional way of granting authority was modified by the new superintendent, who shifted emphasis from the position itself to the competence of the person filling the position. Some cottage parents were given authority to do certain things in their work because they had demonstrated an ability to do it. Tasks such as taking boys to a nearby city, disciplining the boys, and planning cottage schedules and programs were assigned on the basis of ability. Moreover, the giving of advice by social workers and clinical personnel implied to the cottage parents that their role in treatment was a rather minor one. This, too, strained their conceptions of their authority.

Conflicts in the Communication Process. The institution's system of communication also changed. As indicated previously, the former superintendent generally used the official structure of the institution when he communicated with his staff. He had a set of formal regulations and written directions which established policies and procedures for all sorts of eventualities. The greater the recurrent problems and uncertainties the institution experienced, the more emphasis he placed on orders, elaborate directives, and contingency plans. He attempted to reduce some of the operating procedures in-

---

[4] In several articles, Donald R. Cressey has described some of the confusion experienced by the guards of a treatment-oriented prison due to contradictory goals that had been set for them to achieve. These conflicting goals resulted in vague and conflicting directions to guide their work and failed to provied a system of criteria by which the guards' work could be evaluated. These problems were also present in our institution. However, they may have been complicated by the process of change. For details of Cressey's observations, see Donald R. Cressey, "Contradictory Directives in Complex Organizations: The Case of the Prison," *Administrative Science Quarterly,* 4 (June, 1959), 1–9; and "Achievement of an Unstated Organizational Goal: An Observation on Prisons," *Pacific Sociological Review,* 1 (Fall, 1958), 43–49.

volved in written directives by passing "the word" through official channels. Communication from the department heads to the superintendent was accomplished mainly through verbal reports. Senior cottage parents made reports directly to him.

The new superintendent communicated directly with all of the institutional staff, as well as with the boys. This open and direct procedure led all employees to believe he was accessible and had sincere interests in their work and problems. However, this direct system of communication meant that information was sometimes given to subordinates before it was given to senior cottage parents. Occasionally, boys obtained information in advance of the staff. Generally speaking, cottage parents were puzzled and confused by the new system of communication. Moreover, they often were jealous of the social work and clinical personnel, believing that they had access to the superintendent and greater influence on him.

Conflicts in the Organization of Work. The earlier division of work was relatively simple. The levels of hierarchy in the organization were few and precisely defined, and specialization within each stratum of the hierarchy was almost nonexistent. The skills required of the cottage parents were general. The personnel possessing these skills were directly available from the community. In this situation, training and conferences to discuss ways of improving work with the boys were not necessary. Cottage parents practices continued over the years without a major evaluation and became the traditional and the customary way of doing things.

Introduction of social work and clinical personnel disrupted these various time-honored concepts of cottage parents' work. In the new program, the cottage parents were viewed as having insufficient technical knowledge and skill and as in need of training, consultation, and technical supervision. They were limited to counseling boys on day-to-day problems, while problems of a personal or emotional nature became the province of the social workers, psychologists, and psychiatrists.[5] Similarly, the cottage parents were seen as in need of

---

[5] Difficulties are bound to occur in any area of professionalization when professionalization of the field of service has not gained general acceptance. The situation becomes increasingly more difficult when there is no general agreement on the appropriate professional functions of the various specialities operating in a given field. See, for example, Lloyd E. Ohlin, Herman Piven, and Donnell M. Pappenfort, "Major Dilemmas of the Social Worker in Probation and Parole," *National Probation and Parole Association Journal,* 2 (July, 1956), 211–225. This problem is discussed for corrections

education about theories of delinquency causation, use of attitudes in relationships with delinquents, use of arts and crafts in cottage leisure-time programs, etc. Further, in some cases the cottage parents' relationships with some of the boys were such that it was believed that the cottage parents needed consultation and close supervision if they were to do their work effectively.

Conflicts in the Allocation of Prestige.   When the authority and duties of the cottage parent were traditional and fixed, their prestige was well-defined and secure. But as the basis for prestige shifted from length of the period of employment and number of boys under supervision to educational achievement, skill in working with boys and degree of identification with the new program, the cottage parents became insecure. One thing was clear, however. Members of the social work and clinical staff, even with very limited experience, were accorded higher prestige than were cottage parents with years of experience. Moreover, within the cottage parent ranks, newer members who were identified with the new program and had some college education were accorded higher prestige than those cottage parents who had held the higher-ranked cottage positions and had had more institutional experience.

This situation produced considerable tension in the institution. The prestige of some of the cottage parents dropped from a previous high, and this situation was aggravated by the fact that the degree of prestige and respect accorded to a cottage parent was not always in accord with the responsibilities carried. The differential in the responsibilities of older cottage parents for security of the institution and care of the delinquents, as compared to the responsibilities of the newly-employed technical staff, further complicated the situation.

Role Conflicts.   Some of the roles the cottage parents were expected to assume in the new program were in sharp conflict with roles played previously. Further, some aspects of the new roles were

generally by Donald R. Cressey, "Professional Correctional Work and Professional Work in Correction," *National Probation and Parole Journal,* 5 (January, 1959), 1–15.

The intense problems that may result over varying conceptions about the respective tasks of the cottage parents and the social workers, psychologists and psychiatrists, are discussed by George H. Weber, "Conflict Between Professional and Non-Professional Personnel In Institutional Delinquency Treatment," *Journal of Criminal Law and Criminology,* 48 (June, 1957), 26–43.

not specified in a form such that the cottage parents could understand what was expected of them. This variance and vagueness confused the cottage parents. Three principal types of role conflicts occurred.

Conflict Between Roles of the Different Programs. In the previous program, cottage parents were required to be custodians, supervisors, disciplinarians, and housekeepers. These interrelated roles, emphasizing the functions of security and detention, direction and surveillance, enforcement of order, upkeep of the cottage, and requisition of clothing for the boys and supplies for the cottage, were generally consistent with each other in terms of the purposes they were supposed to achieve. Generally, cottage parents were to gain compliance from the boys by means of securing custody and by directing and suppressing the boys' behavior. In the new program, in direct contrast, they were to give the boys freedom and to encourage them to pursue socially-constructive behavior through participation in a variety of socially-acceptable activities. Previously, the cottage parent "told" the boys what to do and if they didn't comply, they were punished. In the new program, they were expected to understand the boys, counsel with them, and use various attitudes such as active friendliness and firmness to influence their behavior. This meant that they were to participate in active give-and-take with the boys, accepting some aggressive and other behavior that might be distasteful to them.

Antagonism Between Roles of the New Program. In the new program, it was necessary for cottage parents to continue their custodial and security functions, but they became confused when they attempted to integrate their custodial role and their treatment role. For example, they were puzzled about the extent to which they should be permissive and encourage or permit spontaneous behavior, and about the extent to which they should be actively friendly. They had similar questions about the degree to which they should be suppressive, setting the limits of the boys' behavior. The cottage parents were perplexed when the boys responded to friendly, encouraging, and supportive efforts with strong, aggressive reactions. This confusion was intensified when they found they had to manage some of this aggressive behavior by suppression, just as they had in the earlier program. They also faced dilemmas about which roles they should play in working with dependent and withdrawn boys. Sometimes the cottage parents saw unusually immature behavior emerge as they attempted to meet the boys' needs for nurturance by counselling them and giving them other personal attention. They recognized that a regression sometimes occurred as a step in the total treatment process; however, they had difficulty accepting it and questioned the efficacy of a program that accepted any such behavior. Rather, they concluded that the boys were less apt to regress if they were held strictly accountable for their behavior.

Role Conflicts with the Social Work and Clinical Personnel. Initially, the cottage parent saw the work of the clinical and social work staff as superfluous. They had always done the diagnostic and treatment work, though it had never been called that. Consequently, there were some problems, especially early in the program, as the cottage parents objected to the "duplicating" work of the social work and clinical staff, and as these technical people pressed for the legitimacy of their work. The cottage parents gradually came to recognize the contribution of the social work and clinical staff, and the potential that their own work had for making a contribution to the new diagnostic and treatment procedures. After they were given an orientation to the formal diagnostic procedures of the clinical team and were instructed regarding the part they could play in the diagnoses, particularly by their observations of the boys, the cottage parents began to see themselves as possessing a new diagnostic role.

A similar development occurred in the area of treatment. Following some instruction on the clinical techniques they could use in their work, such as the use of different attitudes in relating to the boys and the contributions that counseling with the boys could make, the cottage parents began to feel they had a real part in the treatment program. They also became impressed with some of the clinical staff's accomplishments through their interviews with the children. These experiences changed the concepts that the cottage parents had of their own roles and of the roles of the social work and clinical people. However, this did not bring about the desired teamwork. Disagreements occurred about the extent to which treatment recommendations, developed at the diagnostic and review committee meetings mainly by the technical people, applied to the cottage parents' daily work with the boys. The cottage parents viewed the information that was developed at these meetings and conferences as helpful and directing in a general way, but the social work and clinical staff believed that application of these findings should be binding and specific.

SOME EMOTIONAL REACTIONS OF THE COTTAGE PARENTS

Under the organizational conditions that have been described, a variety of emotional reactions were expressed by the cottage staff. The several emotional reactions that have been selected for presentation and the defensive reactions that follow appeared to occur sufficiently often and to be intense enough as to affect the process of change in the institution, as well as the treatment process. It will be recalled that the cottage parents were screened before they were employed and were a group of relatively normal people. The emotional and defensive reactions of this group to the behavior of the delinquents and to the conflicts that the change in organizations provoked do not represent the reactions of a group of neurotic people.[6]

Reactions of Aggression. The cottage parents expressed anger toward the delinquent children in a variety of ways and in varying degrees of intensity ranging from mild displeasure, as in Mr. L.'s characteristic frown at an erratic screaming, shouting, or continuous loud noise, all the way to the infliction of some bodily blow or some other type of pain, as in Mrs. F.'s impulsive slapping of a boy for the use of vulgar language. As these illustrations suggest, the cottage parents's aggression were also expressed in varying degrees of directness or indirectness. Some direct modes were consciously sly; others were expressed unwittingly. To illustrate: Mr. A. would not permit Jim to participate in cottage basketball even though it had been recommended as a part of his treatment and Jim was enthusiastic about playing. Mr. A. knowingly distorted the reason for not allowing Jim to play when he winked and said, "Jim doesn't feel well; he can't hear. I guess we'll just keep him out of the game for a while." Actually, Jim's hearing was excellent, but he had been diagnosed as having a serious compulsive disorder such that once he began doing something, he had difficulty stopping. In the cottage, this characteristic, coupled with an enthusiasm for basketball, had brought Jim into trouble with Mr. A., who was confused about how he should attempt to influence the boys' behavior under the new program. Jim had not

---

[6] For analysis of some aspects of individual and organizational influences on staff conflicts, see the Comments section in *Children,* 5 (May–June, 1958), 119, where Donald R. Cressey discusses Lloyd E. Ohlin's paper, "The Reduction of Role-Conflict in Institutional Staff," *Children,* 5 (March–April, 1958), 65–69.

stopped bouncing a ball after several requests from Mr. A., so he was eliminated from the activity and ridiculed before the other boys.

Another cottage parent did not seem to be aware of the aggressiveness of his reactions. Clarence had periods when he was moody and other periods when he was very active. These shifts in behavior angered Mr. C. because he was without any diagnostic training and believed Clarence was faking them. However, for several months Clarence had seemed to improve, and it was agreed in staff committee that he should be given a pass into town. After breakfast on the day he was to go to town, Clarence lingered to talk with a supervisor in the dining room and was late arriving at the cottage. He failed to notice Mr. C.'s involvement with another boy and interrupted their conversation, asking for a clean pair of trousers. Angered by the boy's lateness and by his demanding and changeable personality, Mr. C. withdrew the promised pass. He explained, "He doesn't seem quite ready, and may not make it in town." In so doing, Mr. C. did not acknowledge his own anger directly but attributed his action instead to an alleged manifestation of a serious adjustment problem.

All of these cottage parents had expressed great concern about the permissiveness of the new program. Mr. L. and Mrs. F. were on edge about it. Mr. A., ill-equipped to handle a complex treatment problem and angered by it, knowingly maneuvered to circumvent the program while Mr. C., confused by a diagnostic approach to problems and angered by the boy, seemed to maneuver unwittingly to circumvent it.

Threats to a cottage parent's authority, discipline, and respect are apparent in the following two cases. (1) Larry refused to get up the first morning he was at the school, saying he wasn't used to getting up at that hour and no one could make him. Mr. S., the cottage parent, became angry and ordered him out of bed. Larry complied in a belligerent manner, so Mr. S. struck him. (2) Ronald was a disorganized boy who was diagnosed as being in poor contact with reality. He was almost always the last to assemble for group activities. Mr. R. interpreted this "slowness" as a flout to his authority. One day, as the cottage group waited for Ronald before going into lunch, Mr. R. expressed his displeasure about Ronald. Ronald came out of the washroom in time to overhear him, and Mr. R. become quite upset. The boys began to laugh at the situation, and Ronald joined in. At this point, Mr. R. grabbed Ronald, shook him severely and shoved him in the direction of the group.

The cottage parents often over-reacted to threats to their authority by the boys. They were highly sensitive in this respect because the administration had limited their authority but had left them with the responsibility for maintaining good order. Also, the social service and clinical personnel had questioned their ability to handle what authority had been left to them. This problem was further complicated because the boys were aware of some of these staff differences and frequently tested out the limits of the cottage parents' authority and control.

The cottage parents also expressed some anger directly at the administration, social work, and clinical personnel. However, most of the cottage parents' dissatisfactions with these personnel and their policies were expressed through failing to cooperate with them or by avoiding their direction. They also discharged these feelings through grumbling among themselves. Direct expressions are illustrated by Mrs. R.'s anger when she confronted the superintendent about cottage trouble brought on by a change in the pass policy for the boys, Mr. C.'s indignant resignation after he failed to gain support from the social worker and superintendent for his threat to restrict a boy, Mrs. A.'s vehemence in accusing the superintendent of showing favoritism because the new professional people were paid considerably higher salaries, and Mr. R.'s continual failure to send the boys in his cottage for diagnostic or treatment interviews.

Reactions of Jealousy. The cottage parents' jealousy of the children was sometimes contained in expressions of anger toward them. Like the reactions of aggression, jealousy was manifested in many ways and with different degrees of intensity, ranging from Mr. M.'s quiet sulking about having to shift his working hours in order to provide activities for the children on weekends to Mrs. G.'s dramatic walk to the head of the cafeteria line and her demand to be served a particular portion of chicken even though the superintendent had issued the policy that the staff would be served in the order of their arrival in the dining room and had requested them not to file in ahead of the boys.

The subtlety of jealousy varied from parent to parent. Mrs. M., with her kindly manner but cold remarks expressed a somewhat subtle form of jealousy. She would repeatedly comment, "The children don't seem as well-behaved as they used to, it seems to me they are upset all the time. I do believe too much consideration is given to them. That's one thing that doesn't happen to us." Mrs. R. was more outspoken. On one occasion, she said, "These kids make me envious when they get everyone to listen to them pouring out their troubles. I wish I got that much attention."

The changed policies of the institution played a strong part in bringing about the cottage parents' feelings of jealousy. The school increased its concern about the welfare, happiness, and treatment of each child, but less attention was given to the cottage parents. In line with these practices, the cottage parents were expected to give more attention to the children and to demand less affection, loyalty, and deference from them. The cottage parents' jealousies were frequently related to their unwillingness to accept some of the institution's changed policies, particularly those pertaining to the organization of their work. These forces culminated in their complaints that the children received too much attention, recognition, freedom, or other good things. They felt that some of this nurture should be given to them.

The cottage parents' personal feelings of jealousy were generally expressed to their friends or acted out against the boys. When they were conveyed to the superintendent, the feelings of jealousy were usually somewhat disguised because they were combined with concern that privileges and services for the boys were harming them.

Reactions of Fear and Anxiety. Some of the cottage parents developed fears, in varying degrees of intensity, of certain children or situations they saw as being dangerous. For example, Mrs. M. was heard to say, "You know, I'm afraid of Alvin. He knocks things around and when I try to correct him, he goes into a rage and threatens me. At first, it didn't bother me but every time this happens now, I get more scared." Or Mr. A.'s statement, "I hate to say it, but I am afraid of Jerry. There's something about him—he's just too quiet. I know there is something going on there. I'd bet that it won't be long and something will break—a runaway, maybe a fight, or some stealing. It's beginning to put me on edge. I'm going to have to move in on him."

Others developed anxiety from the pressure of their own ideas and impulses. This was reflected in Mr. J.'s statement, "I am afraid I'm going to lash out and hurt that boy one of these days." In the same conversation, Mr. C. responded by saying, "I know what you mean. There is something about that kid that gives me an uneasy, wary feeling. I'd like to get him out of my cottage. I know we are supposed to welcome these boys and make them feel at home but I don't feel that way about this one and so that makes it still harder."

Often fear and anxiety were experienced simultaneously by the cottage parents. For example, some cottage parents feared an attack from a delinquent but at the same time their intense, overwhelming anger and accompanying impulses to eliminate the threatening delinquent by beating him made them anxious. To illustrate, Mr. R. said, "First I was afraid of him when he came at me; then I was afraid I would really hurt him if I hit him." Another cottage parent added to the conversation, "Things sure get built up. You get fussed and uneasy about what the boy is doing. That's enough; but then you've got to watch yourself so you don't make the mistake of getting too tough."

The fear or anxiety precipitated by the boys were experienced in different ways and to different degrees by the cottage parents. Some expressed vague feelings of uneasiness, while others described much stronger feelings. Still others, when they were anxious or fearful, showed some tremor, faltering in their speech, or general tenseness. Illustrations of some of these observations can be seen in the following examples. Gene was committed to the institution for striking a filling-station attendant over the head with a stove poker. He proved to be unmanageable at the school. One evening he got into a serious fight in the cottage. When he attempted to gouge the other boy's eyes out, the cottage group turned on Gene and began to beat him. He ran across the cottage to Mr. I., who had just come in the door. Mr. I. stopped the group and attempted to work out the problem. Following the incident, Mr. I. said, "I was scared. I didn't know what they were going to do." As he continued to talk with considerable emotion, his hands trembled and several times his voice cracked.

The case of John is an illustration of the fear and anxiety that delinquent behavior can produce in a lesser degree. John was a severe behavior problem in his neighborhood, and following a series of aggressive and destructive incidents, he was sent to the school. He would not participate in the cottage activities. Rather, he sat in a chair away from the group and constantly watched Mrs. C., the cottage parent, who developed an uneasy feeling about what John was thinking and what he might do.

It was possible to note a relationship among the anxieties and fears of the cottage parents, the treatment organization, and the behavior of the boys. During the interim of change from the old to the new treatment organization, many definite procedures to handle problem behavior were dropped, and vague and general objectives were sometimes offered, as new procedures were being developed. This left the cottage parents with shifting guides, fuzzy goals, and an organizational structure that seemed on shaky grounds. It made them anxious. This kind of relationship was involved in the cottage parents' basic skepticism about the permissiveness of the new program and their doubts about whether the administrators would back them up when they disciplined the boys. If a boy had been punished, the cottage parents sometimes became greatly concerned, believing that their actions might imply a lack of capability in handling the problems more constructively. In other instances, they were anxious about what were the best things to do for the boys and feared being censured by the administrators and professional personnel. Some saw the standards of work required by a treatment program as being so high that anything they did would be wrong.

The case of George is an illustration of the anxiety and indecision that an indefinite treatment policy provoked in a cottage parent. George was diagnosed as a highly impulsive, shrewd and hostile boy who was not concerned about the general welfare of others. One day, he put pressure on Mr. J. to allow him to work as cottage monitor, which ordinarily was not permitted. He did this suavely, by assuming certain privileges and applying pressures both subtle and direct. Mr. J. knew he was letting George go too far and felt uneasy about the increasing demands, but he did not know how to deal with him. He thought being firm with George was the best approach, yet he believed this would result in some serious misbehavior which might require physical restraint. He feared criticism from the administration if this should happen. In the meantime, Mr. J.'s fear and anxiety about the situation increased.

Reactions of Discouragement. Some cottage parents felt discouraged, disheartened and hopeless about their efforts to "treat" delinquents. When they were discouraged or despondent, they worked in a listless, perfunctory, and routine way. Some made an effort to disguise their discouragement, but others did not. As these feelings intensified, cottage parents became more disinterested and did only the most necessary things to maintain the routine of the cottage.

Discouragement and listlessness usually occurred after a series of disappointing and painful experiences in which the cottage parents felt they had failed in their work. For example, when a boy ran away from the institution, the person in charge of the cottage from which the youngster escaped was likely to view his own failure to maintain custody as a disappointing and painful experience. Similarly, the return of parole violators precipitated attitudes of discouragement, as did boys who shrewdly tried to mislead or manipulate the cottage parents, play them off against each other or against some other staff member or child. These attitudes also arose when cottage parents perceived that the institution was unable to place or parole those boys whom the cottage parent felt were ready to be placed. Defiant behavior, after the cottage parents had made genuine effort to help a boy, was another depressing experience. A similar reaction was provoked when the boys flouted the cottage parents' efforts to carry on a constructive program.

The new institutional organization stimulated discouragement among the cottage parents, especially when its philosophy and goals led the cottage parents to develop unrealistic expectations from their work. As a result, they often felt that they were not performing as expected in the new program. These feelings were also associated with fear that their work might be such that they would lose the support and interest of the superintendent and other staff members. More generally, cottage parents were discouraged by their declining prestige in the institution, lack of a career opportunity beyond cottage work, low salaries, and general conditions of work.

SOME DEFENSIVE BEHAVIOR OF COTTAGE PARENTS[7]

The cottage parents employed a variety of defensive mechanisms to relieve the feelings of anxiety, fear, aggression, discouragement, or jealousy that they experienced in their relationship with the delinquent boys. They also used some of these same defensive mechanisms to help them handle the problems they encountered in trying to perform their jobs under the new treatment program, and to gain some satisfactions from these jobs. Avoidance, repression, rationalization, projection, reversal, withdrawal, compensation, displacement, development of physical ailments, and repression occurred frequently. The extent to which these mechanisms were expressed reflected the strain under which the cottage parents were functioning. These mechanisms, which are common in "everyday life," were so pronounced

[7] The concept of defensive behavior is drawn mainly from Anna Freud, *The Ego and Mechanisms of Defense* (New York: International Universities Press, 1946).

that they took on unusual proportions as the cottage parents attempted to cope with the situations confronting them. Cottage parents used a number of the defensive mechanisms at the same time, but for purposes of analysis the reactions will be discussed separately.

Avoidance. By ignoring, denying, making excuses, and failing to "face up" to the problems that the behavior of the boys and the difficulties of working under the new program presented, the cottage parents pretended that conflicts did not exist, that their job was a relatively stable and comfortable one, and that some of the behavior of the delinquents in their care did not upset them. Some chose to maintain an ignorance about the facts of any misbehavior that would present a conflict for them. Others chose to be ignorant of memoranda issued by the superintendent that defined various aspects of the cottage program. Still others ignored recommendations of the clinical staff and behaved in a manner which had been customary in the old treatment organization. The following case illustrates the ignoring, denying, and excuse-making of a cottage parent in relationship to the superintendent, as well as to the boys.

Mr. G. was scheduled to supervise the playground outside his cottage after the evening meal. However, this assignment occurred after the cottage parent had already worked a full day. Further, it was a period of high activity for the boys—a period when they needed considerable leadership and supervision. The playground was located in an area that was not observable from the administration building nor from the other cottages. After a particularly difficult day, Mr. G. sent the boys to the playground alone and remained in the cottage, even though he knew that he was supposed to supervise the playground and was aware of the need for his help in organizing the games and handling any trouble that might arise. Several boys returned to the cottage to complain about the lack of discipline on the playground. Although Mr. G. was not busy in the cottage and seemed somewhat concerned about the trouble, he responded by wearily shrugging his shoulders, implying that he was unable to handle the situation. The boys returned to the playground, and Mr. G. continued to ignore the behavior and problems of the play-area.

As indicated, some cottage parents avoided problems by denying their existence. They denied having negative ideas and feelings about the change in program, yet they complained bitterly about the problems they experienced in trying to make the program work. An incident involving Mr. R. illustrates this kind of avoidance. The new program emphasized treating each boy as an individual in the institution.

Among several things, each boy was given a set of "dress-up" clothing. The boys chose the clothing themselves, and there was a wide variation in style and color. It was difficult to keep ownership of this clothing clear, principally because adequate storage space was not available. On one occasion, several boys in a cottage were unable to find their "dress-up" shirts. They reported this to Mr. R. and also told him that they had seen a particular boy in the cottage with one of the missing shirts. Mr. R. was irritated by this information but he never checked on the matter, although this type of problem was common to a cottage. Instead, he denied that the shirts could have been stolen, expressed futility about attempting to keep track of the clothing, and then told the boys that this was a problem they should solve themselves.

These avoidance-mechanisms were used by some cottage parents to such an extent that they failed to face up to problems involved in rather routine work tasks. For example, some boys excitedly reported to Mr. L. a fight in another part of the cottage. On a common sense basis, such a report should have been Mr. L.'s cue to check the troubled situation. Although the youngsters approached Mr. L. and shouted the trouble to him, he ignored them, muttered something about the boys' continual fighting, and continued to put clothing on the shelves of a storage closet. Several boys stopped the fight, but one boy was so badly beaten that he had to be taken to the infirmary for medical attention. This brought the incident to the attention of the superintendent, who called Mr. L. to his office. Mr. L. reported that he had heard nothing unusual, at least nothing to indicate that a fight was taking place. He went on to point out that he was busy putting clothing away and did not know of the problem until some of the boys told him somebody was hurt. When questioned further on the matter, particularly about the boys reporting the fight to him, Mr. L. said the boys had many complaints and consequently he did not pay a great deal of attention to this particular one. The superintendent stated that the loudness of the noise and the boys' complaints seemed an adequate basis for an investigation. Mr. L. then excused his lack of response to the situation by saying that the boys had been fighting all their lives and undoubtedly would continue to fight over irrelevant matters, so there was little reason to intervene in the current fight. When pressed still further, Mr. L. commented that the boy who was hurt had it coming to him, and furthermore, this was a consequence of a more permissive program.

Much of the cottage parents' avoidance stemmed from their lack of knowledge and skill as to what should be done. They particularly lacked the versatility required to switch from a supervisory role to that of recreational leader or counselor. They were made anxious by these job expectations and consequently avoided dealing with many types of problems. In some instances they were tired or overworked and simply avoided as many problems as they could. In other instances, as in the case of Mr. L., the cottage parents were prone to utilize the boys as monitors to supplement their supervision. This practice stemmed from the previous militaristic program where monitors were regularly made "non-commissioned" officers and had some authority. The system also had certain practical values, for it helped the overworked cottage parents meet their duties.

Repression and Suppression. The persistently aggressive, destructive, scheming, and defiant behavior of many of the delinquents frequently stimulated similar behavior among the cottage parents. They had a difficult task that required the utmost patience and forebearance. It was not unusual for delinquent behavior to arouse responses which cottage parents usually were able to repress more or less successfully. The continual aggravation of latent conflicts and feelings caused by the boys' disturbed behavior, and the psychodynamic interpretations of behavior being given by the clinical staff, had some striking manifestations.

For example, Mr. L. had a domineering, aggressive older brother. When an older and stronger boy gave any sign that he might intimidate or pick on a younger boy, Mr. L. sometimes found it very difficult to control his anger. Mr. L. had only a vague awareness of this particular tendency. He was intellectually aware of the psychoanalytic idea that one's own point of view is highly influenced by his family relationships in early formative years. At a meeting in which staff members were discussing the problem of older boys picking on younger boys, Mr. L. became very active in the conversation and complained strongly about some of the abuse he had suffered from his older brother. He seemed to be very tense as he made this point, but he did not carry the association further. In dropping the subject, many of the memories and strong feelings about his early experiences with his brother probably remained repressed, and his over-concern about domination of younger boys by older boys continued.

Another illustration of repression by a cottage parent and how it related to behavior of one of the boys was seen in an incident involving Mrs. J. Mrs. J.'s first marriage had ended in divorce, her ex-husband failing to fulfill his obligation to support the children. Mrs. J. made arrangements for the children, secured employment, and tried to put the whole affair out of her mind. Several years later she remarried, and after the children were grown she and her second husband were employed by the training school. Although Mrs. J.'s work was satisfactory, when a boy became disturbed because of trouble between his parents, she usually shared his disturbance; significantly, if a boy became upset because of some other condition, Mrs. J. did not seem to be as bothered. One boy, William, had been making satisfactory progress at the institution until he learned (through another boy's parents who were visiting the school) that his father had deserted the family. William did not share the information with anyone. He began to withdraw, was deferent but sullen to Mrs. J., and stayed away from her husband. Initially, Mrs. J. was concerned but unperturbed by this behavior and attempted to work with the boy. After about a week, William's mother wrote him a letter informing him of the father's desertion. Mrs. J. learned of the situation from reading the incoming mail. She became highly incensed and demanded that the superintendent ask the police in William's home community to bring the father back to face his responsibility. The superintendent observed that Mrs. J.'s reaction seemed to involve more than the objective aspects of William's situation, and he asked her to discuss the problem with the social worker handling William's case. During these discussions, Mrs. J. brought out some of her own previous difficulties and queried the worker as to whether these might have had any bearing on her present point of view. She said that she hadn't thought about her first marriage for some time, but that recently it had been on her mind a lot and she was aware that sometimes painful experiences in life stay with one more than one might think.

In contrast to repression (pressing various powerful memories, feelings, and urges back into the unconscious without conscious knowledge of doing so) suppression involves conscious and deliberate renunciation of problems. This mechanism also was used frequently by cottage parents, sometimes because they did not know what else to do with their problems. For example, Mr. J. once said, "I know that Jim will be terribly wild again when he comes back to the cottage. This is one case where I wish the people up in the administration building could tell me what to do. I'm just going to put it out of my mind."

On one occasion, Mr. A. said, "Sure, I know Larry is beginning to break down because he knows his folks don't want him. I keep giving him time and attention but this thing is wearing me out. The people up in counseling tell me to keep right on, but I need more than that to go on. I'm going to try to forget this whole thing, at least for a while."

The defense-mechanism of suppression was used when cottage parents attempted to cope with some of their feelings of uneasiness, anxiety, and uncertainty about their work and their future, as well as in coping with the problems of specific boys. Mr. N. revealed this when he said, "I've been in this work for six years now. I like it, but it's gotten so that it's taking more out of me than I have to give. Sometimes I wonder what else I can do. Guess I'll try to forget it for awhile and figure it all out later." A similar effort was being made by Mrs. E. when she said, "I'm not going to think of it now, but I don't know how I can keep on working when things aren't more definite."

Repression particularly and suppression to some extent seemed to be precipitated when the treatment organization's permissiveness allowed the children to be more expressive but at the same time required the cottage parents to be in greater control of themselves. This switch was a particular hardship on the cottage parents because they had to hold their impulses and reactions to the boy's behavior in check.

Rationalization. The cottage parents often framed facts in ways that reduced the size of the problems confronting them or "eliminated" them altogether. In doing this, they seemed to be distorting the facts in a problem situation and organizing them to simplify the situations they faced. The cottage parents' justifications often reflected their conceptions of delinquency treatment and their roles in it. Failures in communication between the cottage parents and the clinical and social work staff were often apparent in their rationalizations. Rationalizations were particularly noticeable as the cottage parents attempted to develop a logical basis for punitive treatment of the boys in the face of the superintendent's, social workers', and clinical staff's efforts to get them to be more tolerant and understanding. The cottage parents' tendencies to rationalize were also apparent as they attempted to handle organizational problems arising from the introduction of the new program.

Many of the cottage parents "explained away" their stern and aggressive management of the children with simple arguments. Mrs. H. struck Bill in the face for muttering and cursing to himself when she had asked him to remake his bed. In discussing this with another cottage parent, she justified her action on the ground that the blow would help Bill learn to do a better job in making his bed, appreciate cleanliness generally, and respect authority. She said, "These kids have come from homes where nothing is taken care of and they don't care about anybody; they have no respect for anything. So when Bill got surly, I hit him. It should teach him when nothing else will. I know the people up in the superintendent's office don't want it handled this way but I have to run the cottage and keep order. This is my job. If they want to show me exactly how to do this in language I can understand, O.K. Otherwise I'll run the cottage and they can do their own work."

An incident involving Mr. M. also illustrates the rationalization of punitive measures. When Ed returned to the school after running away, Mr. M. gave him a whipping. It was Ed's sixth runaway and seemed to be related to his concern about home. Mr. M. rationalized his whipping by saying, "Children learn to leave a hot stove alone, so why not make the punishment for running away just as hot?" When confronted with an opposing point of view by the superintendent, Mr. M. shifted his rationalization and justified his whipping of Ed on the basis that "this is a hard world and these boys will have to learn to take the knocks." Perhaps Mr. M. was only reflecting a general community attitude and the philosophy of the previous program that the guilty must be punished. However, Mr. M. was overlooking the fact that Ed had a long history of hard knocks and had not "learned" from them.

It was not uncommon to hear the cottage parents rationalize their participation, or lack of it, in the institutional program. Their knowledge of the work of the clinical staff was very inadequate and loaded with misinformation and bias. They had received little or no information or training along clinical lines and the new treatment program was more threatening than challenging to them. Some of the cottage parents explained away their failure to cooperate with the new staff with reasoning which seemed illogical to the new staff. To illustrate, the cottage parents often withheld important observations of the delinquents from the clinical staff on the ground that the clinical staff would use the information against the boys, that they would confront the boys with this information in their interviews with them, or that they would recommend lengthy stays in the institution for the boys if they learned of any problems in connection with them. Also, they rationalized their failure to accept recommendations and suggestions made by the clinical staff on the ground that their own experience and skill were superior to that of the technical staff. They believed that the social work and clinical personnel were trying to direct them without the intimate knowledge and tested skills of a cottage parent. Their rationalizations reflected the basically different conceptions that the cottage parents and the personnel representing the new treatment organization held about the way the institution should organize its work. Also apparent were their different ideas as to the roles the cottage parents ought to be playing.

Projection. When the cottage parents ascribed their own negative and unacceptable wishes and thought to other staff members, to the institution, or to the boys, they avoided recognizing these unacceptable ideas and feelings as their own and thus could avoid handling them directly. In employing this defense of projection, they either made themselves objects of special consideration or lack of consideration, of favor or disfavor, whichever seemed to help. In all cases, they tried to become the recipient of attention.

It was not uncommon for the cottage parents to blame the boys for many of the troubles they had in running the cottage. The boys became scapegoats. Mr. F. was a relief cottage parent who could manage the cottage adequately if a strict routine were observed. In the absence of the cottage parent, Mr. F., who was not up to the responsibility, was asked to take the boys in his cottage into town to the movies. The boys threw popcorn, whistled in the movies, and bothered several teen-aged girls sitting near them. Mr. F. waited before taking and direct action, hoping that the show would interest the boys and that they would stop. When this did not occur and the group became more openly aggressive, he went from one boy to another, frantically asking them to stop. This action had little effect, and he finally withdrew them from the theater and returned them to the school. Mr. F. was bitter. He said the boys were untrustworthy and uncooperative and he vowed never to take them to the movies again. He refused to accept any of the responsibility for the boys' behavior and placed the blame for the entire experience on the boys. He could not admit that he had not prepared the boys for the trip, except to threaten them to "stay in line." He refused to recognize his own lack of leadership. The new treatment organization's contribution to this problem was twofold: first, it allowed a man to be assigned to a task beyond his capability; and second, as products of its permissive program, the boys were naturally greater risks for this type of behavior. Further, the screening for the experience of a movie in town was inadequate.

Reversal. In reversal, the actor develops behaviors that seem diametrically opposed to his unconscious wishes. By means of reversals, cottage parents protected themselves from admitting some of the negative feelings they had toward the change in program or toward the boys. They did not have to admit or express their conflicts if they exhibited diametrically opposite behavior. Mrs. H. was unusually tolerant of the boys' aggressive and irresponsible behavior, but this tolerance seemed to come with a real effort and sometimes relationships with the boys were strained. The clinical personnel believed that her tolerance actually was a reversal of her own underlying aggressive feelings and her conflict over accepting the boys. Further, they thought that her reversal of real feelings was not entirely effective and that her dislike for some of the boys broke through occasionally. One day a boy who had run away and stolen a car was returned to Mrs. H.'s cottage. She said to him, among other things, "I've been fed up with you for a long time. I've tried not to show it, but now you either get along or I will make arrangements to send you elsewhere." She then turned to the group of boys who were observing them and threatened, "And that goes for the rest of you, too."

Some cottage parents invoked the reversal mechanism when they talked about their work. Sometimes they talked in glowing terms to all about their new role in the treatment organization, but they also complained about being used as messenger boys, dispatchers, and receivers of boys at the cottages. In conferences with the superintendent and in staff committees, some cottage parents who constantly expressed negative feelings toward boys in the cottages would reverse themselves and assume positive attitudes. For example, in her work with the boys, Mrs. A. was aggressive and rejecting. However, in staff conferences where her recommendations were scrutinized by the superintendent and the social and clinical personnel, and where her recommendations were important in determining whether boys would go on a pass or be placed out of the institution, she would reverse her former opinions and express high praise for the boys. Similarly, Mr. R. reported to a staff meeting that several boys had run away from his cottage during the previous night and had stolen a car in their flight. He looked tired, discouraged and generally downcast. Just a week previously, Mr. R. had requested that two of these three boys be remanded to the court. Yet after Mr. R. reported the runaways, without any change of expression he talked about the unusually good qualities of the boys and their ultimate good future.

The treatment organization furthered duplicity in the cottage parents. In many instances, it set up unrealistic demands and tasks for the cottage parents to fulfill, and then failed to provide adequate organizational training and promotional opportunities. Finally, the organization generally placed professional personnel in positions of authority and prestige, and the cottage parents felt compelled to respond positively to them, irrespective of what they thought or how they felt about them.

Withdrawal. Simple withdrawal in the form of shifting from one activity to another, such as leaving a group of noisy, aggressive boys and visiting boys whose behavior was more congenial, occurred frequently. Withdrawals of greater significance, involving escape from job responsibilities, also occurred. More than occasionally, cottage parents stayed away from their shifts of work or worked their shift in a half-hearted, superficial way. Their reasons for absences and lack of enthusiasm on the job were usually vague and could not be considered legitimate excuses under the personnel rules. However, it was difficult for the cottage parents to continually work at their maximum of efficiency when they felt their jobs to be of less importance under the new treatment organization than previously.

The cottage parents avoided participating in personally irritating or threatening situations that required responsible personal contact. They also withdrew from demands and threats by boys in their charge, as in the following case. New boys were kept in a reception cottage for two weeks. During this period they were studied and oriented to the institution, and decisions were made about their particular institutional program. During his two weeks in the cottage, one boy frequently got into fights with other boys and threatened the staff when they attempted to correct him. His reputation spread through the institution, and the cottage parents speculated about who would get him. When Mr. B. learned that the decision to assign the boy to his cottage had been made at the clinical staff meeting, he did not work for several days. He reported that he was ill and went hunting. In talking with friends, Mr. B. said he couldn't face taking the boy into his cottage.

When the new program was introduced, some of the cottage

parents withdrew completely by resigning. Others were not as free to do this because of economic reasons or strong personal commitments to do this type of work. Others coupled their efforts to withdraw from a difficult work situation with efforts to develop a more favorable work environment. Thus, they requested that their work be limited in some way, asked to work with selected groups of children such as those of a particular age or with a certain stability of behavior, or requested shifts during which the work was lighter.

Mrs. K. had been working on the afternoon and evening shift (3:00 to 10:00 P.M.) as a cottage parent for several months. She had been employed to supplement the regular cottage parents during this period of high activity in the cottage. Ideally, during this time, the cottage parent would develop and supervise activities in the cottage, receive the boys from school, and send boys out to work. One afternoon several boys came from school, complained about one of their teachers, and asked Mrs. K. if they could quit school. Two other boys asked to remain in the cottage rather than go to their work, claiming that they were overworked. At this point, the telephone rang and Mrs. K. learned from the principal of the school that the boys complaining about school had refused to do their assigned work during one of the afternoon classes. The principal asked Mrs. K. to talk with the boys about their negative attitudes. While Mrs. K. was engaged in the telephone conversation, an argument broke out among the boys over recreational equipment so she interrupted her conversation to quiet them. She resumed her conversation but suggested that the problem be discussed later because of present cottage demands. Exasperated but determined, she then got the boys started in various activities, walked to the administration building, saw the superintendent and asked him to assign her to a shift on which there would be less trouble.

It should be mentioned here that Mrs. K. was doing no more or less work than any of the other cottage parents employed at the institution. However, in many instances the work demands on the cottage parents were excessive. They had too many boys to handle and too many tasks. Also, there were definite organizational limitations. For example, the institution had a limited appropriation within which it had to operate. This restricted the number of cottage parents and other personnel it could employ.

Compensation. Obviously, some of the cottage parents did not gain much satisfaction from their work with the boys. In order to compensate for this lack of satisfaction, they exerted themselves in one or a limited number of areas of cottage work that were attractive to them, and neglected those which were not. For example, some cottage parents enjoyed and concentrated on the housekeeping activities and neglected their work with the boys; others behaved in the opposite way by spending an excessive amount of time in recreational activities with the boys and neglecting other aspects of their work. However, the most striking use of this mechanism was the cottage parents' constant efforts to create the impression that they were important, intelligent, and highly-skilled workers. The new treatment organization stimulated their feelings of insecurity about their jobs. As a result, they felt compelled to make this extra effort to handle their feelings of insecurity, as well as favorably to influence the administration and clinical and social work personnel.

Displacement.   When upset about the behavior of certain boys or about particular aspects of the treatment program, cottage parents often transferred their feelings to other boys or staff or work situations. Hence, some of their attitudes toward certain delinquents and staff were quite inappropriate. Some cottage parents, for example, were provoked and angered by the prestige and apparent authority of the social work and clinical personnel but did not express their anger directly because they feared some kind of censure from them. Instead, they seemed to direct their feelings to the boys who seemed least likely to strike back. Or they might displace their feelings onto some other staff member whom they might blame for something seemingly unimportant.

Mrs. M. had often said she was irked by the diagnosis and treatment plans set forth by the professional staff for Bill. They saw him as reacting aggressively to defend himself from unrealistic fears, and they prescribed that cottage parents should be friendly but firm with him when he became aggressive. Mrs. M. was unsympathetic to Bill, who in her opinion really belonged in the reformatory because of his continuing aggressiveness. Mrs. M. talked with Bill's social worker, after he fought with another boy. Bill had also made a vague threat to hurt Mrs. M. when she was correcting him. The social worker encouraged Mrs. M. to express herself; however, he suggested that she continue working with Bill. He also stated he would not support extreme punishment for him at this time. This recommendation was contrary to Mrs. M.'s conviction that Bill should be returned to the court. Believing that she could not press her idea, she passively agreed to be patient with Bill and returned to the cottage. Obviously upset, Mrs. M. walked into the reading room of the cottage, noted several boys who were quietly reading, and severely reprimanded them because they had scattered the newspapers on several tables.

Displacement took other forms. Cottage parents who had a difficult day at their work would complain about the food at the school cafeteria, which was usually excellent, instead of attacking the social work and clinical staff who had been responsible for having the staff dining room closed, requiring that the staff eat in the same room as the boys. This policy was aimed toward improving the relations between the staff and the boys and helping to close the gap between them.

Other cottage parents complained about the maintenance and repair given their cottages, which in reality was good, instead of complaining about the extensive improvements that had been made on the clinical offices.

Older cottage parents frequently found the staff conferences, which had been instituted as a part of the new treatment organization, threatening and anxiety-arousing experiences, and it was not uncommon for them to displace their feelings on the boys by issuing rather absurd orders demanding strict quietness or threatening to restrict the boys for trivial reasons, as shown in the preceding case of Mrs. M.

Development of Physical Ailments. Some of the cottage parents, disturbed by their changing work environment and the destructive behavior of many of the delinquents, developed pains and ills that seemed to have no organic basis. Previously there had been less aggressive behavior because the organizational structure was more suppressive. Furthermore, the directions governing the cottage parents' management of this behavior had allowed them to express their own anger, as well as other feelings. The current methods encouraged them to be "permissive but firm." Many of them were untutored as to "how" to do this if physical punishment, isolation, etc., were not allowed.

The cottage parents complained of such conditions as nervous stomach, intestinal cramps, palpitations of the heart, headaches, painful backaches, etc. Without full diagnostic studies, we cannot be sure that the ailments were not organic. However, it could be observed that Mrs. R. regularly developed headaches at those times when she was to share the morning supervision of the boys in the dining room, and that Mrs. A. always complained of a sore back when she was

expected to help take the boys on a picnic or some other type of
outing—activities in which the boys were often difficult to control.

More complex developments were seen in the problems of several
other people. After working with a group of particularly aggressive
boys for several months, Mrs. B. began to complain about some vague
pains in her abdomen. She consulted her physician who could detect
nothing organically wrong with her although the pains had become
complicated with diarrhoea. In discussing her illness with Mr. C. she
said, "Sometimes I get so mad at those boys who won't do what they
are asked to do that my stomach justs hurts. I could just cat-dirt on
them." Mr. P. also apparently developed a physical reaction to problem situations. The skin on his hands broke out in a fine eruption
which over a period of several days turned into small blisters. Again
no physical basis could be established for these eruptions. He sensed
the relationship between the onset of his skin disorder and his tension
when he recalled the anxiety he experienced in attempting to manage
the boys when they tended to disregard and openly flout his direction.

The Return to Previous Practices.   When the new program was
introduced, many cottage parents changed their work practices and
adapted to the requirements of the new approach, as they understood
them. However, when the demands of the jobs became great and
frustrations became intense, some of the cottage parents returned to
their previous ways of doing things. Almost all reminisced about the
"good old days" when cottage work seemed simple, but some went
beyond this. For example, Mr. J. tried having the boys help in the
planning and carrying out of recreational activities, but when this
task became too involved he returned to the practice of specifying
what activities were to be included and who could participate in
them. He complained that it was too "mixed up" when the boys
participated, and besides, "The kids didn't know what they wanted."
Mr. J. made the decision to run the recreational program himself
after a heated argument among the boys on the cottage recreational
committee over the type of activities to be organized for a weekend.
Mr. J. refused to recognize the argument as a problem he should
work through with the boys. The large number of impulsive boys in
Mr. J.'s cottage and their unfamiliarity with such planning contributed
to the situation.

Another return to previous practices occurred when Mr. A. began
to carry a small leather strap in his back pocket, as he had done in
the earlier period. He defended his return to former work habits by

saying that he felt the boys were getting too surly. Similarly, Mr. C. returned to his former practice of making the boys line up to be counted before going to bed. After several of them had run away immediately before bed-time, Mr. M. decided to quit trying to talk anything over with the boys. He gave this as the reason: "They begin to think you're soft, and the first thing you know they are running all over you." Mr. M. had not been trained to reflect on his manner of talking to the boys and did not realize that he was expected to check and see if the boys were really flouting his authority. A friendly, supportive, institutional environment was desirable. However, the rationale of the casework or psychiatric interview could not be extended to become the pervasive influence in guiding the cottage parents' work. Further, those elements of the interview technique believed to be applicable to cottage tasks had not been delineated or communicated to the cottage parents in a clear and deliberate way.

Sublimation and Perfectionism. Frequently some of the cottage parents seemed to sublimate some of their feelings and aggressiveness into an additional determination to understand a situation more fully or to cope with it in accordance with treatment principles. For example, Mr. R. was perceptibly angered by the outburst of fighting in his cottage but after stopping the fight by telling the boys to break it up, he said, "If I do anything today, it's going to be getting an afternoon schedule set up to take better care of this problem of fighting. Now, let's sit down right now and draw up some preliminary plans so that we can talk this thing over with the rest of the boys this afternoon."

Another illustration of an apparent effort to sublimate impulses into socially acceptable behavior was seen in the reflections Mr. A. made in his apartment after several boys had run away from his cottage. He said, "These runaways may not be such a bad thing for the individual boy to do, but runaways are not good for the school's reputation and they make me mad as ——. I'm saying now that we better get busy and set up a better program to keep these kids around. You know, we don't do much for them; sometimes we don't even give them much supervision, and we had better get a better program under way. What would you say about meeting with Mr. —— (superintendent) to do something about this?"

Sometimes the sublimation of the cottage parents developed into a type of perfectionism. For example, Mr. L. seemed to be sublimating many of his aggressive feelings about the boys when he required them to behave in an exemplary way and keep the cottage immaculately clean. Mr. C. was another case in point. He seemed to direct many of his aggressive feelings about the boys into a determination that the boys would participate in and achieve victory in the sports program of the cottage.

NEW ORGANIZATIONAL PROBLEMS

Confusion, conflict, and turbulence within the institutional structure were associated with the process of change from a suppressive, custodial program to one emphasizing treatment of the delinquent. This was the organizational condition to which the cottage parents were reacting. Their reactions to this and to the behavior of the delinquents in this environment, and their inability to cope with the problems facing them created new organizational problems.

The Institutional Goals Were Questioned. The strong reactions of the cottage parents raised serious questions about the compatibility of the institution's treatment goal and its goals of custody and security. To the administrators and clinicians, these seemed compatible in theory, for it could be said that the boys needed varying degrees of security, depending on individual needs, for purposes of treatment. But refinements of this general idea were needed, and a whole host of details were overlooked. Among the more important questions not answered in our period of observations were: What degrees of security are necessary for what kinds of delinquents? What degrees of security are required for delinquents in the different phases of progress in their treatment? What type and how much physical security (locked doors, fenced grounds), coupled with what kind and how much of a particular management approach (firmness, strict observance of the cottage rules), will provide the desired degree of security, and, associated with what other methods, will provide the positive setting?

The cottage parents' complaints and turbulent behavior raised these questions directly and by implication. They were perplexed and disturbed by the new organization's philosophy that their greatest holding force on the boys was their relationship with them. As a directive for behavior, this philosophy was overly general and overlooked many necessary details. It did not specify how to establish and sustain a positive relationship with different types of delinquent boys; what to do when boys do not respond to the cottage parents efforts; what to do in periods of stress when a positive relationship is least binding; and when to invoke other types of security measures, and what types. Left without specific directions, and caught between the conflicts of new and old organizations, the cottage parents floundered. This was perceived by the boys, who exploited cottage parents' indecision by aggresive behavior and by running away.

The Administrative Structure Was Shaken. The organizational machinery that was continued or set up to facilitate change and administer the program—the system of authority and supervision, the channels of communication, the organization of work, and the system for allocating prestige and assigning roles—all had difficulty in functioning. The cottage parents' reactions to and through the structure threatened its continuance.

Many of the traditional patterns were disturbed or broken, and their influence in governing the operations of the institution was greatly reduced. The new organization had made progress in implementing its program, but it floundered. Many of the cottage parents were demoralized because they considered the new organization to be indifferent to their needs. Further, they questioned whether anything could be accomplished in the institution, which they now believed to be very unpredictable and lacking in system. The superintendent raised the question of whether the treatment goals of the new organization were slipping further away, rather than being realized. He pressed the social work and clinical personnel with this issue. These staff members had become more aware of the cottage parents' problems and of some of the larger organizational problems; however, they continued to be highly critical. Their response to the superintendent was complex. Stricter demands, coupled with inservice training, should be made on the cottage parents. This implied that the already overworked superintendent should extend and intensify his efforts. The superintendent reacted with some discouragement and with a sense of futility. He felt that the social work and clinical personnel pressed him to accomplish many things through administrative direction that they should be achieving through consultation. Further, he was perplexed by this pressure and believed the specialized staff's support for implementing the new treatment organization was limited.

The Authority and Supervision Were Questioned. Administrative authority and supervision were questioned and directly challenged by cottage parents. They alternately wavered between rejecting some of the administration's policies and procedures, and demanding overly-specific techniques that they could use in working with the distrubed behavior of the delinquents. This direct challenge by the cottage parents, like their generally disturbed behavior, was of great concern to the administrators. The superintendent urged the social work and clinical personnel to give greater consideration to the cottage parents' ideas and feelings, particularly at case conferences where major decisions were made about a boy's institutional program or after-care. He also gave the cottage program a new status by designating it "Department of Group Life" and placing it on the same organizational level as the Social Work and Clinical Department. The new department was headed by a group social-worker who was cognizant of the cottage parents' problems and able to deal with them. Through him, cottage parents were given a stronger voice in broad administrative matters and in planning. They also were given greater authority in their work with the boys. Although the consulting function of the social and clinical people was affirmed, the professional personnel were requested to refrain from giving implicit directions or orders in consultations.

The Channels of Communication Were Disrupted. The channels of communication were disrupted by the cottage parents as they frequently circumvented the established lines of communication or withheld information they felt would put them in a poor light. Emotional reactions sometimes distorted the meaning of information contained in many of their reports and conversations. Moreover, some emotionally-charged ideas necessary for the operation of the institution were repressed. The structure of the organization was weakened by this confusion in the communication system. The superintendent, as well as the heads of the education and social services departments, were often misled when they accepted the cottage parents' communications at face value. When they examined these communications analytically, they were amazed at the shifting and sorting, as well as interpreting, that was necessary to gain a fairly correct notion about what was actually happening. For example, the emotional coloring given by many cottage parents in reports on boys' behavior or general cottage problems often gave the impression of a serious or crisis situation when, in reality, this was not the case. The social work and clinical personnel also contributed to the mixed-up content communications. They often used technical language that was not understood by the cottage parents. Sometimes it misled them.

In view of these problems, the superintendent was faced with the necessity of developing a more effective system of communication. One objective in establishing the Department of Group Life was improved communications, for the department head was to serve as a communication bridge between the superintendent and the cottage parents. Structurally, this removed the superintendent from the direct and detailed participation and communication in the cottage parents' daily activity which had been required of the old superintendent. The social workers were to continue working directly with the cottage parents and with the boys as assigned, and to work with the clinical staff on a consulting basis. The director of Group Life would work with the social workers, clinicians, and superintendent on planning and administrative matters. Lastly, the head of the Department of Group Life was to work with the cottage parents on their cottage program and the management of special problems.

The Division of Work Was Rejected.   The institution was faced with resolving the organization problems resulting from its division of labor under the new treatment organization, particularly those problems stemming from the cottage parents' rejection of refined job specifications. As care and custody of the delinquents was de-emphasized, cottage parents charged that their positions were being relegated to a low status. Some maintained that they were charged with the major responsibility for maintaining custody of the boys but were given little or no authority for doing so. This was largely true. As specialties were added to the institution staff, many cottage functions were placed elsewhere. However, activities that required the highest degree of security remained in the cottages. For example, cottage parents supervised those activities scheduled for late afternoon and evening hours—periods of the day when the boys were most likely to run away. Also, the cottage parents were to insure that the boys met their total schedule, and they were held responsible for the boys' movement from and to the cottages. Nevertheless, the cottage parents' actions, especially those involving the use of authority, were restricted and closely scrutinized. Corporal punishment was forbidden, and reprimands, chastisement, and threats were discouraged. The cottage parents no longer had the major voice in determining whether the boys could, on the basis of their behavior, participate in various recreational and other "extra-curricular" activities on the grounds, go on passes into the community, or be released on the parole. In the new organization, these decisions were made by the staff at case conferences. The cottage parents complained bitterly that diagnostic, planning, and counseling functions were being usurped by the social work and clinical staff and that recreation was being taken over by the recreational specialists and teachers. These complaints, together with demands by the social work and clinical staff that some of the work traditionally carried out by cottage parents be assigned to them, complicated the organization of the institution's work.

Administrators responded by developing detailed job specifications for cottage parents, social workers, and clinicians, and then attempted the more difficult task of getting the various personnel to accept them. Cottage parents were given a stronger voice in decisions about individual cases and (through their department head) in planning and broad administrative matters. The consulting function of the social and clinical people was affirmed, but the procedures guiding the cottage parents' participation in counseling the boys were clarified and broadened. The cottage parents were encouraged to listen to the boys' personal problems if the boys felt like talking, and they were given some instruction on other counseling techniques. The problem of when to refer boys to the social workers was clarified.

The Status of the Cottage Parents Was Threatened. The administration was interested in according prestige to personnel with formal training, since training implied both an ability to understand the various facets of a boy's problem and skill in helping with the problem. Strong identification and association with the treatment program were also valued highly by the institutional authorities. Implicitly, at least, the administration placed a disproportionate amount of favor on personnel holding social work, clinical, and, to an extent, teaching positions. The cottage parents decried this situation, grumbled about it among themselves, and brought it to the attention of the administration. The superintendent reassured them, but this reassurance wore off rather quickly because the social work and clinical people retained the major decision-making powers and because they had better working conditions and salaries than the cottage parents. Consequently, the administrators had to find ways of returning lost prestige to the cottage parents and ways of making the cottage parents believe that administrators really believed them to be important. As indicated earlier, the cottage parents' status was finally improved by establishing a new department, giving greater recognition to their opinions in case conferences, and delegating more responsibility and authority to them in their work with the boys. Their salaries were raised, and additional personnel were made available to the cottages during periods of high activities, such as weekends and evening hours.

The Role of the Cottage Parent Changed. The administrators were faced with the general task of developing a new role for the cottage parents. This required an examination of recruitment and selection procedures, training processes, and motivation problems. While the superintendent, social workers, and clinicians were trying to stimulate cottage parents to develop a professional point of view, the specific tasks of the cottage parents were constantly changing under the impact of the treatment program, indicating a need for continuing in-service training of the cottage parents.

The administrators had made a genuine effort to recruit the best cottage parents they could. However, low salaries and poor working conditions made it difficult to attract and hold the type of cottage parents the superintendent, social workers and clinical staff envisioned as they talked about the future of the new treatment organization. The new organization did respond to the cottage parents' demands for help in doing their work. Serious efforts to convey the new treatment ideas were made, but the cottage parents were not particularly interested. Their demand was for training in specific skills to be used in working with the boys. The resistance of many of the cottage parents to the new treatment organization continued to block their complete acceptance of the new treatment ideas.

The Institutional Means Were Put to Serious Test. The cottage parents were to provide an accepting and helpful "climate" for the boys and were to help them establish acceptable habits, learn certain social and recreational skills, and accept the rules of the institution and society. They were to accomplish these goals by providing the boys with a "total group-living experience," which meant establishing routines for daily living, meeting school and work schedules, offering recreational and work activities, and encouraging a positive give-and-take among the boys. They also were to influence the boys by directing their activities, by the deliberate use of various attitudes, and by counseling.

But the cottage parents often were unable to maintain the routines of the cottage. They experienced serious trouble in getting the boys to cooperate and to develop a sense of fair play in recreational and leisure-time activities, as well as in the work they were required to do in the cottage. They did not always know in what situations they should be permissive and in what situations they should be firm. As a result, the total treatment organization was threatened. The cottage parents' emotional and defensive reactions were frequently incongruous with the reactions that were necessary if the boys were to be helped. These reactions had ramifications in the educational, social work, and clinical programs because cottage living was a basic part of the total program. A boy could not learn in school if he was improperly managed in the cottage, nor could he be successfully treated by the social work and clinical personnel if his cottage life was turbulent.

These problems reflected the wide gap in the field of institutional delinquency treatment between the conceptualization of principles and objectives, on the one hand, and the skills, knowledge, and attitudes necessary for their successful execution, on the other. Several changes, in addition to those already mentioned, were made by the new treatment organization to facilitate effective cottage parent functioning. The superintendent, social workers, and clinicians changed their expectations about the role of cottage parents. A more tolerant and supportive attitude was taken. They were given more latitude in their work, and their judgments were no longer subject to severe and critical analyses. They were encouraged to be more accepting of the boys, and to make an effort to understand them and work with them patiently. However, they were also encouraged to be natural and spontaneous in their actions, rather than behave in a way that was artificial and unnatural in order to carry out a particular recommendation in detail. Emotional and defensive behavior among the cottage parents diminished as a consequence.

6

STANTON WHEELER

| | | | | | | | | | |

Role Conflict in Correctional Communities

Studies of role relations in correctional communities point to the existence of value conflicts between inmates, custody staff, and treatment staff. Attention has been directed primarily to the effects of an inmate culture that poses a direct challenge and attack on the values of the prison administration.[1] The conflict between inmates and staff has been complicated in recent years by the addition of treatment personnel whose objectives may diverge from those of the custodians. The presence of three sub-units with differing interests and values places severe limits on the ability of the organization to define or achieve its major objectives.[2]

The purpose of this chapter is to extend our understanding of the nature and effects of role conflict in the prison, and to point to some conditions that may be important in reducing the conflict. The chapter reports the results of an empirical study of role conflict between

[1] Lloyd E. Ohlin, *Sociology and the Field of Corrections* (New York: Russell Sage Foundation, 1956), 27–32. A recent analysis and extensive bibliography of studies of the inmate culture appears in Gresham M. Sykes and Sheldon L. Messinger, "The Inmate Social System," in Richard A. Cloward, Donald R. Cressey, George H. Grosser, Richard McCleery, Lloyd E. Ohlin, Gresham M. Sykes and Sheldon Messinger, *Theoretical Studies in Social Organization of the Prison* (New York: Social Science Research Council, 1960), 5–19.

[2] Donald R. Cressey, "Limitations on Organization of Treatment in the Modern Prison," *ibid.*, pp. 78–110.

inmates and staff in a state reformatory.[3] Specifically, the study examines (1) the degree of conflict between inmates and staff in their privately expressed conceptions of appropriate conduct in the institution, and (2) the differences in perceptions, by inmates and staff members, of the attitudes that personnel and inmates are believed to have about appropriate conduct. The results suggest that there is less conflict between inmates and staff on a private attitudinal level than is usually reported on the basis of observational accounts. The social organization of the institution operates, however, to create a *perception* of severe conflict in role expectations. These perceptions guide the behavior of members of the organization, and are therefore an important force in the life of the correctional community. Since the bias in perception of social roles is a product of the institution's social structure, changes in the perception of those roles require changes in the social organization of the institution.

The chapter is organized in four sections. The first reviews the setting and the research design of the study. The second reports the major findings regarding private and perceived role expectations. A third section presents an attempt to account for the systematic bias in the perception of social roles by utilizing data on the social organization of the community. A final section suggests some conditions under which the inmate culture and social structure might be modified.

Research Setting and Method

The research was conducted at a reformatory for male offenders convicted of felony by Superior Court action and sentenced by the court to an adult correctional institution within the state. Although located in the west, the physical plant is roughly typical of many northern state institutions designed to handle younger, "more tractable" men ranging in age from 16 to 30. It is a walled, close-custody institution, although there are the usual provisions for medium and minimum custody assignments. The institution has a maximum capac-

[3] This chapter draws upon data gathered in a study of a state reformatory: Stanton Wheeler, *Social Organization in a Correctional Community* (Unpublished Ph.D. dissertation, University of Washington, 1958). I am indebted to Clarence C. Schrag for aid in the formulation of the problem, and to Harold Garfinkel and Howard E. Freeman for critical readings of portions of this chapter.

ity of 800 inmates, and, at the time of the study, had an institutional population of roughly 750.

The formal organization is similar to that usually found in close-custody prisons, including, of course, the caste division between rulers and ruled. Among the staff there is a further division of labor typically found in prisons, with a separation of staff under two associate superintendents: one responsible for custody, and one responsible for treatment. The custody-treatment division is further indicated by different styles of dress, different labels, and differences in the form of organization. Major departments within the treatment division include reception and guidance, classification and parole, education and vocational training, and religious services.

Changes in program established some three years before the study included the addition of reception and guidance units staffed by sociologists or social workers, a clinical psychologist, and a vocational counselor. All incoming inmates are processed through the unit and are later seen by members of the classification and parole staff. Thus, the inmates have been exposed to treatment staff members on a routine basis, though few of them have had any kind of intensive treatment.

Inmates included in the study group were selected on a random sampling basis from each of the major housing units in the institution. The sampling rate differed for each unit, since some of the units have relatively small numbers of inmates (those comprising custodial segregation, reception, and honor farm, for example). The research required a fairly large absolute number of inmates from each of the units. The sample design called for selection of 259 inmates. Dropouts and administrative scheduling problems reduced the final sample to 242, from which 237 usable questionnaires were returned, or 92 percent of the target sample.

The design called for a complete enumeration of custody and treatment staff members. Usable questionnaires were obtained from 18 of the 21 treatment staff employees, (86 percent), and 81 of 111 members of the custody staff (73 percent). No apparent biases existed between the tested and the untested groups.

The study required a research instrument which would yield (1) the privately expressed evaluations of inmate and staff conduct by inmates, custody and treatment personnel; (2) the perception of the evaluations held by members of each group. The approach adopted was similar to that used by Stouffer in the investigation of role conflict.[4] Hypothetical situations were developed from incidents that have occurred in penal institutions—situations that were known to occur with enough frequency to elicit realistic responses. In some of the situations, inmates are the central characters, and respondents were asked to evaluate the inmates' conduct. These situations provide evidence regarding consensus and conflict in the definition of appropriate inmate behavior. Other situations have staff members as the central figures, and are used to assess consensus and conflict in attitudes toward staff.

Two forms of response were used to elicit privately expressed evaluations. For some of the items, the respondents were asked to indicate their approval or disapproval of the behavior engaged in by the principal actor in the situation. Other items left the action unresolved, and required respondents to make a forced choice between two opposed alternatives. The following are examples of each of these items:

> Inmate Dooley gets cut in a knife fight with another inmate. Dooley is called before a disciplinary committee. The committee asks him to tell them who he was fighting with. He refuses to name the other inmate.
>
> How do you personally feel about Dooley's refusal to name the other inmate?
>
> _____ Strongly approve of Dooley's action
> _____ Approve of Dooley's action
> _____ Disapprove of Dooley's action
> _____ Strongly disapprove of Dooley's action

> Inmates Brown and Henry are planning an escape. They threaten inmate Smith with a beating unless he steals a crowbar for them from the tool shop where he works. He thinks they mean business. While he is trying to smuggle the crowbar into the cell house, he is caught by an officer, and Smith is charged with planning to escape. If he doesn't describe the whole situation, he may lose up to a year of good time. He can avoid it by blaming Brown and Henry.
>
> What should inmate Smith do?
>
> _____ He should clear himself by telling about the escape plans of Brown and Henry.
> _____ He should keep quiet, and take the punishment himself.

[4] Samuel A. Stouffer, "An Analysis of Conflicting Social Norms," *American Sociological Review,* 14 (December, 1949), 707–717.

All of these situations were designed to reveal the private expressions of approval or disapproval given by inmates and staff—a measure of role expectations as privately reported by the respondents.

In order to assess the *perception* of inmate expectations, respondents were asked to estimate the proportion of inmates who would approve of the action taken by the inmate in each story. For example, following the "knifing" situation reported above, all groups of respondents were asked the following question:

How many reformatory inmates do you think would *approve* of Dooley's action?

_____ Almost all of them would approve.
_____ About three-fourths of them would approve.
_____ About half of them would approve.
_____ About one-fourth of them would approve.
_____ Almost none of them would approve.

In the situations used for assessing norms applied to staff members, each group of respondents was asked to estimate (1) the proportion of *custody* staff members who would take a given action, and (2) the proportion of *treatment* staff members who would take that action. The form was identical to that used for inmates.

The questionnaires were administered to groups of from ten to twenty inmates at a time. Staff members responded during in-service training classes. All replies were anonymous. The seating arrangement precluded observation of any other person's response. After each administration, the groups were encouraged to discuss the items and the reasons for adopting one or another choice. Discussions were lively and indicated general agreement among both inmates and staff that the situations were highly realistic.

All findings are reported in terms of differences between the three groups of respondents. For privately expressed attitudes, all comparisons are based on differences in the proportions selecting one of the two alternatives presented for each situation.[5] Differences in the perception of group opinion are based on the median perceptions for each group. The relationship between private opinions and perceived group opinion is established by comparing the proportion who actually

[5] For the treatment and custody staff responses, the best estimate for the population is the proportion yielded by the sample. For inmates, the population proportion is estimated from the sample proportion weighted by the contribution of each sampling unit to the total inmate population. For details on sampling procedure, see Wheeler, *op. cit.,* pp. 26–32.

choose a given response with the median estimate of that proportion made by the three groups of respondents.[6] This enables an assessment of the direction and degree of bias in the perception of group opinion.

RESULTS

Expectations Applied to Inmates

Six of the stories had inmates as the central action figures. The situations tap aspects of inmate behavior that are assumed to come under some form of normative regulation by both inmates and staff. In addition to the two situations previously cited (to be referred to as the "knifing" and "escape" stories) the following four were used:

> Inmates Smith and Long are very good friends. Smith has a five dollar bill that was smuggled into the institution by a visitor. Smith tells Long he thinks the officers are suspicious, and asks Long to hide the money for him for a few days. Long takes the money and carefully hides it.

> An inmate, without thinking, commits a minor rule infraction. He is given a "write-up" by a correctional officer who saw the violation. Later three other inmates are talking to each other about it. Two of them criticize the officer. The third inmate, Sykes, defends the officer, saying the officer was only doing his duty.

> Inmate Martin goes before a committee that makes job assignments. He is given a choice between two jobs. One job would call for hard work, but it would give Martin training that might be useful to him on the outside. The other job would allow Martin to do easier time in the institution. But it provides no training for a job on the outside. Martin decides to take the easier job.

> Johnson, an inmate, learns that the institution has a group therapy program for interested inmates. He thinks the program might help him understand his problems. He asks a member of the treatment staff if he can get into the program.

[6] Conversion of the median perception to a percentage estimate was accomplished by assuming that the categories "three-fourths," "one-half," and "one-fourth" are mid-points of intervals with a width of 25 percentage units; the "almost all" and "almost none" categories having widths of 12.5 percentage units. The median perception was then converted to an estimate of the percentage of inmates who would approve of a particular action, using standard procedures for interpolation.

The situations were constructed to vary in the extent to which they involve participation in treatment programs, and in the extent to which the action taken by the inmate is likely to have direct consequences for other inmates. Responses of inmates, custody staff and treatment staff members are presented in Table 1.[7]

TABLE 1

APPROVAL OF INMATE BEHAVIOR BY INMATES, CUSTODY STAFF, AND TREATMENT STAFF

Situation	Percent inmate approval	Percent custody staff approval	Percent treatment staff approval	Percent difference between staff & inmates*
Knifing	89%	51%	61%	33%
Escape	30	82	78	50
Money	61	4	—	59
Rule infraction	47	85	100	45
Classification	31	6	—	28
Therapy	99	99	100	1

* Percentage difference was calculated by subtracting the inmate percentage from the mean of the percents for custody and treatment staff.

Inmate responses to these situations reveal something of the nature and range of private attitudes or expectations in the prison community. The "knifing" and "escape" situations reveal the strong support given to the maxim, "Don't inform." Almost 90 percent of the inmates in the "knifing" situation approve of the inmate's refusal to name his attacker. And even though inmate Smith is forced to participate in the escape plot, fully 70 percent of the inmates feel that he should keep quiet, and serve the extra time.

The money situation taps another aspect of inmate loyalty. Failure to protect the friend may or may not result in staff action against the friend. Yet roughly 60 percent of the inmates would expect a

[7] In this and the following tables, *n*'s are not reported, as the proportion of no responses was extremely small. For all tables presented, treatment staff responses are based on an *n* of 18; custody staff responses on an *n* of 79–81; inmate responses on an *n* of 231–237. The results can best be evaluated by their consistency rather than by tests of significance for specific items.

party to such a relationship to protect his friend, even though violating major institution rules to do so. While the minority opinion
here is larger than in the "ratting" situations, the majority still support deviance from staff policy.

The "rule-infraction" situation produced no observable consensus
among inmate respondents. Inmate comments about this situation
suggest that expectations are conditional on the reputation of the
officer. If he is defined by inmates as a trouble-maker or "all bull,"
any inmate who came to his support would be censured by other
inmates. If he is defined as a square-shooter who is fair and impartial
in his relationships with inmates, support for the officer would not
be disapproved.

The remaining two situations are different from the others, especially from the "knifing" and "escape" situations, in that the action
of the inmate has no direct effect on the lives of other inmates—
no one stands to lose by the inmate's decision. In these situations, the
modal response of inmates is favorable to staff programs. While a
large minority approved of the inmate's taking an easier job rather
than one that might prepare him for release, virtually all inmates
approved of the offender who sought help for his problems by participating in group therapy programs.[8]

To the extent that responses to these situations tap the role of
inmate as that role is privately defined by inmates, certain general
conclusions can be drawn. The results give strong support to observations on the importance of loyalty relations among inmates—particularly the norms against ratting. The greatest discrepancy between
inmates and staff occurs when the action has some direct consequence
for other inmates. This is consistent with Schrag's finding that "the
greatest social error is to cause someone to serve a longer sentence."[9]
But the inmate role is not consistently defined in opposition to staff
standards. Private expectations tend toward the norms of staff members in situations where individual decisions are unlikely to have any
adverse effect on other inmates.

[8] In the discussions following administration of the questionnaire, many
inmates were quick to mention that *they* didn't need therapy, but weren't
opposed to it for those who did. Others added that therapy is fine so long
as the group doesn't turn into a "rat-club." Some of the support accorded
group therapy programs in the abstract is undoubtedly withdrawn in the
concrete situation, when therapy may become re-defined as another form of
ratting.

[9] Clarence C. Schrag, *Social Types in a Prison Community* (Unpublished
master's thesis, University of Washington, 1944), 46.

These findings do not mean that the support indicated in the private expressions of opinion is acted upon by inmates. The data refer only to what inmates privately feel about inmates' actions. The results do suggest that there may be a considerable latent support for conventional values. The problem of treatment for many inmates may lie less in converting them from a criminal to a noncriminal value system and more in activating and reinforcing attitudes which already may be present on a private attitudinal level. Yet, as we shall see later, there are powerful forces operating to inhibit the expression of conventional values.

Staff definitions of proper inmate behavior reveal a high degree of consensus both within and between the custodial and treatment staffs. As expected, custody and treatment staff members are nearly unanimous in their approval of inmates who obey the rules, give support to the staff, and make constructive use of their prison term. The only departure from this pattern of consensus occurs in the "ratting" situations. Significantly, over half of both the custody and treatment staff indicate *approval* of the inmate who refuses to inform in the "knifing" situation, and roughly 20 percent of the staff give a similar response to the more extreme "escape" story. Arguments that inmate norms against informing are arraigned against the norms of the staff assume that staff members, in fact, are favorably predisposed to informers. Again, on the private level of expression, the data call this assumption into question. Whatever formal policy may be, staff members appear to be ambivalent about the informer. The conflict was expressed by a staff member who remarked, "Hell, I don't like rats any more than the inmates do, but if I think an inmate has inside dope on an escape plan, gambling, or something, I've got to ask him."

The lack of clear-cut approval for the informer undoubtedly reflects in part the generally low esteem accorded informers in the broader society. Beyond that, however, there is a suggestion that it is generated within the institution. Accommodation is a two-way process. It is significant that the staff lacks consensus at precisely the point where inmate norms appear to be most strongly held.

Perception of Inmate Expectations

This section reports findings on the *perception* of inmate standards. The perception index refers to the estimate of how inmates actually feel about the actions in the stories. It is not a statement as to how they should feel, nor how they will actually behave. Table 2 lists the median estimate of the percentage of inmates who would approve of the conduct in the hypothetical situation. In the "money" situation, for example, the average inmate estimate is that 83 percent of the inmates would approve of Long's hiding the money for Smith.

TABLE 2

INMATE, CUSTODY STAFF, AND TREATMENT STAFF
PERCEPTIONS OF INMATE OPINION*

Situation	*Inmate perception*	*Custody staff perception*	*Treatment staff perception*
Knifing	91%	91%	92%
Escape	8	9	28
Money	83	74	71
Rule infraction	15	22	25
Classification	54	54	52
Therapy	63	59	64

* Percentages of inmates who would approve of the conduct of the inmate in the situation. (Further description of statistical procedure in footnote 5.)

There is a high degree of agreement between the three groups in their perception of inmate standards. Inmates and custody staff in particular show marked similarity. The perceptions differ by more than 15 percent in only one situation. It appears that inmates and custody staff are perceiving the same social world with respect to inmate expectations, despite the differences in their official roles and in the sources of their knowledge. Moreover, the norms are perceived to be opposed to staff expectations. Only in the "therapy" situation, do custody and inmates perceive that the majority of inmates hold attitudes similar to those of staff members. Treatment staff perceptions showed a small but consistent departure from this pattern. In five of the six situations, their estimates are closer than the estimates of custody and inmates to the norms actually held by staff members. The treatment staff has a more optimistic view of inmate attitudes.

Bias in the Perception of Inmate Expectations

Comparison of the findings reported in the first two tables shows the relationship between privately expressed opinions of inmates and staff, and perceived inmate opinion. The data are portrayed in

TABLE 3

ACTUAL APPROVAL BY INMATES AND STAFF COMPARED WITH PERCEIVED INMATE APPROVAL

KNIFING SITUATION

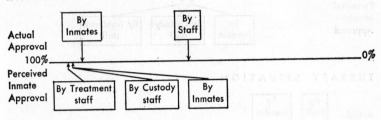

ESCAPE SITUATION*

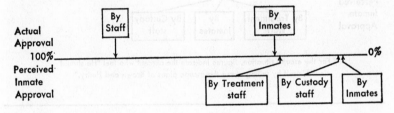

MONEY SITUATION

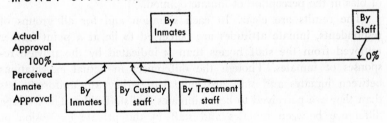

RULE INFRACTION SITUATION

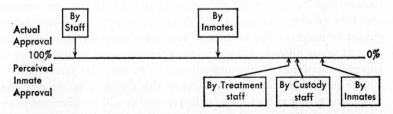

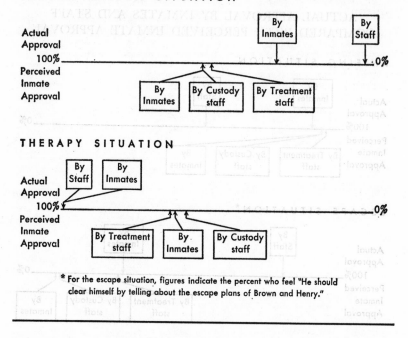

CLASSIFICATION SITUATION

THERAPY SITUATION

* For the escape situation, figures indicate the percent who feel "He should clear himself by telling about the escape plans of Brown and Henry."

Table 3. The comparison allows assessment of the degree and direction of bias in the perception of inmate opinion.

The results are clear. In each situation and for all groups of respondents, inmate attitudes are perceived to lie at a point farther removed from the staff norms than is indicated by the private responses of inmates. Though the differences in actual expectations between inmates and staff are quite large, they are uniformly less than they are perceived to be by inmates and staff alike. The average difference between inmates and staff in the private expression of appropriate inmate conduct is 36 percent. The differences are perceived to be greater than that by some 20 percent in the case of inmate and custody staff perceptions, and by 15 percent among members of the treatment staff. The image of an inmate society guided by norms hostile to those of staff members receives only partial support when differences in *private expectations* are reviewed, but it appears to operate clearly and strongly in guiding the *perceptions* of inmate standards. The consequences of this finding and some of the conditions giving rise to the bias in perception will be discussed after examining similar data drawn from staff behavior situations.

Expectations Applied to Staff Members

Three hypothetical situations are used to study expectations regarding the behavior of staff members. One situation places a treatment staff member in the dilemma of whether to reveal information about an inmate to other officials of the institution, when such information might be the source of action taken against the inmate. The situation reads:

> An inmate, Burns, meets frequently with a psychologist, Roberts. During one of their meetings, Burns tells the psychologist, Roberts, about a burglary offense Burns committed before being sentenced to the institution. The offense has not been solved by police, and the psychologist, Roberts, is the only one who knows about it.
>
> What should the psychologist, Roberts, do?
>
> _____ He should keep the information to himself.
> _____ He should make an official report about the information.

The situation involves the familiar conflict between professional ethics regarding confidentiality and obligations to the law-enforcement aspect of correctional work.

A second situation concerns a correctional officer rather than a treatment staff member. The officer's choice is between rigid adherence to formal rules and authority, compared with adoption of a permissive, counseling role. The situation is as follows:

> A correctional officer, Adams, observes a fight between two inmates. The inmates apologize, and say they are sorry. The officer, Adams, knows that both inmates have clean conduct records, that they are due to go before the parole board for a time cut soon, and that a write-up on their records might mean that they would not get a time cut from the board.
>
> What should the correctional officer, Adams, do?
>
> _____ He should investigate, and if the fight was nothing serious, forget about it.
> _____ He should give the inmates a write-up, and let them take the consequences.

The third situation assesses expectations regarding maintenance of custodial security when other objectives might call for relaxation of such security. It reads as follows:

The classification committee is considering a request from Jones, an inmate, for reduction in custody from close custody to medium custody. Jones has about eighteen months left to serve before he is scheduled for parole. He has a very good record in the institution. But he once escaped while serving a sentence in another reformatory.

What do you think the classification committee should do?

_____ Assign Jones to medium custody.
_____ Leave Jones on close custody.

The three situations will be briefly referred to as the "psychologist" situation, the "correctional-officer" situation, and the "classification-committee" situation. Table 4 lists the responses for inmates, custody staff and treatment staff personnel. The results leave little doubt as to inmate definitions of proper staff action. As expected, inmates give consistent and strong approval to the least severe staff response.

TABLE 4

APPROVAL OF STAFF BEHAVIOR BY INMATES, CUSTODY STAFF, AND TREATMENT STAFF

Situation	Percent inmate approval	Percent custody staff approval	Percent treatment staff approval
Psychologist should keep information to himself	88%	33%	44%
Correctional officer should investigate and forget it	97	69	56
Classification committee should assign to medium custody	93	74	83

The pattern of custodial and treatment staff responses is more complex. Ambiguity of staff norms is suggested by the fact that neither custody nor treatment staff members show a high degree of consensus in their role expectations. Only the treatment staff's response to the "classification-committee" story yields as many as 80 percent of either group of staff members in agreement as to appropriate staff conduct.[10]

[10] The figure for the treatment staff in the "psychologist" situation conceals an important split between subgroups. Seven of the nine guidance and

Moreover, the differences *between* custody and treatment are very small. Indeed, in the "correctional-officer" story the treatment staff gives a less "permissive" response than does the custody staff. Thus instead of finding homogeneity within each staff grouping and conflict between the staffs, precisely the reverse is found. The data do not fit the usual image of marked conflict between custodial and professional roles.[11]

Two features of the institution should be considered in accounting for the ambiguity in definitions of staff roles and the lack of conflict between custody and treatment. First, the institution has shifted in recent years toward a more "treatment-oriented" philosophy. The addition of reception-guidance units and the expansion of classification and parole brought a number of treatment personnel into the institution for the first time. The shift was supported by the central office. Furthermore, there had been a number of changes in personnel at the upper level of custody; the custodial structure was essentially fluid. Thus the introduction of treatment staff occurred in a context of other changes, and failed to meet a stable core of resistance. The variation of response within the ranks of custody may reflect the evolving though as yet only partial movement toward a new orientation. An alternative interpretation equally consistent with the data is that ambiguity in the definition of staff roles may be endemic to any institution that moves away from a strictly custodial program.[12]

A second feature of the custody-treatment relationship may help explain the absence of marked conflict between the two groups. Most of the treatment staff members were young and relatively new to the

---

classification personnel approved of the psychologist keeping quiet; eight of the nine education personnel felt the psychologist should make a report. Except for this item, the two segments of the treatment staff were in marked agreement. This item, however, is the only one that directly taps the professional standard of "privileged communication," and suggests the possible conflicts that may surround this area of role definitions.

[11] The items, of course, are too few and too narrow in range to permit any firm conclusions about the degree of conflict between custody and treatment. But other parts of the study give further evidence of a lack of value conflict. For example, 67 percent of the custody staff and 72 percent of the treatment staff, ranked "rehabilitation" as the most important objective of the institution. A larger proportion of custody than of treatment staff members felt that treatment programs could be successful for "the great majority of inmates," and that most inmates "desire to improve themselves" while in the institution.

[12] Cressey, *op. cit.*, pp. 93–110.

correctional field. Although well trained in behavioral sciences, they lacked the wealth of "common-sense" experience held by many of the custodial staff. They did not care to be labeled as starry-eyed men who failed to see the "basic realities" of the prison. Custody staff members, on the other hand, were well aware of the educational background of treatment personnel, and were not disposed to be viewed as ignorant and punitive guards. Moreover, both groups were expected to cooperate in establishing a stable institutional program. The hypothesis is that when the introduction of treatment staff occurs in a context of genuine support from correctional officials outside the institution and at a point of fluidity in the custodial structure, both custody and treatment personnel will face a strain to appear competent in dealing with many aspects of institutional life. The strain may be resolved as each group learns from the other in the process of working out a new program. This process should function to reduce the initial conflict between custodial and therapeutic roles, while at the same time producing ambiguity in the definition of those roles.

Perception of Staff Expectations

For the three "staff-behavior" situations, respondents were asked to estimate the expectations of custody and treatment staff members. Table 5 lists the expectations as perceived by inmates, custody staff and treatment staff personnel. The interpretation of the percentage figures is the same as in Table 2. For example, the median inmate estimate is that 13 percent of the custody staff would feel that the psychologist "should keep the information to himself."

Perhaps the most striking finding is that although custody and treatment staff members consistently view the treatment staff as more permissive in their orientation, this differentiation is completley lacking among inmates. Inmates perceive the norms of custodial and treatment staff personnel to be identical, and to lean strongly in the custodial direction.

There is a realistic basis for inmates' identification of treatment with custody. The functions usually performed by the treatment staff consist largely of institutional housekeeping—writing of diagnostic reports used mainly to aid in making decisions regarding custodial security, preparing progress reports for the classification committee and parole board, screening of mail and visiting lists, and the like. Although such activities may require psychological training, their consequence is largely custodial. Most inmates are acutely aware of

TABLE 5

INMATE, CUSTODY STAFF, AND TREATMENT STAFF
PERCEPTIONS OF STAFF OPINION

	INMATE PERCEPTION		CUSTODY PERCEPTION		TREATMENT PERCEPTION	
	of Custody	*of Treatment*	*of Custody*	*of Treatment*	*of Custody*	*of Treatment*
Psychologist should keep information to himself	13%	12%	19%	30%	36%	58%
Correctional officer should investigate and forget it	32	34	57	70	56	62
Classification committee should assign to medium custody	41	42	63	74	50	70

that fact. In the words of one inmate to a member of the treatment staff, "You case workers are nothin' but educated screws."

Some treatment staff members in this institution tried to dissociate themselves from the custodial role. While they agreed with the necessity of custodial security measures, they felt the identification with such programs limited their value as therapeutic agents. Thus one social worker refused to serve on the disciplinary committee for fear inmates would identify him with custody. The data from this study suggest that efforts to cast off the custodial image go largely unnoticed by the bulk of the inmate population.[13]

Bias in the Perception of Staff Expectations

Tables 6 and 7 portray the relationship between staff expectations and the perception of those expectations by the three groups of respondents.

[13] There may, of course, be *other* bases of differentiation between custody and treatment—along a dimension of who can be "conned" most easily, for example. See Lloyd W. McCorkle and Richard Korn, "Resocialization Within Walls," *Annals of The American Academy of Political and Social Science,* 293 (May, 1954), 88–98.

TABLE 6

ACTUAL APPROVAL BY CUSTODY STAFF AND INMATES COMPARED WITH PERCEIVED CUSTODY STAFF APPROVAL

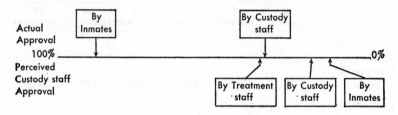

PSYCHOLOGIST: "SHOULD KEEP THE INFORMATION TO HIMSELF"

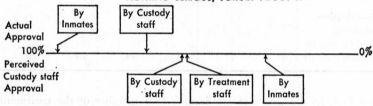

CORRECTIONAL OFFICER: "SHOULD INVESTIGATE AND IF FIGHT WAS NOTHING SERIOUS, FORGET ABOUT IT"

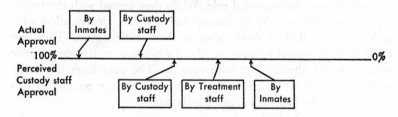

CLASSIFICATION COMMITTEE: "SHOULD ASSIGN JONES TO MEDIUM CUSTODY"

When custodial norms are the object of perception, all groups perceive those norms as further removed from inmate standards than is indicated by the private reports of members of the custodial staff. The average custodial officer has opinions that are closer to those of inmates than they are perceived to be by inmates or by staff members. This pattern holds over all situations for inmate and custody staff perceptions, and in two of the three situations for the perceptions of treatment staff members. When treatment staff expectations are the object of perception, as reported in Table 7, the overperception of conflict holds throughout for inmates, in two of the three situations for custody, and in one of the three stories for the treatment staff. Thus there is greater variation in the perception of treatment staff opinion than in the perception of either custodial or inmate opinion. Treatment staff members tend to view their own opinions as closer

TABLE 7

ACTUAL APPROVAL BY TREATMENT STAFF AND
INMATES COMPARED WITH PERCEIVED
TREATMENT STAFF APPROVAL

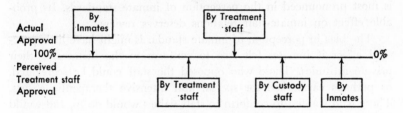

PSYCHOLOGIST: "SHOULD KEEP THE INFORMATION TO HIMSELF"

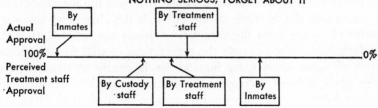

CORRECTIONAL OFFICER: "SHOULD INVESTIGATE AND IF FIGHT WAS
NOTHING SERIOUS, FORGET ABOUT IT"

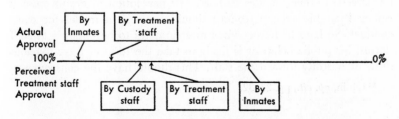

CLASSIFICATION COMMITTEE: "SHOULD ASSIGN JONES TO MEDIUM CUSTODY"

to inmate standards than either of the other groups. Throughout the comparison of perceived and privately reported expectations, the only deviation from the pattern of overperception of conflict occurs in the treatment staff's estimates of treatment staff opinion.

Overperception of Conflict in Staff-Inmate Expectations

The most consistent finding revealed in the comparison of private with perceived opinions is the strong tendency toward overperception of conflict in the role expectations of staff and inmates. To be sure, a considerable degree of conflict is revealed in the private expectations of inmates and staff. Such conflict is usually found in organizations with a caste-like division between superordinate and subordinate positions; especially when those in the subordinate position are involuntary participants in the system. But the *degree* of conflict is systematically perceived to be greater than it actually is. The tendency is most pronounced in the perception of inmate standards. Its probable effect on inmate-staff relations deserves review.

The bias in perception of inmate standards might have little practical effect if inmates felt free to conform to the dictates of their private attitudes. Those who opposed the staff could be segregated, or perhaps earmarked for special and intensive therapeutic efforts. Those who wanted to conform to staff values would do so, and would easily be recruited into staff programs designed for their benefit. This is the kind of process which supposedly operates in the ideal free community, where members can choose the company they keep. But a paramount characteristic of the prison is the absence of any easy means of escape from the expectations others are believed to hold. In fact, it is easier to evade the expectations of staff members than those of other inmates, for inmates are in nearly constant contact with their fellows; moreover, the informal sanctions available to inmate leaders are in many ways more powerful than those of the staff.[14]

Thus, the inmate is under pressure to conform to the expectations he perceives other inmates to hold. His perception of group opinion rather than his private feelings should serve as a model for overt conduct. So long as he perceives most inmates to be opposed to staff norms, his public behavior is likely to take the form of a conspicuous show of hostility toward the staff. This should have the consequences

[14] Ohlin, *op. cit.*, pp. 27–32.

of heightening the overt conflict between inmates and staff, and reinforcing others' perceptions of the norms as hostile to staff values. A further consequence is that of strengthening the position and power of those who actually *are* in opposition to the staff. Since their norms may be perceived to be the operating norms of the system, their power as sanctioning agents is increased. Their dominance exceeds their numbers. Finally, it has the consequence of preventing the development of organized opposition to the inmate culture among those who privately dissent from its maxims. How are they to find out that others have similar ideas when they are afraid to express their sentiments?

The condition described above appears to be quite general in correctional institutions. Cloward, in a study of a military prison, noted the frequency with which men concealed their desires for restoration from others, producing a pattern (which the data in this study strongly confirm) of "pluralistic ignorance"—the men were unaware of the number of others who felt as they did.[15] Ohlin notes that inmates who are willing to give support for conventional values often feel unsafe in doing so.[16]

These accounts and the data from this study suggest that a principal problem for correctional administrators is the presence of a perceived inmate culture that operates in opposition to the conventional orientations of staff members. Some suggestions of ways to neutralize the effect of the perceived inmate culture emerge from analysis of the conditions giving rise to the systematic bias in perception.

SOURCES OF THE BIAS IN PERCEPTION OF GROUP OPINION

Two very general models have been invoked to account for systematic biases in social perception. The first of these is a social psychological model which stresses social pressures acting upon individuals, giving rise to needs to distort or selectively perceive the social world. A variety of social and personal characteristics have been

[15] Helen Witmer and Ruth Kotinsky, Eds., *New Perspectives for Research on Juvenile Delinquency* (Washington, D.C.: Children's Bureau Publication Number 356, 1956), 80–91.

[16] Ohlin, *op. cit.*, p. 30.

shown to be related to accuracy of social perception, both in judging the attributes of individuals, and, more relevant to the present study, in the assessment of group characteristics.[17]

We may be sure that many of these processes are operating within the prison to produce biases in inmate and staff-member perceptions of each other. Many inmates enter the institution with a deep reservoir of hostility to authority which may lead them to view staff attitudes and opinions as highly opposed to their own. Staff members, dealing daily with troublesome inmates in a caste relationship, may come to view them as hostile and defiant with regard to any intentions of the staff. The degree of conflict between inmates and staff found in most of our penal institutions could easily lead to a negative stereotyping process, which may account for a greater perceived than actual conflict in attitudes and opinions between staff and inmates.

Other social psychological processes may operate to create biases in the perception of opinions of one's *own* group. For example, one mechanism by which an inmate may protect his self-esteem as judged by conventional standards is to deny that he is a "typical" inmate by selectively perceiving other inmates' attitudes as being more hostile to society than his own. Staff members, for their part, are in constant contact with inmates who are adept at pointing to the evils and inconsistencies of imprisonment. Under pressure to be accepted by inmates as "regular Joes" they may come to view themselves as more responsive and understanding than other staff members, hence perceiving that the others hold more hostile views toward inmates than they do.

A second model invoked to account for biases in social perception begins by questioning an assumption implicit in the "selective perception" approach. This is the assumption that the opinions and attitudes being perceived are freely observable, such that any error in perception must rest with the perceiver. This model (which might be called "selective visibility" to distinguish it from selective perception) focuses on the social processes which make for the observability

[17] For a review of some of the studies and their results, see Jerome Bruner and Renato Tagiuri, "The Perception of People," in Gardner Lindzey, Ed., *Handbook of Social Psychology,* Volume II (Cambridge: Addison-Wesley Press, 1954), 634–655. Attempts to develop more refined measures of accuracy of perception of group opinion than those used in the present study are reported in David C. McClelland, Alfred L. Baldwin, Urie Bronfenbrenner and Fred L. Strodtbeck, *Talent and Society* (Princeton: D. Van Nostrand Company, 1958), 29–111.

of the opinions and attitudes in the first place.[18] In complex organizations such as prisons, some members occupy more visible positions in the social structure than others. If the opinions of visible members are different from those of others in the organization, it is likely to be the opinions of the most visible members that serve as a basis for the perception of general group opinion.

This second model focuses, then, on what opinions are available to be perceived, rather than on what the perceiver does in selecting from the available material. It directs attention to the positions persons occupy in the social structure of the organization, and the resulting visibility (or lack of it) of their attitudes, opinions, and values. Applying these ideas to our finding that both inmates and staff tended to perceive inmate norms to be further removed from those of staff than the inmates actually indicated, we should find that the organization of the prison operates in such a way as to place antisocial inmates in highly visible positions; the norms and attitudes held by them should serve disproportionately as a source for the perception of general inmate standards.

There would seem to be at least four features of the social structure of prisons that serve to differentiate inmates according to their visibility. Three of these features are common to any large-scale organization; the fourth is applicable particularly to certain types of organization rather than others. First, visibility is a function of the position a person occupies in the formal and informal status system of the organization. Persons in positions of high status initiate interaction for a wider range of persons than those in low-status positions. Moreover, since the opinions of high-status persons usually carry authority, others are more motivated to learn their opinions and norms than those of low-status members. Applying this reasoning to the reformatory, we should expect that the perception of inmate norms is closer to the actual opinions of high-status inmates than to those of low-status inmates.

A second criterion of visibility is location in the spatial and temporal life of the organization. Persons who are located at the "center" of the organization's communications network and those who are allowed relatively free movement through the organization have a wider audience for their opinions and norms than do physically

[18] The following discussion of visibility draws heavily from Robert K. Merton, *Social Theory and Social Structure,* Revised Edition (Glencoe: Free Press, 1957), 335–357.

immobile persons or those far removed from the center of operations. In addition, those who have been in the organization for a long period of time, as distinguished from newcomers, have had more opportunities to make their opinions known, and hence can serve as objects for the perception of group opinion. We should find, then, that in prison the perception of inmate opinion is closer to the opinions of highly mobile inmates, inmates located in the center of the institution and inmates who have served longer sentences than to opinions of those who are not in these more visible positions.[19]

A third criterion of visibility focuses less on the position occupied by persons, more on their verbal output. Independent of other aspects of position, we should find that persons who are gregarious, who tend to talk often, are more "visible" than those who withdraw from social interaction, simply because the latter fail to make their opinions known. Applied to the prison, we expect that gregarious inmates serve as a basis for the perception of group norms more than do nongregarious inmates.

Finally, there is an attribute of the organization as a whole which relates to visibility. Organizations whose bureaucratic form follows what Gouldner outlines as a "punishment-centered bureaucracy" direct members to the observation of rule-violating behavior—a systematic attentiveness to the norms and values of those who violate the organization's proscriptions, with an under-emphasis on the opinions and attitudes of those who conform.[20] Although current correctional ideology calls for an emphasis on treatment, there can be little doubt that reformatories and prisons tend toward the "punishment-centered" type of bureaucracy. The interests of the public in custodial

---

[19] Support for the propositions about the effect of social status and ecological structure comes from a variety of small group studies. See Lindzey, *op. cit.*, pp. 786–832.

[20] Alvin W. Gouldner, *Patterns of Industrial Bureaucracy* (Glencoe: Free Press, 1954), 207–228. All of the types of bureaucracy noted by Gouldner may be found in the reformatory, and one may question the judgment that the major pull is toward the "punishment-centered" type. The attempt to shift the image away from a punitive-custodial emphasis is evident in a changed vocabulary—the "fish tank" is now the "reception-guidance unit," the disciplinary segregation block has become an "adjustment unit," and what was once isolation or simply "the hole" is now referred to as "quiet cells." But the custodial staff outnumbers the "treatment" staff by five or six to one, the disciplinary committee (now the "adjustment" committee) meets daily, and no member of the staff leaves until the "count" is cleared. At least these were the conditions that prevailed when the data for the present study were gathered.

security and of the state in maintaining a "quiet" institution with few escapes and insurrections operate to make both staff members and inmates highly concerned with those who are the greatest threat to custodial security. This leads us to expect that perceived inmate opinions are closer to the actual opinions held by recalcitrant inmates than to those who abide by the institution's rules.

By drawing upon data gathered in conjunction with the present research we can make a rough test for the operation of differential visibility as a mechanism making for an overperception of conflict between inmates and staff. The test is restricted to accounting for the bias in perception of inmate standards, since material on the staff is less complete. The data available for each of the dimensions included the following:

1. Social status:
   a) formal status—inmates who had served on the inmate council versus all others.
   b) informal status—inmates who reported being leaders or men to whom others came for advice versus those that did not describe themselves in this manner.

2. Spatial and temporal location:
   a) physical mobility—inmates assigned to work crews permitting freedom of movement through the institution, or a wide range of contacts with other inmates, versus those assigned to work-crews which limited their freedom of movement.
   b) ecological centrality—inmates assigned to central housing units versus those assigned to the reception, segregation, or honor farm units.
   c) temporal location—inmates who had served longer than average sentences versus those who had served shorter than average sentences.

3. Gregariousness:
   a) inmates who reported making three or more friends in the inmate population versus those reporting fewer or no friends.
   b) inmates who reported spending their free time in contacts with many other inmates versus those who spent their free time mostly by themselves.

4. Punishment-centered bureaucracy:
   a) inmates who were housed in the disciplinary segregation cell block versus all others.
   b) inmates who had received three or more conduct-infraction reports versus those who had received fewer such reports.

The visibility hypothesis asserts that the median estimate of inmate norms should be closer to the opinions actually held by the "high-visibility" group in each case.

The hypotheses were tested by using the four hypothetical situations in which there was considerable variation in inmate opinion; the "money," "escape," "rule infraction," and "classification" situations. For each item, the high- and low-visibility groups were compared. There were thirty-six separate tests (four each for the nine hypotheses). Thirty-four of the thirty-six were in the expected direction—the median perception of inmate opinion is closer to the actual opinion of the more visible group. There was one error in the case of the mobility hypothesis and one error in the second of the gregariousness hypotheses. The test was crude, for the number of cases was too small to permit holding constant visibility on other criteria while examining it on one. Within this major limitation, the results provide support for the hypothesis of differential visibility as a factor accounting for the bias in perception of inmate opinion.

The degree of fit between perceptions and opinions varies for the different criteria of visibility. The two criteria providing the closest approximation are formal social-status, and being housed in the punishment section. Inmate estimates of group opinion differed from the actual opinions of inmate council members by an average of 10 percent over the four situations, and from the opinions of the disciplinary cases by seven percent; the perceptions differed from the opinions of the total inmate body, however, by 25 percent.

A further test of the visibility hypothesis was made by classifying inmates according to the *number* of visible positions they occupied. Complete data were available for 153 inmates housed in the two major cell blocks of the institution. Of these, roughly 15 percent were in visible positions on at least five of the criteria of visibility. The median perception of inmate norms is strikingly close to the norms actually expressed by these highly visible inmates. The median perceptions for the total inmate sample were: money, 83 percent; escape, eight percent; rule-infraction, 15 percent; classification, 54 percent. The actual opinions of the most visible inmates were 82 percent, 5 percent, 27 percent, and 59 percent, respectively. Thus the data lend further support to the notion that opinions of the most visible inmates serve as the perceived opinions for the broader inmate society.

The findings on visibility among inmates apply in many respects to staff members; they, too, are likely to have contacts with members of the inmate council, and with inmates housed near the centers of communication. Other results from this study suggest in addition that the more nonconforming inmates (from the staff viewpoint) receive information about staff policies from cell block officers and other interpersonal means of communication, while those who conform to staff expectations more frequently cite formal sources, such as the superintendent's radio program. Supplementary to this, custody staff members who felt they had more contact with inmates than the average custodial officer perceived inmate norms to be more opposed to those of the staff. These results suggest that the custodial staff system and the inmate system may be linked through the roles played by highly involved and visible inmates.

We conclude that much of the strength of the inmate culture may reside in the ability of anti-staff oriented inmates to attain positions of high visibility within the inmate system, thereby generating and reinforcing the image of a culture in marked conflict with the values of the administration. Although there is latent support for conventional orientations among many inmates, their actions may more closely model the opinions of the highly visible minority, thus creating conflict over and above that called for by the actual differences in values of inmates and staff. The combination of heightened sensitivity to the custodial requirements of the reformatory and an informal inmate structure placing those most opposed to staff values in positions of visibility and power may be the primary conditions operating among both inmates and staff to produce a conflict which exceeds the actual differences between the two groups.

It is, of course, impossible to know whether these results and interpretations hold for other types of correctional communities. The results seem consistent with the findings of Cloward in his study of a military prison, with Schrag's results drawn from a state penitentiary, and with the earlier analysis of inmate leadership by Clemmer.[21] The most important practical question which emerges from these studies

---

[21] Cloward, *op. cit.*, 90–91; Clarence C. Schrag, "Leadership Among Prison Inmates," *American Sociological Review*, 19 (February, 1954), 27–32; Donald Clemmer, *The Prison Community*, New Edition (New York: Rinehart and Co., 1958), 111–148.

The patterns of pluralistic ignorance and differential visibility are likely to be found in any social structure whose leaders use coercive power. Accounts of Soviet refugees give evidence of the importance of pluralistic ignorance as one mechanism preventing the development of organized resistance against the Soviet regime. See Raymond A. Bauer, Alex Inkeles, and Clyde Kluckhohn, *How the Soviet System Works* (New York: Vintage Books, 1950), 261–263.

concerns the inevitability of the process by which those inmates most opposed to conventional values emerge into positions of visibility and power in the inmate system. Is it possible to modify the inmate social structure such that the administration can begin its work in creating value shifts among inmates without the added burden of functioning in an environment which appears to magnify the actual differences between inmates and staff? A firm answer to this question requires more knowledge than we now possess about the conditions under which the inmate social structure develops. Some tentative suggestions will be discussed in the concluding section of this chapter.

MODIFYING THE INMATE SOCIAL STRUCTURE

The consistency with which the inmate status and power structure gives support to an anti-staff position suggests that the structure is responding to some very stable elements that may be extremely difficult to change. A chief limitation clearly derives from the requirements for custodial security. So long as prisons are expected to protect the broader society, there are severe restrictions on the kinds of changes which the organization can undertake. Within the limits imposed by the custodial function, however, there are other conditions that may be subject to control by correctional authorities.

One of these conditions is the series of deprivations which accompany the loss of freedom. Sykes and Messinger have outlined the many deprivations which frequently accompany imprisonment, including the lack of autonomy, absence of physical comforts and the lack of normal heterosexual contacts, all of which constitute an attack upon the inmate's self-conception.[22] They suggest that the inmate social system functions to offset the "pains of imprisonment" by establishing a solidary system which legitimizes opposition to the staff, provides a basis for self-esteem, and enables inmates to gain amenities not allowed by the official system.

The hypothesis implicit in the analysis of Sykes and Messinger is that the inmate system will be controlled by those most hostile to staff interests in treatment and rehabilitation so long as the pains of imprisonment are not reduced by the official system. Perhaps this reduction of deprivations is one of the important features of minimum

[22] Sykes and Messinger, *op. cit.*, pp. 13–18.

custody institutions such as the California Institution for Men.[23] The relaxation of immediate concern for custodial security, the many programs available to inmates, and the systematic strengthening of ties to the outside world through family-visiting programs may serve to reduce many of the deprivations faced by inmates in maximum security institutions. The Norfolk Prison Colony in Massachusetts, with its novel attempt to provide for secure custody by tight control at the perimeter of the institution while allowing for greater freedom of movement and more natural surroundings inside the perimeter, provides one example of an attempt to reduce the deprivations of imprisonment while maintaining custodial control. Qualitative evaluations suggest that the traditional "inmate culture" is less in evidence than in other close-custody institutions, though this may be due more to the process of inmate selection than to the program itself.[24]

A related difficulty facing attempts to manipulate the inmate social structure is that those inmates who have thoroughly internalized a criminal value system probably benefit the most from an inmate culture based on antipathy toward the staff. They are likely to be most motivated to assume positions of influence and power. In addition, they may be the men most fully prepared by past experience to assume leadership roles. While little is known about the relationship between roles played inside and outside the prison, there is a strong suggestion that the visible inmates are those who have had most experience in exploitative and manipulative roles prior to imprisonment—those most schooled in techniques of aggression and deceit. The combination of greater motivation and more well-developed skills among the more criminalistic inmates suggests the difficulties facing administrative attempts to decrease their visibility and power.

That such attempts can be at least partially successful is evident in McCleery's recent report of changes over time in the inmate culture of a maximum security institution.[25] By opening new channels

[23] Kenyon J. Scudder, *Prisoners Are People* (New York: Doubleday and Co., 1952).

[24] A account of some of the problems and results over the early years of the program is found in Walter H. Commons, Thomas Yahkub and Edwin Powers, *The Development of Penological Treatment At Norfolk Prison Colony in Massachusetts* (New York: Bureau of Social Hygiene, 1940), 71–208.

[25] Richard McCleery, "Communication Patterns as Bases of Systems of Authority and Power," in Cloward, Cressey, Grosser, McCleery, Ohlin, Sykes and Messinger, *op. cit.*, pp. 49–77. See also McCleery's Chapter 4, above.

of communication through which the staff could present its definitions to inmates and by closing off the sources of information which had given the old guard among inmates and custody staff an advantage in the prediction of events, the staff was able to create a qualitative change in the inmate social structure. There was less emphasis on the "rat" concept, greater participation in treatment activities, and a closer liaison between inmates and the treatment staff. Although the possibilities of utilizing the staff's power to control communications and inmate assignments have yet to be explored fully, the experience reported by McCleery is a hopeful sign.

McCleery's report illustrates another problem in bringing about desired changes in the inmate social structure. As he notes, the changes in the distribution of knowledge and power among inmates require changes in the patterns of communication of staff members as well. Although the custodial staff and inmate systems may be in conflict on the level of values, the two groups both profit from a stable institutional operation. Others have noted a frequent pattern of accommodation between inmates and custodial staff whereby the staff uses the inmate elite as a source of social control over other inmates, in return for protection of the inmate leaders' position of power and visibility.[26] Thus a further condition for successful manipulation of the inmate social structure may well be a consistent program of training and education for the correctional officers, with particular emphasis on the nature of inmate society and on the dangers inherent in certain types of accommodation between correctional officers and inmates.

This very brief review suggests, then, that changes in the inmate system might result from (1) reduction of deprivations which accompany confinement, (2) changes in the communication patterns between inmates and staff, and (3) programs of staff training designed to offset the patterns of accommodation through which the more negativistic inmates are supported in their positions of power and visibility. Comparative analyses of correctional systems which differ in these respects might show a corresponding variation in the inmate culture. In addition there are variations in the structural characteristics of inmate populations that probably make it easier to introduce changes in some institutions than in others. For example, reformatories

---

[26] Richard A. Cloward, "Social Control in the Prison," *Ibid.*, pp. 41–43; see, also, Gresham M. Sykes, *The Society of Captives* (Princeton: Princeton University Press, 1958), 40–83.

differ in a number of ways from penitentiaries, apart from any differences in the value-orientations of their inmates. The inmate population of reformatories is typically younger, and therefore, perhaps more malleable. Reformatories also have a higher rate of turnover, which may produce a less stable and solid social structure—one which is less resistant to organizational change.

Verification of these suggested relationships requires studies that depart from the usual analyses of single institutions at one point in time. It also requires the development of objective techniques for assessing the inmate social structure and culture—techniques that can be applied across a range of different types of correctional communities. The detailed accounts of single institutions repeatedly show the impact of the inmate culture and social organization. But they are unsuited to the test of the most important practical and theoretical hypotheses about the conditions under which the structure might be modified. The need for tools that enable objective comparisons between institutions is particularly apparent at the present time, when correctional systems increasingly depart from the model of a pure custodial operation. Development and application of such tools should result in a significant advance toward a more adequate sociology of prisons.

7

RICHARD H. MC CLEERY

| | | | | | | | | | |

Authoritarianism and the Belief
System of Incorrigibles

The present chapter concentrates intensive inquiry on a small proportion of the prison's population and a small part of its physical area. However, the incorrigible unit and its occupants receive a disproportionate amount of attention from those charged with the government of the prison. The conditions which appear within the incorrigible unit deserve the close attention of those who would examine the prison as a system of social control, and their significance may be outlined under three headings.

1. *The incorrigible unit is an integral part of the prison as a system of social control.*

As a prison within a prison, a maximum sanction, the incorrigible unit serves as a last resort of the governors and as a deterrent to the inmates in the control of behavior throughout the prison in general. The anticipation of possible assignment there functions as an internal constraint for the majority of men in the general population, and its significance for them may be measured by the prominent mention it receives in the myths and rumors of the prison yard. When the prison is relatively stable, and inmate attitudes are tolerant of the administration, inmate society will ascribe the status of "dangerous outcast" to the incorrigibles. Under conditions of instability and tension, however, occupants of the incorrigible unit may be regarded as "Promethean

heroes" by the rest of the inmate community. Always a powder magazine of emotional energy and accumulated frustration in their com-
pressed unit, the incorrigibles represent the potential for an explosive
riot in the institution if events provide the spark.

2. *The incorrigible unit maximizes the variables of external constraint in a system of social control and permits examination of their
consequences.*

Any system of social control is a complex of external constraints
and sanctions plus internalized controls in some uncertain proportion.
The theory of *imprisonment* turns on the idea that men with minimal
or defective self-controls must be confined in situations which supply
that deficiency with a maximum of external constraints. The logic
of that position seems to be beyond question. The different and, perhaps, more mystical theory of *punishment* turns on the idea that a
given set of external constraints and sanctions will have predictable
consequences in the reinforcement of internalized values or self-
controls. The substance of the idea is contained in the phrase, "Punishment will teach him a lesson."

The concept of a reciprocal relationship between external and internal controls, however, admits of the possibility that a maximization
of external constraints will be associated with distortion, deterioration,
or atrophy of internalized controls. That alternative is rudely summed
up by incorrigibles as, "Too much time in the unit will drive a man
stir crazy!" Life in the incorrigible unit intensifies certain critical
qualities of the prison experience in general. It provides a logical
extreme of regimentation and an opportunity to study its consequences
which is as free from the impact of intervening variables as the wit
of authority can devise. As a result of the structured nature of the
unit situation and its isolation from both the prison yard and the
world beyond, the patterns of interaction and belief which do emerge
there correspond closely to the characteristics of the situation.

3. *The incorrigibles themselves provide an insight into both the
attitudes and processes of extreme alienation—a relatively uncompromised culture of criminality.*

The same logic that governs study of the prison as a "society in
microcosm" or a relatively self-contained interactional system applies
with double force to this isolation unit within the institution. Whatever the social limitations of men placed in the unit may be at the

outset, certain standard changes occur during their confinement, and much of their social activity is directed toward keeping such changes under some measure of control. Research, focusing on the relationship between behaviors and the conditions of confinement, can explore the possibility that certain behaviors and attitudes are "created by" the punitive conditions themselves. In the course of our study, widely separated groups of incorrigibles reported coherent and quite similar concepts of criminality. These concepts, reported in full in the following pages, defined the conditions of being a criminal as a state of mind or a conscious act of will. Unlike a majority of inmates, who would dissociate themselves from criminality, the incorrigibles identified themselves as criminals without reservation. The study of incorrigible groups, thus, permits observation of the manner in which self-perception is incorporated in behavior and belief.

Despite the elements of significance noted above for the study of incorrigible groups, little systematic or extended study of their behavior has been reported.[1] The relative poverty of this material, as contrasted with the wealth of research on the prison and the prisoner community in general, may be attributed to a combination of theoretical and technical limitations. Certain theoretical limitations must be noted as qualifications on the adequacy of this report. First, the collection of data requires the cooperation of some of the most hostile and uncooperative persons to be discovered anywhere. The following material dwells on procedures and procedural problems at some length in an effort to indicate the barriers of resentment which must be breached in an effort to gain rapport. Second, even after the researcher has established some measure of confidence, the respondents' emotional and intellectual limitations restrict the application of standard, systematic instruments of inquiry. The analysis of data must depend as much on the interpretation of cell-block gossip and "grapevine" as on the formal and scheduled elements of study. Finally, the impossibility of separating the study entirely from the prison's system of authority dictates certain reservations as to its conclusions.

The technical obstacles to research in the incorrigible unit are equally obvious. Any modification of the routines of control there con-

---

[1] Observations drawn from the context of specific programs are cited throughout this chapter where they apply to points at issue. Two works of general significance for the problem here are: Maurice L. Farber, "Suffering and Time Perspective of the Prisoner," *University of Iowa Studies in Child Welfare,* XX (1944), 155–227; and Jerome G. Sacks, *Troublemaking in Prison* (Washington, D.C.: Catholic University, 1942).

stitutes both a serious administrative burden (in one prison, two guards must be specially detailed to supervise anyone entering or leaving the unit) and a potential threat to security. Where administrative theory denies even the possibility of interaction and communication patterns among the isolated incorrigibles, approval of the research represents a considerable concession. In view of these difficulties, we are deeply indebted to the institutional officials who cooperated to keep technical obstacles to a minimum and made the research possible.

The present study of incorrigibles is drawn from a larger research program which examined prison government and the inmate communities in two maximum security institutions: the Central Prison, Raleigh, North Carolina, and Oahu Prison in the then territory of Hawaii.[2] The object of the larger study was to compare inmate behavior, attitudes and beliefs under authoritarian and liberal prison regimes. The research, which extended over three months in Central Prison and one year in Oahu Prison, involved systematic comparisons of incorrigible groups and the general inmate populations in each prison as well as comparisons between the two institutions.

STEEL, CONCRETE, AND SHADOWS

The prison, even in its larger dimensions, is a world of steel, concrete and shadows—a society of gray and lonely men in which love and laughter remain as hollow echoes of the past. Yet within that larger pattern of punishment and control, there are patches where its hard, sharp lines are softened by a plot of grass. There are times when the hardened world of social relationships is lightened by moods of affection or respect, and hours when the metallic clang of grated

[2] A general report of the work in Central Prison appears in *The Strange Journey* (University of North Carolina Extension Bulletin, March, 1953). A more extended discussion of administrative procedures and their relation to social structure and belief in the inmate community is published in my *Policy Change in Prison Management* (Michigan State University Governmental Research Bureau, 1957). The separate studies are drawn together and treated in detail in the unpublished dissertation, "Power, Communications, and the Social Order: A Study of Prison Government" (University of North Carolina, 1956). The over-all research program, covering several penal institutions and extending over a period of three years, was supported by the University of North Carolina and by a grant from the Doris Duke Foundation, administered by the Institute for Research in Social Sciences of the University of North Carolina.

doors fades into the background of an old song, softly played. Even prison rules, which regiment the day with lines of sullen, silent men, relax at evening time. Then the outcasts from the larger world mingle in what is called the "freedom of the yard," exchange pictures, form private cliques and petty conspiracies, trade from an always surprising accumulation of private goods, and order their affairs in terms of patterns that constitute the prison community. The yard is the forum and the market place of the prison community.

In the prison world, however, there is still another degree of extreme constraint—a corner in which the steel, the concrete, and the shadows converge into a massive and gloomy cell block. Its walls are thicker, its bars more closely spaced, and its regimentation more exacting. This most heavily guarded section is the incorrigible unit. Confined in individual cells within that unit are rows of men removed from contact with free society and the prison community by every device available to the management of the institution. For months or, in some cases, even years, these isolated men live in a perceptual universe which consists of the steel walls of their cells and the more barren wall beyond the grated cell door. The stark simplicity of life in the incorrigible unit combines the qualities of a nightmare with those of an extremely rational, and artificial, logic. In the ordered squares of steel, restriction and a denial of individuality reach an extreme that cannot be extended, even in one's imagination. The governing of men within this unit becomes in part a prototype and in part a fantastic caricature of the authoritarian situation.

It is not so much in the ordered knowledge of social science as in the farthest flights of the imagination that suggestions for understanding the social psychology of the incorrigible unit may be found. One of the most perceptive of these flights is Plato's allegory of the cave. He creates an image of prisoners chained so that they see nothing but shadows on a distant wall, and hear only the echoes of other voices. This is almost a description of incorrigible prisoners who in reality are prevented from seeing one another, but whose shadows are projected outward from their cells. To them, like Plato's imaginary prisoners, the truth can be nothing but the shadow of images.[3] These are men who live on a level of reality different from that of the world outside, men whose life in the shadows gives them a most uncertain contact with reality at best.

Another perceptive flight of the imagination has been recorded by a contemporary artist. William Steig has drawn a cartoon showing

[3] Plato, *The Republic,* vii, 514–515.

a small box turned on its side with a glowering little man huddled inside. The thought of that little man is expressed in the caption of the sketch, "People are no damn good!"[4] There is a relationship between the peculiar view of the world given to the men inclosed in a box and the philosophy he holds about the world. Both Plato and Steig provide fundamental insights into the character of life in the incorrigible cells.

A Social Laboratory. The particular significance of incorrigible units to this research lies in the fact that they provided "laboratories" for the study of small-group interaction in an extreme authoritarian situation. On the assumption that criminal behavior represents some ideological or attitudinal departure from the normal, these desperate men might be thought of as standing at the extreme of distance from the normal—a distance somehow proportionate to the extraordinary setting in which they live. In North Carolina, at least, assignment to the incorrigible unit was based on attitude as much as on behavior. We sought out the beliefs and perspectives of prisoners on a wide range of problems related to law enforcement and social control. The responses of incorrigible inmates to a series of questions about the causes and control of crime served to identify their position on just those matters in which they might be presumed to differ most completely from the conventional point of view.

A Trouble Spot. An element of special significance to penal administration lies in the position which incorrigible units have occupied in riots. Very often the shock wave of hysteria and violence that occasionally erupts in prisons has originated in an incorrigible section. The explosion in Michigan's Jackson Prison, one of the most destructive in penal history, began in its segregation section, Cell Block 15. John Martin's detailed report of that riot provides one of the rare descriptions written of life in an incorrigible unit. The unit, as Martin describes it, is almost identical to those providing the setting for this study, except that it was on a larger scale.[5] Study of the social processes and beliefs examined here may provide an insight into the roots from which the fury of riot springs.

A Demonstration Project. There is an intrinsic significance to the beliefs and outlook reported by incorrigibles. They are men who have had and are having the most immediate and direct experience of

[4] William Steig, *The Lonely Ones* (New York: Duell, Sloan and Pearce, 1942), 78–79.

[5] John B. Martin, *Break Down the Walls* (New York: Ballantine Books, 1954), 55–98.

punishment. Whatever the hopes of those who advocate punitive sanctions as a means of controlling behavior, and whatever the logic, facts, and theory of those who oppose the use of such sanctions, the experience of incorrigibles is relevant. Donald Rasmussen has written, in connection with a study of inmates in Illinois, "A prisoner does have a perspective of the penal and parole systems that no one else can get, and, therefore, his expressions are necessary in order to have a complete description of the entire penal and parole systems."[6] The men who took part in our study were told that their participation might make a real contribution to a more rational and effective treatment of men in trouble everywhere. That statement was made in all sincerity.

ELEMENTS OF AUTHORITARIAN CONTROL

In neither of the prisons studied was the incorrigible unit the primary punitive sanction. Each institution had its row of block cells adjacent to the incorrigible section, and additional facilities in which a man could be broken by the withdrawal of food and other privileges, or, in Central Prison, by more direct means. In both Oahu Prison and Central Prison there was a certain ambivalence in the attitude of officials toward the units. Some officers saw confinement in them as straightforward and uncompromised punishment; other officials took the position that such confinement was simply "administrative segregation." (The latter position was popular in North Carolina, where inmates were placed in the unit on an indefinite or permanent basis.) The American Prison Association officially recognizes this difference:

> It may seem like hairsplitting to those who have no experience in institutional work to differentiate between administrative segregation and punitive segregation . . . It may be said that [administrative] segregation is also punitive segregation in its effect, but its intent is protection of the inmate and the institution rather than punishment of the individual. It is essential that inmates understand their new status and the purpose behind it.[7]

Whatever distinctions may officially be made, and whatever the distinctions made by administrators of the prisons studied, the inmates

[6] Donald Rasmussen, "Prisoner Opinions About Parole," *American Sociological Review*, V (August, 1940), 594.

[7] *A Manual of Correctional Standards* (New York: The American Prison Association, 1954), 358.

understood only that they were being punished. Neither of the units provided the facilities for recreation, education, religion, work, supervision, or counseling which standards prescribe for "administrative segregation."[8] Yet both units also compromised absolute conditions of punishment in view of the length of time for which men were confined. Reading, writing, smoking were permitted, within limits. Thus, unit confinement was, in fact, punishment. However, when confinement was prolonged over many months and into years, it became a way of life rather than just a special experience of punishment.

Authoritarian Qualities. As a way of life, the incorrigible unit displays some of the characteristics of authoritarian social systems in an extreme degree. One of these characteristics is the use of force. This does not mean that the inmates were systematically flogged or physically tortured. The force used is not the dynamic energy of the whip: it is the static power of tool-proof steel cells. The inflexible restraint of a square of steel is a directly-felt physical experience. As time turns the thumbscrew of that square down closer on the mind, the pain may express itself in a physical sensation. When, as often happens, the isolated inmate beats his own head and hands against the walls, the bloody results cannot be easily distinguished from brutality.

A second characteristic of authoritarian systems is regimentation and depersonalization, both of which mark the incorrigible unit. Life goes on in absolutely unchanging routines. The guard pads by the cells with clocklike regularity, and all but the most elementary physical processes are ordered in complete detail. Unlike life in some fantastically "ideal" authoritarian state, however, regimentation does not take the form of a variety of disciplined behaviors. Its form is the removal of alternatives for behavior. There is no type of work or social activity which will enable the prisoner to create an experiential product and give expression to his own individuality. Only thought and a small selection of carefully screened reading matter are available to give a man a vehicle for achievement or the development of personality. Absolute conformity is the only type of behavior that gains official approval, and such approval can be expressed only by a promise, stated or implied, that deprivations will be reduced at some distant future time. The system of government is geared to compel a vegetable-like level of existence.

An additional characteristic of the incorrigible unit is the ever present eye of authority. Advertisements in the trade magazines of

[8] *Ibid.,* p. 360.

penology have featured an invention which smacks of fiction and fantasy—a television device that produces, on a central control panel, a picture of the activities in every cell. An identical device and the psychology of those on whom it was turned provide a central theme in George Orwell's imaginative story of an absolute dictatorship.[9] In neither of the incorrigible units studied was absolutism equipped with such a technical convenience. In its place, there were rules which required the guard to look into each individual cell at frequent intervals. The constant presence of repressive authority was a dominant fact in the experience of the men.

An equally important characteristic is the unresponsiveness of the governing authority. Guards in the incorrigible units are only slightly less bound by regimentation and regulations than the men they watch. It is not within the guard's discretion to answer the requests of the men, and the rules of his post prohibit him from approaching the front of the cells close enough that he can be seized. Few requests made by inmates could be granted under such circumstances, but even those that were possible to grant gain little response. The units are detached from the communication and the habit patterns of the main prison to essentially the same degree that they are segregated physically. Requests for writing paper, interviews, medicine, or a new light bulb often fail to enter into the communication channels of the larger prison, and hence bring no response. Factors of social and physical distance, convenience, and security combine to lower the degree of responsiveness to men in the units even below that applying to men in the prison yard.

A final authoritarian characteristic of the units is uncertainty and indefiniteness. However personally responsible the men of the units may be for the situation in which they are placed, their future is removed from their effective control. Particularly in the case of Central Prison, the period of men's confinement in the unit depended on the will of persons on whom they had no influence and was decided on the basis of factors which they did not understand.

The amount of uncertainty in the situation was one of the important differences between the Oahu Prison and Central Prison incorrigible units, which were very similar in most respects.[10] In Cen-

[9] George Orwell, *Nineteen Eighty-Four* (New York: Harcourt, Brace, 1949).

[10] In the context of the larger research program, Oahu Prison was sharply contrasted with Central Prison in its use of liberal concepts of prison govern-

tral Prison, men were committed to the unit on an indefinite basis, but they were led to believe that an improved attitude would gain their release. However, no indication was given of what constituted such an attitudinal change, nor of the process by which such change would be communicated to those who made the decisions on the future of the man. Men were released from the unit at times, but the criteria which guided such decisions were unknown to the man released, the other men in the unit, and the research worker who studied them. The effect was to create the impression of a completely arbitrary and mysterious use of power in Central Prison.[11]

Confinement in the incorrigible unit at Oahu Prison was also indefinite, for each case was subject to periodic review, and a variable number of days-per-month might be allowed to the credit of the man who was reviewed. However, a maximum length of sentence was set at the time of confinement, and this sentence was respected by the officials. A first escape attempt brought an eighteen month period of confinement, and men who attempted to escape a second time were confined for three years. Assault brought the relatively short sentence of one year, but on no occasions were men confined for less than three months. Reductions in the length of such sentences were earned entirely on the basis of conformity to known rules. There was some appearance of arbitrariness and inconsistency in sentences for actions other than escape and in the varied interpretations placed on the same behavior by different guards. Reductions in sentences seemed to be based on highly intangible considerations which included "attitude." However, the existence of a known maximum limit on the length of the punishment contributed a degree of certainty not present in Central Prison.

Distinctions. There were other differences. For a few minutes each day, men in Oahu Prison would be permitted to come out of their cells, and one man would be allowed to remain out long enough to mop the corridor or perform some other janitorial task. Letters written to the officials at Oahu Prison often received an eventual acknowledgment, and visits to the unit by top level officials were

---

ment with the general inmate population. This contrast did not extend to the management of the incorrigible unit, however, and the standard operating procedures of the two units were nearly identical.

[11] See the discussion of "absolute predictability" and "absolute unpredictability" in Chapter 3, pp. 115–122, above.

more frequent at Oahu than at Central. While these visits seldom changed conditions in any positive way, they gave the men an important sense that they were not completely forgotten by the governing powers. Another difference arose from the fact that regulations against marking the walls had been overlooked for some time in Oahu Prison. Drawings on cell walls ranged from accurate reproductions of the girl on a matchbook cover to a wall-sized mural of impressive quality done in pencil, cigarette ash, food juice, and, after its main outlines had appeared, a crayon provided by a guard. This art, like the cave drawing of primitives, expressed the personality of the occupants, and often seemed to represent a wishful manipulation of symbols for desired objects.

The presence of an exercise yard and its use weekly by most of the men in Oahu Prison was also an important difference. The chance to see grass, sunlight, and the sky, if only for a few minutes, was an important privilege after months of cell confinement. A final difference in the two situations was relevant to the procedures of our study, rather than substantive. In both prisons the incorrigibles were divided into two sections, but in Central Prison the two groups could be brought together for the period of the study sessions, making a single group averaging fifteen men. In Oahu Prison separate sessions were held with the two groups of between six and eight participants. This was a difference imposed by security considerations.

It is difficult to define the amount of difference between the two units, for there is no common standard of measurement that would have meaning in the outside world. To a casual outsider passing through and judging in ordinary terms, the rows of men in solitary cells would seem identical. To the man who daily counts the number of rivets in the steel walls around him or studies the geometry of shadow patterns cast by the bars, the prospect of a cell change may be a crucial life experience. Thus, the differences may seem insignificantly small from one point of view and "catastrophic" from another. At Christmas time in Oahu Prison, a prisoner conceived the idea of tearing a piece of paper into the shape of a bell and hanging it over his cell door by a thread pulled from his shirt. The idea was copied by other men in his section, and the guard permitted the paper bells to remain until after New Year's Day. Such fads did not occur, and probably were not allowed to occur, at Central Prison. This illustrates some difference in permissiveness in the two situations. There is no way to indicate the impact of that difference from the point of view of the man in the cell.

Other Extremes. There is a small body of literature available on the individual and social behaviors which appear in the type of extreme authoritarian situation represented by incorrigible units. This material is drawn primarily from observations of Nazi concentration camps. An article by Theodore Abel supports the basic assumption of the present study, namely that the nature of the governing process, at least in extreme cases, determines basic social relationships in the group governed:

> One of the more interesting observations is the fact that in every one of the more than two hundred large concentration camps, identical patterns of reaction developed among inmates in spite of the virtual absence of contact between them as well as the heterogeneity of their populations.[12]

Abel notes that the reaction patterns stem from adjustment to the destruction of all previous group relationships and from the limitations on the absolute controls which the rulers tried to establish. He also observes the similarity of the behavior exhibited by those at the top of the hierarchy of inmates to the behavior of the officials, a phenomenon that appears frequently in prison society.[13]

In an article based primarily on observation of women concentration camp inmates but including some study of male prisoners, Herbert Bloch reports that the efforts of the German officials to brand the inmates as criminals were resisted by the inmates and failed completely. Most inmates saw themselves as victims of fate, martyrs, and persons superior to their captors. Bloch makes the following comment on the camps as "social laboratories":

> What happens to the untrammeled socius when the usual social framework is removed? What happens when the inculcated propensity for conforming to well established channels of routine in human intercourse is denied these patterned outlets? It transpired that what developed was a process of "desocialization," resulting in a primal state of human association. It is possible to conceive of this as a heuristic prototype for comparative study with institutionalized and more normal patterns of groupings, leadership, and hierarchical class structure.[14]

[12] Theodore Abel, "The Sociology of Concentration Camps," *Social Forces,* XXX (December, 1951), 153. See also Donald R. Cressey and Witold Krassowski, "Inmate Organization and Anomie in American Prisons and Soviet Labor Camps," *Social Problems,* 5 (Winter, 1957–58), 217–230.

[13] Abel, *op. cit.,* p. 154.

[14] Herbert A. Bloch, "The Personality of Inmates of Concentration Camps," *The American Journal of Sociology,* LII (January, 1947), 355.

The Nazi concentration camps included a number of intellectuals in their populations, and that fact has produced some sociological study of inmate behavior by inmates themselves. Bruno Bettelheim's reports on the behavior of leaders, the processes of adjustment, the brutalization of social relationships, mass fantasy, and regressive phenomena are perhaps the most extensive of these.[15] Curt Bondy, another ex-inmate, has written on the spread of rumor, emotional epidemics, and the drive for dominance resulting from calculated degradation. Bondy admits to an approval of the indeterminate sentence in his earlier days as a criminologist. His conclusion after experience in the camp was that the indefinite sentence, like all forms of uncertainty, exercises a "depraving effect on the personality of the internees."[16]

The dominant characteristics of the incorrigible units studied were expressed in the presence of force, authority, regimentation, and uncertainty in the relations of the subjects to the governing officials. These, plus the factor of isolation, gave the units a number of qualities in common with concentration camps; both types of institution represent extreme instances of an authoritarian system of social control.

THE APPROACH

In each case, the study of incorrigible groups was preceded by general observation of prison culture under extreme conditions and by acquaintance with some inmate leaders in the prison. Although the details of the approach varied to a small degree in the two cases, the variation was only that required in the different situations to achieve a certain relationship with the men. In order to explain the nature of the approach and the relationship it was designed to achieve, it is necessary to anticipate some of the later analysis of inmate behavior in the units. The problems of gaining confidence and establishing communication provide insights into the social structure and attitudes of the incorrigible groups.

Relation to Power. In a social group completely dominated by

[15] Bruno Bettelheim, "Individual and Mass Behavior in Extreme Situations," *The Journal of Abnormal and Social Psychology,* XXXVIII (October, 1943), 417–452.

[16] Curt Bondy, "Problems of Internment Camps," *The Journal of Abnormal and Social Psychology,* XXXVIII (October, 1943), 465.

official power, every response to the ruling class and to persons associated with the ruling class is dictated in great part by the power relationship. The two basic alternatives presented to the investigator were (1) to exploit a relationship with the power system in order to enlist a more active response from the men—for example, to have more men fill out questionnaires; or (2) to dissociate himself from the official power structure as far as possible. There was no middle course such as that which might distinguish government-sponsored and private research in the outside world. Nothing was permitted to exist in the closed environments of the incorrigible units without official approval, and the prisoners were highly conscious of that fact.

The second alternative was chosen. We disclaimed any official power, influence, connection, or sympathy with officials and illustrated the relationship of the study to the University in every possible way. This was not a position to be asserted at the start of the sessions and ignored after that time; there was a continuing process of reinforcement throughout the study. The investigator deferred to the guard's requirements with apparent ill-will, in order to demonstrate that his power was less than that of the guard in the situation. However, he halted discussions whenever the guard came within hearing range and made obvious use of every possible technique to protect the confidence of the prisoners. Note-paper bearing the letterhead of the University of North Carolina and the Institute for Research in Social Sciences was used on every occasion possible, thus establishing the notion that the research was sponsored by an outside agency. As an incentive to participation, the point was made that the research might be of value to prisoners and men in trouble somewhere, but it was clearly and regularly asserted that there was no prospect of any aid or benefit to the participants directly.

In short, while it was not possible to dissociate the study and the investigator entirely from the power structure of prison administration, an effort was made to neutralize the relationship to power by exploiting the prestige of the University and to minimize the appearance of power in the hands of the investigator. This element of the procedure gives a foundation to the hope that the responses of the men were not dictated by a calculated effort to manipulate power by means of their relationship with the research worker. However, the extent to which the situation and social relationships of the men were dominated by the factor of power makes it probable that the responses were conditioned in some way by a perception of the study as high or low in the order of power. The differences in the two prisons prevented the investigator from approaching the men in exactly the same way, but the investigator's behavior in both incorrigible units was calculated to create and maintain an identical appearance of the relationship of the study to the administration.

Participation. Participation in the study was voluntary. The only incentive provided was the hope that the work would lead to more rational treatment of other men and to more effective means of preventing children from getting into trouble. Concern for children seemed to be the most frequent motive for participation, but an undeniable attraction of the study was the opportunity it gave the men to leave their cells for short periods. This boredom with ordinary routine and the rare opportunity for self-expression which the discussion group provided were added incentives for the majority of men.

In neither unit did the study groups include the entire population. In Central Prison the study group averaged around 70 percent of the unit population, and all the leaders were active members. In Oahu Prison every man in the unit gave some support to the project. Also, active participation was higher in discussion and in returning questionnaires than was the case in Central Prison. However, one of the high-status inmates participated fitfully at best; he was conducting a hunger strike when the study began, and he later manifested extreme symptoms of mental breakdown and regression which cost him his leadership position by the time our work was concluded.

The majority in each case was given a veto on participation by any member whom they distrusted or whom they felt could not contribute to an intelligent discussion of the problems proposed. This veto was not exercised formally by the Oahu Prison group, although low-status members were subordinated in active participation. The men in the Central Prison unit refused to permit the participation of some individuals whom they considered "rats." In both cases, the men who agreed to participate were permitted to define their own degree of cooperation and its terms. They might attend the discussion without contributing. They might speak in the discussion without filling in any parts of the questionnaire of which they were skeptical. We hope that anything lost by those allowances was more than equaled by a gain in the validity and reliability of the replies given. These precautions, taken to insure willing sincerity, may seem too elaborate by outside standards, but they were required by the atmosphere of suspicion and hostility which permeated the units. Even with these precautions, the men who cooperated did so with a feeling that it was dangerous to speak the truth as they saw it and with a conscious resolve to assume that risk. The opportunity to speak freely and to make the choice involved in responding was, by itself, a pleasant experience to some men.

The actual work of the groups was done at a table placed in the corridor in front of the cells and at the opposite end of the cell block from where the guard was stationed. The table, of dining-hall size, was large enough to accommodate the entire group which met for discussion sessions. The presence of the meeting place in the corridor was an advantage not shared by all studies of prisoner attitudes. It provided a setting in which the men were accustomed to speak frankly and in which they did not feel the discomfort of unfamiliar surroundings.

Problems. In the first approach to the incorrigibles at Central Prison, we took advantage of inmate acquaintances made some months before. A series of adult-education programs in the camps of the prison system had been conducted earlier, and, acting on the assumption that a successful prison program must be acceptable to inmate leaders, several leaders had been asked to assist with the planning. Some of these leaders, who were approached on the advice of the prison physician, were old-time prisoners with records of serious violence and disciplinary trouble in the institution. They gave meaningful help with the design of the camp programs and later were sent letters of appreciation by the University. These letters contributed to their status with their fellows as word of the camp programs returned to Central Prison. Thus, the inmate leaders held cordial feelings toward the University, and they cooperated willingly when they were asked to aid with the Central Prison study. Among other things, they provided introductions to high-status figures in the incorrigible unit and insight into some of the power relationships there.

Despite this background, establishing a study group was difficult. In a serious procedural error, one man from each of the two sections of the incorrigible unit was called to a group meeting with two leaders from the yard. This meeting was held in the visiting room and ended with both men definitely committing themselves to assisting with the study. On returning to the incorrigible unit, each man was faced with the task of explaining the project to his fellows and gaining their support. This task was complicated in one of the sections by the fact that the consultant selected had recently lost much of the status which had once given him a top-leadership position in his group. In both cases, the attempt to win the interest of others was met by flat failure, and when the research worker entered the unit two days later to begin the work, the two men who had promised to help refused even to discuss the matter.

In the face of this refusal, the research worker could only wait in idiotic silence for some explanation, knowing that the entire project hung on a thin thread. The culture of the unit prohibited any move that would grant information to "free people," but after a wait of about an hour the explanation came. The group felt the entire project was a trap set to get the men to give information which would be used against them. The inmates were convinced that the administration would stop at nothing to ferret out their thoughts and punish them for their attitudes. The fact that the inmate assistants had gone out of the unit to the visiting room and returned with such a proposition placed each of them under suspicion of having sold out to the administration. Even the man who was held in the highest respect by his associates had lost considerable stature as a result of his suggestion, and both men resented the research worker for having compromised them to such an extent.

The first experience drove home a lesson that was not ignored thereafter. Conversation with an inmate must take place in the area occupied by the group and within hearing of his associates if suspicion is to be minimized. In the face of apparent failure, the investigator could do nothing better than spend the afternoon in the unit in idle and friendly conversation, conversation which, in inmate terms, did not have an "angle." Such an approach from an outsider was a unique experience in the lives of the lonely men in the unit, and one which soon produced a much warmer relationship. It appeared that there might still be prospects of gaining cooperation. A second lesson from the experience was that no motive or interest of science, however lofty, provides a substitute for direct, personal, nonexploitive interest in the men as a means of gaining their cooperation. During the course of the later study sessions, each hour of formal group study was matched by an hour of informal and friendly visiting, which often proved more productive.

A return visit on a later day was spent in getting acquainted with the men in the cells personally and talking about whatever matters were of interest to them. At that time, the two men who had been tapped as leaders suggested that the study sessions might possibly be arranged. They supplied the names of others whom they felt should be consulted, and a picture of the leadership structure of the sections began to emerge. The men thought to be power figures were then asked to suggest how the study might be initiated. On their suggestion, the group in each section was assembled to hear the project explained, on the condition that they not be required to speak. Four men were not invited because it also was suggested that the group would not meet if they were extended invitations. The separate meetings were held, and at the end of the explanation the research worker withdrew while the men voted on whether or not to take part in the project. After the leaders, who were now apparent, had said a few words the vote was unanimous for approval in each section. The first meeting was scheduled for the following week.

When the investigator returned at the scheduled time, he was again met with flat and unanimous refusal to participate. After another long wait for reasons, it was stated that the explanation given to the two sections had been different. No difference had been intended and we could recall none, but on further discussion minor differences in wording and detail were accurately reported and the talks given to the two groups compared. It is significant that the two groups had been completely segregated between the time of the explanations and the time of our return. The two sections were separated by several feet of concrete and steel, yet what had been said in each section was known with the most detailed accuracy in the other. After further discussion, clarification of the previous explanation, and requests for help directed at the leaders, the project was again approved by vote. In the discussion, we emphasized that little help could be expected from men who were afraid of their own shadows and who felt that there might be danger involved. The men responded to the latter idea more favorably than they had responded to earlier assurances of confidentiality.

The problems of the approach to the Central Prison group illustrate what can hardly be conveyed in a direct statement—the hostility and suspicion which were a central feature of the atmosphere in the incorrigible unit. Extreme suspiciousness was expressed in the conviction of the group that dictaphones were planted in the cell block and that some of their own group might be "rats" stationed to hear the discussions. Such suspicion constituted a limiting factor in procedure as well as a finding of the study.

Cooperation of the group in the incorrigible unit at Oahu Prison was easier to obtain, in part because of the lessons learned in Central Prison. Two months were spent in the prison before work in the incorrigible unit was begun. This experience provided an orientation to life in the prison as a whole and some knowledge of relationships in the unit. Friendships were established with several men, and an introduction to the men in the incorrigible unit was provided by one of these men, who slugged an official and received a one year sentence. After he had an opportunity to enter into the social processes of the unit, the investigator visited him in confinement. His cell was between those of the two most dominant figures in his section, and he persuaded those leaders to take the initiative in gaining support for the study.

Each member of the group was told the outline for the study, and all explanations were made in identical terms. The prestige of the two leaders in the first section was sufficient to stimulate participation in the second. The man who held the highest status in that second section became deeply interested in the work and was the most active participant in the unit. There were indications that the basic hostility and suspicion which had provided such a barrier in Central Prison were largely offset in Oahu. The suspicion was there, and it expressed itself in many hesitations and the failure to deal with some of the questions raised, but at no point did it seriously threaten the existence of the study. On the other hand, the topics studied in Oahu Prison did not provoke, on the whole, the intensity of interest and violent reactions which often marked the Central Prison group, and a problem of sustaining interest appeared.

Methods and Materials. The details of the group-discussion procedure used in the incorrigible units were identical in both prisons and with those used in study of groups from the prison yards. The only change made in the mimeographed materials used by the study groups was the substitution of "Territory" for "State" or "North Carolina" where that change applied. A series of problems in law enforcement, social control, and penology were presented for study and discussion by the group. The series constituted a simplified seminar in criminology designed for presentation in sixteen sessions. Two-hour meetings were held twice each week with the groups, and some topics not completed in one session were carried over to an extra meeting. The format involved presentation of material in the form of a life story of a man in trouble. After two introductory topics to establish definitions and working procedures, the series dealt with causes and methods of control of delinquency, police and judicial administration, admission, orientation and classification in prison, discipline, and penal rehabilitation.

Questionnaires on which respondents checked alternatives were distributed in order to record the beliefs and preferences of inmates and to provide a framework for discussion; they were not distributed as attitude tests. However, a number of questions posed alternatives which seemed to range on a scale of hostility and resentment toward society and institutions such as police departments and prisons. Other questions provided alternatives which seemed to range from an extreme at which responsibility for crime was accepted by the individual to an extreme at which such responsibility was projected on others. In most questions, at least one alternative was intended to allow expression of cynicism and bitterness. The first application of these questionnaires in Central Prison indicated that some items were unsatisfactory, but the schedules were not changed because we wanted to present identical stimuli to all groups. Some of the "forced choice items" provided a useful stimulus to discussion as the men took the opportunity to quarrel with the question.

Participants were asked to criticize and/or elaborate the ideas presented. This was a fairly complex assignment and was repeated at the start of each session. The men were told that the number of children who got into trouble was increasing every year, and that society did not seem to have the answers which could prevent that trouble. At every stage in the process of law enforcement, the unsolved problems resulted in tragic failures and untold misery. It was suggested that a major part of society's problems might come from a failure to understand the experiences of men in trouble and to see the problems from their point of view. The idea was advanced that a combination of social theory and experience might achieve solutions that neither was able to accomplish alone. The men were asked to consider the problems, not from the point of view of their own experience alone, but from that of all the other men in trouble whom they had known. The justification for selecting this group as helpers was given as the fact that they had more experience with trouble than any others. By repeating the assignment at intervals and drawing attention to the questions posed, it was possible to control to a considerable degree the tendency of the incorrigible unit meetings to deteriorate into "gripe sessions."

The investigator acted as moderator. He tried to keep his own participation at a minimum and limited to asserting the questions rather than proposing particular solutions. The list of questions was taken up item by item, and general discussion occurred near the end of each session. The moderator made only brief notes during the discussion sessions because of the suspicion which extensive note-taking aroused, but these notes were expanded as soon as possible after the sessions were completed. The men were encouraged to write as extensively as they would on problems raised, and a number of carefully prepared essays were produced. These were often thinly disguised bills-of-complaint based on the writer's case. However, discussion of some items in the questionnaires provided evidence of a high degree of consensus within the group, and reasoned defenses of the answers given indicated that the questions had touched on definite tendencies to act, an essential element of "attitude."

The issues raised most clearly in the group discussions were explored in greater detail by discussions and interviews with the leaders in each group. Questionnaire items were scored in the presence of the group and with the assistance of the men in a number of cases, and unsolved problems were returned to the group for further discussion.

One additional point must be noted. These were not men with academic backgrounds to aid them with test-taking techniques. The task of choosing one best alternative from a list often struck them as unreasonable when other alternatives also contained elements of truth. Selection of two or three alternatives was common. Scoring, then, involved giving one-half or one-third weight to distributed markings. Discussion of the problems of crime with these men indicated in many cases that their refusal to identify single causes was more reasonable than the expectation that they should.

THE SOCIAL SYSTEM

Our conclusions about the social life of the incorrigible units are based on a number of hours spent in casual visiting and interviewing as well as on study of behavior occurring in the group discussions. Interviews with the guards served as a check on many of the observations made directly in the units. In addition to these observations, an insight into unit life under the most repressive conditions was provided by a thirty-one page, single-spaced, typewritten document found in the archives of Oahu Prison.[17] This document was the official transcript of testimony taken in an investigation into social relationships which had matured into a fight in the incorrigible unit in 1939. The present section will first consider the common characteristics of social life in the units and then note certain elements which distinguish the social systems of the two prisons.

Although the basic physical conditions of life are the same for each man who is confined in the incorrigible unit, a distinct social structure is apparent. Some men are recognized as leaders, others are rejected as social outcasts. The majority of men are quite conscious of their place in the group. With the exception of those who are on the lowest level of the social scale, the men form an obvious identification with the group, and this identification seems to increase with the degree of isolation from the rest of the prison or outside world. In Central Prison, a man deliberately committed an offense in order to be returned to the incorrigible group, giving up an attractive spot in the outer prison to do so. Although this is the only case in which rejoining the group was obviously deliberate, other indications, confirmed by interviews with the men, suggest that the unit has an attraction stronger than its severe conditions for some men who have found a sense of membership in the society there.

The sense of belonging to a distinct group does not prevent a bitter atmosphere of hostility and resentment within the group itself. Hostility is directed toward low-status members and scapegoats. Also, the men of the unit identify themselves with inmates generally, but

[17] In 1939, the incorrigible unit at Oahu Prison was the same physical facility now in use. Only two inadequate meals were provided, other privileges were reduced in proportion, sentences were indefinite, and one of the members of the group investigated was the last man to be flogged at Oahu Prison. At that time the men were permitted out of their cells to eat, and a fight started at meal time. The officer who investigated the fight questioned the nine inmates and the guard on duty. The two participants told opposite stories, but their testimony indicated that the fight had been building up over a period of time. On that basis the officer spent many hours questioning each man on the tier separately about the social relationships and problems there. While the pages contain scores of references to the word "rat" and expressed aversion to "ratting," the men talked about the unit, its communications, and the autocracy which prevailed in its informal, social system. This valuable body of data served as a check on the observations of the present study and added weight to parts of its analysis and conclusions.

there are a number of indications that they think of themselves as a select group and see other prisoners in the yard as weak and frightened. They see their own group as somehow set apart by the test of strength they are meeting and by punishment which they define as persecution. The group will accept men of very low intelligence or obvious mental disorder, but it rejects the weak and the penitent. A consciousness of informers dominates the thinking of the group, and the hatred vented against a weakling who is desperate for release is associated with a fear that he may turn informer to gain his freedom.

Leadership. There is nothing to be gained, and, perhaps, much to be lost by an inmate who would set himself up as the leader of the incorrigible group. The leaders who emerge apparently do nothing to seek that distinction, and conscious efforts to exert leadership by men who lack the proper qualification brings them little but humiliation. The mantle of leadership is bestowed, like a hereditary crown, on men who fulfill traditional requirements of the group. The leaders in each of the four sections of the incorrigible units appeared to be quiet and restrained men. In only one of the sections did the leader appear to be the most physically powerful of the members in the group. The more volatile and aggressive men ranged themselves as lieutenants to the leaders. The leaders were trim, well-conditioned men with a reputation for being able to fight if necessary but not "bulls of the block."

In each case the leaders were men who had demonstrated courage and had been involved in dramatic misbehaviors, but many of their associates could claim as much distinction. They were above the average for their group in intelligence but they were not the most intelligent members. The primary condition which seemed to be involved in leadership was a relationship to power. This was not simply the ability to command power or exert force among their associates, although such rights came with their office. Leadership came to those with reputations of exerting power in the past, and even more important, to those who also demonstrated an ability to resist power in the present. Leaders were respected for their ability to take punishment without breaking. The greatest fear expressed by incorrigible leaders in interviews was that they might "crack up" under the strain of long confinement. In the presence of the group, however, they maintained an appearance of philosophical calm and adjustment to their situation.

The ability to take punishment "like men" could not be demonstrated in a brief period under incorrigible unit conditions. Each leader was one of the senior men in his section. In North Carolina, a Negro who had remained defiant through a reported 26 days in "the hole" (solitary confinement) and repeated beatings was held in high respect by the predominately Southern, white, members of his group. It appears that leadership among the incorrigibles is a form of adjustment to a situation in which power is monopolized by the ruling class.

It is the leaders' subordinates, not the leaders themselves, who express overt hostility in the most violently aggressive terms. The leaders are moderates who temper the more extreme statements of others, and it appears that one function of leadership is moderation of quarrels and mediation between the group and power. The leaders exercise a limited degree of control and discipline over their groups, and this control usually stops the group just short of conflict with the officials. At the same time, the leaders enjoy a relative freedom from the group code which prohibits speaking to officials. In each section studied, interaction between the group and officials seemed to go most frequently through the leader.

In one of the two instances in which a revolt against leadership was observed, the man displaced was one whose discussions with officials were believed to have worked unfavorably for the group. In what seems to be a general characteristic of the extremely authoritarian situation, the old leader was completely rejected, scapegoated, and ostracized by all but a small minority, despite the fact that the group had earlier accepted his practice of speaking with officials. He did not become a participant in the discussions of his unit because, as he said, it would have been necessary for him to fight certain other inmates. Another leader either broke down mentally or attempted to create the impression of mental breakdown in hopes of being transferred from the units. The judgment of his fellows was that, given either alternative, he had failed to stand up under punishment; he was completely rejected. The only incidents of violence which appeared among the groups studied came in connection with changing leadership or in expression of hostility against scapegoats who were excluded from the group by definition.

Communication. An illustration of the highly developed communication system operated by the incorrigible group was reported above, when we described the unauthorized contacts made between the two sections of the unit in Central Prison. Instruments of communication are as complex as the system of plumbing and ventilation, and information not intended for the ears of the guard must follow intricate channels. The system of communication is closely related to status; low-status men are ignored or by-passed by the system.[18] The scapegoat finds his questions unanswered and his comments not passed on beyond the adjoining cell. The comments and interpretations given by the high-status member, on the other hand, receive circulation throughout the group.

Communication content focuses on the affairs of the unit, and, to a lesser degree, on the prison generally. Sports events and other entertainment from the outside world, which hold an interest for the men in the yard, have little place in the communication of the unit group. Almost the only news from the outside world which circulates among those men is information on court cases and police reports. On such subject matter the group keeps itself well informed, and in its discussions of current information is used as a basis for bias against the police, court, and parole authorities. New men in the unit are questioned in minute detail about the affairs of the yard, and this questioning gives the regular members a chance to evaluate the new men. Social acceptance tends to be slow, and it accompanies absorption of the new man into the communication system.

A great amount of interest and attention centers on food, even where the diet is adequate. There is speculation on the next meal, evaluation of the last, and complaint about unequal distribution. One of the continuing sources of trouble and hostility is suspicion that the food is not divided fairly. Food is the only form of gratification offered the men, and it becomes the principal issue in their lives. Other elements of communication content are scandal and gossip about guards and officials. Every type of story which will tend to question the integrity of the officials is told and retold; the stories often carry the implication of homosexuality. Finally, there is discussion of official policy. On one hand, the men are convinced that they are buried and

[18] A close connection between power or status and a capacity to transmit definitions which serve as the premises of behavior for others appeared in all the prison communities studied and seems to be a fundamental characteristic of any closed or censored system of communication. See Richard M. McCleery, "Communication Patterns as a Basis for a System of Authority and Power," Chapter 3 in Richard A. Cloward, Donald R. Cressey, George H. Grosser, Richard McCleery, Lloyd E. Ohlin, Gresham M. Sykes and Sheldon L. Messinger, *Theoretical Studies in Social Organization of the Prison* (New York: Social Science Research Council, 1960).

forgotten by the administration. On the other hand, there is a conviction that the administration is so concerned about them that it
may plant spies or microphones at any time in order to learn what
they are thinking and punish them for it.

In the formal work of the discussion groups, the bulk of the
communication was carried on by a few men. The majority sat back
and listened. Some of those who had the most interest and the most
to contribute to the discussion lacked the status to gain a hearing.
They often wrote their comments on neatly printed, carefully ruled
sheets of paper which they turned in after the session. Expressions
of bitterness and hostility, or apparent examples of injustice, gained
the obvious approval of the group. When these were based on the
individual's personal case, however, they did not meet with the same
approval, and the group withdrew its attention and ignored men who
monopolized discussion with private gripes.

As indicated, the leaders acted as moderators in the discussions.
They had less to say than their lieutenants, and they usually waited
until other expressions had been made before giving their opinions.
After the opinion of the leader had been given it usually was futile
to expect any further debate on the issue. Their comments showed a
greater capacity to generalize, interpret, and rationalize the more
particular resentments expressed by the others. Although the summary
statements of the leaders provided the last word in group discussion,
they did not seem to exert strong influence on the responses given to
the questions posed for a written answer. Men would sometimes con-
cede a point in open debate and then would continue to assert their
position in the written answers.

Summary.   In summary, the social system of each section in the
incorrigible units appears to be a rigid hierarchy. Leadership is related
to seniority, a reputation for toughness as expressed in both the ability
to exert power and to take punishment, and a relatively moderate
position in relation to the officials. The leaders are permitted more
frequent contacts with the officials than are other group members,
but such permission contains the seeds of revolt, which flower when
the contacts become unsatisfactory to the group. The loss of high
status brings with it complete rejection, including ostracism from
the patterns of communication. These tendencies seem to be expressed
in each section of the units in both prisons considered.

There are clear differences and distinctions, however. In the unit
in which confinement was indefinite and its reasons less clearly

defined, leadership by one man in each section was more pronounced, and the hostility and rejection expressed against suspected "rats" was the most dominant characteristic of the social system. A sense of persecution, identification with the persecuted group, and hostility toward outsiders (factors which will be considered more fully in connection with discussion of the belief system) were expressed more dramatically in the group to whom confinement appeared most arbitrary. Both groups were oriented to the value of not breaking under punishment. Yet the tendency to break down mentally and emotionally appeared most clearly in the Central Prison unit. Men on the verge of cracking were compelled by the value system to express their strength and defiance of the officials. This took a variety of forms, but the most conventional form in the units, as in prisons generally, is destruction of everything breakable in the cell. Since the plumbing facilities are about the only breakable things available, ripping the toilet out by its roots and smashing it has become a stereotyped means of expressing strength and defiance. This form of expression was frequently used in North Carolina; and while the number of cells without plumbing testifies to its use in Oahu Prison in times past, at the time of the study such behavior in Oahu's unit was very rare.

THE WORLD OF THE INDIVIDUAL

Just as the world of the incorrigible group provides a strange model of an extreme type of social condition, the world of the individual in the unit reflects elements which characterize the group itself. Identification and description of these elements as they appear in the world of individuals may provide a foundation for understanding the beliefs and behaviors of the larger group.

There is considerable range of individual differences in the responses of men confined in the units. Some show every evidence of wishing to conform to the demands of the prison, and they display very little involvement in the social life of the unit. They may continue for several months with only a peripheral relationship to social process and beliefs held by their associates. For a time such an individual may exhibit penitence to an outside person and may express to him an apparently sincere regret for whatever misdeed placed him in punishment. Such attitudes of penitence are not expressed in communicating with fellows; on the contrary, in order to maintain any status in the group he must publicly express hostility and bitterness toward officials. The rather private attitude of penitence does not bring any sign of response from the officials, for they are placed at such a distance that they do not know of its existence. But public attitudes of hostility do bring response and approval from men in adjoining cells and from leaders. In this situation, the man's penitence is replaced by a feeling of humiliation and resentment at the absence of any official recognition for that sentiment, and he tends to become indoctrinated with the attitudes of the group. Interviews in both Central Prison and Oahu Prison indicate that the early period of confinement brings a personal desire to conform to the regulations of the prison, and that this attitude passes into an increasing hostility as time goes on. Observation suggests that the increased hostility is related to increased acceptance by the group.

There are some men who do not conform to the above pattern, however. Something about their offense or the extent to which they resist the dominant patterns of belief of the group casts them in the role of the social isolates. They may criticize the thinking of the group too strongly on their arrival and, as a result, be ostracized from the communication system. They may behave in such a way as to create a suspicion that they are "rats." Other isolates are rejected leaders who have been cast out of the group. Still others seem to become isolates simply because they find complete withdrawal to be pleasant. Although the majority of the men welcomed the group discussion sessions as an opportunity to come out of their cells, visit friends, express hostility, and gain a feeling of contributing to something of significance, the isolates did not come out. Some even resented the light and the sounds of the unit life. Isolation and withdrawal were more common and extreme in Central Prison, but evidence of a common pattern appeared in both units. The pattern is likely to mature into either homicidal or suicidal behavior.

It was possible to interview some of the most extremely withdrawn individuals in their cells. The problem of gaining rapport was difficult in all cases and insuperable in some. In two cases, resistance was overcome by eating food which the individual believed was poisoned. In others, a relationship was established by discussing highly abstract philosophical and theological issues with men who displayed a background of intensive reading in those fields. In these discussions the men always tended to focus on their particular situation, and the discussions provide the basis for the following sketch of the world as it appears to the totally isolated individual. It should be noted that prison officials regarded some of the individuals as mentally unbalanced. It must be conceded that these men were at least out of touch with reality as it is ordinarily perceived.

The isolate sees himself at the center of a great, complex creation. He sees the unyielding, physical mass of the unit extending away from him, and he is the only person in that perceptual field. He has a sense that there is something personal about the world around him and a feeling that it was created for him alone. Where the prohibition against defacing property has been enforced and the walls are a blank expanse, he has no sense of the men who have occupied the cell before him or of others who will follow. He thus has a tremendously exaggerated conception of his own importance. At the same time, the isolate who is in lingering touch with reality realizes that he is being confined, restricted, and punished. The cold, hard world, which he feels was created especially for him, seems to be created for his particular discomfort. It is a cross which he must bear bravely and without yielding. If the cause of the harshness of his world is sin, he does not feel that the sin is his own. The cause of the evil is the will of the "rat" or official who put him in the unit. To his mind, nothing that he has done or could have done is sufficient cause of what he feels is an omnipotent power focused on his personal oppression. As the isolated individual loses touch with others in the unit, his conviction that he is being privately persecuted increases. His feeling that he has been betrayed by a "rat" and persecuted by those in power may increase until he forgets entirely the reason for his confinement. Seeing no limit to the extent of the power exercised against him by an evil and mysterious force, he will assume that his food is poisoned and that some "rat" or secret device is being used to seek out his inner thoughts so that his punishment can be increased.

Within the strange creation which is the world as the isolate experiences it, he is the master of all he surveys. He surveys very little, but within his cell there is no occasion to compromise his own interests with those of another. He is alone in his perceptual world. However insecure he may be outside his cell, and however much he may feel compelled to move things within that cell in order to assert his mastery, he is absolutely dominant in the cell. He may not want to come out. There is no criticism of him or his ideas. As time goes on he magnifies his own importance and the extent to which he is persecuted. He elaborates one of the stories of official wrongdoing which circulate in the unit communication process until it becomes a fantastic tale of corruption. Believing his own invention, the inmate becomes convinced that he need only communicate his knowledge to the outside world and the administration will be dismissed in disgrace. The hours, days, and months which go into the development of these illusions are seldom interrupted by contact with reality or challenging skepticism. The isolate has no one but himself to convince that he is free of blame and the victim of a complex plot. He is under powerful compulsions to believe all that he has created, and in order to protect this private conception of his world he may withdraw even more completely, often by creating disturbance which stimulates removal to a dark cell. Either there or in his regular cell, he is apt to undergo something which he regards as an intense and personally justifying religious experience.

A fairly common product of this condition is a note written to the Warden on paper which is perfectly ruled and exactly lettered. The note, with minor variations, will express the idea that the inmate has information which gives him complete power over the prison system. It will assert that unless the Warden stops "them" from trying to poison or hurt him, the inmate and God will destroy the system. If these notes find their way through official channels, the inmate may be transferred to a mental hospital where his condition is diagnosed apart from the situation that produced it. Prison inmates, however, recognize the condition as an extreme form of a common affliction they call "stir crazy." In its extreme form it manifests itself in the individual's not wanting to be released from the prison, or from the incorrigible unit, or from his isolation cell. More rational inmates fear and resist going "stir crazy," but they do not resent it in others. They recognize it as a way of adjusting to confinement and distinguish it from the "cracking up," which comes with inability to take punishment.

In summary, the extremely isolated individual has what might be termed delusions of grandeur and power, and he holds an unshakeable conviction of his own rightness in the zealous manner that other persons hold religious convictions.[19] While a very small increase in the amount of social contact permitted and the exactness with which

[19] The characteristics of the isolated incorrigible are similar to those associated with paranoid-schizophrenic syndrome. For a discussion of paranoid-schizophrenia as a protection against and a result of pressures and conflicts in the isolate's situation, see George Winokur, "A Conceptual Scheme for Psychiatric Syndromes," *American Journal of Psychotherapy,* IX (July, 1955), 403*f*.

the situation is defined is accompanied by a striking decline in the most extreme characteristics mentioned, these individual behaviors and definitions appeared in both prison situations studied. These characteristics of the isolated individual appear to be expressed in the social psychology of the isolated incorrigible group.

THE BELIEF SYSTEM

The incorrigible prisoners who were released from their cells and who assembled at the discussion tables in the corridors expressed little disagreement among themselves on basic issues. After a definitive statement had been made by one of the recognized leaders, there was little further discussion. Attempts to set up opposing positions by means of drawing out an elaboration of potentially conflicting statements usually ended in the collapse of discussion on the point. In individual interviews, as indicated, the men often displayed more insight and less hostility than in the group discussions. Also, written answers to problem questions showed more divergence from group norms than did verbal expressions by the same individuals before the group.

Norman Polansky has suggested two alternative courses of behavior for prisoners under extreme pressure. In one alternative, they might be drawn closer into a unified group. In the other, group organization might disintegrate under pressure. His study indicates that the latter alternative is taken in repressive prisons:

> In prisons of stricter discipline, and in spite of the practical difficulties of communicating with each other in such places, there is a greater tendency toward fighting and internal dissension among the inmates. We find too, that the inmate "politician" group tends to be more resented, and that the other inmates are generally less well-liked.[20]

The present study confirms the finding of greater hostility in the more repressive situation. The hostility of the inmates toward the type of person represented by the "politician" in Polansky's statement was intense in the units. However, this did not seem to take the form of conflict between members of the group. The norms and stand-

[20] Norman A. Polansky, "The Prison as an Autocracy," *Journal of Criminal Law and Criminology,* XXXIII (May–June, 1942), 20–21.

ards of the group were so sharply drawn that the distinction between members and nonmembers was absolute. Thus the hostility was projected outward to nonmembers. Requirements of the code, such as the prohibition against speaking to the guards, were so strict that men often failed to live up to them and, in consequence, were deprived of group membership and subjected to the hostility of those remaining in the group. The rejected men were defined as deviates from the norm. The conflict within inmate society came as a result of the intensity with which the code was maintained and the amount of conformity that it required, rather than from a breakdown of the code under repressive conditions.

The discussions provided a means of releasing tensions.[21] The attitudes and ideas expressed seemed closely related to the amount of tension in the unit, and expressions on every subject became more bitter when some particular event aroused the hostility of the group. In Central Prison, the execution of one of the inmates from the nearby death-row tier brought the group to a point of almost hysterical hatred against the prison in its next discussion period. In both units, the imposition of punishment which the group considered unfair charged the discussions with great hostility. One study of prisons made the following observations about group therapy in prisons:

> As in all groups, leaders emerge, and in a prison group you may be sure that the first to manifest leadership will be the most hostile and aggressive members. These will compete among themselves for eventual leadership, though earlier they will cling together against authority.[22]

This observation about leadership was not witnessed in the present study, probably because the groups were structured before the discussions began. The most hostile and aggressive members of the incorrigible groups were the first to give opinions but these men did not enter into a competition for leadership; after their extreme opinions had been presented they seemed willing to accept the more moderate statements of the leaders.

The belief system of the incorrigibles, therefore, appeared to be

[21] *Cf.* Robert C. Lappen, "They Talk Out Tensions," *State Government,* XXVI (May, 1953), 140*ff*.

[22] Samuel B. Hadden, "Group Therapy in Prisons," *Proceedings of the Seventy-Eighth Annual Congress of Correction of the American Prison Association* (New York: The American Prison Association, 1948), 181.

distorted by feelings of resentment and influenced to an extreme degree by their own group membership. In spite of this, the beliefs were not simply inventions that proved satisfying in the situation. They were based on actual events or incidents that were subject to interpretation or misinterpretation. Some event reported in the press or some incident in the prison might be woven into the foundations of the belief system without understanding of the larger issues involved. An event which the men in the units used to support a sense of outrage might be a matter of indifference to the prisoners in the yard. The incorrigibles were under greater compulsions to justify themselves by conceptions making them appear to be more sinned against than sinning. At the same time, their isolation separated them from the prison's more complex system of communication, which served to place events in a somewhat larger perspective for others. All the incorrigibles were, somewhat like the isolates, separated from the processes of interaction which might criticize their selection and use of particular events in ways which were most satisfying to their more intense psychological needs. Often the events at the foundation of beliefs in the units were insignificant details which men in the yard had nearly forgotten or interpreted in a vastly different way. The prison was condemned for practices which had long since passed away even in the most severe institution, and in Oahu Prison conceptions of the police were based on abuses which seem to have been eliminated in a "clean up" eight years previously.

Concepts of Crime. The first of the discussions in the series involved a definition of crime. The majority of the incorrigibles showed agreement with other prisoners by selecting a definition stating that crime is a conscious act that injures all of society. They indicated less preference than the more cynical inmates in the yard for a legalistic definition of crime as simply an act prohibited by statute. However, they also selected a definition of crime as a sinful and immoral act prohibited by the Bible. Discussions brought out the fact that the incorrigibles define crime largely in moral and ethical terms. The emphasis in their definition is on the element of deliberation and intent rather than on the act itself. At the same time, however, the incorrigibles categorize more specific acts as crimes than do prisoners in the yard.

The concept of society held by incorrigibles appears to reflect their own isolation. Their idea of society had the connotation of "high society," and they had little sense of identification with that group. "Society" and "the public" were hostile groups taking revenge on the criminal. To a much greater extent than the men in the prison yard, they had a sense of being cast out and rejected. The distinction between "we" and "they" was strongest among the men in the unit. We have already indicated that seeking the cooperation of these men in the study "for the good of society" was a tactical error. They were willing to help the research worker personally, and they were particularly willing to help for the sake of preventing children from getting into trouble, but they had no inclination to help society. Their feeling of being rejected by society appeared to be a major element in their justification of acts which they believed to be morally wrong, but which, nevertheless, were viewed as "against society." They seemed to feel that acts which were intrinsically evil and violent became justified by the existence of a state of war which society had legally declared against them. This phenomenon is similar to the practice described as "rejecting the rejectors."[23]

The Criminal. The incorrigible groups were not inclined to recognize any basic difference between criminals and noncriminals. As they saw it, being a criminal was a matter of personal decision. They recognized that a criminal has attitudes different from those of the average person, but, unlike other prisoners who saw this as a basic distinction, they considered the difference to lie in the fact that distinctive attitudes had been deliberately chosen. The men made it clear that a man does not become a criminal simply because he has committed an offense. They felt that the man who is "driven" or in some way "compelled" to commit an offense is usually sorry for his action immediately afterward, and an excellent subject for correction by guidance and help at that moment. In their opinion, any person might be led to commit an illegal act by passion, circumstance, or accident. Several of the men wrote notes to the effect that all men are potential criminals.

In Central Prison, the incorrigibles almost violently held the opinion that the circumstantial, "noncriminal" offender was apt to be abused and unfairly treated by law-enforcement officials. He was ill-treated and, perhaps, beaten by the police if he failed to cooperate completely with the process of vengeance directed against him. His misfortune was exploited by attorneys for both the prosecution and

[23] Lloyd W. McCorkle and Richard Korn, "Resocialization Within Walls," *Annals of the American Academy of Political and Social Science,* 293 (1954), 88–98.

the defense, working in combination. He was summarily processed through a court which did not extend a presumption of his innocence, which took the word of every man against him without hearing his own, which was operated with a mysterious language and procedures not explained to him, and which gave both its verdict and its sentence without consideration for the reasons he had behaved as he did. Then he was cast into a prison which exploited his labor under the most abusive conditions and restricted the outside contacts which he felt contained the only hope of his rehabilitation. Under such circumstances, the offender who had been prepared to admit his error and change his ways becomes bitter and resentful. He decides to "get even" for his unjust treatment and take reprisals through further crime at the first opportunity. It is with this decision that a man becomes a criminal.

The force with which the above argument was presented in the first discussions, the frequency with which it appeared thereafter, the regularity of its form, and the similarity of the statements written on the reverse side of several returned papers indicate that it is a culturally-shared formula. Central to this thinking is a sharp and bitter sense of injustice.

Law Enforcement. In a general survey of law-enforcement procedures, the unit men displayed all the standard resentments that inmates hold against police, prosecution, and parole officials. However, there were some differences between the attitudes of incorrigibles and prisoners in the yard. Unit men felt more strongly that the basic rules and procedures of justice were sound and good. As a general rule, they were less inclined to suggest changes in court procedures. An exception to this was in connection with the rules of evidence. As indicated, unit men felt that they had never had the opportunity to explain their position and communicate the reasons which seemed sufficient to them for what they had done. While incorrigible prisoners were conservative about the system of justice, they felt that the system was distorted and manipulated against them by professionals who took personal profit from the imposition of misery. They felt that the accused person had basic rights and protections in the system which were ignored and taken away by the lawyers who dominated the courts.

While the hostility against the legal profession took somewhat different forms in the two prisons studied, lawyers were the focus of the most intense resentments felt by the men. Thus, resentment against attorneys was significantly stronger than the dislike felt for guards and prison officials. The unit men were in favor of the grand jury and trial jury systems principally because they offered protection from the lawyers whom the men felt had a personal and political stake in convicting the accused. They felt that laymen were more apt to be guided by considerations of justice and not professional advancement or politics, and that participation of laymen in the trial was a means of thwarting the designs of the professionals.

Crime Prevention. Sessions in the causes and prevention of crime indicated that the men in the unit held more clear-cut conceptions on this subject than prisoners in the yard. The theory expressed made a sharp distinction between "underlying" or "predisposing" causes and "precipitating" causes. The causes recognized as predisposing were poverty and lack of education. Consistently, the measures of prevention most frequently recommended by unit men were of vocational training and improved educational facilities. Yet the men recognized that most of the poor and ignorant people in the world do not get into trouble, and they used precipitating factors to complete their theory. They felt that there is a great deal of injustice and abuse in the world, and that this falls most frequently on the poor. Wealthy and educated people have ways of protecting themselves from abuse and ways of expressing their resentment if the abuses strike them. The poor are defenseless, and the only way available to them for striking back against injustice is crime. Not all of the poor and ignorant are abused, and hence not all become criminals. In Central Prison, the group included Negroes in the class of persons who have no defense or means of expression for their resentments.

The men saw the elimination of poverty and ignorance, and the elimination of abuse, as alternatives for the prevention of crime. The latter alternative was preferred, but many men regarded it as less probable than the former. The general theory of crime and its prevention expressed itself in a variety of ways. One of these was the belief that a program of rehabilitation should include study of constitutional law, thus giving the inmates an opportunity to protect themselves from injustice and abuse. Ideas about crime and prevention that did not square with their generally-held theory received little attention from the group. They had little patience with theories holding that infantile experiences determine misbehavior. While they recognize the existence of emotional disturbances in children, and in themselves, they felt that there were any number of possible outlets for the behavior of the disturbed person, and that most of these were constructive or acceptable. The evil does not lie in the energy generated by emotional disturbance, but in the abuses which turn that energy into crime. This way of thinking is a corollary of their idea that a person is driven into crime; it is a way of thinking which denies personal responsibility.

Police and Courts. Sessions held on the question of whether police work is work in crime prevention provided an opportunity to explore conceptions of the police. The extent to which all prisoners made an issue of police brutality and the wealth of illustration which they supplied were sufficient to convince the investigator that there is some foundation in fact for their claims. In any event, the belief that the police physically abuse offenders, in combination with the conviction that force justifies force in return, became a major foundation stone for their explanations of criminal behavior. Despite the belief that police in general are brutal, there was little resentment against the arresting officer. He was considered a tool in a system over which he has no control, and his actions are attributed to some undefined "they" who demand that the police get a conviction for every crime. All inmate groups expressed a preference for the F.B.I. over local officers. This preference, held as strongly by men who had come in contact with federal officers as by others, was based on the belief that the F.B.I. is outside the reach of local politics and that it conducts impartial investigations rather than investigations designed to convict the accused.

At every point at which politics appeared to be related to the law-enforcement process as the incorrigibles saw it, there was a marked increase in feelings of bitterness and resentment. Thus, attitudes about "politics" affected feelings about both the police and the courts.[24] There was little resentment against the men in law enforcement work who have a regular job to do at a regular salary unless those men were perceived as personally hostile and biased. Hostility against the judge was rarely expressed, although some men were serving extremely long sentences. Public prosecutors were disliked

---

[24] It is very hard to convey the meaning of the term "politics," as it is used by inmates and some officials. Politics is a dirty word, pronounced as though it were an epithet. It stands for the manipulation of people, but it takes on special connotation in a prison situation where all manipulation is exploitive. In the more liberal prison situation studied here, however, the use of the term was not much different from that used in the traditional prison.

more than other officials, principally because the men believed that prosecutors will deliberately convict defendants whether they are guilty or not, in order to build up a record for political purposes. They believed that the prosecutor, as the key figure in the trial, should present both sides of the case in an impartial way, and it was obvious to them that he does not.

It should be noted that almost all the incorrigibles were convicted on pleas of "guilty," often after what was taken to be a promise of consideration from police and prosecution officials. They did not have a defense, and according to their reports, they had little opportunity to speak at the trial. They had no conception of what the rights of the accused are until they came to prison and studied law as it is taught in the prison yard. Gradually, they came to believe that they were tricked and cheated of rights to defend and explain themselves. It is but a step from that belief to the feeling that they were convicted because they had no defense, not because they had committed a crime.

The men in the units had an extremely idealistic conception of rights and protections provided by the Constitution. To them, the Constitution is the protector of the poor against every type of abuse and exploitation. They had very little idea of its content or the extent to which it controls criminal process in the State or the Territory.[25] It is an imaginary standard by which they measure reality, and reality fails that test. Prisoners in the yard are very often cynical, practical men who have a very low opinion of the integrity of the government and the legal system, but they feel little bitterness. They take the workings of the system for granted and adjust as best as they can. To the incorrigibles, on the other hand, all reality is a betrayal of the ideal. They cling to a private conception of justice and right that justifies their own conduct and maintains their own self-respect. Not content to maintain this private sense of justice as a personal standard, they project it into the Constitution or into religion and bitterly condemn the rest of the world for not living up to it. Although the men in the unit had a higher estimate than did the men in the yard of the number of correct verdicts handed down in the courts, they expressed a greater resentment against the courts for not achieving a perfect justice.

In the most repressive of the unit situations, the men were bitterly

[25] When inmates referred to the Constitution, it was always to the Constitution of the United States, not to that of North Carolina or the Territory's Organic Act.

antagonistic against Communism and expressed the most complete devotion to the American ideal as they conceived it. They listed Communism among the major crimes—along with perjury, murder and rape. Men in the units also conceived of themselves as being more religious than most persons. They openly expressed a faith in God, but they were often opposed to churches and ministers. They had less regard for the institutional religious program than did other prisoners, and they were openly skeptical of the motives of inmates who attended and took part in religious activities.

The Idea of Justice. Because the incorrigibles' ideal conceptions of justice and right were not of this world, it was difficult to form an exact definition of what they involved. One element was the idea of an eye for an eye. Force and abuse should be repaid in the same coin, and one injustice deserves another. The men believed in force and punishment as a means to compel behavior, though this belief was not clearly reflected in their prescriptions on how to deal with offenders. They preached tolerance, understanding, and a second chance in many cases where they identified themselves with the offender, but they turned to force and fear as means of enforcing the standards which they established for the law enforcement process. They felt that punishment is necessary in order to maintain conformity.

However, they also believed that the punishment should be exactly measured and equal for all individuals committing the same offense.[26] Rules, including criminal laws, should consist of detailed specifications that cover every possible case. In comparing situations where their punishment was indefinite with situations in which it was more exactly stated, their preference for certainty was clear. They wanted to know exactly where they stood and what the limits were in their relationship to authority.

The Prison World. The type of thinking applied to the outside world was also applied to the prison world. They felt that a man has a right to know exactly where he stands. Where the prison pro-

---

[26] The incorrigibles, who are not without charity and concern for the individual, here fall into contradictions which confuse other inmates to a lesser degree. They want individualized treatment of crime and a consideration of personal factors in the offense. However, this wish conflicts with the great need for a definite and rigid relationship with authority which can come only if both rules and penalties for rule-violation are precisely defined and stipulated in advance. *Cf.*, Donald R. Cressey, "Limitations on the Organization of Treatment in the Modern Prison," Chapter 4 in Cloward and others, *op. cit.*

vided the exact definition of the situation, they expressed far less hostility against it. The resentment which the men felt against the prison was less, in general, than that expressed against police and court officials. While they charged prison guards with a number of abuses, they did not express the amount of hostility against them that they held for some of the higher custodial officers. Some of the guards who were cordial and pleasant were well liked, though they were seen in terms of stereotyped conceptions of guards. The unit inmates felt that the guards are stupid, and they thought of them as "hacks" or "screws," but they recognized that the guards exercise very little discretion in the rules that they enforce. Therefore, they reserved what hostility they felt against guards for those who acted in a biased way or attempted to change established rules and customs.

Some officials who occupied more responsible positions were more resented than guards, but others were more respected. One of the standing complaints was that higher officers did not inspect their area and talk with them. Any contact with top officials was a very important event to men in the units, but feelings about such contacts were ambivalent. The group values required an expression of hostility to the officials, yet the men wanted to communicate. In Central Prison, where hostility toward officials was strongest, the action of a high official who sent marked Bibles to two of the most bitter men had an effect of breaking them away from the thinking of the group for some time. Rehabilitation programs were condemned as farcical, yet members of the rehabilitation staff were resented for not extending their training and help to the men in the units. While in particular cases it is difficult to divorce the perception of positions from the perception of individuals who occupied the positions, it appears that officials with greater power and authority were more respected than those with less power, even though the latter were charged with responsibilities for helping inmates.

Admission. Unit inmates condemned the admission and orientation process of both prisons for its failure to let the new man understand exactly what his position was within the system. This attitude, again, seems to reflect a strong desire for certainty. The thinking of the men about the classification programs of the two institutions is not comparable because of substantial differences in the two programs and a lack of understanding of the program by inmates in Central Prison. In connection with studies on classification, however, the men were asked to estimate the number of men who would be classed in each of several categories according to the "reason" for their crimes. Unit men placed more men under the headings "Crimes Caused by Poverty" and "Resentment Toward Authority" than did men from the yard. They were generally less favorable to classifying men on the basis of attitudes or attitude tests than were men in the prison yard.

Discipline. Like all other prisoners, the men in the units objected more to the way disciplinary cases are handled than to the punishments meted out. The incorrigibles believed that punishments are necessary, and none of them felt that the most severe punishments were too severe. As indicated, being able to take punishment was high on their scale of values. Yet they felt that all punishment was exemplary rather than corrective, and they insisted that punishment should stop short of destroying the mind of the individual. When asked to describe ways of making punishments more fair they could only suggest that they be made consistent for like offenses, but they were inconsistent in wanting a psychological report, as well as the offense, to be considered in setting the punishment. They preferred a disciplinary committee to a system in which one man acted as disciplinarian, and yet they wanted one man to assume full, personal responsibility for what was done. They felt that divided responsibility led to decisions which were both more arbitrary and more severe, principally because punishments assigned by the committee relieved any individual member of personal responsibility for the destructive effect of the group.

Some of the antagonism toward the rehabilitation program stemmed from a belief that the program did not provide any help for them. Rehabilitative efforts in the two prisons differed to a degree which made detailed comparisons impossible, but in neither case did the concept of rehabilitation employed by the institution seem realistic to the men. Prisoners in the units held concepts of the causes of crime, as outlined above, which made vocational training a critical element in rehabilitation, and they thought that existing programs were extraordinarily ineffective. An unrealistic standard of efficiency in rehabilitation was maintained, and the efforts of officials responsible for rehabilitation were critically and unfavorably compared with this standard.

Thus, in this area as in others, men who were out of touch with reality imposed ideal standards on practice and were violently critical of practice which failed to achieve those standards. Nevertheless, the standards were conservative and conventional. Men in the units were less apt than men in the yard to suggest radical departures and new innovations for prison and law enforcement practice. Their demands on justice were that every accused person should have a jury trial and a defense, that every man should be entitled to a full hearing and receive absolutely equal treatment. They were especially concerned that there be known limits established and maintained, that officials should keep their word, and that men should not be punished over and over again for the same offense. The men in the units were not radicals. While their beliefs about the system of justice amounted to a theory of class oppression, they did not hold this radical doctrine but turned for their defense to what they thought were the rights embodied in the Constitution and in American ideals.

Differences. Although we have emphasized similarities, we have also shown that there were substantial differences in the beliefs of the men in the two units, both in substance and in the intensity with which they were held. This finding is contrary to our expectations, which were influenced by the remarkable similarity of the two situations. In retrospect, it appears that the following differences in the two units have significant effects on beliefs and attitudes. In Central Prison the men were confined to the incorrigible unit indefinitely, while in Oahu Prison they were held for a known term. In Central Prison the men were isolated from all formal contacts with the main prison yard, although informal channels of communication were maintained. In Oahu Prison, the mimeographed news sheet published by inmates in the yard was delivered in the unit. As a result of a more relaxed official policy, there was more communication between the inmates and guards in Oahu Prison than in Central Prison. These were the only apparent major differences in the two situations.

These differences seemed to be reflected in differences in the degrees of general tension and hostility in the belief systems of the men in the two units. Oahu incorrigibles held much less hostile feelings toward the guard, despite the fact that their value system, like the one in Central Prison, compelled them to oppose him or swear at him in order to express formal defiance. Punishment seen as arbitrary and unfair produced an almost hysterical resentment in both units, but the fairness of punishments for a number of offenses was more readily conceded in Oahu. The most striking difference was the relative absence of the "rat" concept in the thinking of Oahu incorrigibles. The document recovered from 1939 indicates that the idea of "rats" was as dominant in the thinking of the men in the Oahu Prison unit at that time as it was in Central Prison when the study was made. Oahu men still have the idea that a "rat" is a vicious, evil thing which should be destroyed, but they do not live in constant fear that they are being spied on.[27] This difference in the two units is attributable to differences in the extent of communication with prisoners in the yard and with guards and officials.

Ideas about the police and the courts were very similar in the two units, but thinking about the prison itself was much more tolerant, more flexible, and more fact-oriented in Oahu. Instances of total withdrawal into a world of private fantasy were less frequent in Oahu Prison and there was less evidence of "prison psychosis." In Central Prison, occasional instances of violent aggression directed against the guards had made the officers hostile to the men. In Oahu Prison, this aggressiveness was not as great, and the unit guards were more sympathetic toward the prisoners than other officials of the institution. Decreased aggression by prisoners appeared to have set up a circular procedure which further increased communication, decreased hostility, and modified some of the more severe regulations. Inmates had less feeling of being totally rejected and forgotten by officials. It appears that the degree of communication and degree of definiteness in the situation both are associated with the kinds of beliefs and behaviors exhibited by the men.

ANALYSIS

Curt Bondy's observations on the effects of isolation in the internment camps seem to apply to confinement in incorrigible units. Isolation brings disregard for appearances and decency; fantastic stories spread, and there are wild dreams and emotional epidemics. "Social degradation" brings envy and hate, compensatory mechanisms in lying and boasting, and the urge to dominance.[28] Alexander Leighton has warned against underestimating the danger of circum-

---

[27] The change in the beliefs of the Oahu Prison incorrigibles parallels changes in attitudes in the general prison community, where preoccupation with "rats" substantially decreased with development of a more open system of communication. See McCleery, *Policy Change in Prison Management, op. cit.*

[28] Bondy, *op. cit.*, pp. 461–465.

stances which foster repeated frustration, inconsistent desires, or uncertainty; and he points out the danger of ignoring complaints which are an indication of psychological needs.[29] The present study underlines the importance of uncertainty as a critical factor related to hostility and aggressiveness. As Leighton has observed, this aggression combined with fear produces "pathological" rumors of atrocities, betrayals, and plots and attacks on persons who have little to do with the causes of stress.[30] While hostility was greatly increased in the more arbitrary and ill-defined situation, it was not directed against figures in the prison who held formal authority and power to the same extent that it was directed toward those who had responsibilities without power. Officials charged with rehabilitative functions were more resented and criticized than those who held custodial powers.

In the extremely authoritarian atmosphere characterizing the units, the men set up an extremely rigid and demanding code of conduct for themselves and others. Hostility was expressed against those who failed to conform to these rigid standards. Where individual expression was most restricted, the hostility appeared to be turned inward by the individual upon himself. Dabrowski writes that introverted, schizoid individuals often take self-mutilation as a means of liberating the self from unbearable tensions—the physical pain becoming a compensatory substitute for psychic pain or shame.[31] While the type of person confined in incorrigible units seems to be more prone to withdrawal, self-mutilation, and aggression than other prisoners, it also appears that the nature of the authoritarian situation and the belief system contribute to such behavior patterns.

Cornelius Wholey has given technical language to the notion held by the men of their going "stir crazy" by stating that the more extreme and repressive prison enivronment creates a "general paranoid or persecutory reaction" which he calls "prison psychosis."[32] Sutherland and Cressey have suggested that reactions to extreme repression in prison can be either apathetic or aggressive. "Either reaction to the system of rigid discipline tends to become something

[29] Alexander H. Leighton, *The Governing of Men* (Princeton, N.J.: Princeton University Press, 1945), 262.

[30] *Ibid.*, p. 268.

[31] Casmir Dabrowski, "Psychological Bases of Self-Mutilation," translated by William Thau, *Genetic Psychology Monographs* XIX (1937), 12.

[32] Cornelius C. Wholey, "Psychiatric Report of Study of Psychopathic Inmates of a Penitentiary," *Journal of Criminal Law and Criminology,* XXVIII (May–June, 1937), 55.

very much like insanity—either apathy, listlessness, vagaries, or else irritability, hatred, and nervous instability."[33] Jaco's description of the social world of the schizophrenic comes close to describing the reality experience by men in incorrigible units, isolated from all outside contact:

> The pathogenic effects of social isolation have long been recognized by specialists in personal and social disorganization. Faris has connected social isolation specifically with the onset of schizophrenia, the most common type of mental disorder. The schizophrenic is generally depicted as one who lives in a mental world of his own fancy, a sort of "pseudo-community" inhabited by creatures whom the schizophrenic considers desirable or perhaps at least subject to his control.[34]

Similarly, Bonner has identified a number of sociological aspects of paranoia, and pointed out that "a family pattern of suppression, cruelty, domination, and criticism is found in a very large number of paranoic cases."[35] At least the characteristics of suppression, domination, and condemnation are a part of the social environment of the men in the incorrigible units. The major products of their adjustment to that environment are a social order which emphasizes conformity and hierarchy plus a belief system which provides self-justification.

Certain general conclusions may be drawn from study of the most extreme authoritarian situations in prisons, and these conclusions seem to apply to the culture of entire prisons as well. In cases where men are governed with repression, restriction, and regimentation, both the social system and the belief system seem to become extremely rigid. Neither ambiguity nor nonconformity can be tolerated by the social group. The social structure is sharply defined as a rigid hierarchy. The belief system is equally rigid and dogmatic. It is protected from criticism by a withdrawal of communication processes, in a kind of informal system of censorship against hostile ideas, from those who do not conform to the group belief.

When this authoritarian situation becomes uncertain and ill-defined, the hostility and aggression of the group become extreme.

---

[33] Edwin H. Sutherland and Donald R. Cressey, *Principles of Criminology* (5th Edition; New York: J. B. Lippincott Company, 1955), 473.

[34] E. Gartly Jaco, "The Social Isolation Hypothesis and Schizophrenia," *American Sociological Review*, XIX (October, 1954), 567.

[35] Hubert Bonner, "Sociological Aspects of Paranoia," *The American Journal of Sociology*, LVI (November, 1950), 255.

It appears that rigidity of belief and social structure are fiercely defended as a means of providing the sense of certainty and emotional security which is missing in the formal situation. Men are only slowly admitted into the fellowship of the group, and leadership falls to those who prove their strength in relation to the dominant power governing the men. Yet such proof of strength is not active rebellion. One proves himself by adjusting to the situation on the best possible terms and draining off the hostility of the group by verbalizations which give satisfaction. The authoritarian situation produces a group which feels that it is made up of men who are select, especially important, and better than others who have not suffered the same trials. The leader exemplifies this conception and gives it expression. When any person behaves in a way that challenges the group's conception of itself, his action is defined as betrayal. Because the leader is the figure who mediates between the group and power, and is consequently extended a greater freedom of action, his position is unstable. He is expected to manipulate power, but he is rejected if his manipulations are not satisfying.

The belief system of incorrigible groups is conservative and conventional. The thinking is moralistic rather than pragmatic, probably because a function of the belief system is to provide self-justification to a group that is being condemned. The belief system is not tempered by practical considerations or the need successfully to seek physical objectives. A sense of rightness and justification can be achieved in a psychologically intolerable situation if the men believe that others are more evil than they are. They seize every scrap of evidence suggesting that those responsible for their confinement were, and are, motivated by a desire to persecute them for personal gain. In the environment in which they are placed, justice is represented by power and force. As they come to the conviction that justice is with them, they are prepared to exercise force in the defense of what they believe to be right.

These aspects in the social life of incorrigible units may offer insights into the occasional eruptions of collective violence in such units, and in prisons generally. The sequence leading to violence may take the following course. Men are placed in a rigid and repressive situation in which power is the dominant element, and their society becomes an adjustment to power. Power is formally identified with justice and right, so that the men respect both inmates and officials who exercise it. At the same time, the men use highly idealized conventional values to erect a belief system that characterizes them as a select and persecuted minority. As a consequence of formal isolation and informal censorship of criticism, nothing challenges this belief system, and it becomes a theoretical basis for revolt. In a stable situation, both the belief system and the social system are relatively satisfying means of adjustment—the group has a conservative rather than a revolutionary foundation. However, in an arbitrary and undefined situation, an extreme amount of hostility is created, and it serves to defend and reaffirm both the social system based on power and the belief system. If an unstable and aggressive individual rises to power or to a position of leadership on the wave of that hostility, the group is ready for open rebellion.

There seems to be a close relationship between maximal external constraint and the internalized values which complete the system of social control in incorrigible units. The extreme authoritarian system does not lead to the complete personal demoralization which might logically be expected. In a majority of individuals, the counterpart of authoritarian controls appears to be a rigid, moral idealism and a compulsive conformity. Such behavior patterns protect and justify the individual's personality in the face of hostile forces. Neither the idealism nor the conformity seem to be useful devices for adjusting to the demands of the broader society. Thus, the over-all impact of the incorrigible unit in penal practice probably is one that intensifies tendencies to criminal attitudes and behavior.

PART THREE

REHABILITATION IN THE

PRISON COMMUNITY

8

CLARENCE SCHRAG

| | | | | | | | | | |

Some Foundations for a
Theory of Correction*

CRIMINOLOGY AND CORRECTION

One of the major objectives of criminology is the formulation of concepts, postulates, and theories that are useful in the analysis of correctional problems and policies. However, progress toward this goal has been difficult and unsteady. Attempted practical applications of criminology have frequently been hindered by the inadequacies of its theories, especially its vaguely defined concepts and its loosely connected postulates.

Some scholars have constructed criminological theories of great generality without relating them to relevant factual information, while other researchers have accumulated hordes of descriptive data without regard for their theoretical integration. Neither approach seems likely to produce generalizations that are verifiable and significant for the field of correction.

Theories that are not supported by empirical evidence may be

* The author gratefully acknowledges his indebtedness to several of his colleagues for many of the ideas and research materials reported here. Particularly significant in this regard are the unpublished works of Peter Garabedian (University of Arizona), John Kinch (San Francisco State College), Duane Strinden (Seattle Public Schools), Stanton Wheeler (Harvard University), and Donald Garrity (San Francisco State College). These persons are of course in no way responsible for any defects in the chapter.

309

little more than wishful thinking. Conversely, descriptive data that are not organized in terms of some guiding theory may be hard to distinguish from undisciplined observations. Clearly, progress in scientific criminology entails the mutual development of both theory and validating evidence.

It seems probable that the desired rapprochement between system builders and data gatherers can be facilitated by consolidation of theories for which some supportive evidence is available. Such consolidation, if successful, should increase the orderliness of factual assertions regarding crime and should also provide a logical basis for predicting previously unobserved facts about criminal behavior.

However, the attempted consolidation of theories may produce some rather drastic revisions of existing concepts and postulates. Since theories have occasionally been regarded as the somewhat sacred domain of their originators, deliberate revision and reformulation have perhaps been less common than extended discussions regarding the meanings of the theories or the intentions of the theorists. Justification for the proposed revisions therefore requires that we keep clearly in mind the functions of theory in empirical science.

The Nature of Criminological Theory.[1] Criminological theory does not concern itself simply with description of criminal behavior. Rather, it involves searching for principles or generalizations which allow us to predict and to control criminality. Principles and generalizations are "if . . . then . . ." statements asserting certain interrelationships between criminal actions and the various conditions under which these actions may be expected to occur. If the generalizations are sufficiently detailed and accurate, then observation of the specified conditions should enable us to predict the resulting criminal behavior.

Control of crime is believed to be possible when the variables on which prediction is based are subject to deliberate modification. By changing the statuses of persons or groups with respect to the variables that are associated with criminality, designated changes presumably

---

[1] Problems of theory construction are nicely presented in Carl G. Hempel, "Fundamentals of Concept Formation in Empirical Science," *International Encyclopedia of Unified Science,* vol. 2, no. 7, University of Chicago Press, 1952; Karl R. Popper, *The Logic of Scientific Discovery* (New York: Basic Books, 1959); and Llewellyn Gross, *et al., Symposium on Sociological Theory* (Evanston: Row, Peterson, and Company, 1959). A very brief but relevant discussion is found in C. Schrag, "Comments on the General Theory of Action," *Alpha Kappa Deltan* (Winter, 1959), 46–52.

can be produced in the amount or the nature of criminal behavior. This, at least, is the assumption involved in applications of criminological theory to the field of correction.

The *concepts* of a theory identify the phenomena with which the theory is concerned. In criminology, concepts designate certain kinds of crimes and other related variables. Generally, modes of criminality comprise the dependent variable which is to be predicted by taking into account the asserted relationships between crime and various independent variables, such as goals, motives, attitudes, self-conceptions, social positions, and other personal or social factors. When a theory is fully developed, the interrelationships among all of the variables, both dependent and independent, are completely specified. In this case, decisions concerning the variables to be treated as dependent and independent are matters of choice that are determined by the problem at hand. Moreover, the concepts of a theory should identify the conditions under which the asserted relationships between dependent and independent variables are expected to hold true.

Postulates are statements describing the empirical interconnections that supposedly exist among the variables of a theory. Whereas concepts, as already mentioned, identify the phenomena encompassed by a theory, postulates make claims concerning the interrelations among these phenomena. While the meanings of concepts are established by definition and convention, the accuracy of postulates and of hypotheses derived from the postulates can be ascertained only by the observation of relevant data. Considered jointly, concepts and postulates should provide a graphic picture of how crimes are believed to be linked up with certain environmental conditions.

Improper use of concepts and postulates seems to occur with unfortunate frequency in criminological theories. For example, relations among variables are sometimes assumed by definition or fiat when they should be hypothesized and confirmed by careful observation. Thus, the notion that criminals are sick persons implies that we can identify the symptoms of a disease which is peculiar to criminal offenders. Confirmation of this idea requires that a certain sickness be defined independently of crime and that an observable relationship between these two phenomena be demonstrated. However, advocates of this view seem inclined to use the idea as an explanation for crime without going through the necessary processes of definition and verification.

Again, some theorists, often called functionalists, assume that all social groups and organizations serve essential functions.[2] Were it not for the functions served, it is held, the groups would not long endure. These theorists may attempt to explain the nature and existence of prisons and other correctional programs by asserting that such programs fulfill necessary social functions, including punishment, rehabilitation, expression of mass resentment against the criminal, and so on. But this assertion, unless tested by reliable data, does not show that the agencies actually serve the functions claimed, that the functions are served effectively, or that the same functions could not better be served by other agencies and programs.

The difficulty with some functionalist arguments and the idea that criminals are ill is that they take for granted certain relations among variables without requiring objective substantiation for their claims. Similar criticism, we believe, is relevant to the idea that prison officials have unlimited power, that social relations between prison officials and inmates result in corruption of authority, or that the impact of prison culture upon the individual inmate is necessarily harmful. These popular criminological conceptions will be discussed later in more detail.[3]

Criteria for Determining the Adequacy of Criminological Theories. Faith in the claims of a theory should not be a matter of creed or dogma but a result of the preponderance of supportive evidence. Sometimes postulates can be tested directly by pitting their claims against the relations that can be reliably observed among the variables in question. Perhaps more frequently, however, theories are evaluated in terms of observations that verify some of the hypotheses which can be logically derived from the postulates. If the hypotheses are confirmed by reliable evidence, faith in the utility of the theory is enhanced accordingly.

Estimation of the degree of confidence warranted by a given theory requires that researchers come to an agreement regarding at least three crucial issues dealing with the application of the theory to concrete situations.

First among the issues involved in the evaluation of a theory is the

[2] For a critical review of functionalism see Kingsley Davis, "The Myth of Functional Analysis," *American Sociological Review*, 24 (1959), 757–772. Formal evaluations are found in Gross, *op. cit.*, ch. 9, "The Logic of Functional Analysis," by Carl G. Hempel, and in Ernest Nagel, *Logic Without Metaphysics* (Glencoe: Free Press, 1957), 247–283.

[3] See the section on The Correctional Community, p. 331 below.

boundary problem. The boundaries of a theory are determined by the definitions assigned to the concepts. Definitions should enable researchers unequivocally to agree on the phenomena to be included within the meanings of the various concepts and to set aside those events that fall outside the scope of the theory. If agreement on these matters cannot be attained, the theory cannot be consistently applied or evaluated.

Second is the problem of truth claims. The claims of a theory are contained in the postulates and in hypotheses that can be derived from the postulates. These statements assert the kinds and degrees of relationships that are expected to prevail among the phenomena falling within the scope of the theory. If a theory is to be applied systematically to concrete situations, then the empirical propositions that are derived from the theory must be unambiguous and testable.

Third is the congruence problem. Empirical adequacy of a theory, in the final analysis, is estimated by the degree of agreement between hypotheses and relevant observations. Ideally, the claims of a theory should be valid indicators of the phenomena the theory purports to represent, although precise standards of accuracy have not yet been established in the field of criminology. In general, congruence is lacking when the picture portrayed by a theory is not consistent with the experience of qualified observers.

Criminological theories vary widely in their resolutions of problems concerning boundaries, claims, and congruence. While we cannot review the literature here, certain impressionistic conclusions gained from an examination of current theories are nevertheless presented. For example, the more popular theories are apparently those that cover the greatest variety of criminal behaviors, even though a larger number of restricted theories may be encountered. Furthermore, it seems that the greater the range of behavior with which a theory is concerned, the fewer the relevant conditions cited and the more general the definitions of these conditions. Again, the narrower the scope of the theory, the greater the number of conditions and the more specific their definitions. This suggests that the requirements for congruence between theoretical claims and empirical observations may not be so exacting for theories covering a wide range of criminality as they are for theories covering more specific offense categories. However, congruence for many theories, both broad and narrow, cannot be determined because the concepts are unclear and/or the postulates are ambiguous.

Science, of course, aims at predicting a maximum range of phenomena with a minimum number of postulates and conditions. But premature extension of the scope of a theory tends to result in trite or banal assertions that cannot be confirmed or denied by empirical evidence. For example, "the individual internalizes the norms of his social group," and "stimulus patterns that are active at the time of a response eventually acquire the capacity to elicit that response," are illustrations of such arguments that are sometimes found in theoretical discussions.

Highly abstract and generalized arguments, such as those mentioned above, are attractive because they seem to circumscribe a wide range of behavior and to involve a minimal number of restricting conditions. Their attractiveness is deceptive, however, because they fail to specify precisely the phenomena with which they are concerned or to indicate the conditions under which they can be tested. Consequently, such arguments obviously need to be greatly clarified and elaborated before they can be utilized effectively in theoretical discourse.

In contrast to theories that fail to make sufficient specification of the phenomena falling within their scope are those that greatly restrict the range of behavior and maximize the number of relevant conditions. The multiple-factor theory of crime causation is a good example of overspecification, as are a number of clinical theories stressing the individualistic approach. These theories, in effect, assert that for any given mode of behavior there is an endless variety of possible causal determinants. Since each case covered by these theories is regarded as being essentially unique, the problem of deciding upon truth claims is a complex and seemingly hopeless task. Therefore, the prospects for testing postulates or hypotheses implied by these theories are extremely limited.

The above impressions, if valid, suggest an issue additional to those already mentioned. That is, they signify the need for a realistic balance between concepts designating behavioral variables to be predicted and those identifying the independent variables and conditions that are presumed to have an important bearing on the prediction process. Balance is particularly significant in the early stages of theory construction since decisions are then made concerning the concepts to be included. While the criteria for evaluating balance may be largely matters of taste, the obvious excesses previously noted indicate the desirability of moderation with respect to the complexity of theoretical proposals. A few concepts that have clear and verifiable empirical interconnections generate far greater predictive power than does a vast array of loosely connected concepts.

In summary, the attempted consolidation of concepts and postulates should be aimed at resolving some of the issues dealing with balance, boundaries, claims, and congruence. Progressive reconstruction of criminological theory requires the simultaneous consideration of all of these problems.

CRIMINOLOGICAL THEORY: SOME SOURCES AND CONVERGENCES

Sources of Contemporary Criminological Theory. Tracing the histories and interdependencies of ideas is always hazardous. This is especially the case in a relatively new field such as correctional research. We therefore cautiously venture the opinion that contemporary correctional research reflects the influence of three major theoretical sources. Specifically, we refer to Sutherland's arguments regarding differential association, Durkheim's views on anomie, Weber's analyses of bureaucratic organizations, and to the works of students of these authors.[4] Let us very briefly outline some of the chief arguments involved in these theories.

Differential association. The theory of differential association develops the idea that criminal values and attitudes are transmitted through social contacts.[5] It does not explain the origin or genesis of criminal behavior. Rather, it assumes the existence of a criminal culture that contradicts the norms of the broader community and commands the allegiance of criminals and other law violators.[6] This criminalistic element within our culture is viewed as being highly organized and possessing its own values, codes, and enforcement methods.

Those persons who have the closest contacts with patterns of crime and the most tenuous contacts with anticriminal patterns are regarded as most likely to exhibit criminal behavior. Although early

[4] Except for the lack of space, the works of Clifford Shaw and others, as well as certain developments growing out of parole prediction and actuarial research in the field of correction, would be included.

[5] Edwin H. Sutherland and Donald R. Cressey, *Principles of Criminology,* Sixth Edition (New York: Lippincott, 1960), ch. 4.

[6] Edwin H. Sutherland, *The Professional Thief* (Chicago: University of Chicago Press, 1937).

formulations of the theory stressed frequency and consistency of con·tact as the main causal factors,[7] later adaptations of it placed greater emphasis on a number of contact variables, including priority, duration, and intensity.[8] The most recent reformulations have given the theory a more interactionist orientation by taking into account the self-conceptions of criminal offenders[9] and the degree to which different persons identify with criminal behavior patterns.[10]

Anomie. Durkheim's theory of deviant behavior assumes that methods used in the attainment of social goals, although they ordinarily are effectively regulated by tradition and convention, are sometimes freed from social restraints.[11] Restraints are likely to be ineffective in times of crisis, under rapidly changing social conditions, and when great discrepancies occur between goals or aspirations and prospects for their attainment.

Disparities between goals and means of attainment, for example, are common during periods of economic depression or extraordinary prosperity. Again, the attainment of aspirations may be very difficult in rapidly expanding technologies or under social philosophies calling for perpetual progress. Durkheim also noted that relative emancipation from conventional regulations is characteristic of persons occupying certain social positions.

The result of social disruptions and incongruities such as those mentioned is a state of de-regulation, normlessness, or anomie in which deviant behavior is greatly encouraged.[12] Thus, the theory of anomie considers deviant behavior as a product of social influences, and it minimizes the causal role of personal predilections.

Disparities between culturally prescribed goals and alternative

[7] Edwin H. Sutherland, *Principles of Criminology,* Third Edition (New York: Lippincott, 1939), ch. 1.

[8] *Ibid.,* Fourth Edition, 1947, ch. 1.

[9] Donald R. Cressey, "The Differential Association Theory and Compulsive Crimes," *Journal of Criminal Law, Criminology, and Police Science,* 44 (1954), 29–40; also the same author's "Changing Criminals: The Application of the Theory of Differential Association," *American Journal of Sociology,* 61 (1955), 116–120.

[10] Daniel Glaser, "Criminality Theories and Behavioral Images," *American Journal of Sociology,* 61 (1956), 433–444.

[11] Emile Durkheim, *Suicide,* translated by J. A. Spaulding and George Simpson (Glencoe: Free Press, 1951).

[12] *Ibid.,* especially pp. 247–257.

means for their attainment are utilized by Merton in classifying several types of deviant behavior.[13] Goals and means may be accepted or rejected by different cultures, societies, groups, or individuals. For example, emphasis on goals may be so great that the means for acquiring them are virtually disregarded. The consequence in this instance is innovation, or the employment of unconventional methods for the achievement of goals. Conversely, devotion to conventional means may be such that goals are assigned relatively insignificant values. Ritualistic conformance to custom is then observed. Rejection of both goals and means results in retreatist behavior, such as isolation, withdrawal, or psychosis. Rebellion, according to Merton, entails the substitution of unconventional goals and means for more traditional objectives and methods.

Since access to alternative means of goal attainment varies among the members of a society, the above scheme provides a basis for predicting observed forms of deviant behavior.[14] This is more apparent if it is assumed that in our culture both legitimate and illegitimate means have been institutionalized, an assumption that can well be justified in terms of Sutherland's account of criminal culture. Thus, Cloward argues that our ordinary criminals are persons who have been deprived of access to legitimate means for achieving success but who have regular access to illegitimate avenues towards success goals. He further maintains that persons who are bereft of both legitimate and illegitimate success routes are likely to engage in drug addiction, alcoholism, and other forms of retreatist behavior.[15] Consolidation of the conceptions of Sutherland, Durkheim, and Merton offers some promise for the prediction of specific types of deviance and criminality.

Perhaps the fullest extension of the notions of differential association and anomie, along with certain psychogenic arguments, is found in the theory of working-class delinquency as propounded by Albert

[13] Robert K. Merton, *Social Theory and Social Structure,* Revised Edition (Glencoe: Free Press, 1957), especially chapters 4 and 5.

[14] Merton's work is here interpreted as an embryo theory rather than a classification system. For a contrary view see Robert Dubin, "Deviant Behavior and Social Structure: Continuities in Social Theory," *American Sociological Review,* 24 (1959), 147–164.

[15] Richard A. Cloward, "Illegitimate Means, Anomie, and Deviant Behavior," *American Sociological Review,* 24 (1959), 164–176. See also Richard A. Cloward and Lloyd E. Ohlin, *Delinquency and Opportunity: A Theory of Delinquent Gangs* (Glencoe: Free Press, 1960).

Cohen.[16] The theory holds that juvenile members of the lower classes are systematically frustrated in their efforts to gain security and stature in conventional middle-class society. However, instead of succumbing to de-regulation and anomie, these persons develop a subculture that provides opportunities for mutual strivings toward unconventional goals.

Youths of the lower classes find sympathetic understanding in delinquent gangs composed largely of others who share similar problems of adjustment. Interaction among gang members encourages innovation and rebellion, helps to establish norms for innovative behavior organized around officially proscribed goals, and promotes self-conceptions that facilitate identification with deviant norms and nonconformist groups. The psychological process of reaction-formation results in the inversion of conventional goals and values. Assignment of negative values to middle-class practices enables gang members to reject the society from which they have been rejected. Hence, the culture of delinquent gangs encourages, and provides opportunities for, the expression of malicious, negativistic, and nonutilitarian conduct.[17]

Bureaucracy and formal organization. The above cursory review indicates that for several decades criminology has been greatly influenced by the works of Sutherland and Durkheim. In contrast, the impact of Weber seems to have been more recent and less direct.[18] Nevertheless, the problems of concern to Weber have special significance for the field of correction, and it appears likely that they will receive closer attention in the immediate future.

Weber studied the rise of bureaucracy in modern society, its typical structures and procedures, its widespread social ramifications, and its

[16] Albert K. Cohen, *Delinquent Boys: The Culture of the Gang* (Glencoe: Free Press, 1955). For an extension and modification of Cohen's theory see Albert K. Cohen and James F. Short, "Research in Delinquent Subcultures," *Journal of Social Issues,* 14 (1958), 20–37.

[17] Cohen, *op. cit.,* especially ch. 2.

[18] Weber's influence on correctional research seems to have been mediated primarily by the work of Talcott Parsons. See especially T. Parsons, *The Structure of Social Action* (Glencoe: Free Press, 1949); and "Suggestions for a Sociological Approach to a Theory of Organization," *Administrative Science Quarterly,* 1 (1956), 63–85. See also Alvin W. Gouldner, *Patterns of Industrial Bureaucracy* (Glencoe: Free Press, 1954); and Peter M. Blau, *Bureaucracy in Modern Society* (New York: Random House, 1956).

effects on individual freedom.[19] Modern bureaucracy is fostered by the employment of science and technical knowledge in the management of human affairs. With the advancement of science, tradition gives way to formal or legal organizations in which human efforts are deliberately and rationally coordinated in the pursuit of explicitly-stated objectives. These are the general topics with which Weber's theory of formal organization is concerned.

Achievement of the goals of an organization depends upon the difficulties inherent in the assigned task and the availability of necessary knowledge, skills, and other resources. These factors may be regarded as external to the organization in question. But even more important, in the long run, are factors operating within the organization. Foremost among the internal determinants of organizational efficiency are member consensus with respect to goals and objectives, coordination of member activities, and relative utilization of available skills and resources.

Bureaucratic mobilization of human and material resources, as Weber saw it, calls for the employment of a special class of administrators who are responsible for the policies of the organization. It also calls for a hierarchical arrangement of staff positions in order to provide clear and consistent lines of communication and authority. In addition, bureaucracy demands a finely graded system of member rewards based on assigned duties and responsibilities.

The blueprint of bureaucracy is that of a machine. The role played by each member is geared to the activities of other members by means of official rules and regulations. So long as all members perform according to instructions, the organization operates with clock-like precision.

However, there are many things that can go wrong with the bureaucratic machine. For example, there is a notable tendency for the organization to lose sight of its avowed objectives. Once an organization is established, it seems to acquire the primary function of perpetuating itself. Activities aimed at maintaining the organization may overshadow the efforts directed at the original goals and objectives. In such a case regulations acquire a sacred character, blind

---

[19] Talcott Parsons, Ed., *Max Weber: The Theory of Social and Economic Organization* (London: Oxford University Press, 1947), and H. H. Gerth and C. W. Mills, *From Max Weber: Essays in Sociology* (London: Oxford University Press, 1946).

obedience gains recognition as a virtue, and loyalty to staff members is interpreted as evidence of personal integrity. Procedures that were formerly employed for the achievement of external objectives come to be regarded as ends in themselves.

As a result of the pressures mentioned above, there frequently evolves a system of unofficial controls that may have little similarity to the original, rationally planned, official program.[20]

Many corollaries concerning Weber's theory of bureaucracy can be observed in correctional research, especially in studies of the "informal" society of prisoners,[21] the conflicts between "formal" and "informal" prison social systems,[22] the role of communication in the establishment and maintenance of staff authority,[23] the effects of divergent administrative policies on staff and inmate behavior,[24] the

---

[20] Ambiguities in the conception of "informal organization" are well indicated in Stanley H. Udy, "Bureaucracy and Rationality in Weber's Organization Theory," *American Sociological Review,* 24 (1959), 791–795.

[21] Donald Clemmer, *The Prison Community,* New Edition (New York: Rinehart, 1958); and Gresham M. Sykes, *The Society of Captives* (Princeton: Princeton University Press, 1958). See also Gresham M. Sykes, "Men, Merchants, and Toughs: A Study of Reactions to Imprisonment," *Social Problems,* 4 (1956), 130–138; Norman S. Hayner and Ellis Ash, "The Prison Community as a Social Group," *American Sociological Review,* 4 (1939), 362–369; Hans Reimer, "Socialization in the Prison Community," *Proceedings of the American Prison Association,* 1937, 151–155.

[22] Erving Goffman, "On the Characteristics of Total Institutions," in *Symposium on Preventive and Social Psychiatry* (Washington: Government Printing Office, 1957), 43–84; Lloyd W. McCorkle and Richard Korn, "Resocialization Within Walls," *Annals of the American Academy of Political and Social Science,* 293 (1954), 88–98; Richard R. Korn and Lloyd W. McCorkle, *Criminology and Penology* (New York: Henry Holt and Company, 1959), chapters 21 and 22; Frank Tannenbaum, *Crime and the Community* (New York: Ginn and Company, 1938), especially ch. 27; Donald R. Cressey, "Achievement of an Unstated Organizational Goal: An Observation on Prisons," *Pacific Sociological Review,* 1 (1958), 43–49; Donald R. Cressey and Witold Krassowski, "Inmate Organization and Anomie in American Prisons and Soviet Labor Camps," *Social Problems,* 5 (1957–8), 217–230; Johan Galtung, "The Functions of a Prison," *Social Problems,* 6 (1958), 127–140; Norman Polansky, "The Prison as an Autocracy," *Journal of Criminal Law and Criminology,* 33 (1942), 16–22.

[23] Richard H. McCleery, *Policy Change in Prison Management* (East Lansing: Michigan State University Governmental Research Bureau, 1957).

[24] S. Kirsen Weinberg, "Aspects of the Prison's Social Structure," *American Journal of Sociology,* 47 (1942), 717–726; Harvey Powelson and Reinhart Bendix, "Psychiatry in Prison," *Psychiatry,* 14 (1951), 73–86; Gresham

causes of prison riots,[25] and the impact of custodial emphasis versus treatment emphasis on staff-inmate relations and on inmate leadership phenomena.[26] These studies indicate some of the advantages to be gained from the consolidation of organization theory and criminological theory in correctional research.

Now the various theories mentioned have serious logical and empirical defects. Indeed, none of them appears to meet even minimal standards for balance, boundaries, claims, and congruence. Differential association, for example, does not clearly specify the kinds of crime that fall within its scope. It does not provide satisfactory definitions or empirical measures for frequency, duration, priority, or intensity of contact. Moreover, it does not claim any observable interconnections among these contact variables.

Because the major contact variables are not tied together by postulates, the deductive capacity of the theory of differential association is limited and its verification is greatly complicated. That is, the assertion of an expected correlation between crime rates and intensity of criminal contacts, for example, makes no claims concerning the relationship between crime and any of the other contact variables.

M. Sykes, "The Corruption of Authority and Rehabilitation," *Social Forces,* 34 (1956), 257–262; S. B. Peizer, E. B. Lewis, and R. W. Scollon, "Correctional Rehabilitation as a Function of Interpersonal Relations," *Journal of Criminal Law, Criminology, and Police Science,* 46 (1956), 632–640; L. E. Ohlin, H. Piven, and D. M. Pappenfort, "Major Dilemmas of the Social Worker in Probation and Parole," *National Probation and Parole Journal,* 2 (1956), 211–225; George H. Weber, "Conflicts Between Professional and Nonprofessional Personnel in Institutional Delinquency Treatment," *Journal of Criminal Law, Criminology, and Police Science,* 48 (1957), 26–43.

[25] F. E. Hartung and M. Floch, "A Socio-Psychological Analysis of Prison Riots," *Journal of Criminal Law, Criminology, and Police Science,* 47 (1956), 51–57; G. M. Sykes, *op. cit.,* ch. 6; J. B. Martin, *Break Down the Walls* (New York: Ballantine Books, 1954); Lloyd E. Ohlin, *Sociology and the Field of Corrections* (New York: Russell Sage Foundation, 1956), 22–26; *Prison Riots and Disturbances* (New York: American Prison Association, 1953); "Aftermath of Riot," *The Prison Journal,* 34 (1954), entire issue; Austin H. MacCormick, "Behind the Prison Riots," *Annals of the American Academy of Political and Social Science,* 293 (1954), 17–27; Vernon Fox, *Violence Behind Bars* (New York: Vantage Press, 1956; P. McGraw and W. McGraw, *Assignment: Prison Riots* (New York: Henry Holt and Company, 1954).

[26] Oscar Grusky, "Organizational Goals and the Behavior of Informal Leaders," *American Journal of Sociology,* 65 (1959), 59–67; Clarence Schrag, "Leadership Among Prison Inmates," *American Sociological Review,* 19 (1954), 37–42.

It follows that if the intensity hypothesis were empirically confirmed, its confirmation would have no definite bearing on the validity of the remaining hypotheses. Consequently, the theory lacks internal structure, and it is best viewed as a series of loosely connected hypotheses.[27]

Technical inadequacies noted in the theory of differential association could be illustrated equally well with reference to most of the other theories mentioned. Vaguely defined and loosely connected concepts are the rule rather than the exception. This, of course, is not surprising. Theories in criminology, and in the other social sciences as well, have not yet attained very high standards of logical and empirical adequacy. Knowledge in this field does not seem to have matured sufficiently for the construction of comprehensive theories with precise and reliable concepts, unequivocal postulates, and formally derived theorems.

How to make the transition from vague and uncertain generalities to precise and verifiable arguments is one of the major issues confronting criminology. It has already been suggested that consolidation of the concepts and the postulates implied by current theories may provide one of the more hopeful methods for assisting this transition. Therefore, our primary interest here is in examining current theories to see if there are any parallels or convergences in concepts and postulates that might serve as a basis for the desired consolidation.

Trends in the Definition and Use of Basic Concepts. Rather distinctive trends and convergences can be observed, we believe, in the use of concepts such as crime, culture, society, and the social self. Significant changes have occurred in the meanings of these terms and in the way they are interconnected.

Conceptions of criminality. Early studies viewed crime as autonomous behavior resulting from the malicious intent or the perverse will of the individual offender. Treatment of the isolated offender was indicated by this view. Concurrent with this view was the rapid growth of American correctional institutions under the well-known Pennsylvania and Auburn systems of prison administration.

---

[27] For some of the difficulties encountered in pragmatic applications of differential association see especially Donald R. Cressey, "Application and Verification of the Differential Association Theory," *Journal of Criminal Law, Criminology, and Police Science,* 43 (1952), 43–52. See also Donald R. Cressey, *Other People's Money* (Glencoe: Free Press, 1953); and James F. Short, "Differential Association and Delinquency," *Social Problems,* 4 (1957), 233–239.

However, reliable evidence increasingly indicated that individualized treatment is not a very effective method of crime control. It also became apparent that crime often involves the cooperative effort of several persons, that its incidence is exceptionally high in certain kinds of neighborhoods and communities, and that it is sometimes fostered and protected by the cultures of delinquent gangs and of other dissentient social organizations. These findings suggested that greater emphasis should be placed on social factors in crime causation and crime control, and this no doubt encouraged the conceptualization of criminal subcultures and the utilization of various techniques of group therapy. The advent of the group approach signifies a fundamental revision in our basic assumptions concerning crime and its treatment.

Another revolution in definitions and assumptions regarding crime appears to be in process. That is, criminogenic forces are now anticipated in all segments of society and are no longer conceived as traits that are restricted to criminal subcultures and other deviant organizations. Increasing attention is being devoted to white-collar crime, to the contributory roles often played by the victims of criminal offenses, and to indications of fairly strong community support for certain kinds of organized crime and for some forms of political-criminal collusion.

More significantly, there is widespread concern over the behavior of reputable persons and the practices of legitimate organizations as possible sources of criminalistic influence. With this in mind, various phases of social life are being subjected to public scrutiny, especially in areas involving government, communications, labor and industry. Investigators are perhaps less interested in uncovering illegal activities than in determining if there are systematic violations of public standards of justice and decency. The main contention of these investigators is, in effect, that respected persons and essential social agencies may be carriers of criminalistic values and attitudes, that contradictory goals or discrepancies between goals and opportunities for their attainment may contribute to criminality, and that society in the last analysis is the patient in need of treatment if the crime problem is to be alleviated.

Some important general trends are reflected in the changing conceptions of criminality. Rationalism has given way to the view that behavior is frequently affected by nondeliberative and irrational influences. Activities that once were regarded as autonomous are now seen in a broader perspective as both products of and contributors to the social climate of the community. Goals and motives that were formerly interpreted as characteristics of individuals are now commonly accredited to custom, tradition, and other social factors.

Conceptions of culture. Trends in the use of many other sociological concepts seem to parallel those outlined above.[28] Thus culture was early conceived as a superorganic entity, that is, a universal pattern of behavior to be clearly distinguished from the beliefs and actions of given individuals. It was further assumed that culture is rationally designed to satisfy man's essential needs, that an inherent strain toward consistency produces progressive integration of the cultural pattern, and that increasingly effective solutions to problems of human survival are almost inevitable. All of these views have been substantially revised in more recent theoretical formulations.

Recent formulations consider culture to be a historical accretion comprised of the symbols and other artifacts that grow out of human interaction. These symbols and artifacts serve as a medium of communication and as focal points for the organization of human behavior. Through symbols, slogans, proverbs, and other normative devices, culture defines and organizes the chief goals of human conduct. Likewise, culture identifies the alternative means by which achievement of these goals may be expected.

However, goals and means can be mutually exclusive or contradictory forces. They need not always exert pressures toward consistency and integration. The systematic exploits of organized criminals are as much a part of culture as are the retaliatory efforts of police, courts, and other official agencies.

Since culture is no longer viewed as an integrated whole consisting of interlocking parts, it follows that cultural influences may be as much dysfunctional as functional in their impact on designated goals such as crime control, for example. In other words, the current view is that culture reflects not only the progressive accomplishments of mankind but also the most grievous of human errors and blunders.

Society and social systems. While culture variously defines and

[28] Although wide variations in the definitions of sociological concepts must be admitted, we have attempted to follow fairly closely the conceptual frameworks of Talcott Parsons and Robert K. Merton. See especially Talcott Parsons and E. A. Shils, Eds., *Toward a General Theory of Action* (Cambridge: Harvard University Press, 1951); and Robert K. Merton, *Social Theory and Social Structure* (Glencoe: Free Press, 1957).

organizes the means and ends of social action, it remains for societies or social systems to regulate the contacts and communications that occur among groups and individuals. Contact, communication, and interaction make possible the orderly pursuit of cultural objectives.

Social contacts are not random events that follow the probabilities of chance. Neither are they dictated by the capricious choices of individuals. Instead, the different members of a community are systematically connected with each other according to their social positions and their assigned roles.

The implied rules that regulate the contacts among a certain group of persons comprises a designated social system; and a description of the contacts and communications among these persons, organized in terms of their statuses and roles, is a description of that social system.

For example, the accessibility of an administrative official, such as a prison superintendent, is vastly different for correctional officers than it is for prison inmates. Systematic differences occur in the frequency of contacts, in the channels by which contacts are established, in the roles played by the respective partners, in the attitudes of deference or authority that may be exhibited, and in the range of permissible topics of discussion. Similar variations occur among the remaining members of the prison community, depending upon their assigned roles and social positions. The implied rules that govern these variations—that is, the principles that describe the observed pattern of contacts—comprise the prison's social system.

It is clear that the social system regulates the contents of social contacts, or the messages and communications contained therein, as well as it regulates the degree of accessibility of different persons to each other. Thus, prison superintendents, in their contacts with other staff members, are usually receivers of information and givers of advice and orders. By contrast, custodial officers, in contacts with their superiors, are givers of observational reports and receivers of advice and orders. It follows that social relations with other persons vary for any given individual according to his position in the hierarchical arrangement of roles and statuses within the community.

Status is ordinarily defined in terms of the power, prestige, and authority assigned to a given social position. Persons occupying positions of high status may have distinctive advantages in the accessibility of other individuals, in organizing the activities of others, and in commanding their support and allegiance. Moreover, high status usually entails access to knowledge, skills, and other social and cultural resources that may be inaccessible to persons of lower rank. This means that the ease and assurance with which certain goals may be attained are importantly related to variations in social status. The establishment of some congruence between cultural goals and means for achieving them is therefore one of the fundamental problems to be faced by any goal-oriented social organization.

Interrelations of culture and social systems. The implementation of cultural goals and values is at least partly dependent upon the social systems that regulate contacts and communications within a given community. Let us return to the prison for an illustration. The role of the custodial officer is to transmit reliable reports of first-hand observations and to exhibit incontestable fidelity in carrying out orders received from higher authorities. Conversely, the role of the prison superintendent is to digest and evaluate reports from diverse sources so as to initiate and maintain policies that are successful in attaining the goals that are prescribed for the institution, namely, the cultural goals of custody, therapy, protection of society, and reinforcement of noncriminal norms and values. Both the rank-and-file officers and the top-level administrators work within a situation that is defined for them by the broader community. In this way the mechanisms of prison administration are essentially related to cultural goals and objectives.

If our analysis has merit, then the common conception of the prison as a cultural island existing in isolation from civilian norms and values is far from accurate. The same thing holds for the presumed autonomy of prison society. A significant topic for investigation, then, is the reciprocal relationship between civilian normative codes and the behavior of prison inmates and officials.

The social self. Investigation of the impact of social and cultural factors upon the behavior of the individual makes it advisable first to identify the relevant behavioral variables. That is, we need to indicate those aspects of an individual's behavior that are expected to be most directly related to social and cultural influences. The concept that has perhaps been used with greatest frequency for this purpose is the social self, a term that has recently entered significantly into criminological discussions.[29]

[29] W. C. Reckless, S. Dinitz, and E. Murray, "Self Concept as an Insulator Against Delinquency," *American Sociological Review*, 21 (1956), 744–746; W. C. Reckless, S. Dinitz, and B. Kay, "The Self Component in Potential Delinquency and Potential Non-Delinquency," *American Sociological Review*,

"Self" refers primarily to the way a person evaluates his own performance and perceives his relations with others. Two major lines of reasoning have utilized the self concept. First, it is held that self evaluations often exert a determining influence on an individual's overt actions. If a given person conceives of himself as a doctor, a lawyer, or a thief, for example, then his overt behavior can be expected to reflect that conception.

Secondly, the accuracy of a person's self evaluations is believed largely to determine the efficiency with which he can function in his interpersonal relations.[30] Thus, leaders and other influential persons are supposed to excel in their evaluative skills and abilities. Although common-sense evidence lends considerable support to these contentions, there are also some important objections that remain to be answered.[31]

For example, the behavior of a given individual seems to be as closely related to the attitudes of others towards him as it is to his self evaluations.[32] Consequently, the joint effect of self evaluations and the evaluations of others would appear to be at least as significant for purposes of analysis as are self evaluations per se. In addition, the assessment of accuracy in self evaluations runs into some knotty problems of measurement.

To be sure, evaluations of one's own performance and one's relations with others presumably can vary in degree of accuracy. This presumption, however, implies that there are standards of judgment

---

22 (1957), 566–570; W. C. Reckless, S. Dinitz, and E. Murray, "The 'Good' Boy in a High Delinquency Area," *Journal of Criminal Law, Criminology, and Police Science,* 48 (1957), 18–25; Harrison Gough, "A Sociological Theory of Psychopathy," *American Journal of Sociology,* 53 (1948), 359–366; H. Gough and D. Peterson, "The Identification and Measurement of Factors in Crime and Delinquency," *Journal of Consulting Psychology,* 16 (1952), 207–212.

30 See, for example, Leonard S. Cottrell, "Some Neglected Problems in Social Psychology," *American Sociological Review,* 15 (1950), 705–713, and J. S. Bruner and R. Tagiuri, "The Perception of People," in G. Lindzay, editor, *Handbook of Social Psychology* (Addison-Wesley Publishing Company, 1954), vol. 2, 634–654.

31 U. Bronfenbrenner, J. Harding, and M. Gallwey, "The Measurement of Skill in Social Perception," in D. C. McClelland, A. L. Baldwin, U. Bronfenbrenner, and F. L. Strodtbeck, *Talent and Society* (New York: D. Van Nostrand Company, 1958), 29–111.

32 The findings reported by Reckless and his students, *op. cit.,* suggest this view.

which can be used in assessing the evaluations made by any given individual. It is with respect to these standards of judgment that basic questions of measurement arise.

Numerous attempts have been made to develop objective measures of accuracy in self evaluations. Nevertheless, the procedures most frequently adopted are based upon the consensus obtained from ratings made by persons who are selected to act as judges.[33] That is, a given subject's ratings of himself are compared with ratings of him that are made by a group of judges. Or the subject's ratings of other persons are compared with the ratings those persons make of themselves. Finally, the subject's ratings of another person are compared with ratings of that person made by a group of judges.

All of the above measures, of course, make the assumption that consensus among judges can serve legitimately as a standard of accuracy. However, there is good evidence that the ratings of judges are influenced by social and cultural factors other than the judges' knowledge of the person being rated.[34] Thus, the standard of accuracy may be expected to vary according to the methods used in selecting the judges. A measurement device that fluctuates according to the persons who use it can hardly be employed for purposes of validation.

For the reasons mentioned, we feel that conventional attempts to validate self evaluations by the use of judges may tend to obscure more significant questions dealing with the interrelations between self evaluations and social positions or cultural forces. Instead of trying to decide if given evaluations are accurate or inaccurate, for example, it would be more appropriate to investigate variations in self evaluations among persons occupying different social positions. Also, self evaluations may vary according to the degree of attachment to various cultural goals and objectives. Furthermore, the ratings of judges who are carefully selected in terms of their social positions or their cultural attachments may reveal how evaluations of a given person are dependent upon the perspectives of the judges who are

[33] See especially the various works of L. S. Cottrell and R. F. Dymond.

[34] N. L. Gage, "Judging Interests from Expressive Behavior," *Psychological Monographs*, 66 (1952), no. 18; N. L. Gage and L. J. Cronbach, "Conceptual and Methodological Problems in Interpersonal Perception," *Psychological Review*, 62 (1955), 411–422; A. H. Hastorf and I. E. Bender, "A Caution Respecting the Measurement of Empathic Ability," *Journal of Abnormal and Social Psychology*, 47 (1952), 574–576; H. C. Lindgren and J. Robinson, "The Evaluation of Dymond's Test of Insight and Empathy," *Journal of Consulting Psychology*, 17 (1953), 172–176.

doing the ratings.[35] This approach, while it may not solve the problem of validation, should help us to establish empirical connections among some of the basic concepts of criminology.

The preceding discussion proposes that a fair amount of criminological knowledge can be organized around postulated relationships among cultural norms, social systems, and self conceptions. We turn now to a conceptual framework based on this assumption and supported by a series of studies of correctional institutions in a Western state.[36]

In the studies cited, the actions of staff members and inmates are related, first of all, to the goals and norms of the broader civilian community as well as to the cultural forces that are more indigenous to the correctional institutions in question. Culture, according to the framework used, is comprised of normative patterns that are founded in symbols and other products of human interaction. Normative devices, such as symbols and slogans, define and order the goals of human conduct. Furthermore, these devices may establish conventional expectations regarding the behavior of a given individual in a specific situation.[37] In some situations and for given individuals the expected behavior may be illegitimate or illegal with respect to the

[35] Reliability and validity of sociometric tests and devices for the measurement of interpersonal relations are discussed in G. Lindzay, *op. cit.*, by G. Lindzay and E. F. Borgatta, "Sociometric Measurement," especially pp. 420–424. See also "Technical Recommendations for Psychological Tests and Diagnostic Techniques," *Psychological Bulletin*, 51 (1954), no. 2, part 2.

[36] The studies are reported in a series of M.A. and Ph.D. theses at the University of Washington. See Peter G. Garabedian, *Western Penitentiary: A Study in Social Organization*, 1959; John W. Kinch, *Certain Social-Psychological Aspects of Types of Juvenile Delinquents*, 1959; Duane Strinden, *Parole Prediction Using Criminological Theory and Manifold Classification Techniques*, 1959; Stanton Wheeler, *Social Organization in a Correctional Community*, 1958; Donald L. Garrity, *The Effects of Length of Incarceration Upon Parole Adjustment and Estimation of Optimum Sentence*, 1956; Stanton Wheeler, *Evaluation of Parole Prediction Techniques*, 1956; Bernard C. Kirby, *Parole Prediction Using the Discriminant Function*, 1953; Clarence Schrag, *Crimeville: A Sociometric Study of a Prison Community*, 1950; Clarence Schrag, *Social Types in a Prison Community*, 1944.

[37] An interesting account of social and cultural factors involved in unstructured or tacit communication is found in Thomas C. Schelling, "Bargaining, Communication, and Limited War," *Journal of Conflict Resolution*, 1 (1957), 19–36; also Thomas C. Schelling, "The Strategy of Conflict: Prospectus for a Reorientation of Game Theory," *Journal of Conflict Resolution*, 2 (1958), 203–264.

ethical or official codes of the community. Antisocial attitudes and criminal skills and abilities are by no means restricted to the criminal segment of the community. Therefore, criminal behavior may be an integral part of the cultural system.

Secondly, staff and inmate behavior patterns are related to different roles and positions that are observed within the social systems of the institutions studied. Social systems are delineated by the contacts and interactions that are observed among the members of a given community. Opportunities for contact and interaction vary for different individuals according to their social positions and their assigned roles. Thus, the structure of social roles and positions within a given community determines the relative degree to which the various members have access to legitimate and illegitimate means of goal attainment.

In addition, the above conceptions of culture and social systems clearly imply that the various members of a given community may exhibit important differences in their cognitive knowledge of alternative means of goal achievement, in their affective attachments to these alternatives, and in their access to social and cultural resources that make possible the employment of the varied alternatives. Presumably, objective measures of knowledge, attachments, and accessibility can be made. It follows that these measures should be useful in predicting the behavior of given individuals, assuming that performance depends upon ability, opportunity, and relevant attitudes. Consequently, these three variables are related to a number of other behavioral indexes in the studies mentioned.

A third focus of attention in the studies cited is the connection between self evaluations and other activities of staff members and inmates. For example, attempts are made to observe the ways in which different inmates conceive of their statuses in the civilian community, their statuses in the society of prisoners, their knowledge of criminal techniques and values, and their intrapersonal adjustments as reflected in levels of aspiration and anxiety. These aspects of the social self are related to positions within the prison's social system, to inmate perceptions of prison goals, and to perceptions of the roles of staff members and inmates.

Furthermore, the empirical interconnections among the different variables mentioned are examined for any signs of consistency or uniformity. The result is a typological system that seems to reveal, at least in a crude and preliminary fashion, some of the ways in which cultural, social, and personal variables are empirically interrelated within the institutions investigated. While the findings in support of the conceptual framework are by no means conclusive, they appear to warrant further study by suggesting certain refinements in the concepts and the postulates of contemporary criminological theory.

We turn now to a summary of the major findings, considering first the structure of the prison community and then the main patterns of inmate adaptation.

THE CORRECTIONAL COMMUNITY[38]

Cultural Determinants of Correctional Policy. Problems of criminality and activities of criminals have attained such prominence in contemporary social life that nearly all persons have some conception of the methods or techniques of crime, the supposed causes of crime, and tactics of crime control. Common conceptions of criminality exert an important influence on the activities of correctional administrators because administrators regard themselves as representatives of the broader community in their dealings with criminals. Moreover, they are so regarded by the members of the broader community. Correctional officials, in other words, carry a public trust, and their duties and responsibilities are defined for them in terms of conventional beliefs concerning criminal behavior. Thus, the objectives and policies of correctional institutions are largely reflections of beliefs and values that are indigenous to the broader community.

If their objectives deviate very far from those of the broader community, correctional officials encounter various forms of public opposition. Consequently, the assessment of changes or trends in public expectations is an inevitable and important task for the correctional official. To the extent that social conventions are supportive of confused or contradictory correctional objectives, it may be expected that prison policies will reflect these confusions and contradictions.

According to available evidence, the foremost responsibilities assigned to prison officials are maintenance of custodial security and protection of society against convicted offenders.[39] Therapy comes

[38] This section is an elaboration of "Social Role, Social Position, and Prison Social Structure," paper presented to the American Correctional Association, Miami, Florida, September, 1959.

[39] Garabedian, *op. cit.*, ch. 3.

next. "You can't treat the prisoners if you can't keep them," and similar mottoes indicate the relative values ordinarily attached to treatment and custody. Among the goals that receive weaker public endorsements, although they are strongly invoked in special cases and in times of crisis, are deterrence of potential offenders and reinforcement of cultural norms and values.

While the relative importance attached to different correctional objectives may vary somewhat in different segments of the community, the protective functions of correctional institutions are usually given the highest rankings, followed by the therapeutic or restorative functions, and finally the integrative functions. Moreover, staff members of correctional institutions, in general, follow the same order of rankings, the primary exception being that top-level administrative officials who have been indoctrinated in modern treatment philosophy tend to place a higher premium on therapy.[40]

Like the goals and objectives of correctional institutions, the policies of such organizations are greatly influenced by conventional assumptions concerning criminal behavior. Correctional programs are founded on a public conception of the criminal as a person who habitually engages in deliberative misconduct. In fact, the conception of malicious intent is an essential ingredient of criminal conduct as defined by statute. Furthermore, persons who are regarded as being incapable of willful wrongdoing, namely, children and the insane, do not ordinarily come under the purview of criminal law or under the correctional policies that are presumably designed for deliberative offenders.

Although the above conception of criminal behavior may be gradually changing under the impact of contemporary explanations of human conduct, it seems clear that the bulk of opinion and the weight of official and legal doctrine are still largely in support of the traditional notion that the criminal knows the difference between right and wrong, that he makes a rational and considered decision against the moral order, and that his choice is subject to voluntary control. Criminals and prisoners, in other words, are believed to be capable of conformity but disposed to play the role of the rebel. Prisoners consequently are expected to exhibit antisocial attitudes and to be resistive and unruly in their contacts with correctional authorities. To the degree that prisoner roles are conditioned by the tradi-

[40] *Ibid.*, pp. 38–44.

tional assumptions mentioned, these assumptions may be expected to strengthen the staff-inmate conflicts and the negativistic attitudes of prisoners that have been so frequently noted in correctional research.

The role of the prison official, as perceived in the broader community, also reflects the influence of the assumptions mentioned above. In effect, inmates are absolved of any responsibility for prison programs and policies; and officials are held fully accountable for the attainment of correctional objectives, the maintenance of plant and equipment, the protection of inmate health and welfare, and the enforcement of inmate conformity and obedience.[41]

The focus of traditional prison policies is the enforcement of compliance and obedience despite the expected opposition of the inmates. Strict surveillance and punitive actions are deemed necessary to show the prisoner that society is stronger than he is. Force and restraints, according to the view that seems dominant in the broader community, should only be used when necessary to maintain control; but they should always be available in sufficient degree to insure the maintenance of control. Thus, correctional institutions are frequently viewed as autonomous societies having police powers sufficient for the prompt detection of any rule violations and for rigorous enforcement of official rules and regulations.

The prison world, as seen from a conventional perspective, is a world of conflict between forces of good and of evil. Prisoners are expected to exercise their antisocial propensities if they can get away with it. Officers are, or are expected to be, the sentinels of the good society who carry the full authority of the official community in their relations with the inmate caste. Their first objective is to obtain by means of external constraints the compliance that prisoners are disinclined to display voluntarily.

Significantly, the traditional view of the prison is also the view of most staff members and inmates. Striking similarities can be noted in the previously mentioned assumptions and in the way staff members and inmates perceive their own social roles and the roles of each other.

To illustrate, staff members and inmates were questioned concerning various possible solutions to problematic situations that frequently arise in correctional institutions. In addition to stating their own preferred solutions to the problems, officers and inmates indicated

[41] We are concerned with assumptions regarding staff and inmate roles in the traditional close-custody prison. Role definitions vary according to the kind of correctional institution in question.

the solutions that they thought would be adopted by most officers and by most inmates. Then the observed preferences of the two groups were compared with their anticipated preferences.[42]

Responses to the questionnaires clearly show that the role of the inmate is quite uniformly perceived as an "antisocial" role, whereas the role of the officer is just as consistently perceived as an "authoritarian" role. That is, both staff members and inmates regularly overestimate the number of antisocial solutions to prison problems that are actually chosen by the inmates. Likewise, both staff members and inmates, in attempting to anticipate the solutions that are chosen with greatest frequency by staff members, consistently assign to prison officials a higher degree of authoritarianism than is warranted by their actual choices. Moreover, differences in the role of the inmate as perceived by officers and by the inmates themselves are relatively minor. The same thing holds for the role of the officer.

The conclusion suggested is that staff members and inmates share perceptual distortions in such a manner that they see the differences in their assigned roles as being greatly exaggerated. These distortions tend to reinforce the traditions of conflict between the two groups. Furthermore, the distortions are in complete accord with the conventional view of the prison as a world of conflict. It may consequently be assumed that the distortions reflect the influence of cultural factors upon the cognitive behavior of staff members and inmates. The cultural expectation of staff-inmate conflict impregnates the perceptions of the members of the prison community, and in this way it may function as a self-fulfilling prophecy.

The strategies for "reforming," "rehabilitating," "treating," or "correcting" criminals in institutions also are greatly influenced by the assumptions of persons in the broader society, and these assumptions have been importantly revised during the course of correctional history. Early efforts were to be aimed at "breaking the will" of the offender. Current conceptions of treatment place greater emphasis upon the inculcation of useful habits, such as thriftiness and industriousness, and the acquisition of social and occupational skills. Thus, the treatment function of the prison is to make available to inmates a variety of facilities, including programs of academic and vocational training, medical care, religious instruction, counseling, and parole planning, to mention only the standard treatment devices.

[42] Wheeler, *Social Organization in a Correctional Community, op. cit.,* ch. 3. See, also, ch. 6, above.

But the assumption that it is entirely up to the inmate to take advantage of treatment opportunities if he is so inclined is still an important feature of treatment philosophy. Behavior is still regarded as primarily a matter of personal volition. Reorganization of attitudes and modification of affective attachments to objects and persons in the social environment are generally viewed as personal issues over which prison policies have little control. The possibility of redefining the roles and changing the social positions of inmates by means of administrative procedures receives relatively little consideration, although some efforts along these lines are being initiated through various forms of group therapy.

In other words, a systematic and convincing rationale for the use of modern methods of therapy has not yet made its way very effectively into the philosophy of correctional administration. This is especially true of the traditional close-custody prison. In many cases, treatment programs seem primarily designed to bolster staff and inmate morale, to institutionalize the rewards for obedience and conformity, to improve housekeeping practices, and to serve other custodial functions. The relationship of treatment to the acceptance of civilian responsibilities after the inmate is released from the institution gets less attention than the immediate effects of treatment upon problems of prison management.

Primacy of the protective functions of correctional institutions is perhaps inevitably reflected in administrative practice. Nevertheless, some institutions are placing great stress upon treatment programs even though they violate some of the conventional expectations concerning correctional objectives. For example, inmates in certain institutions are held largely responsible for their own welfare, or they may be encouraged to participate in decisions regarding institutional policy, and attempts have been made to create staff and inmate climates in which the expectation of cooperation and mutual effort is the rule rather than the exception.[43]

However, such radical departures from convention as those mentioned above appear to gain community support only if there is full assurance that traditional close-custody programs will be available for the more belligerent offenders. In addition, the greater visibility

---

[43] See, for example, Lloyd W. McCorkle, Albert Elias, and F. Lovell Bixby, *The Highfields Story* (New York: Henry Holt and Company, 1958); and "Group Counseling in Prison," *Proceedings of the American Correctional Association,* 1955, 51–60.

of custodial criteria, such as escapes and riots, means that even in treatment-oriented institutions new programs are likely to be evaluated in great measure by their impact on the frequency of custodial incidents.

Administrative Organization of the Prison. The structure of prison administration is organized around conventional definitions of correctional objectives and conventional assumptions concerning criminal behavior. More specifically, the administrative structure of the prison is comprised of a hierarchy of offices or staff positions, each of which implies certain duties and responsibilities, and a chain of command linking the various offices in a rationally predetermined manner. The immediate objective of this structure is the attainment of uniform compliance to a set of official rules and regulations that designates the behavior expected of staff members and inmates.

The articulation of authority patterns and staff positions provides a powerful and intricately balanced mechanism for manufacturing policy decisions. Everyday observations of inmate behavior are reported from the lower levels of command up the ladder to higher levels, where the numerous reports are collated and official decisions are made. Then directives and supportive information, sanctioned by top-level administrators, flow back down the ladder in a unilateral sequence, from division chief to supervisor to officer and, in turn, to the inmates. Hence, the typical communication pattern in the close-custody prison is for reports of a first-hand factual nature to move upward in the chain of command and for policies, directives, and interpretations of factual materials to move down the ranks of employees.

Despite the clear logic of its structure, there may be significant defects in the system of unilateral authority relations. First, the system assumes that officers are fully committed to the objectives and policies announced by the chief administrator. Secondly, it assumes that the administrative machinery of the prison embodies the power and authority of the broader community in dealing with the inmates. Thirdly, it assumes that inmates occupy a caste-like status that deprives them of any influence in the determination of policy. None of these assumptions is very realistic if judged in terms of social activities that are normally observed in the prison community. Let us briefly examine these assumptions in the order mentioned.

Alienation of the officer. Instead of insuring agreement between rank-and-file officers and top-level administrators, the unilateral flow of authority and communication may tend to produce a considerable barrier between the low-ranking officer's world of everyday experience and the picture of that world as it is viewed from the top levels of command.

Frequently persons in highest authority are far removed from the scene of contact between staff members and inmates where the relative worthiness of alternative policies is most clearly revealed. Administrative decisions regarding specific situations are based chiefly on facts reported by subordinates. Therefore, administrative judgments are sometimes jeopardized by the distortions of fact that tend to occur when reports are repeatedly reviewed, digested, and passed upward through the ranks of the administrative hierarchy. In addition, the highest authorities may be among the last persons to learn about the impact of their decisions upon the relations between staff members and inmates. Generally, the higher the rank of the administrative officer, the greater his dependence on reports of the observations of others and the less direct the sources of his information.

Again, the officers who are most immediately affected by correctional policies are the ones who play the least part in policy formation. The task of low-ranking officers is to carry out orders, not to evaluate them. Feedback, such as criticism of directives received, is minimized, and in some institutions no official procedure for such reverse flow of communication is available. When reverse flow of critical comment is tolerated, it is often restricted to informal relations among trusted associates and is not treated as a matter of policy. Failure of unilateral communication to exploit the possibilities of feedback encourages the development of unofficial channels for the diffusion of messages. This may seriously interfere with the operation of the formal machinery of administration.

Official communication, based on the unilateral design, seems to be at a distinct disadvantage when competing with the mutual give-and-take that characterizes unofficial relations among officers or between officers and inmates. Two factors are of special significance in this connection. First, official directives generally assume the form of unqualified and universal imperatives. This results from the tendency for rationalizations, justifications, and elaborations to get lost or misinterpreted as the directives filter down the ranks of the administrative hierarchy. Secondly, for every official directive that is issued there is likely to be an unofficial interpretation which results from comments and discussions occurring outside the official channels of communication. For subordinate officials, it is perhaps the unofficial version that has the more comprehensible meaning and fits the directive into the over-all plan of prison administration. If this is the case, the unilateral system of communication, instead of eliminating the influence of hearsay and rumor, may tend to make unofficial messages an essential part of the officer's conception of prison policy.

Allegiance to the official administration may be less important to the subordinate officer than are his many involvements in the unofficial conventions of the prison community. His knowledge of the official program is sometimes limited to the specific rules and regulations that are his immediate concern. His information about prison affairs comes primarily from sources other than those that are officially prescribed. For example, over half of the subordinate officers in a state prison were unaware of the existence of a certain group therapy program that had been in operation for more than nine months.[44] And the majority of those officers who knew about the program stated that they had learned of it from inmates or fellow officers rather than from their superiors.

In many institutions, the status of subordinate officers is essentially connected with their lack of official information, their limited influence, and their minimal participation in matters of administrative policy. Attitudes of detachment and feelings of powerlessness or meaninglessness with respect to the official program are also commonly noted. Objective factors related to the status of subordinate officers tend to reinforce their feelings of powerlessness, and vice versa. The result is that officers of the lower ranks frequently are alienated from the official program. This is reflected, for example, in the negative correlation that is observed between the length of service of low-ranking officers and the degree of their confidence in prison treatment programs.[45]

The illusion of unlimited authority. Because of the primacy of custodial functions, the greatest concern of prison administrators is the constant threat of prisoner escapes and uprisings. Major techniques for the control of inmate rebellions are, first, the show of force and, secondly, appeals to the inmates based on the notion that the prison's administration embodies the power and authority of the political state.

However, neither technique seems to be nearly as effective in

[44] Garabedian, *op. cit.,* p. 186.
[45] *Ibid.,* ch. 3.

organizing the routine activities of the prison community as are the unofficial alliances between staff members and inmates. Routine activities of the prison are largely governed by a system of symbiotic social relations that is designed to eliminate the necessity of force except in emergencies. This symbiotic system is based on certain fundamental weaknesses in the official structure of prison administration.

First of all, the repeated use of force is often self-defeating. Its cost is excessive in terms of manpower and material resources. It is detrimental to inmate morale and interest in staff-inmate harmony. Force begets force in the sense that officers who are employed in the continued use of force are thereby deprived of the major social means for obtaining voluntary inmate cooperation.[46] This is largely the reason for the traditional separation of custodial and therapeutic functions in the close-custody prison.

A more crucial reason for restraint in the employment of force is that public opinion generally denies the necessity of its continued use in correctional institutions. Withdrawal of public support from correctional administrations that are founded on repetitious displays of official violence has occurred with increasing frequency during the course of our penal history. For example, the use of force in the recent wave of prison riots almost always resulted in public inquiries into the complaints of the rioting prisoners. These inquiries clearly revealed that public opinion was by no means unanimous in its support of prison policies, a situation that was apparently anticipated by the riot leaders and may have contributed to their rebellions.

While social conventions hold administrators responsible for the conduct of prison inmates, they also assume that strict surveillance and rigorous enforcement of appropriate penalties should make major displays of violence a rare occurrence. Consequently, most prison administrators, in order to maintain their official positions, must utilize devices other than violence in gaining inmate conformity and obedience. Force, then, is increasingly regarded as a device to be used as a last resort in case of emergency. Its public justification is sometimes threatened by the conventional belief that efficient prison administration should make its use unnecessary.

For the above reasons, the appeal to authority is a far more prev-

---

[46] The institutionalization of influence patterns among inmates and staff members is discussed in Goffman, *op. cit.*, especially pp. 66–81. See also chapter 2, above.

alent mechanism of official control. However, the functions of authority in the prison community are also subject to common misunderstanding. Authority is based on the assumption that persons in subordinate positions will voluntarily submit to the dictates of their superiors. But authority is effective only if subordinates share the social perspectives of their superiors. Our discussion of alienation has already suggested that officers occupying different ranks in the administrative hierarchy do not necessarily share similar views of the official program.

It is sometimes naïvely assumed that an officer's instruction to an inmate carries the full sanction of the prison's administration and that the officer's failure to enforce his order is evidence of the "corruption" of his authority. This is not necessarily the case. It would be far more realistic frankly to admit that the officer's control over an inmate depends primarily on his skills of persuasion and leadership.

Consider, for example, the alternative procedures that are available to an officer in the event that an inmate refuses to obey his command. First, he might resort to physical force. Generally, there are official regulations that restrict the use of force except in cases of attempted escape or threatened bodily injury. These regulations are designed to prevent unnecessary use of force. Therefore, if the officer uses force, he must justify his actions to his superiors in the same way that his superiors need to justify violence in the face of public opinion. His superiors are likely to hold the common opinion that effective leadership and preventative methods should make force unnecessary. Repeated involvement in violence against inmates is consequently likely to result in termination of the officer's employment by the institution.

Again, the officer may use the more common procedure of reporting inmate misconduct to his superiors. Penalties against the inmate may then be determined by a disciplinary committee. However, should the committee receive an extraordinary number of complaints or reports from a given officer, this too may be interpreted as evidence of incompetence on the part of the officer. Inmates, of course, are fully aware of the role they play in the official evaluation of an officer's services. Thus continued employment of a given officer depends largely upon the degree of voluntary cooperation that he can win from the inmates. Skill in interpersonal relations is more important in this situation than is the "corruption" of highly restricted authority, and the idea that officials have unlimited authority is simply not consistent with the essential evidence.

The fiction of official autonomy. Another defect of the unilateral system of communication and authority is the assumption that prison policies are autonomous and uninfluenced by inmate pressures. Official policy views the prisoner as being habitually antisocial and inclined to violate regulations if he can get away with it. Further, policy holds that the only defensible role for the officer to play is to enforce all rules to the letter and "let the chips fall where they may." Since the inmates are not involved in the formulation of policy, their only opportunity for influencing the administration of the institution is in the area of policy enforcement. Therefore, if the rules are enforced without deviation, complete domination over the inmates presumably can be gained.

For instance, rules aimed at curbing food pilferage may define as contraband all items of prison fare that are found in any place other than the mess-hall. As a consequence, any inmate found in possession of unauthorized food is officially presumed to be guilty of theft or somehow involved in the food racket. Excuses don't count.

Similar presumptions of guilt operate with respect to other rules and regulations. The apparent purpose of the presumptions is to base the decision of guilt upon objective factors and to eliminate problems of judgment concerning extenuating circumstances. In this way it is believed that the possibility of inmate influence in the dispensation of prison justice will be minimized.

However, undeviating enforcement of all rules can involve an officer in the repeated employment of force and/or the issuance of innumerable rule-infraction reports. The practical effect, in either case, may be to create official doubts concerning the officer's competence, as has already been mentioned. Furthermore, the officer may have full knowledge of extenuating circumstances in certain cases and may therefore disagree with the official presumption of guilt. If the officer takes into consideration the alleviating conditions and gives the inmate a "break," he is in danger of official reprimand. In addition, toleration of rule infractions in the face of a policy of complete enforcement makes the officer vulnerable to charges of collusion with the inmates. This is precisely the point at which conniving inmates seek to "get something on" the officer, to be held against him later in more important situations and progressively to bring him under inmate domination.

The traditional policy of complete rule enforcement breaks down because it does not allow room for individual judgment concerning the circumstances related to rule violations. It places the officer in a fine dilemma. As a practical matter the officer can neither enforce all rules to the letter nor can he admit that he tolerates certain rule violations. This is why many correctional institutions, including some close-custody prisons, are developing mechanisms for taking into account the circumstances related to rule violations. However, all of these mechanisms, so far as can be ascertained, involve distinctive modifications of the unilateral system of communication; they either give the officer considerable discretion in reporting violations, a procedure that is euphemistically called "counseling," or they provide for the inmate an official opportunity to defend his actions.

Nevertheless, insistence upon unilateral relations among staff members and between staff members and inmates, rather than paucity of treatment facilities, is the feature most characteristic of the traditional close-custody prison. Restrictions against feedback and participation in policy formation, of course, are extended to the inmate population. However, such restrictions apparently run counter to some of the assumptions underlying modern therapeutic techniques. Modern methods of group therapy and guided participation in programming activities, for example, encourage the inmate to evaluate and perhaps initially to criticize the behavior standards that he is expected eventually to adopt as his own. Frank expression of skepticism and freedom of discussion, instead of insuring rejection of social norms, are believed to improve the inmate's understanding of social controls and to further the development of self-imposed discipline.

If the above analysis of defects in traditional prison policies is valid, then it seems clear that the unilateral organization of the close-custody prison may place severe limitations upon the treatment potential of our prisons and may provide a greater barrier against the resocialization of the offender than do the bars and walls that attract such adverse comment. How to modify traditional policy so as to integrate the roles of inmates and officers within a more efficient official organization continues to be one of the most difficult problems of prison administration.

Some Aspects of Prisoner Society. Juxtaposed with the official organization of the prison is an unofficial social system originating within the institution and regulating inmate conduct with respect to focal issues, such as length of sentence, relations among prisoners, contacts with staff members and other civilians, food, sex, and health, among others.[47] The unofficial system, contrary to administrative rules

---

[47] Schrag, *Social Types in a Prison Community*, ch. 4.

and regulations, does not demand uniformity of behavior. Rather, it recognizes alternative roles that inmates may play with respect to each of the focal issues.

In various subtle ways the unofficial social system encourages reciprocal, complementary, or symbiotic relationships among inmates and between inmates and officers. Behavior prescriptions are based on interlocking role alternatives that are organized around the focal issues. Alternative roles are allocated among the inmates so as to maintain a fairly stable social equilibrium within the society of prisoners. To illustrate, consider some of the alternative roles that are organized around the procurement of illicit foods. Codes of conduct pertaining to food pilferage differ for "scores" (spontaneous or unplanned thefts) and "routes" (highly organized thefts). An inmate who "scores for food" may consume it or share it with friends, perhaps for past or expected favors, but he is not expected to sell it. Food obtained through organized theft is ordinarily sold in the illicit food racket.

Sale of pilfered food is regulated by an intricate division of labor and responsibility based on a network of symbiotic roles. Designated inmates are assigned the job of obtaining the food and delivering it to distributors. Distributors, in turn, may sell on credit to trusted inmate customers. Or the food may be sold on a cash basis to inmates from whom knowledge of procurement techniques is carefully concealed. Roles affiliated with the food racket are further delineated in terms of the kinds and quantities of foods stolen; in terms of the food sources, such as the officer's mess or the inmate's mess, for example; and, finally, in terms of the methods of distribution and exchange.

Only those inmates who are involved in the food racket, of course, need to know the details of the system. Designation of role incumbents is handled informally, chiefly by mutual agreement among the persons concerned. But once a role has been assumed, it places upon the incumbent fairly precise requirements regarding his relations with others who participate in the racket, and with nonparticipating inmates and staff members as well. Furthermore, the amount of knowledge and skill required of an inmate depends upon the degree of his involvement in the racket. The food racket may be so well organized, however, that if all persons involved in it know and fulfill their assignments, the pilferage system can operate with an efficiency that is alarming and costly to the prison's administration.

Maintenance of a *sub rosa* organization such as the food racket requires that inmates be capable of assessing the probable behavior and the loyalty attachments of their fellows. Roles and statuses must generally be appropriate to the skills and interests of the persons involved. Errors made by the inmates in the assignment of roles ordinarily work to the advantage of the prison's administration and its officials. In order to minimize such errors, a fairly elaborate system of role allocations is set into operation not only with respect to food pilferage but in all areas of behavior related to the focal issues.[48]

Allocation of roles is based on evidence regarding the affective orientations of the inmates, the accuracy and consistency of their perceptions of role requirements, and the degree of agreement between their perceived role requirements and their performance. Role allocations not only reflect the assessments and expectations of fellow inmates relative to the person in question, but they also in a large measure determine this person's opportunities for future social contacts and his access to information and to other social resources.

Evidence relevant to role assignments is obtained from observations made during initiation ceremonies and from a variety of contrived testing situations that accompany the introduction of an inmate into the prisoner community. The process of role allocation commonly proceeds in a standardized sequence of events. First, a degree of consensus is attained regarding the inmate's relative loyalties to the administration and to his fellow prisoners. Attempts are made to determine whether a given inmate generally evaluates situations according to the codes of prisoner society or according to the dictates of the officials. Then, the inmate's knowledge of prisoner roles and his skill in dealing with problematic situations are carefully examined. Knowledge of prisoner society indicates a given inmate's potential for aiding or obstructing the goals and strategies of his fellow prisoners. Finally, the consistency, reliability, and integrity of the inmate's behavior are investigated in a variety of contrived situations. Within six months, or so, after the inmate's admission into the institution, his major roles in the prisoner community seem to have been pretty well established. Role assignments, of course, are sometimes modified through a continuous re-evaluation of the inmate's performance, but the frequency of such modifications is usually not great enough to disturb the social equilibrium.[49]

In addition to exercising great care in the allocation of roles, especially in areas involving high risk of detection by the officials, inmate society sets up expectations of mutual care and protection

[48] *Ibid.*, especially pp. 43–54.
[49] *Ibid.*

among the prisoners. These expectations, of course, conflict with the official suggestion to "do your own time," and they provide a basis for strong inmate morale in the face of persistent staff opposition. Roles played by prisoners with respect to forbidden activities create sets of mutual obligations that define conceptions of loyalty and protect organized rackets from interference by nonparticipating inmates or staff members. The rule that an inmate should not do anything to interfere with another's participation in forbidden activities is apparently the strongest commandment in the prisoner's code of conduct.[50]

For example, inmates engaged in the food racket, in order to maintain a climate favorable to the continuation of this enterprise, may be expected to support and protect various other forbidden activities. Inmates who profit from such support or nonintervention are required to reciprocate in like manner. A system of largely unspoken but finely graded reciprocities of this kind tends to integrate prisoner society in its opposition to the prison's official administration.

But the system of inmate reciprocities, like the official system of unilateral communications, is vulnerable in crucial ways to outside interference. Deviations from the system, although they may be largely concealed from many of the inmates, are as much the rule as the exception. One problem is competition among inmates who are striving for higher status and authority within the society of prisoners. Again, the system is far less autonomous than the inmates would like to believe; and whenever it is disrupted by official intervention, there is great difficulty in determining exactly what went wrong. Finally, many of the inmates refrain from full involvement in the system; they may feel an allegiance to the official codes or they may be greatly influenced by official rewards and punishments. All of this lessens the effectiveness of the social controls that are primarily accessible to the prisoners.

The result is that neither the official system nor the society of prisoners can long retain dominance in the prison community. Symbiotic relationships tend to develop in such a way that, although the integrity of the two systems may be retained on the surface, the behavior of an inmate or a staff member in almost any given case is determined by intersecting influences that cannot be realistically accredited solely to either system. It is to this topic that we now turn our attention.

[50] Wheeler, *op. cit.*, p. 54.

PATTERNS OF INMATE ADAPTATION[51]

Sets of role alternatives, as previously indicated, reflect the organization of inmate behavior with regard to given focal issues. The conception of a social system, however, signifies a higher level of organization than that dealing with specific issues. Society, as an abstract concept, implies that the role alternatives assumed by given individuals with respect to various issues are interrelated in a more or less systematic manner. Thus, the pragmatic problem related to the concept of the social system is for research to determine the empirical regularities, if any, among sets of role alternatives. We call such regularities role configurations.

Major Role Configurations. Role configuration implies that a particular alternative regarding a given focal issue will be empirically connected with a certain alternative related to a second issue. A straightforward empirical procedure for identifying configurations of role alternatives would be to list all logically possible combinations of alternatives and then determine the frequencies with which the combinations occur. This procedure is unrealistic, of course, because the combinations rapidly reach staggering proportions and the relevant observational data are not available. An alternative procedure is to focus attention on the role configurations that are implied in the prison's symbolic system, including its argot, proverbs, legends and beliefs.

Prison argot makes many sharp distinctions between alternatives, which define the separate roles organized around a given issue, and configurations, which specify sets of alternatives that are perceived as being interrelated. "Merchant" for example, denotes the salesman role in a variety of situations, whereas "food peddler" identifies a single role alternative. The "merchant" configuration cuts across a number of focal issues. It is involved in a variety of *sub rosa* organizations and consequently arouses stronger inmate support or opposition. The term, as it seems to be used in prison, does not merely label a given role alternative, but implies that several alternatives are empirically connected.

It is immediately apparent, however, that inmates may erroneously perceive a particular set of role alternatives as being interrelated.

[51] Some of the material in this section is adapted from a paper, "Preliminary Criminal Typology," presented to the American Sociological Association, Chicago, Illinois, September, 1959.

Therefore, a distinction should be made between perceived relationships and confirmed or empirically verified relationships among role alternatives. Likewise, it is necessary to distinguish between normative statements, or behavior *pre*scriptions, and statements about overt performance, or behavior *de*scriptions. Since these distinctions are not ordinarily made in the use of prison language, great caution must be observed in relying upon the prison's symbolic system as a guide in the identification of role configurations.

Keeping in mind the perceived-confirmed and the prescribed-performed dichotomies mentioned above, a number of cross-tabulations were made of roles that are supposed to be interrelated according to prison argot, proverbs and legends. Several configurations were found that cut across a number of issues within the prison community. Most important, in our opinion, is a set of configurations that deals primarily with issues involving social relations among inmates, contacts with staff members, and access to the civilian world. The set includes four major configurations, to which are attached the prison labels "square John," "right guy," "con politician," and "outlaw."[52]

Briefly, inmates who fall within the "square John" configuration consistently define role requirements in terms of the prison's official social system. By contrast, "right guys" just as regularly perceive requirements according to the norms of prisoner society. "Con politicians" shift their frame of reference from staff norms to inmate norms with great alacrity. "Outlaws," deficient in aptitude for identification, are in a perpetual anarchistic rebellion against both normative systems and against affective involvements in general.

Whereas the above argot labels refer to specific sets of interconnected role alternatives, our interest is in developing a typological system relating these role configurations to other social or cultural aspects of the prison community. In order to emphasize this distinction, a shift from argot labels to a more neutral terminology seems advisable. Consequently, the terms *prosocial, antisocial, pseudosocial,* and *asocial,* will hereafter be used in lieu of the argot labels in the respective order in which they have appeared. These role configurations, in the interest of brevity, will be called, collectively, social types.

Career Variables. To investigate the assumption that there are distinctive variations in the careers of the various social types, groups of inmates belonging to different types were interviewed and their

---

[52] Schrag, *op. cit.,* chapters 5–9.

case-histories were carefully examined.[53] Clear distinctions were noted in the criminal records of the social types, their family and community experiences, and their attitudes towards crime and society. Major findings are summarized below.

Prosocial inmates are most frequently convicted of violent crimes against the person, such as homicide and assault, or naïve property offenses, chiefly forgery. Few have prior arrests, and their criminal careers are initiated relatively late in life. Their offenses are situational. That is, the offenses reflect extraordinary social pressures frequently involving real or imagined misbehavior on the part of a spouse or of close friends.

While in prison, prosocial inmates maintain strong ties with family and civilian associates, and they are sympathetic and cooperative toward prison officials. Generally supportive of established authority, they believe in the efficacy of punishment, show strong guilt for their offenses, and expect to pay for their crimes in order to renew civilian life with a clean slate. Naïve about illegal techniques and strategies, they have little knowledge of, or contact with, organized crime.

Antisocial inmates are highly recidivistic, their careers frequently progressing through stages of truancy, expressive theft with other gang members, instrumental theft involving contacts with "fences" and other organized criminals, and culminating in patterns of unsophisticated crimes, such as robbery, assault, and burglary.

Coming chiefly from families having other delinquent members and living in underprivileged urban areas, antisocial inmates frequently earn a livelihood via contacts with organized crime, but do not often rise to positions of power in this field. Rebellion against conventional norms has continuity in their careers and is noted in their educational, occupational, and marital adjustments. Close ties with the parental family were commonly seen, however.

---

[53] *Ibid.* See also Garabedian, *op. cit.*, ch. 5. The findings of these studies seem to be generally consistent with those reported in other typological investigations. See, for example, Lester E. Hewitt and Richard L. Jenkins, *Fundamental Patterns of Maladjustment: The Dynamics of Their Origin* (Springfield: Illinois State Printer, 1947); Albert J. Reiss, "Social Correlates of Psychological Types of Delinquency," *American Sociological Review*, 17 (1952), 710–718; R. Nevitt Sanford, "A Psychoanalytic Study of Three Types of Criminals," *Journal of Criminal Psychopathology*, 5 (1943), 57–68. A good list of references to typological studies is found in Don C. Gibbons and Donald L. Garrity, "Some Suggestions for the Development of Etiological and Treatment Theory in Criminology," *Social Forces*, 38 (1959), 51–58.

In prison, the antisocial offenders continue their close association with criminalistic elements and their rebellion against civil authorities. Their philosophy of life, as reflected in the slogans "only suckers work," "all politicians are crooks," and "big shots and real criminals never get caught," alleviates their sense of guilt and solidifies inmate opposition against the prison's administration.

Pseudosocial inmates are involved primarily in subtle, sophisticated, profit-motivated offenses, such as embezzlement, fraud, and forgery. Relatively few have juvenile records, and onset of criminality often occurs after a position of respectability has already been attained in the civilian community.

Family and community backgrounds are frequently middle-class, but evidence of inconsistent parental discipline and other family disharmony is the most striking feature of their preinstitutional careers. Apparently, pseudosocial offenders acquire their facility in role-playing at an early age, and they are frequently described as having a pleasant, ingratiating manner. Educational and occupational records are far superior to those of antisocial offenders.

In prison, pseudosocial inmates display chameleonic skill in shifting their allegiances from staff members to inmates, and vice versa, according to the exigencies of the moment. Pragmatic and instrumentally oriented, they exploit to their own advantage the conflicts and inconsistencies inherent in the prison's social structure. Although they are recognized to be unreliable, their strategic position between the two social systems makes them the mediators in staff-inmate conflicts and results in rewards, such as relatively short sentences, desirable prison assignments, and reduced custody, among others.

Asocial inmates commit a variety of offenses against persons and property, frequently using bizarre methods without clear motive or reason. Recidivism is extremely high, and there is early evidence of severe behavior disorders, although age at first arrest varies considerably.

Paramount among findings regarding social backgrounds is the seemingly universal evidence of early rejection. Asocial offenders are frequently reared in institutions, shifted around various foster homes, or are otherwise lacking reasonable care and attention from their parents. Social abilities and skills in the use of social symbols are greatly retarded. The careers of asocial offenders are marked by high egocentrism and an inability to profit from past mistakes or to plan for the future. These persons often exhibit an apparent distrust and fear of personal ties of any kind. Their problems are solved by direct and immediate aggression.

In prison, asocial inmates are the undisciplined troublemakers who are chiefly involved in riots, escape plots, and assaults on both inmates and officers. Nevertheless, their lack of capacity for cooperative enterprise means that most of their rebellions are destined for failure.

Several tentative conclusions can be drawn from the above findings. Generally, antisocial offenders are reared in an environment consistently oriented toward illegitimate social norms. Asocial and pseudosocial offenders exhibit defective normative perceptions growing out of early parental rejection and patterns of inconsistent discipline, respectively. They suffer severe personal frustrations at an early age and acquire distinctive adaptation techniques. Prosocial offenders, although utilizing legitimate normative standards, seem unable to cope with intense social pressures or unique personal problems. That persons with such varied problems of adjustment should play distinctively different roles in the prison community does not seem surprising.

Cognitive and Affective Orientations. It will be remembered that staff members and inmates uniformly perceive sharp and consistent distinctions between role requirements that are defined conventionally and those defined in terms of the prisoner social system. The concept of criminal subculture, at least so far as staff and inmate perceptions are concerned, does have specifiable pragmatic meaning as a set of behavior prescriptions. Consequently, criminal subculture, as a deviant or an illegitimate normative system, may be useful in revealing additional distinguishing characteristics among our social types.

Speculation concerning the life organizations of individual offenders and their knowledge of, and attachments to, cultural standards leads to the expectation of systematic variations in the frames of reference employed by the various social types. That is, some types are expected to utilize legitimate norms and others illegitimate norms as frames of reference. Moreover, variations in cognitive and affective orientations toward the two normative systems, unless our speculations lead us astray, should be highly associated with the patterns of personal and social traits that were noted previously.

More specifically, prosocial offenders appear to evaluate problematic situations with reference to legitimate norms, to have greater cognitive understanding of legitimate role requirements than of illegitimate requirements, and generally to apply legitimate norms in specific situations regardless of the personal discomfiture that might result. Conversely, it is expected that antisocial offenders will consistently employ deviant or illegitimate norms as standards of reference, to exhibit detailed cognitive knowledge of illegitimate role requirements, and likewise to display their allegiance to these norms irrespective of the impact on personal goals or objectives. Their general opposition to legitimate means of achievement is expressed figuratively in the motto, "only suckers work." The two types, then, are alike in emphasizing collective values, such as loyalty, mutual aid, and group solidarity, but they differ in the normative systems used as standards of judgment.

Pseudosocial offenders, by contrast, are capable of shifting their normative perspectives according to the availability of instrumental rewards. They stress personal achievements rather than collective goals, exploitative strategies rather than conventional procedures, and affective neutrality rather than strong identifications with persons or social conventions. Their cognitive knowledge and role-playing skills extend to the deviant realm as well as to the conventional one. Above all, to be bound by social conventions or moral commitments is for them a sign of weakness.

Asocial offenders are similarly detached from social conventions and moral commitments. However, in their case, detachment reflects ignorance of role requirements and deficiency in role-playing ability rather than emancipation. Moreover, their conceptions of the illegitimate system appear to be as much distorted as their conceptions of legitimate norms. They are generally incapable of developing affective ties either with prisoners or with officials. Thus, their behavior is ordinarily impulsive and motivated by expressive functions; only rarely does it reveal the deliberative and instrumental characteristics so commonly noted among the pseudosocial inmates.

Information obtained by presenting to staff members and inmates alternative solutions to common prison problems has already been mentioned. The solutions chosen by members of the different social types seem to agree with the above arguments. For example, staff members and prosocial inmates tend to choose the same solutions, while pseudosocial offenders choose solutions representative of both conventional and deviant prescriptions. Antisocial offenders are fairly consistent in following the choice-pattern dictated by the illegitimate normative system. Asocial offenders make the greatest number of irregular choices.[54]

Evidence regarding cognitive knowledge possessed by the social types has been difficult to obtain. However, tests of argot vocabularies suggest that, at the time of admission to the institution, antisocial offenders have the best knowledge of prison lingo. Pseudosocial offenders, though, appear to learn more rapidly and they may eventually attain a higher degree of proficiency. Asocial inmates, perhaps surprisingly, have a less adequate vocabulary, so far as labels for prisoner roles are concerned, than do the prosocial inmates; and both of these groups, of course, have vocabularies inferior to those of the antisocial or pseudosocial inmates. Further empirical investigation is needed, however, to demonstrate important anticipated differences in cognitive knowledge among the social types.

In summary, the social types reveal systematic differences in their cognitive and affective orientations toward the legitimate and illegitimate normative systems that are found in the close-custody prison, especially with respect to their attitudes regarding expressive (group-integrating) and instrumental (goal-achievement) norms. Some of the observed differences are indicated in Table 1, where (X) represents high knowledge or affective support for the norm, and (—) represents limited knowledge or affective rejection.

TABLE 1

COGNITIVE AND AFFECTIVE ATTACHMENTS
OF SOCIAL TYPES

| | Legitimate Norms | | Illegitimate Norms | |
Social type	Cognitive knowledge	Affective attachment	Cognitive knowledge	Affective attachment
Prosocial	X	X	—	—
Antisocial	—	—	X	X
Pseudosocial	X	—	X	—
Asocial	—	—	—	—

Social Contact and Participation. Normative orientations of prison inmates are importantly related to their patterns of social participation. In general, inmates are selectively responsive to those segments of their society that reinforce their own standards of judg-

[54] Garabedian, *op. cit.*, ch. 5.

ment and provide continuity of experience. Persons having similar beliefs and values are sought out and their friendships are cultivated. Encounters with shocking or markedly dissimilar points of view are avoided, if possible. The same factors operate in contacts with staff members. Consequently, members of the various social types, since they are characterized by distinctly different normative orientations, may be expected to exhibit distinctive variations in their patterns of contact and participation within the prison community.

A reasonable expectation, for example, is that prosocial offenders will have extensive contacts with staff members, while their contacts with inmates are restricted largely to other members of the prosocial type. Conversely, antisocial offenders may be expected to have extensive contacts among the inmates, but minimal relations with the staff. Prosocial offenders may have a wider range of contacts involving both staff and inmates, while the asocial inmates may be restricted to fewer relations in either category. The expected patterns are listed in Table 2, assuming that contacts are dichotomized in terms of high and low frequencies, and that the relatively highest frequency of contact for a given social type is marked (X).

TABLE 2

PARTICIPATION PATTERN OF SOCIAL TYPES

	Contact Patterns			
Social type	High staff/ high inmate	High staff/ low inmate	Low staff/ high inmate	Low staff/ low inmate
Prosocial	—	X	—	—
Antisocial	—	—	X	—
Pseudosocial	X	—	—	—
Asocial	—	—	—	X

Direct evidence regarding inmate participation patterns is not yet available. Indirect evidence was obtained, however, by asking a sample of inmates to report the relative amount of their contacts with staff members and other inmates as compared with the contacts of the average inmate. The reported patterns are consistent with those hypothesized, except for the prosocial inmates who reported a somewhat higher amount of inmate contacts than was expected.[55]

[55] *Ibid.,* pp. 115–118.

Amount of contact, however, may have less social significance than the quality of the relationships, such as friendship, animosity, or leader-follower patterns. Evidence pertinent to the quality of interaction comes from a sociometric study in which inmates reported the names of their closest prisoner friends.[56] Friendship choices were classified according to the social type of the respondent and of the person chosen. Major findings are that members of every social type except one select their friends most frequently from their own type. The single exception is again the prosocial offender, who expresses a slight preference for pseudosocial friends over his choice of prosocial friends. In addition, both prosocial and pseudosocial inmates receive fewer choices than would be expected if friendship were independent of social type; whereas antisocial inmates and, to a lesser extent, asocial inmates receive more than their proportionate numbers of choices.[57]

The same study obtained the names of inmates designated as leaders.[58] Most striking among the findings is the high frequency with which asocial inmates are identified as leaders. Even the prosocial and pseudosocial types, despite their sharp cognitive and affective differences as compared with asocial inmates, frequently select asocial inmates as leaders.

The rationale behind such choices may be revealed in a comment made by one of the respondents to the effect that, "One thing clear is that the outlaws aren't going to make any deals with anybody." Evidently the fears and suspicions aroused by members of the other social types result in leadership status for inmates who are incapable of any high degree of mutual effort. Presumably, then, the higher the tensions and anxieties within the prisoner community, the greater the leadership potential of the asocial type.[59]

Thus it appears that while pseudosocial and perhaps prosocial inmates may have a wider range of contacts, the social climate of the close-custody prison provides for the antisocial and asocial inmates a higher social status and involves them more frequently in patterns of friendship and positions of leadership.

Degrees of participation in staff-sponsored activities and treatment programs likewise shows consistent variations among the social types.

[56] Schrag, *Crimeville: A Sociometric Study of a Prison Community, op. cit.*
[57] *Ibid.*, pp. 140–142.
[58] *Ibid.*, pp. 139–140.
[59] This is suggested by a comparison of the present findings and those reported by Grusky, *op. cit.*

Greatest participation in such organized activities, as expected, involves the prosocial offenders, followed in order by the pseudosocial, antisocial, and asocial types. Also, prosocial inmates, to a far greater extent than the others, engage in programs aimed specifically at therapy, while the pseudosocial and antisocial offenders display primary interest in recreation and other expressive functions. The relatively staff-centered orientation of the prosocial inmates is clearly revealed in the data.[60]

Communication patterns mediate the intrapersonal processes of the inmates and their resulting self-conceptions. For example, various dimensions of self-conception are shown to vary according to the inmate's duration of confinement, his pre-institutional criminal record, his normative orientation, and his social position within the prison community. Included among the self-concept dimensions that show the above relationships are the inmate's perception of his own status in prisoner society, perception of the degree of his sophistication regarding criminal activities, and the amount of support he perceives as coming from persons in the civilian environment. These relationships, when measured by brief questionnaires, are not very strong, but they are consistently in the expected direction.[61]

Even among juvenile delinquents, there is evidence, derived from responses to an adjective check-list, that the prosocial delinquent defines the correctional institution and the broader community as supportive agencies. In addition, he conceives of himself as a person who, although generally conventional in his conduct, has made a mistake that requires official attention. By contrast, antisocial delinquents perceive correctional institutions and civilian society as restrictive and antagonistic organizations. They conceive of themselves, in a sense, as leaders of the loyal opposition.[62] Here, then, is another area in which further research is strongly indicated.

Patterns of contact and participation, as has been noted, are good indicators of inmate goals and interests. But they also regulate access to the means of goal achievement. They serve as integrative or divisive social forces that mold the individual according to the group's image of him or contrive his expulsion from the group. In consequence, the prosocial offender, for example, has a relatively clear path to conventional or legitimate behavior. He is divested of loyalty obligations

[60] *Cf.*, Garabedian, *op. cit.*, ch. 5 and Wheeler, *op. cit.*, chapters 4 and 5.
[61] Wheeler, *op. cit.*, chapters 5 and 6.
[62] Kinch, *op. cit.*

toward the inmates, is ill advised concerning the illicit machinations of prisoner society, and in many other subtle ways is deprived of access to the means of goal achievement within the illegitimate social system. However, the ubiquitous pressures of the illegitimate system and the inevitable frustrations produced by his prisoner status make it increasingly difficult for him to maintain his prosocial orientation with the passage of time. Perhaps these are some of the main reasons for the positive correlation that has been observed between the parole violation rates of prosocial offenders and the duration of their confinement.[63]

Participation patterns, then, by regulating access to social means and resources, apparently achieve some modification of inmate normative orientations and behavior standards. The reverse is also true. That is, inmates can sometimes produce changes in prison culture. Generally, prosocial offenders are cultural conservators for whom the stability of even a somewhat oppressive order is preferable to the uncertainties of social revision or experimentation. Pseudosocial inmates, in contrast, are the great innovators. Their exploitative interests, varied resources, and affective neutrality make them the natural catalysts of social invention and change.[64] Antisocial prisoners are rebels who have a cause, namely, the subversion of established authority. Again, the nihilist role is played by asocial inmates, whose language is force, and who are frequently assigned the role of leader in riots, escapes, and similar rebellious activities.

The combined impact of the major role configurations and their related normative systems and participation patterns is to produce the social equilibrium that is commonly observed in the prison community, a fluid and moving equilibrium that enables the society of prisoners to make fairly easy adaptations to the many shocks and strains occasioned by changes in correctional personnel or policies or by other factors over which the inmates exercise relatively little direct control. Equilibrium implies some balance in the way the social types are interrelated, and the evidence outlined above suggests that among the more important balancing mechanisms are factors in the preinstitutional careers of the inmates, their normative orientations, and their patterns of social participation within the prison community.

[63] Garrity, *op. cit.*, and Strinden, *op. cit.*
[64] Garabedian, *op. cit.*, ch. 7.

Conclusion

This report outlines a conceptual framework for the analysis of prison communities by utilizing theories related to the concepts of culture, social system, and the social self. Everyday behavior of staff members and inmates was described in terms of the conventional sociological vocabulary, including terms such as career variables, cognitive and affective orientations, social roles, and patterns of social participation. The concepts were tied together in terms of some postulated empirical regularities among the variables involved. There resulted a typological system that was checked against available evidence from a series of institutional studies, and although the verifications are by no means conclusive they suggest that the system may be of some utility in the analysis of the prison community and may have certain applications in the analysis of deviant behavior outside the correctional setting.

The conceptual scheme is not intended as a classification system, which specifies the logically possible combinations of concepts or variables, but as a typological system, which attempts to formulate the empirical relationships among concepts or variables by designating which of the combinations are expected to occur with high frequency and which ones should occur infrequently or not at all.

The typology, in other words, is an embryo theory that needs further refinement of its concepts and elaboration of its postulates before it can be stated in formal terms as a deductive system. However, the typology does demonstrate, at least provisionally, some potentially important interconnections between different kinds of criminal behavior and certain variables related to the concepts of culture, social system, and self. Furthermore, the component parts of the typology have empirical interrelationships that approximate a closed system. That is, given any two or more parts of the system, the remainder can be predicted with fair accuracy. Thus we feel that the typology merits further study and development as a possible device for meeting some of the theoretical requirements mentioned in the first section of this chapter.

9

DONALD L. GARRITY

| | | | | | | | | | |

The Prison as a Rehabilitation Agency

Most studies of the prison community have been principally concerned with sociological analysis of the prison as a social system, and they have portrayed the social structure, role systems, normative systems, and value orientations of the inmates.[1] In addition, some attention has been given to the pragmatic implications of the data developed. Clemmer, Schrag, and Sykes have been particularly concerned with the implications of their findings for administrative policy. These and other works have developed propositions concerning the effects of the prison community on both the institutional and post-institutional behavior of prisoners. "Common-sense" observations and statements also have contributed to the knowledge about the impact of the prison upon the individual. Yet little attention has been given to an empirical evaluation of these propositions, which is our objective here.

[1] Hans Reimer, "Socialization in the Prison Community," in *Proceedings of the American Prison Association*, 1937, 151–55; Donald Clemmer, *The Prison Community*, New Edition, (New York: Rinehart, 1958); S. Kirson Weinberg, "Aspects of the Prison's Social Structure," *American Journal of Sociology*, 47 (March, 1942), 217–226; Norman S. Hayner and Ellis Ash, "The Prison as a Community," *American Sociological Review*, 5 (April, 1940), 577–583; and "The Prison Community as a Social Group," *American Sociological Review*, 4 (June, 1939), 762–769; Clarence C. Schrag, *Social Types in a Prison Community* (Unpublished M.A. thesis, University of Washington, 1944); Gresham M. Sykes, *The Society of Captives* (Princeton: Princeton University Press, 1958).

The research analyses of the prison community have concentrated on examining conditions which sociological theory suggests are important in the functioning of any social system. Most important among the concepts utilized in structuring the research have been "value," "norm," "position," and "role." The prison social system can be described in terms of the important values around which the thought and action of inmates and custodians are oriented. The normative systems of the prison are listings of the social restrictions and expectations which guide behavior. The system of roles and positions places acting people within the value framework and the normative system. It describes how people may actually interact in everyday life situations within the prison. Observers have often pointed out that the prison is divided into two different but interacting systems, the inmate system and the administrative system.

Schrag, Clemmer, Sykes, and others have pointed out that the inmate social system is dominated by a set of values and norms which are largely antisocial and anti-administration. Time, sex, food, health, leisure, etc. are handled by a set of normative restrictions and expectations which encourage an inmate to "do his own time," recognize the virutes of an alcoholic beverage called "pruno," recognize the necessity of merchants and peddlers, etc. The dominant normative system values criminal behavior, is consistent with the criminal subculture and generally disapproves of friendly and cooperative behavior with the administration.

It is within this fabric that inmate behavior occurs. However, there are variations in the degree of "organization" observed among inmates. Clemmer reported that value and normative ingredients of prison culture are essentially as described above, but he did not find any clear-cut social structure among the inmates. He concluded that the prison community is not characterized by consensus among inmates and that, by and large, prisoners are isolates:

> Contrary to impressions and writings of other investigators, this study found and reported considerable evidence to indicate that consensus, solidarity, and feeling among prisoners has been previously exaggerated.[2]

Clemmer reported further that the population of his prison was divided into three general and relatively vague aggregates which he called the "elite class," the "middle class," and the "hoosier class."

[2] Clemmer, *op. cit.*, p. 322.

This class division was believed to be important only in determining social distance in a very general way; knowledge of it was not viewed as crucial for understanding the dynamics of the prison community or the behavior patterns of particular inmates.[3]

Sykes, on the other hand, reports from his research that a systematic structure of roles can be observed in the prison community and can be used to describe the general behavior patterns of inmates.[4] He found that prison argot labeled and described the position and role behavior of the inmates, and he described eleven roles which he believes form the basic social structure of the prison community.

Schrag described a social system very similar to the one reported by Sykes. He found that the inmate population of his prison tended to be classified in five major types. This typology describes a broad and generic role system which is predictive of the behaviorial tendencies of the inmates. Schrag's typology appears to be broader than Sykes', and it seems to include the argot roles described by Sykes.[5]

The more recent of the three studies suggest, then, that there is a broadly defined social structure in the prison community. This social structure includes a normative system which stems from the common problems of adjustment faced by all of the inmates and tends to be dominated by antisocially-oriented offenders.[6]

Set apart from but interacting with the inmate social system, the administrative structure is composed of a set of somewhat contradictory forms. In its simplest form, the administrative social structure is bifurcated into two substructures each with its own role and normative system. Treatment and custody, the two substructures, are joined together by common tasks and responsibilities and a common set of public expectations. The two systems have distinct and separate role and normative systems which specify different and, in many instances, contradictory expectations for employees.[7]

Interaction between inmates and administrators is dominated and controlled by the social system of each. However, a set of common expectations has developed and these common expectations minimize

[3] *Ibid.*, pp. 107–109.

[4] Sykes, *op. cit.*, pp. 84–108.

[5] Schrag, *op. cit.*, pp. 55–97.

[6] Clarence C. Schrag, "Leadership Among Prison Inmates," *American Sociological Review*, 19 (February, 1954), 37–42.

[7] See Donald R. Cressey, "Contradictory Directives in Complex Organizations: The Case of the Prison," *Administrative Science Quarterly*, 4 (June, 1959), 1–19.

conflict between the two systems and thus maximize the undisturbed continuance of each social system. In the language of inmates, it is basically a "no rap" arrangement. Each group expects the other to refrain from involvement in areas which clearly lie outside its domain. When interaction is necessary, cooperation is expected only to that point where it is fairly certain that little "heat" or displeasure will be incurred from outsiders.

Within social systems defined as loosely as these, it is possible for considerable deviation to occur. Deviations do occur in inmate-inmate, inmate-administration, and administration-administration interaction. However, in all cases the deviation tends to be judged as tolerable or intolerable in terms of a general body of expectations.

Prisons do not uniformly correspond to the description above or to the more detailed descriptions stemming from the formal studies or inmate and administrative social systems. These descriptions seem to be most relevant to maximum security institutions and to apply least adequately to minimum security or open institutions. As the number of institutions increases, as greater selectivity is exercised in assignment of inmates to institutions, and as institutions tend to be organized around relatively new and specialized concepts, the probability that any description will fit all institutions decreases. The diversification of institutions in California may be a case in point. However, the vast majority of prisons do conform within reasonable limits to these descriptions of the prison, and probably they will do so for some time to come.

IMPACT OF THE PRISON

There is general consensus that prison experience is criminogenic in nature. Prisons breed crime. Some years ago, both Tannenbaum and Gillin wrote that exposing an individual to experience in prison increases the probability that he will engage in criminal behavior:

> Every time the apprehension of a child involves throwing him in contact with other young criminals who are confined together there is an increased stimulus in the education for crime. . . . The institutional experience is thus a concentration of stimuli adapted to develop delinquent interests.[8]

[8] Frank Tannenbaum, *Crime and the Community* (Boston: Ginn and Co., 1939), 71.

What monuments of stupidity are these institutions we have built—stupidity not so much of the inmates as of free citizens. What a mockery of science are our prison discipline, our massing of social iniquity in prisons, the good and the bad together in one stupendous potpourri. How silly of us to think that we can prepare men for social life by reversing the ordinary process of socialization.[9]

In his statement, Gillin identifies the process by which prison experience produces its effects—socialization. Prison experiences, like those of the child in family and peer group, may be sufficient to shape attitudes, values, behavior patterns, etc. Although he did not specifically utilize the concept of socialization, Clemmer developed much the same thesis when he described the process of prisonization.

— *Prisonization.* Clemmer defined prisonization as the process of assimilation of the prison culture by inmates as they become acquainted with the prison world.[10] After the inmate is stripped of most of the symbols of personal identity, he begins to attach new meanings to all the conditions of life which were previously taken for granted. These new meanings are provided by the prison culture. Every inmate, Clemmer claims, is exposed to the "universal factors of prisonization."[11] In addition, conditions which maximize prisonization are:

1. A sentence of many years, thus a long subjection to the universal factors of prisonization.
2. A somewhat unstable personality made unstable by an inadequacy of "socialized" relations before commitment, but possessing, nonetheless, a capacity for strong convictions and a particular kind of loyalty.
3. A dearth of positive relations with persons outside the walls.
4. Readiness and a capacity for integration into a prison primary group.
5. A blind, or almost blind, acceptance of the dogmas and mores of the primary group and the general penal population.
6. A chance of placement with other persons of a similar orientation.
7. A readiness to participate in gambling and abnormal sex behavior.[12]

The conditions which allow for minimum prisonization are the reverse of these.

[9] John L. Gillin, *Taming the Criminal* (New York: Macmillan, 1931), 295–296.

[10] Clemmer, *op. cit.*, p. 299.

[11] *Ibid.*, pp. 299–300.

[12] *Ibid.*, pp. 301–302.

The over-all effect of prisonization is to produce a person who generally conforms to the prison expectations and whose behavior upon release is contradictory to anticriminal norms. As Clemmer pointed out:

> Even if no other factor of the prison culture touches the personality of an inmate of many years residence, the influence of these universal factors are sufficient to make a man characteristic of the penal community and probably so disrupt his personality that a happy adjustment in any community becomes next to impossible.[13]

A recent study has given added weight to Clemmer's propositions concerning the process of prisonization.[14] Wheeler found that inmate reactions to certain attitudinal and value situations tended to vary with the amount of time served and with other measures of prisonization. However, he did not investigate the post-release effects of prisonization.

Anomie. The prisonization concept stresses the effect of prison culture on inmates. Some observers have emphasized, alternatively, the apparent high degree of unorganization and individualism among inmates. Clemmer found that 80 percent of the prisoners did not feel themselves a part of any group, and hence existed to varying degrees as isolates.[15] Weinberg's research stressed the poverty of interaction among certain types of inmates and the consequent anonymity which follows from lack of interaction.[16] Cressey and Krassowski have shown that this condition exists in Soviet labor camps as well as in American prisons.[17] They found that while most inmates live in social conditions of anomie, strong tendencies toward organization and interdependence are also present; both conditions are valuable to administrators.

The literature of social psychology suggests that relatively stable and continuous points of reference are necessary if a person is to function as a normal social creature.[18] Isolation from any meaningful reference groups, and interaction on only superficial levels, lead to

---

[13] *Ibid.*, p. 300.

[14] Stanton Wheeler, *Social Organization in a Correctional Community* (Unpublished Ph.D. thesis, University of Washington, 1958).

[15] Clemmer, *op. cit.*, pp. 116–33.

[16] Weinberg, *op. cit.*

[17] Donald R. Cressey and Witold Krassowski, "Inmate Organization and Anomie in American Prisons and Soviet Labor Camps," *Social Problems,* 5 (Winter, 1957–58), 217–23.

[18] *Cf.* Robert E. L. Faris, *Social Psychology* (New York: Ronald Press, 1952), 338–49.

serious personality and social difficulties. An individual who has developed normally and who exhibits relatively stable patterns of behavior may be little affected by relatively short periods of anomie, but prolonged exposure might have important consequences for him. On the other hand, an unstable individual might not be able to withstand the conditions of anomie for even a relatively short period of time. Long periods of exposure to unorganization would be even more serious for the unstable than for the stable personality.

If indeed the prison is a world of anomie for some inmates, continued exposure to such an experience should have a deteriorating effect upon the inmates' abilities to function as normal persons. At a minimum, motivation to participate in any given form of social behavior would be effected. Claims about the effects of physical isolation and solitude in prison form part of the important folk knowledge of corrections.[19] Since a condition of anomie has essentially the same elements as physical isolation, essentially the same consequences might follow.[20] The general predictions from this position would be that prolonged incarceration will result in greater inability to function properly within the prison, and that upon release from the institution numerous adjustment problems will occur. Post-release behavior should be poorer as time spent in the institution increases. We did not specifically test the proposition that anomie has disruptive effects on individual behavior in the institution, but our study does examine the predicted post-institutional consequences of anomie.

IMPRISONMENT AND PAROLE VIOLATION

The concept of prisonization suggests that as time in the prison is extended, prisonization increases. In turn, as prisonization increases the probability of successful adjustment following release decreases. Thus, it is expected that success on parole decreases as time spent in the institution increases, personality becomes less stable, non-prison contacts diminish, the person becomes involved in prison primary groups, tends to accept the norms of the prison, is housed with a cellmate involved in the prison community, and participates in abnormal behavior in the prison.

[19] George Ives, *History of Penal Methods,* (New York: F. A. Stokes Co., 1914), 186–87.
[20] See the discussion in Chapter 7, above.

The concept of prison anomie also leads to the expectation that as exposure to the prison increases the probability of successful adjustment on release decreases.

No study has definitively tested these propositions. Such a test is difficult, if not impossible, because the variables and dimensions of the propositions are not easily operationalized. Empirical analysis can be made only in very general terms, and this was done in a study of a population of inmates released from two Washington prisons over approximately one year.[21] A total of 703 cases were released from one institution and 562 from the other. At the time the data were gathered, all individuals had been on parole for at least one year. In Washington, over 99 percent of all inmates are released on parole. Thus, the parole population studied was almost the total population of releases during the year.

Information on the 1265 men was limited to the data contained in the files of the parole board. These files contain the official records and documents of the board, the institution, and other agencies. They do not contain detailed information concerning the primary associations of the prisoners, measures of his self conception, statements about his role-playing ability, or other facts valuable for research purposes. Although the needs of research and administration may not always coincide, policy and administrative decisions most often deal with the same questions with which the sociologist is concerned. It could be argued that improvement of record systems for research purposes would result in equal improvement for administrative purposes.

The parole performance of each person was recorded. The criterion of adjustment on parole was defined as the issuance or non-issuance of a parole violation warrant.[22] If a warrant was issued, the parole

[21] Donald L. Garrity, *The Effects of Length of Incarceration Upon Parole Adjustment and Estimation of Optimum Sentence: Washington State Correctional Institutions* (Unpublished Ph.D. thesis, University of Washington, 1956).

[22] There are many disadvantages to this definition of parole success or failure, for actions by individual parole officers weigh heavily in determining whether a warrant is issued. There is an unknown amount of variation between parole officers. It would be preferable to use some measure of the actual behavior of the parolee as a criterion. Even better would be some measure of the parolee's efforts to play the role of law-abiding citizen, a measure of the conditions which the parolee encountered in the free community, and a measure of the "therapeutic" assistance he received. Since such measures were not available, issuance of a warrant was accepted as an approximation. For a discussion of these problems see Garrity, *op. cit.*, pp. 51–52.

adjustment was defined as a failure, whether the person was returned to the institution or not. If no warrant was issued, the parole adjustment was defined as a success. Issuing of a warrant was preferable to return to the institution because some parolees committed new offenses in another jurisdiction and were incarcerated in that jurisdiction, and others absconded and remained at large. In a few cases, a warrant was issued in error and later withdrawn. Such cases were considered successful.

Prisonization Considered. No test of prisonization per se was attempted in this study. Rather, the concern was with the purported effect of prisonization on post-release behavior. As indicated previously, Clemmer and others have indicated that prisonization minimizes the probabilities of successful adjustment on parole, probably because antisocial attitudes are assimilated in the prison community.[23] As Clemmer noted, "The phases of prisonization which concern us most are the influences which breed or deepen criminality and antisociality and make the inmate characteristic of the criminalistic ideology in the prison community.[24]

"Time served" was the principal measure of prisonization. If prisonization increases with time, which seems highly probable, parole-violation rates should show a steady and continuing increase as time served in the institution is extended.

Parole-violation rates were computed for categories of parolees who had served various periods of time. The rates for neither institution conformed to the expected pattern. Among parolees from the institution for younger adults, the violation rates went up until a category of men who had served two years was reached, but then the rates decreased rather steadily. Among parolees from the institution for older offenders, the violation rates were highest if release on parole occurred after less than one year in the prison, and then decreased as length of time in the institution increased.

Since it was not possible to construct any reasonable and reliable measure of prisonization, it was assumed that involvement in criminal activity and prison experiences prior to the current incarceration would be directly correlated with degree of prisonization. This assumption may not be completely warranted. Indeed, Clemmer suggests that prisonization is a complex phenomenon which cannot easily be

[23] See the discussion by Edwin H. Sutherland and Donald R. Cressey, *Principles of Criminology,* Sixth Edition, (New York: Lippincott, 1960), 497.
[24] Clemmer, *op. cit.,* p. 300.

described in a set of propositions. Thus, the fact that a person has adopted a criminal pattern of behavior, or has been in prison a number of times, or has served a number of years in one institution, might not always mean that he will be prisonized to a great degree or at a high rate upon incarceration. However, when a relatively large population of individuals is observed, a positive correlation between prisonization and previous criminal career and incarceration should appear.

The variables selected as measures of the individual's involvement in criminal behavior were "prior criminal record," "prior penal commitments," "total time in custody prior to current commitment," "type of criminal career," "type of offense for current commitment," and "age at arrest for current commitment."[25] The first three variables are obvious measures of involvement in criminal behavior. The variables "type of criminal career" and "type of offense" were added because of the well-known differential arrest, conviction, and incarceration practices for different career types and offenses. For example, an individual who has committed a number of robberies is more likely to have been arrested, convicted, and incarcerated on each offense than an individual who has committed an equal number of check-writing offenses. If such differential risks were not handled in some way in the analysis, low-risk individuals with considerable involvement in crime would be classified with individuals who had little involvement in crime but had committed a high-risk offense. Age also determines the possibility of involvement in criminal activities. Relatively young offenders have not had the same opportunity as older offenders for involvement in criminal activity or for incarceration.

The initial analysis was computation of parole-violation rates, by time served, for each of the logical combinations of these six variables. The matrix of obtained violation rates thus show variations by time served for all the combinations of sub-categories of each of the pairs of items. It was expected that as the previous criminal record became more serious, as the number of prior penal commitments increased, and as the total time in custody prior to the current commitment increased, the total violation rate would increase, and that this rate itself would increase systematically with increasing time served.

It was also expected that a differential in violation rates would exist among offenders in terms of type of offense for current commit-

[25] For a definition of these variables see Garrity, *op. cit.*, pp. 79, 231–42.

ment and type of criminal career. The general expectation was that persons convicted of property offenses (burglary, auto theft, grand larceny, etc.) would have higher over-all violation rates than would personal, sex, or other types of offenders. Additionally, it was expected that the violation rates for property offenders would increase markedly with increasing amount of time served, but that the same general pattern of increase would be observed for all types. The same general set of expectations was held for the variable, "type of criminal career." For the variable "age at arrest for current commitment," the expectation was that the most marked increase in violation rates with time served would occur among younger offenders. This, it was believed, would be true because younger offenders are not as committed to any particular system of norms as are older offenders.

In the analysis of pairs of factors, it was expected that each of the above relations would hold, and that the interaction of these factors would clearly indicate the effects of time in the prison community. The analysis was carried out independently for each institution. It was anticipated that the differences in institutional character, if any existed, might show up in differential patterns of post-release success or failure.

Analysis of the variables "type of criminal career" and "previous criminal record" indicated that individuals who had no previous criminal career could nevertheless be classified according to previous criminal record: no record, one misdemeanor, and more than one misdemeanor. The individuals with no previous criminal record (and no criminal career) who served short prison terms had very low violation rates, and as the amount of time served increased, the violation rates decreased to zero. For individuals with a prior record of a misdemeanor, the violation rates were initially very low but rose systematically and steadily with length of time served. For the third group, who had a number of previous misdemeanors, the violation rate was very high for men with short terms and decreased with length of time served. Thus, the violation rates of the men with one misdemeanor were consistent with our expectations, but in the other two cases the rates were in the direction opposite of that expected.

Among individuals with a previous criminal career, only the group whose previous criminal careers involved offenses against property conformed to the expectation. For them, the violation rates were relatively high among those who served short prison terms and increased steadily as length of time in prison increased. As previous involvement in criminal activities increased, the violation rates started higher and were systematically higher with increasing time served. The rates for all other types of previous criminal career and previous criminal record were not consistent with the expectations. Although violation rates rose as previous criminal record became more serious, violation rates for all categories decreased as time served increased. Thus, for individuals with previous records of property offenses the expectations developed by utilizing the concept of prisonization appear to hold; in all other cases the data were not consistent with expectations.

These same general findings were obtained when "type of offense for current commitment" and "previous criminal record" were used. Persons convicted of burglary, larceny, forgery, and auto theft have violation rates which tend to increase systematically with time served. As previous criminal record became more serious, the rates were initially higher and the increase in rates more dramatic. However, persons who had committed an offense against the person, sex offense, or other types of offense had violation rates which were generally lower and did not increase with time served.

When "type of offense" and "prior penal commitment" were utilized, the same general patterns were observed. Although violation rates in general tended to be higher if the institution of previous incarceration confined more mature offenders, only in the case of the property offenders did the violation rates increase with increasing length of time served. An analysis utilizing the variable "total time in custody" prior to current commitment revealed that this variable did not discriminate either in terms of violation rates in general or the violation rates following various periods of incarceration.

When the variable "age at arrest for current commitment" was utilized in connection with "type of offense," it appeared to discriminate among offenders. The level of violation rates tended to be highest for younger offenders and to become lower as age increased. However, when "age at arrest" was analyzed in conjunction with each of the other variables, the discriminating power of the variable "age" tended to be lost.

On the basis of the above findings, we selected for analysis the four variables which appeared to have the greatest discriminating power. These were "type of offense," "previous criminal record," "type of criminal career," and "prior penal commitment." A multiple classification table utilizing these variables was constructed. For both institutions, the analysis indicated that systematic increase in violation rates with increasing time served in prison occurred only among property offenders with a previous criminal record and career of property offenses, or a combination of offenses and a prior commitment to one or more penal institutions. In all other cases, there was no increase or decrease in violation rates as the time in prison increased.

In short, the data did not clearly support the expectations developed from the prisonization concept. It appears from this analysis that the hypothesized post-institutional effects of prisonization appear among property offenders, and the expected pattern is clearer in this one case if the variables "prior penal commitments," "previous criminal record," and "type of criminal career" are also considered. However, manipulation of these variables did not develop the expected trends among other groups of offenders. The consequences of prisonization for post-institutional behavior are not clear. Our data indicate that if prisonization does occur and each person is affected by it to some degree, the post-institutional consequences of this process are quite variable.

Anomie Considered. As indicated previously, the concept "prison anomie" leads to the expectation that as exposure to prison life is increased the probability of success on parole decreases. Also, it is expected that the effects of the prison experience will vary according to the stability of inmates prior to incarceration. The records used did not permit detailed measurement of the personal stability of each offender. Rather, a measure of the probable stability was attempted by utilizing data relating to the social background, personal history, and clinical evaluation upon admission to the prison. It was assumed that personal-history data crudely indicate the stability of a person and that there is an association between degree of social disorganization in the background of a prisoner and his stability. The variables used as indicators of personal and social stability were "family background and delinquency," "employment record," "military record," "marital history," "previous criminal record," "behavior disorder," and "psychiatric classification."[26] The variable "family background and delinquency" is two-dimensional, for it refers to both the socioeconomic status of the parental family and to misconduct by family members in the form of excessive use of alcohol, habitual immorality,

[26] For a definition of these variables see *ibid.*, pp. 231–42.

conviction of crime, and other kinds of delinquency. "Employment record" refers to the stability of the subject's work record and the level of performance on the job, and "behavior disorder" refers to the presence of alcoholism or excessive drunkenness, use of drugs, habitual gambling, homosexual behavior, etc. The categories of psychiatric diagnosis used were: psychotic, pre-psychotic, psychopathic without disorder, psychopathic with sex disorder, senile, neurotic, and no abnormality noted.

Analysis took the form used for prisonization. Pairs of variables were utilized to classify the population, and violation rates were computed according to time served. The results were almost uniformly contradictory to the expectations. When the population of the institution containing younger offenders was classified by "family background and delinquency" and also by "previous criminal record," the violation rates increased as family disorganization increased and the violation rates tended to increase with increasing length of time in prison. This pattern did not appear among parolees from the other institution or among parolees from either institution when other variables were used.

In cases from both institutions it was found that as employment record shows greater instability, the total parole-violation rate tends to go up. However, violation rates computed according to time served were variable. Among men with relatively stable employment records, the violation rates were initially low and remained relatively low no matter how much time was served, but among persons with relatively unstable employment records, the violation rates decreased with increasing time in the prison. Similarly, men with good military records had lower total violation rates than the others, but among the men with poor records, violation rates went down with increasing time in prison, while among the men with better records the violation rate increased with increasing time in prison. Essentially the same results appeared when the populations were classified by behavior disorder and psychiatric category. Men with no observed behavior disorder or psychiatrically-defined abnormality had lower total violation rates than those with behavior disorders and psychiatrically-defined abnormality. But again, the violation rates according to time served increased for the first group and decreased for the second.[27]

In general, the analysis showed positive association between per-

[27] For a detailed discussion of these data see *ibid.*, pp. 134–62.

sonal and social disorganization or stability and parole violation. However, the expected effects of incarceration on the various categories of offenders did not appear. In only one case did the violation rates increase over time. If anything, the data indicated that the extension of prison experience tended to damage the parole performance of those showing greater stability and help the parole performance of those with greater instability. In general then, the observations tended to be contradictory and the reverse of expectation.

AN ALTERNATIVE FORMULATION

It is possible that prisonization cannot occur, or cannot have the predicted effects on parole behavior, in an institution that is characterized by anomie or unorganization. Yet there is evidence that prisonization does occur, despite the lack of general organization among inmates and despite our finding that the data on post-release adjustment were only partially consistent with the expected effects of prisonization. Clemmer developed and emphasized the process of prisonization, but he also characterized the prison as "atomized" because few inmates were intensively or extensively involved in primary group relations. His further claim that little structuring occurred within the prison was based on this same observation. Perhaps the discrepancy occurs because primary relationships were considered necessary to a secondary social structure. Cressey and Krassowski have shown that data on primary interaction might not reveal the presence of a secondary social system, for there are always strong tendencies toward organization and interdependence among inmates, even if a majority of them live in a condition of anomie.[28]

Schrag has further suggested that all inmates face a number of common problems of adjustment as a consequence of imprisonment and that social organization develops as a consequence. When two or more persons perceive that they share a common motivation or problem of action, a basis for meaningful interaction has been established, and from this interaction can emerge the social positions, roles, and norms which comprise social organization.[29] Schrag suggests that the common problems of adjustment which become the principal

[28] Cressey and Krassowski, *op. cit.*, pp. 217–18.
[29] *Op. cit.*, pp. 43–51. See also Muzafer Sherif and Carolyn W. Sherif, *An Outline of Social Psychology* (New York: Harper and Brothers, 1958), 181–208.

axes of prison life are related to time, food, sex, leisure, and health. Sykes has developed the same type of thesis, saying that the "pains of imprisonment," including deprivations of liberty, goods and services, heterosexual relationships, autonomy, and security, provide "the energy for the society of captives as a system of action."[30]

The axial values regarding shared problems or deprivations provide the basis for articulation of the broad normative system or "prison code" which defines positions and roles in a general way but allows enough latitude so that positions and roles take on the character of social worlds themselves. The degree of interposition role consensus in a prison need not be great, and the prison community is thus comprised of a loose structure of positions.[31]

The position of any inmate in the structure depends upon his behavior in reference to the problem areas or areas of deprivation and his loyalty to other inmates. The type of loyalty or attitudinal attachment that an inmate appears to express toward other inmates, the administration, and civilian society seriously affects other inmates' perception of him and the behavior expected of him. As an inmate expresses an attachment to antisocial elements in civilian society, rejection of any attachment to administrative personnel, and an attachment to antisocial inmates, his behavior in reference to the axial values can be predicted by others. Other expressions of loyalty similarly provide a basis for the population to assign each other to categories of positions and to predict the probable role behaviors of individuals. Since the definitions of positions are shared, a system of types of positions and roles appears. Moreover, inmates are also divided into social types, each type denoting a different social world.

Within this kind of social system, variation in behavior can occur as a normal condition of life. The population as a whole is expected to behave uniformly only to the degree necessary for maintaining the value system and the system of types. Beyond this point, the process of social control takes place within the separate categories of inmate types. In such a social structure, individual survival depends largely on conformity to the code of conduct which applies to all, and on receptivity to the social pressures coming from each type. Considerable variance occurs between types.

The social structure of prisons, then, is not necessarily constructed

---

[30] Sykes, *op. cit.*, pp. 63–83.

[31] See the general discussion by Neal Gross, Ward S. Mason, and Alexander W. McEachern, *Explorations in Role Analysis* (New York: John Wiley and Sons, Inc., 1958), 21–47, 95–221.

on a framework of primary groups and primary type social relations. Rather, it is a consequence of differentiated and differentiating aggregates whose members are perceived as sharing certain behavioral inclinations. Role playing becomes extraordinarily important, but successful role playing involves only conformity to the limited prison code and the broad outline of prescriptions and proscriptions for behavior specified by the type within which the person is included. It is possible, therefore, for a person to spend considerable time in prison without any detrimental consequences to himself. Prisonization occurs, but only in the sense that inmates comply to the rules of a loosely organized secondary structure by exhibiting role behavior that is generally consistent with the inmate codes and with a prison type. This kind of compliant behavior need not have any deep personal significance for the individual, for it is not necessary that the individual seriously commit himself to the norms and the role involved.

Social psychologists have established that experiences are most likely to be personally significant and included in an individual's conception of self when they are perceived as relating to interpersonal relationships of a primary nature.[32] Among inmates, then, role behavior has quite different consequences for those who are heavily involved in informal, primary relations with other inmates, as contrasted with those who are only slightly involved in such relationships.[33] Accordingly, prisonization can vary from simply learning compliant role behavior to internalization of the role behavior and a changed self-conception. And if prison expectations and definitions are taken on as part of a self-conception, the consequences for behavior on parole are likely to be quite different from those occurring if prisonization involves only compliant role behavior that has little personal significance.

Such variation would make it possible to find prisonization occurring, as Clemmer and Wheeler did, but also to find that prisonizaton does not always have the predicted effect on post-release adjustment. Inmate life is such that a large proportion of prisoners have very few primary associations, and it is quite correct to call this condition "anomie" or "unorganization." However, such experience need be neither personally disorganizing or detrimental to parole success, for

[32] Faris, *op. cit.*, pp. 165–66.

[33] Ohlin has suggested, consistently, that the prison experience has variable effects on self-conceptions of inmates. Lloyd E. Ohlin, *Sociology and the Field of Corrections* (New York: Russell Sage Foundation, 1956), 33–34.

there may be continuing attachments to groups outside the prison or there may be attachments to prison employees. The concept "reference group" has been developed to emphasize that persons are sometimes influenced more by their motivated relationship to a group than by their actual membership in a group.[34] A reference group provides a person with an orientation and pattern of behavior which is utilized even if he is physically separated from the group and has no real membership in it.

We have shown that inmate populations are arranged into a number of separate social worlds which effectively become membership groups. A member of one of these groups may or may not come to use it as a reference group, but it always is a potential reference group. He may adopt some other inmate group, the administration, or an outside group as a reference group. The character of prison membership groups and thus of potential reference groups is as varied as the types of inmates that are differentiated. If an inmate category or social type is prosocial in character and the individual adopts it as one of his reference groups, the consequences for post-release behavior are likely to be positive. On the other hand, if the inmate social type which is used as the reference group is antisocial in character, the consequences are likely to be negative. This suggests that prediction of the consequences of prison experience for post-release adjustment must take into account the inmates' membership groups and potential reference groups. The social types discovered by Schrag are useful in this connection.[35]

PRISONER ROLES AND PAROLE VIOLATION

Schrag described five social types which comprised the basic distinctions inmates made among themselves: the "right guy," "outlaw," "politician," "square John," and "ding." The "right guy" is an anti-

[34] See Theodore M. Newcomb, *Social Psychology,* (New York: Dryden Press, 1950), 225–32.

[35] *Social Types in a Prison Community, op. cit.* This set of social types seems more useful to our purpose than the set developed by Sykes, for the latter includes types that are "vocational" in nature (the merchant or peddler, for example). Such typology does not emphasize the attitudes, normative orientation, self-conception, loyalty attachments, etc., of the individual. As we stated earlier, Schrag's typology is broader and seems to include the argot roles described by Sykes.

social offender, stable, and oriented to crime, criminals, and inmates. The "outlaw" is an asocial offender, undisciplined, bound by no dence man, is a sophisticated pseudosocial type of offender. The "square John" is prosocial, oriented to society and the prison administration, and without a criminal self-conception. The "ding" category includes socially shunned offenders, the neurotic, psychotic, mentally retarded, and the "rapo" (a non-violent sex offender).

The parolee population previously described was classified using this typology, but since it was impossible to observe the institutional behavior of the parolees, typing was done by means of secondary information contained in the files of the parole board.[36] Before an inmate was placed in a specific category, his file had to indicate that he exhibited *all* the characteristics in one list and a majority of the characteristics in another list. If a parolee had all the necessary characteristics in the first list, but less than the required number of the non-necessary characteristics in the second list, he was labeled a "quasi type." The entire population was sorted for each type; only a small number of cases fit the specifications for more than one type, and in all of these cases the duplication involved a "pure type" who also was a "quasi type" in reference to a different category. The information in the files made it possible to classify about three-fourths of the parolees.

After the typing was complete, an expectation concerning the effects of increased exposure to the prison upon post-release adjustment for each type was formulated. It was expected that the parole violation rates for the "square John" would be very low and would remain low as time served in the institution was extended. A prosocial individual who remains prosocial even while in prison would have a good chance of successful adjustment on parole. A "square John" would use extra-institutional groups, the administration, and/or other "square Johns," as his reference groups. He could be prisonized to the extent that he learned compliant role behavior, but he would cease to be a "square John" if he committed himself fully to the dominant prison code; his conception of self would approach that of the "right guy." The expectation for the category "quasi-square John" was slightly different because many members of this category were persons who had begun to internalize the prison code, thus losing clear

[36] For a more detailed description of this work, see Garrity, *op. cit.*, pp. 163–90.

identity as a "square John." It was expected that the violation rates would be higher than the rates of the "square John" type but lower than the violation rates for the population as a whole. Further, it was expected that the violation rates would increase as time served in the institution increased, for the process of internalizing antisocial norms and attitudes would continue.

The "right guy" is the dominant figure in the prison, and his reference groups are elite prisoners, sophisticated, career-type criminals, and other "right guys." Consequently, we expected that violation rates for this type would be very high. However, it was expected that violation rates would decrease markedly as time in prison increased; because a "right guy" is a stable and deliberative individual, it was expected that continued incarceration would serve to sever his connections with the criminal sub-culture and thus increase the probability of successful parole. Also, it was expected that the pains of imprisonment and pressures by the administration, of which this type of inmate is very much aware, would serve to mature him socially and thus to increase the probability of success. For the "quasi-right guy," it was expected that the violation rates would be relatively high and would increase with time served. It seemed logical that this group included relatively immature criminals who use the period of incarceration to learn criminal techniques and become indoctrinated with the values of the "right guy." If incarceration were sufficiently long, however, the violation rates might begin to decrease, as in the case of the "right guy."

The "outlaw" is without meaningful membership groups or reference groups. He is devoid of loyalty attachments both within and outside the prison. Consequently, it was expected that the violation rates for this group would be very high and would remain high as time served in prison increased.

The "politician" is a chameleon who can conform to the rules of any group but does so only as long as it is to his own best interests. He has no lasting reference groups however. Hence, it was expected that the "politician" and "quasi politician" would have low violation rates in the early time periods but that the rates would increase systematically with time served. Continued exposure to a social situation in which the "politician" played antisocial groups against prosocial groups should be detrimental to successful adjustment on parole.

Because the category "ding" contains a variety of sub-types of individuals who are shunned by other prisoners, separate expectations were formulated for each identifiable sub-type. It was assumed that the pattern of the "square John" would apply to the "rapo." Since the "rapo" is as prosocial as the "square John," it was expected that low-violation rates would be observed at all time periods. The same expectations were held for the mentally deficient and psychotic "ding," on the ground that incarceration was possibly an accidental manifestation of the mental condition and hence should have little effect upon parole adjustment. The expectation for the homosexual "ding" was that the violation rate would be relatively high and remain high with time served; exposure to a homosexual society within which frank acts of homosexual behavior are considered quite normal should increase the probability of failure on parole.

The analysis followed the same general pattern used to study the effects of prisonization and anomie. Violation rates were computed by amount of time served for each of the types. *The data on all types for both institutions were consistent with the expectations.* Further, the untyped parolees from the institution for younger offenders exhibited a pattern of violation rates very similar to that of the "outlaw," while untyped parolees from the institution for older offenders had a pattern that corresponded very closely with that of the "right guy." Although these similarities might be fortuitous, they are consistent with the folklore which maintains that the institution for younger offenders contains a large proportion of unstable, aggressive men, while the institution for older men has a large proportion of mature, stable, antisocial offenders.

SUMMARY AND CONCLUSIONS

The unqualified claims that prisons are breeding grounds for crime and that imprisonment adversely affects all prisoners do not appear to be warranted. Continued prison experience minimizes the chances that some prisoners will refrain from crime upon release, but it increases the chances of successful adjustment in society for others. The data on parole adjustment do not support the general contention that extended exposure to the prison community decreases the chances of successful adjustment on parole. On the contrary, for many classes of offenders increasing length of the period of incarceration either does not affect the chances of successful parole at all or tends to increase the chances of successful parole. In general, it was observed that property offenders corresponded most closely to the expectations developed from the concept of prisonization, that individuals who were most stable appear to be negatively affected by prolonged incarceration, and that individuals who were relatively unstable appear to be positively affected by prolonged incarceration.

Predictions of parole performance developed by utilizing Schrag's inmate typology were supported by the data. From these findings, it is possible to reformulate the statement of the process by which prisonization and anomie are related to post-release behavior. The inmate community is an arrangement of inmate social types, and men of each type have in common the problems of adjustment within the closed social world of the prison. A normative system applying to the behavior of all inmates concerning these commonly shared problems develops, and it is defended and championed by the "right guys." Beyond this, the principal locus of social control is the type category into which the inmate falls, and the amount of social control exerted in each of these social worlds varies.

Since social control is greatest within the "right guy" category, prisonization also should be most rapid there. The antisocial attitudes and values, criminal commitments, etc. which are characteristic of a "right guy" further contribute to the ease with which a "right guy" can conform to the inmate code. Although the "politician" might be expected to become prisonized relatively rapidly, his ambivalent position between inmate and administrative social structures prevents him from doing so. The position of the "square John" in the inmate social order is such that prisonization can only occur very slowly, and never beyond the limits of simple necessity. Similarly, the "outlaw" is an isolate and for that reason he should be only slightly prisonized, despite the fact that his parole violation rates are high.

However the prison might affect the behavior of individuals on parole, it is quite clear that the effects vary according to the roles assigned to inmates by other inmates and by the staff. The day-to-day operations of a prison require the presence of the various types of inmates, and knowledge of these types is a necessary condition to successful predictive statements about parole adjustment. Similarly, rational policy decisions by prison and parole administrators can be

Rehabilitation in the Prison Community

made only if the relationships between prison experiences and post-release adjustment are known. We have suggested that the significant prison experiences are those that affect participation in the various kinds of role behavior that exist in inmate populations. Evaluation of treatment efforts, and proposals for new treatment techniques need to take into account the implications of the inmate social structure for official programs.

10

DANIEL GLASER

and

JOHN R. STRATTON

| | | | | | | | | | |

Measuring Inmate Change in Prison

That inmates change in prison has always been assumed. Clemmer coined the word "prisonization" to designate such change, but he did not define it precisely.[1] Parole and the indeterminate sentence are predicated, in part, on the assumption that change can be discerned while a man is in prison; that is one reason why it is contended that the optimum time to release the inmate can be determined more adequately after he has been confined than at the time of sentencing. Similarly, designation of an appropriate institution and an optimum program for an inmate involves, in part, some assumptions that one can predict if or how the man will change while confined.

As Garrity points out in Chapter 9, the approach to this problem most strongly suggested by sociological literature is to assume that all prisoners become criminally oriented during imprisonment. Prisons have been called "training schools for crime." It has been pointed out that if offenders are thrown into contact primarily with other offenders and are isolated from sources of support for anti-criminal values, one should expect them to become increasingly criminal in their attitudes. This development is fostered also by the fact that it is necessary for

[1] Donald Clemmer, *The Prison Community,* New Edition (New York: Rinehart, 1958), 298 *ff*.

the prisoner to rationalize his being in prison; the status degradation which he experiences in the process of arrest, trial, and incarceration, along with the breaking of family and friendship ties by incarceration, may leave him with a powerful need to enhance his own self-esteem. One form of rationalization is what has been called "rejecting the rejectors," that is, the offender's blaming noncriminal persons for his difficulty. It has been asserted that inmate contact with other prisoners facilitates their sharing of such self-justification in criminality, and that this profoundly impairs their acceptance of prison rehabilitation programs.

While generalizations implying the above are often used in arguments deploring our penal institutions, those involved in correctional work argue that prison can have positive as well as negative consequences for the promotion of conformity to noncriminal behavior norms. It is pointed out that prison provides opportunities to learn occupational skills for those individuals who have had no means of earning a legitimate livelihood at other than unskilled labor. The "success stories" of every warden seem predominantly to concern hardened criminals who became successful mechanics, printers, barbers, or other tradesmen. Academic training is available in many institutions, and some inmates retarded in school on the outside progress in prison through courses ranging from the three Rs to advanced college work. Available recreational time in prison also promotes the development of reading and other conventional leisure-time interests that may carry over to the outside. Prison personnel also point out that in prison men learn to comply with authority, and those who at first have difficulty staying out of fights eventually learn to get along with other men. Inmates with physical defects have these corrected and most leave prison in better physical condition than they entered it. Even some relationships of the offenders with conventional persons outside the prison, such as parents, sometimes seem to improve during the forced separation resulting from imprisonment. Also, ties with criminal peers in and out of prison, which compete with conventional influences, sometimes sharply deteriorate and prove disappointing to an offender while he is confined. It is possible that for many prisoners, sociologists make a profound error in treating prison membership groups as positive reference groups.

Statements like those cited in the foregoing paragraphs can be tossed back and forth, with illustrations from isolated cases, but with very little precise knowledge of the extent of their validity or invalidity. Treatment programs and procedures are suggested, implemented, and revised more on the basis of impressions from striking cases than on the basis of systematic evidence. Before the effectiveness and efficency of various prison and release programs can be assessed, it will be necessary to obtain some measure of their consequences. This means one must determine if they produce change, and if so, what kind of change they produce, how they produce it, and in whom.

This chapter will discuss some of the ways in which theory and research may approach the task of measuring inmate change in prison. It will summarize the results of some relevant research already completed, and will indicate the form in which results are likely to appear from other research still underway.

ANALYSIS OF INMATE ROLES

What would appear to be a frame of reference for determining inmate change in prison is suggested by the various attempts to differentiate distinct social types among inmates. Presumably each type represents a unique pattern of thinking, acting and feeling to which certain inmates gradually are habituated. If this presumption were completely valid, the research task might consist primarily of identifying these types. Several major limitations, however, have prevented the delineation of inmate social types from sufficing for the measurement of inmate change in prison.

One early limitation was ambiguity in conceptualizing social types. Clemmer, in his pioneer study, employed only three categories for differentiating an entire inmate population: the "elite," the "middle class" and the "hoosier." It is clear from his discussion that these are broad and arbitrarily divided prestige strata, rather than unique role behavior patterns. Thus, in an unsystematic manner, he distinguishes some role patterns within his broad categories, such as the "politicians" among the elite.[2]

Schrag was more concerned with using inmate-recognized behavior patterns as his criteria for designation of types. His "right guy," "politician," "outlaw" and "square John" are distinguishable from each other by unique constellations of values and habits. His residual group, the "dings," are not homogeneous, but they are fairly distinct from the four basic categories.[3]

[2] *Ibid.*, pp. 107, 125, *ff.*
[3] Clarence Schrag, "Social Types in a Prison Community, (Unpublished M.A. Thesis, University of Washington, 1944).

Classifiers of inmate social types since Schrag, have recognized his major categories but have described a few other types by focusing on some more specific behavioral dimensions. Thus Morris Caldwell, who departs from Schrag's more pure use of the inmates' own language, designates inmate muscle-development enthusiasts as "Spartans," and he also distinguishes "religionists," "leather-workers" and "moon-shiners".[4] Sykes, in his major work, stresses reliance on prisoner argot for the differentiation of distinct inmate behavior roles, and presents a diverse catalogue, on many behavioral dimensions. Thus inmates are differentiated with respect to homosexuality as "wolves," "fags," or "punks," and they are differentiated by the extent and form of their non-sexual aggression towards others as "ball-busters," "hipsters," "toughs" and "gorillas."[5]

The vagueness of theoretical orientation exhibited by Clemmer and Caldwell in distinguishing social types is relatively absent in Schrag and Sykes. Both of the latter have their conceptual foundations in the analysis of social types by the late Samuel M. Strong and his mentor, the late Louis Wirth. Social types were believed by these theorists to be classifications of role patterns by aspects more significant than those which an outside observer might ascribe, for "social types stand for what the members who live in these various social worlds believe to be critical and important."[6] It is in an effort to capture the inmates' own role differentiations that Schrag and Sykes deliberately cling to the inmates' own designation of these types, and Sykes calls them "argot roles."

A limitation of the social type concept, however, is that these types tend to refer to extreme, rather than average or prevailing, roles in a group. As Strong puts it, social types

> . . . are constructs which the group arrives at by selecting or abstracting accentuated forms of conduct displayed by some of its members and having specific connotations in terms of the interests, concerns, and dispositions of the group. . . . An exaggerated form

[4] Morris G. Caldwell, "Group Dynamics in the Prison Community," *Journal of Criminal Law and Criminology* 46 (January-February, 1956), 648–657.

[5] Gresham M. Sykes, *The Society of Captives* (Princeton: Princeton University Press, 1958), Chapter 5; Gresham M. Sykes, "Men, Merchants and Toughs: A Study of Reactions to Imprisonment," *Social Problems* 4 (October 1956), 130–138.

[6] Samuel M. Strong, "Social Types in a Minority Group," *American Journal of Sociology* 48 (Mar. 1943), p. 564.

of conduct . . . catches the attention of the people, who categorize it . . . e.g., the 'social climber'.[7]

What these social-type analysts seem to have uncovered, but which they apparently did not recognize, is what might be called a "poor man's" or non-academic version of Weber's "ideal type." Like the ideal type, the social type is an abstraction from actual behavior. It selects out for special attention some distinguishing features of behavior which have a strategic function in a social system. It portrays certain role occupants in this system as though they were more consistent in their behavior than all or most persons in these roles are. It then is possible to analyze the causes and consequences of their behavior in the social system by deduction from the attributes ascribed to the pure types. This was done by Weber in analyzing bureaucracy in terms of a "bureaucrat" ideal type; it was done by Sykes, Schrag, and notably by Cloward, in analyzing the prison social system in terms of politicians, merchants, and other inmate types.[8] It is done by all of us in analyzing our daily social life with such social type categories as "eager-beaver," "glad-hander" and "four-flusher"; these exaggerate the behavior of any specific individual, but they give us a sense of comprehending a social reality which would be confused and meaningless unless subjected to some such abstraction and distortion process.

In the experience of the senior writer, in attempting to classify inmates by social typologies, it was easy to find consensus in naming major types, and in identifying inmates who epitomize each type. However, it is noteworthy that inmates usually disagree extensively if asked to type every single person in any particular unit. Furthermore, few inmates will accept an allegation that they fit closely any specific type. It becomes apparent that each type is seen as something of an exaggeration. Also, a majority of types convey derogatory connotation, the most notable exception to this being "right guy." However, should any specific individual claim to be, or be described by others as, a "right guy," a few minutes probing will indicate that even the "right guy" is an idealized—rather than a typical—figure. Focus on any specific individual elicits references to the manner or

---

[7] *Ibid.*, p. 563.

[8] Richard A. Cloward, "Social Control in the Prison," Chapter 2 in Richard A. Cloward, Donald R. Cressey, George H. Grosser, Richard McCleery, Lloyd E. Ohlin, Gresham Sykes and Sheldon Messinger, *Theoretical Studies in Social Organization of the Prison* (New York: Social Science Research Council, 1960); Schrag, *op. cit.*; Sykes, *op. cit.*

time in which his behavior has deviated from the "right guy" standard
to that of a politician, merchant, square, or other type, even when
"on the whole" he is accepted as a "right guy."

The evolution of empirical concepts in social science often starts
with classification of cases into discrete types with respect to some
variable, then progresses to ranking or measuring each case on the
variable, so that more fine discriminations can be made. Only crude
beginnings of the latter operation are available in the measurement
of that inmate behavior which is presumed to change in prison. Two
distinct approaches may be discerned in efforts to deal with this
problem. The first method is to compare direct expressions of attitude
procured from offenders who are at different stages in a correctional
career. We shall call this the "sequential measurement" technique.
A more indirect approach is to compare the post-release behavior of
offenders as a means of assessing the extent to which their behavior
in prison indicated that they were enduringly changed, or as an index
of the effects of different periods of exposure to imprisonment. We
shall call this the "ex post facto comparison" technique.

Sequential measurement

By "sequential measurement" studies we encompass both those in
which the same subjects are seen at different times and those in which
comparisons are made between groups of subjects at different stages
in correctional experience who are believed to have been identical
when first committed.

Fiedler and Bass recently reported a comparison of the responses
of various groups of offenders who were asked to rate themselves, and
others in their group, on pairs of opposite adjectives like "friendly"
and "unfriendly," or "cooperative" and "uncooperative," using six-
point scales between the opposites. Adding these into a "self-esteem
score" by the number of points on the scale selected in the direction
of the favorable adjective in each pair, these authors found that non-
confined offenders rated themselves less favorably than a control group
of non-offenders, but that confined offenders rated themselves significantly more favorably than did non-confined offenders, although not
as favorably as the non-offenders. This same pattern of contrast was
found among juveniles in public schools and state training schools,

and among military personnel in a regular unit and a disciplinary center.

Both a sociological and a psychological explanation are offered by Fiedler and Bass for their findings. The sociological explanation is that with confinement offenders change their reference groups increasingly to their fellow offenders, by comparison with whom they may regard themselves more favorably than they could prior to confinement, when they more often compared themselves with nonoffenders. The psychological explanation is that confinement, as punishment, reduces feelings of guilt, that is, that self-esteem is enhanced by expiation. Both explanations for the findings are speculative, and the findings themselves merit review by panel studies involving successive contacts with the same subjects.[9]

Wheeler studied conformity to conventional norms in inmates of a Washington reformatory by rating each inmate on the extent to which he agreed with the reformatory staff in his responses to questions on the propriety of the behavior of various characters described in anecdotes. These anecdotes reported hypothetical value conflict situations in prison life. As one aspect of this study, Wheeler compared inmates at three stages of prison experience: those in the first six months of confinement, those who had served six months and had at least six months to serve, and those with less than six months left to serve.

We shall limit our reference to Wheeler's findings to two noteworthy features. In the first place, he observed a U-shaped curve, in which conformity to conventional norms was higher at the beginning and at the end of imprisonment than in the middle. This was explained as reflecting progressive change from outsider to fellow inmate reference groups until the last stages of imprisonment, when reference is redirected to outside persons. This explanation was supported by findings that the U-shaped change was least pronounced for those inmates reporting least contact with other inmates.

Wheeler's second finding was that, despite the U-shaped curve, there was a general trend for inmates to move away from conformity to conventional norms with each increment of prison experience. He found that both first termers and recidivists exhibit the U-shaped pat-

[9] Fred E. Fiedler and Alan R. Bass, "Delinquency, Confinement and Interpersonal Perception," Technical Report No. 6, Group Effectiveness Research Laboratory (Urbana: University of Illinois, 1959).

tern, but the recidivists start and finish with lower conformity than the first offenders.[10]

Metaphorically, Wheeler's data suggest that offenders follow a spiral pattern of cyclical movement from conventional to criminal norms, progressively drifting more criminal. Criminality increases with each return to crime, and during much of imprisonment. However, with each return to the conventional world from prison, most offenders become somewhat more conforming to conventional norms, for a while at least. Always there is some possibility of this spiral movement being interrupted by their achieving security, either in the criminal or in the conventional world.

Cloward, in reinterviewing military prisoners every six weeks from commitment to their twenty-fourth week of confinement, noted what he called a strain toward passivity with respect to administration-fostered goals and means, and a strain toward isolation from other inmates. The latter is associated with what he calls "pluralistic ignorance," in that each inmate keeps other inmates ignorant of the extent to which he actually is pursuing conventional goals, by "putting up a front" of greater conformity to inmate norms of opposition to such goals.[11] The latter phenomenon may be responsible for much masking of the upswing in the U-shaped curve indicated in Wheeler's data.

In the four-year research program in the Federal Correctional System directed by Glaser, which at this writing is not half completed, measures of inmate change are sought using a panel approach similar to that of Wheeler. Inmates in five Federal prisons are compared at various stages of sentence completion—after their first week in prison, after six months' incarceration, between the first and last year of expected confinement, and within three months of release. While the findings still are in the first stage of analysis, some preliminary tabulations may be of interest.

When responses to the question "Do you think your sentence was fair," were plotted over the time, the resulting profile indicated that approximately 60 percent of the inmates interviewed within a week of their admission to prison felt that their sentence was fair. However, there was a significant increase in the proportion calling their sentence very unfair as one moved from those interviewed in their first four

[10] Stanton Wheeler, "Social Organization in a Correctional Community" (Unpublished Ph.D. Dissertation, University of Washington, 1958).

[11] Richard A. Cloward, "Social Control and Anomie: A Study of a Prison Community" (Unpublished Ph.D. Dissertation, Columbia University, 1959).

days in prison to those seen in their fifth, sixth or seventh day. Little further change in this attitude was indicated during the first six months of incarceration, but the proportion calling their sentence "fair" dropped to 36 percent by the middle of the sentences. Yet the proportion of inmates interviewed within 90 days of release who described their sentence as fair was 70 percent. The resulting profile is similar to Wheeler's U-shaped curve. It suggests that inmates focus on inmate reference groups very rapidly at first, and continuously during most of their imprisonment, but as release time approaches, most of them assume the perspectives of non-prison reference groups.

Two other indications of this U-shaped curve revealed thus far in the Federal prison panel study may merit mention at this time. First, interest in participating in religious activity was high among inmates on admission, it declined sharply after the first six months, but it rose sharply in the last three months. Also, three-quarters of the inmates ranked learning a trade or improving their academic education high among their interests when they were first received in prison, this proportion decreased significantly during the next six months of confinement, then it rose significantly for inmates in the middle of their sentence. In interpreting these trends, it is hard to disentangle actual reference to outside groups from anticipations that pursuit of conventional interests in prison will facilitate favorable parole consideration.

Some suggestion of reference group influence is provided by other findings. The proportion of inmates who expected post-release assistance mainly from parents or siblings was constant during most of the confinement, but increased slightly near release. The proportion who expected help mainly from their wives decreased as imprisonment progressed, reflecting an increasing proportion of marriages breaking during the husband's confinement. Looking at the other side of the coin, the proportion of inmates who report that their close relatives will "make trouble for them" on release decreases somewhat as release time approaches.

Additional support for a reference group explanation for the U-shaped changes reported during Federal imprisonment is provided by inmate accounts of their orientations to fellow inmates. In the early phases of their incarceration, most inmates in our sample report that they try to stay to themselves as much as possible or to limit their interaction to a few inmate friends. In the middle of their sentence they more frequently report trying to have as many inmate friends as possible. In the last few months, however, they report more of the early pattern of having only limited interaction with other inmates.

Further analysis of the Federal panel data will cover a variety of other interview items and will include separate tabulations for offenders of different criminal record and other background characteristics. We have not yet completed coding and tabulating a considerable body of narrative material, and we are still working on analysis of over a thousand reports by inmates of what they did and what they talked about, hour by hour, in the 24 hours preceding each of our panel interviews.

Ex post facto comparison

Most parole prediction studies have investigated duration of time confined as a possible predictor of post-release behavior. They have invariably found that, taken alone, it is a poor predictor compared to others as readily available. Most findings suggest that the releasees least likely to return to crime are those with the most brief and those with the longest prison confinement. This curvilinear relationship seems to be an artifact of the relationship between criminal record and time served: those with the least prior criminality are released soonest, except for those who have committed murder, who are confined longest, and who also are less often professional criminals than are prisoners in the middle range of time served.

Most parole prediction studies also investigate the relationship to post-release behavior of any manifestation of behavior change during imprisonment which is recorded in prison files. These inquiries also have been relatively fruitless, especially when compared with efforts to relate pre-prison behavior to post-release record. This probably reflects, in part, a lesser influence on post-release behavior of change during any particular imprisonment, as compared with influences of the total life prior to a specific imprisonment. However, the major deficiency probably is the inadequate records available on behavior during imprisonment, the only regularly recorded item being known rule infractions.

While most efforts to correlate such prison behavior records with post-release data have indicated little relationship, our preliminary analysis of file data on a sample of 1956 Federal penitentiary releasees reveals markedly higher post-release success for those whose rule infractions were low or declined towards release, and for those for whom an improvement in over-all "adjustment" was reported by prison officials. This was the best of fifty predictors tested specifically on those penitentiary inmates who had no prior arrests or had a gap of five or more years in their arrest record at some time in the free community. The failure of prison punishment to predict parole outcome very accurately for offenders with much prior confinement may be interpreted as due to the fact that the most criminally oriented inmates are well adjusted to confinement. However, our Federal penitentiary data suggest that development of an ability to conform to prison rules usefully distinguishes the most non-recidivistic of those inmates who, collectively, have the least prior criminal record.

Donald L. Garrity pioneered in the most useful adaptation of parole prediction procedures to measurement of change during imprisonment. After classifying Washington state prisoners by file data presumed to provide very crude indices of Schrag's social types, he tabulated each type's parole violation rate for different periods of confinement. Those presumed to be "square Johns" (no prior record, conformity to prison rules, and constructive use of prison time) had parole violation rates which, though always low, increased with time served. Those believed most resembling the "right guy" (early and persistent criminality, little conventional family influence, and little schooling) had violation rates which, though always high, decreased with time served. For inmates of this "right guy" category in the reformatory, violation rate decreased for increasing duration of time served until the end of the fifth year, then increased; in the penitentiary, violation rates for this category of inmates were lowest if they were released between the tenth and twentieth years of confinement.

Garrity's cases were too few to have much significance for fine time-distinctions in the separate presumed social type differentiations. However, summarizing the trends over all types, he concluded that the greater the amount of stability prior to incarceration, the more an increase in duration of incarceration was associated with an increase in post-release failure, but the greater the instability before prison, the more continued imprisonment was associated with increased post-release success.[12]

[12] Donald L. Garrity, "The Effects of Length of Incarceration Upon Parole Adjustment and Estimate of Optimum Sentence: Washington Correctional Institutions" (Unpublished Ph.D. Dissertation, University of Washington, 1956); Donald L. Garrity, "Statistics for Administrative and Policy Decisions, I," *California Youth Authority Quarterly,* 10 (Fall 1957), 40–47; and Chapter 9, above.

Our preliminary analysis of post-release outcome for a small sample of 1956 Federal penitentiary releasees supports Garrity's conclusions. For the most successful major releasee group (those with no prior arrest or a gap of five or more years in their arrest record), 100 percent were successful of 13 released within a year after imprisonment, 96 percent were successful of 28 released during the second year, and only 77 percent were successful of 35 confined over two years. The least successful major releasee categories were those who were not able to avoid arrest for a period as long as five years in the free community, and who had two or more years of imprisonment prior to the commitment from which they were released. The success rates for this group increased with time served from 38 percent for those released in their first year of confinement to 48 percent for those released after serving over two years. Information has not yet been available on enough cases in such research to permit fine differentiations by type of offender, by prison program, or by time served. However, the consistency of findings thus far suggests that more work with this ex post facto comparison procedure can be very productive of valid and useful generalizations on inmate changes during imprisonment.

Summary and Conclusions

Practical application of sociological knowledge to judicial and correctional decisions depends greatly on ability to measure inmate change in prison. Differentiation of prisoner behavior on the basis of inmate social types has directed attention to polar patterns, but prisoners display some attributes of several patterns. This suggests the need for differentiating inmates by finer gradations of crucial variables.

Two approaches to discernment of change on specific variables were described. The first is sequential measurement of characteristics of inmates at different stages in correctional experience. The second ex post facto correlation of post-release behavior with length of exposure to imprisonment, or with manifestations of behavior recorded during imprisonment. Research on both of these methods still is highly limited, but results already are of considerable interest and suggest great promise in further efforts.